ALSO BY SOLOMON VOLKOV

Conversations with Joseph Brodsky

St. Petersburg: A Cultural History

*From Russia to the West: The Musical Memoirs and
Reminiscences of Nathan Milstein*

*Balanchine's Tchaikovsky: Conversations with
Balanchine on His Life, Ballet and Music*

Testimony: The Memoirs of Dmitri Shostakovich

SHOSTAKOVICH
and
STALIN

SHOSTAKOVICH
and
STALIN

The Extraordinary
Relationship
Between the Great
Composer and the
Brutal Dictator

SOLOMON
VOLKOV

*Translated from
the Russian by
Antonina W. Bouis*

ALFRED A.
KNOPF
NEW YORK
2004

THIS IS A BORZOI BOOK
PUBLISHED BY ALFRED A. KNOPF

All photographs are from the personal collection
of Solomon Volkov.

ISBN: 0-375-41082-1
LC: 2003115653

Manufactured in the United States of America

First Edition

Contents

Preface

If you don't count the mythic Greek singer Orpheus, probably no one suffered more for his music than the Soviet composer Dmitri Shostakovich. He was branded an "anti-people" musician,[1] and his work was dismissed as "an intentionally discordant, muddled flow of sound."[2] For many years, Shostakovich and his family balanced precariously on the edge of catastrophe, under constant threat of arrest, exile, or worse.

This was because the abuse came directly from the Supreme Leader of his homeland—Joseph Stalin himself. To be sure, it was also accompanied by state prizes and carefully doled-out encouragement. Unfortunately, one never knew when lightning would strike. This made Shostakovich's life a living hell for many years.

These were unimaginably cruel times, when Shostakovich's friends, patrons, and family members suddenly disappeared, drawn into the maelstrom of Stalinist repression. How, under these circumstances, Shostakovich managed not only to keep his sanity, but also to write some of the most enduring, almost shockingly expressive, and at the same time touchingly humane music of the twentieth century constitutes the story of this book. It gives the fullest account yet of the arguably unprecedented duel between the composer and Joseph Stalin, the country's Communist tsar and Shostakovich's personal tormentor. In fact, it is the first such book-length account in any language.

After my arrival in the United States in 1976, I heard Shostakovich's work performed countless times in Western concert halls, and I often wondered: Why this rapt attention from the public? Why does palpable tension envelop audiences who know little or nothing about the conditions under which these tormented and tormenting sounds were created?

We in the USSR grew up with Shostakovich's music practically under our skin. Its gloomy melodies, trampling rhythms, and bellowing orchestral writing perfectly suited our moods and inner thoughts, which we tried to conceal from the watchful eyes and long ears of the Soviet authorities.

But here in the democratic West, Shostakovich's music could easily be dismissed as importunate, primitive, and bombastic. And in fact, many professionals—composers and musicologists especially—expressed these disparaging views of Shostakovich, castigating him for his apparent squareness. It was primarily the performers and listeners who ultimately saved the composer's reputation. Audiences flocked to performances of Shostakovich's works, clearly finding in them some vitally needed emotional sustenance.

A perceptive explanation for their reaction was recently offered by the American writer Lawrence Hansen. Shostakovich's music tapped "into our most fundamental, primal fear: the destruction of the self by outside forces, the fear of life being pointless and meaningless, the sheer evil that may be found in one's fellow man." He added that Shostakovich "offers a terrifying yet cathartic emotional roller-coaster ride."[3]

And yet the man behind this powerfully direct oeuvre remained an enigma, just a fuzzy image of an artist disappearing into the Stalinist landscape, an image that could morph, in the spirit of American science fiction, into the likeness of the observer. Especially handicapping in this respect was the absence of a firm factual backdrop, integrated into a broader political and cultural picture of the times.

I am presenting the most detailed reconstruction to date of the two pivotal events that connected Shostakovich and Stalin: Stalin's denunciation of Shostakovich's great opera *Lady Macbeth of Mtsensk* in 1936 and the Communist Party resolution of 1948 censuring Shostakovich and other leading Soviet composers. Particularly close attention is given to the 1936 affair, which in the annals of the twentieth century came to symbolize the extent to which an oppressive state can manipulate culture.

I also make the case for Stalin's writing or dictating the infamous 1936 *Pravda* editorial "Muddle Instead of Music," which attacked Shostakovich savagely, and I attribute, for the first time, other important unsigned texts to him. I cannot underscore enough how personal and sometimes obsessive was Stalin's involvement in micromanaging Soviet culture in general and Shostakovich in particular.

All this is important because the prevailing contemporary thinking is uncomfortable assigning too much credit to any one personality and tends to overrate the influence of a faceless bureaucracy in matters political and cultural. Yet the notion of the cult of personality is not without foundation.

I had no plans for the present book, having for many years turned down offers to write Shostakovich's biography. What finally persuaded me was the distortion of Shostakovich's image that started to take hold long after Stalin's abuse of him was relegated to the proverbial "dustbin of history."

It was in United States academic circles, of all places, that Shostakovich was proclaimed (allegedly ironically) to be "perhaps Soviet Russia's most loyal musical son,"[4] and his opera *Lady Macbeth of Mtsensk* denounced (decidedly without a trace of irony) as "a profoundly inhumane work of art," with the damning conclusion that "its technique of dehumanizing victims is the perennial method of those who would perpetrate and justify genocide . . . if ever an opera deserved to be banned, it was this one."[5]

After this resolutely expressed but somewhat belated solidarity with the Stalinist views of Shostakovich as the ultimate "anti-people" composer, other learned voices describing him merely as a "wuss,"[6] "cowardly,"[7] and "a mediocre human being,"[8] and bemoaning his "moral impotence and servile complicity"[9] could be perceived as almost harmless.

Yet I felt they all sounded equally false. This picture of Shostakovich, pretending to be objective and therefore relying heavily on his official declarations, looked to me and many of my compatriot musicians as crooked as any of the Soviet concoctions about the composer. This was not a portrait of the Shostakovich we knew, but an ideologically biased contraption which little resembled the seemingly fragile and unassuming man who nevertheless cut a complex and contradictory but ultimately courageous figure and whose music electrified and terrified audiences worldwide: not a victim but, rather, a victor, though definitely scarred for life by his ordeal.

Debates around Shostakovich's image and his oeuvre are no less intense now than in his lifetime. This is no quirk of fate. We live in highly politicized times. Confrontations about Shostakovich continue to start over aesthetic issues but quickly cut to the political bone.

It was often noted that the composer's *profession de foi* was confrontation with evil and the defense of man. (The same could be said about Dostoevsky, also a highly politicized figure.) When I came to the West more than a quarter-century ago, such a creative motto sounded hopelessly passé and was frowned upon. Not anymore.

Looking at our troubled horizon today, we could use the dark glass of Shostakovich's music and swim with him in overwhelming waves of torment, grief, and unrelieved angst. But with him we also experience revulsion in the face of evil, deep sorrow for its victims, and the strengthening resolve to overcome it. Therein lies at least one of the reasons that will keep Shostakovich's music center stage in contemporary culture. It will serve for a long time to come as a prime example of politically engaged art of the highest order.

It was my privilege to observe Shostakovich closely in the last several years of his life, while collaborating with him on his memoirs, *Testimony*. During this time I started to formulate an overall description of him that seemed to fit the extreme polarities of his personality and to encompass the multitudes it contained (as in Walt Whitman's oft-quoted self-description).

This was a paradigm of the *yurodivy*, or holy fool—a peculiarly Russian figure, present on the historical scene from the eleventh century to the end of the eighteenth. As scholars point out, *yurodivye* were the people's "conscience personified," boldly speaking out as the oppressed masses suffered in silence and daring to confront even the feared Russian tyrants like Ivan the Terrible. Their diatribes against the rulers were strange and unpredictable, but powerful and memorable.

I elaborated on how Shostakovich was a present-day *yurodivy* in the introduction to *Testimony* (published in 1979)[10] and in an essay about Shostakovich and Dostoevsky published in 1980.[11] *Testimony* aroused controversy that still has not abated, and has forced me over the years to define the *yurodivy* idea more precisely. I concluded that in all probability Shostakovich was influenced not by a real-life *yurodivy*, but followed the fictional model first presented by Alexander Pushkin in his tragedy *Boris Godunov* (1824) and then magnified in the opera of the same title (after Pushkin) by Modest Mussorgsky (1869–1872).

As I show in this book, both Pushkin and Mussorgsky treated the character of the *yurodivy* in their work as the thinly disguised, largely autobiographical embodiment of the figure of the artist, who—in the name of the downtrodden people—speaks dangerous but necessary truths to the face of the tsar. This was the role that Shostakovich assumed as his life model, which also included two other fictional "masks" from *Boris Godunov:* those of the Chronicler and the Pretender. In adopting, as they suited him, all three masks and juggling them for many years, Shostakovich placed himself as a true successor to Pushkin's and Mussorgsky's Russian tradition of artistic dialogue and confrontation with the tsar.

So this interpretation of Shostakovich's tortured and difficult personality seems to me more all-encompassing and, at the same time, more nuanced than the one I offered in the introduction to *Testimony.* It is presented here for the first time.

Over the years, Shostakovich's views, as I faithfully recorded them in *Testimony,* became confused—intentionally by some, out of sloppiness by others—with my own views and positions. For example, Shostakovich's scornful descriptions of Stalin as a total ignoramus in all matters cultural were sometimes ascribed to me. As the reader of the present book will see, I don't share the composer's somewhat immoderate (albeit understandable) opinions on this and some other matters. On the other hand, I've personally heard a music commentator declaring jovially on National Public Radio that "Shostakovich all his life called himself a *yurodivy.*" Hardly.

In an effort to clarify this confusion and to draw a distinguishing line between *Testimony* and this book, I've kept quotes from *Testimony* and from my personal conversations with Shostakovich to a minimum. But of course, everything in the present work is informed by these conversations and by the insight they afforded me into the composer's psyche, his worldview, and his way of being.

This is why as a motto to this book I've adopted the humble but still proud words of the widow of poet Osip Mandelstam, Nadezhda, a contemporary of Shostakovich: "A person with inner freedom, memory, and fear is that reed, that twig that changes the direction of a rushing river." This observation will always remind me of why Shostakovich's life and work became of such burning importance to so many of his contemporaries.

This is a book of cultural history. Therefore, I do not engage in analysis of Shostakovich's music, concentrating instead on the political and cultural circumstances of the Stalin era and the dictator's relationship with the leading creative figures of the day, an area that is still insufficiently researched and understood. I describe this relationship as a shifting, mutable one, not fixed and frozen. Besides Shostakovich himself, many distinguished personalities helped me in my efforts to shed light on this period. For understanding the workings of Stalin's cultural politics and navigating the maze of published pronouncements and documents, conversations with Anna Akhmatova, Lili Brik, Sergei Yutkevich, Viktor Shklovsky, Anatoli Rybakov, and Maya Plisetskaya were of immense value. Russian archives of Stalin's era are still far from open, but I made full use of some recent important publications of previously classified materials.

Some rare insights into Shostakovich's patterns and inclinations were generously given to me by Berthe Malko, Gabriel Glikman, and Yevgeny Yevtushenko and by musicians who premiered some of his greatest works—David Oistrakh, Kirill Kondrashin, Mstislav Rostropovich, Rudolf Barshai, and Yevgeny Nesterenko. I am also grateful to Kurt Sanderling, Lazar Gosman, Vladimir Ashkenazy, Yuri Temirkanov, Valery Gergiev, Mariss Jansons, Vladimir Spivakov, and Gidon Kremer for discussing with me some important aspects of the Shostakovich phenomenon. Of special significance were the opinions of composers: Georgy Sviridov, Rodion Shchedrin, Alfred Schnittke, Giya Kancheli, Alexandre Rabinovitch, and Peteris Vasks.

I am also immensely indebted to Maxim Shostakovich for sharing with me his unique knowledge of his father.

The twentieth century could be dubbed the propaganda century. Published and broadcast cultural content was wielded as a potent political weapon; words became political currency; and the gap between what was proclaimed in public and spoken in private grew greater than ever before.

Because of that, the interpretation of official Soviet documents and press is an especially intricate and delicate craft, an example of which for me was the book by Lazar Fleishman, *Boris Pasternak v tridtsatye gody* [Boris Pasternak in the Thirties] (Jerusalem, 1984). To Professor Fleishman, who also happens to be a childhood friend, I owe gratitude for additional advice and help, as I do to Professor Timothy L. Jackson, Professor Allan B. Ho, Dmitry Feofanov, Ian Macdonald, Dr. Vladimir Zak, and Andrei Bitov.

Many aspects of the present book were first discussed with my dear friends Grisha and Alexandra Bruskin. And my heartfelt thanks go to my wife, Marianna, who recorded and transcribed many interviews for this book. I am also very grateful to my translator, Antonina W. Bouis, with whom collaborating is always a pleasure, and to my formidable editor at Knopf, Ashbel Green, and his assistant, Luba Ostashevsky, for their unflagging support and informed help with the manuscript.

SHOSTAKOVICH
and
STALIN

Prologue   Tsars and Poets

On Wednesday, 8 September 1826, Moscow was in a whirlwind of festivities: the ancient capital of the Russian Empire was in its second month of opulent coronation celebrations. The new monarch, Nicholas I, came to Moscow from St. Petersburg after the execution of five prominent Decembrists—noblemen revolutionaries who headed the failed attempt on 14 December 1825 to stop Nicholas from ascending the throne. On 13 July 1826, Pavel Pestel, Kondratii Ryleev, Sergei Muravyev-Apostol, Mikhail Bestuzhev-Ryumin, and Petr Kakhovsky were hanged. The military governor general of St. Petersburg reported to Nicholas I: "Through the inexperience of our executioners and lack of knowledge on how to build scaffolds, at the first attempt three, to wit: Ryleev, Kakhovsky, and Muravyev, broke off, but were quickly hanged again and received their deserved death. About which I report loyally to Your Majesty."[1] Nicholas's mother, Maria Fedorovna, wrote in relief after the execution to one of her confidants: "Thank God, everything went peacefully, everything is all right. May God forgive the executed and may the Final Judgment be merciful with them. I thanked God on my knees. I believe that by God's Mercy, Nicholas will reign in peace and quiet from now on."[2]

For Nicholas I, the rebellion was one of the most horrible events of his life, a nightmare to which he returned frequently. He had been on the brink of defeat and humiliation then. "The most amazing thing," the emperor would say later, "was that they did not kill me that day." He was convinced that Providence had saved him so that he could become the head of Russia and lead the country with an iron hand down the road to law and order, victories and glory. He was truly God's Anointed.

That September Wednesday the emperor's schedule was tight, as usual. In the morning he and the Prince of Prussia came out onto Ivanov Square for the changing of the guard; then he received the military governor general of Moscow for his report. After that, Nicholas I met in the Kremlin with the leaders of the Moscow Assembly of the Nobility; then came several top officials with reports, including the chief of the Gendarme Corps, Alexander Benckendorff. That day, the official *Moskovskie Vedomosti* printed the royal decree on the establishment with Benckendorff at its head of the Third Department of His Imperial Majesty's Personal Chancellery—the modernized version of the Russian secret police.

Among other appointments, between lunch with the Prussian prince and a ball given in honor of important foreign guests by the French ambassador at the marvelous palace of Prince Kurakin, there was an audience planned with Alexander Pushkin, a young but already nationally known poet. Nicholas I's older brother, the late emperor Alexander I, had been very angered by Pushkin—dissolute, audacious, haughty, flooding Russia with outrageous poetry—and had exiled the poet twice, once to the south of the empire, and then to the backwaters of the countryside, to the estate of his parents in Pskov Province, under the supervision of the local authorities. Many of the arrested participants of the December uprising were found to have handwritten copies of Pushkin's antigovernment verses in their homes. A man who had such influence over the minds of his countrymen was dangerous, and he had to be dealt with—attentively, dispassionately, but decisively and firmly.

Pushkin, who had been summoned abruptly on the tsar's orders from his village exile to Moscow (it took four days by horse), was brought to the Kremlin after four p.m. The autocrat and the poet were meeting face to face for the first time. It was a historic moment, whose importance both men appreciated.

Pushkin's fate hung by a thread. It was impossible to imagine two more disparate people: Pushkin, short, unattractive, but with an animated and expressive face, curly-haired and dusky (a reminder of his

African heritage), never known for the elegance of his dress and now in rumpled and dusty traveling clothes, unshaven and chilled, stood before the tall, handsome, broad-chested emperor, only three years his senior, with an aquiline profile, always regal in bearing and most observant of people's appearance and elegance. Their clash seemed inevitable.

But just the contrary occurred. After a long tête-à-tête, the tsar and the poet emerged from the office, and there were tears in Pushkin's eyes—the poet was touched, profoundly agitated and happy. In his turn, Nicholas I came to the conclusion that Pushkin was "the wisest man in Russia."[3] Now he called him "my Pushkin."

What did they talk about? It began with the tsar's question: "What would you have done if you had been in St. Petersburg on December 14?"

"I would have stood in the ranks of the rebels," Pushkin replied without hesitation. Those words could have been fatal for the poet. But Pushkin's intuition had suggested the right path: Nicholas I valued direct and honest people. His respect for Pushkin grew even greater when in response to the tsar's question if his thinking had changed and he would give his word to act differently now, the poet vacillated. Only after a long silence did he extend his hand to the emperor and promise "to change."

As a contemporary of Pushkin's wrote enviously, "His intelligent, frank, and respectfully bold speech pleased the Sovereign. He is permitted to live where he wants and publish what he wants. The Tsar has taken on being his censor with the condition that he not abuse this gift of total freedom and remain to the end of his life under the personal patronage of the Tsar."[4]

All of Moscow learned instantly about this significant meeting. A secret agent of the Third Department related in a special report that "everyone is sincerely happy over the Emperor's generosity and benevolence, which, without a doubt, will have the happiest consequences for Russian literature."[5] If Pushkin had only known how ungenerous Nicholas I would be, how little benevolence he would show for "the wisest man in Russia," how picky, rancorous, envious of another's fame, indifferent to Pushkin's poetry, manipulative, and cruel he would prove to be in the coming years! In other words, he was a politician, a real politician, for whom culture was merely a way of achieving his goals, and an unreliable and suspect way at that. Pushkin was killed in a duel, and Nicholas I will always be blamed for it. The poet's funeral was organized under strict official supervision. At the church services there were reportedly more gendarmes and police than mourners. The farewell to Pushkin was turned into a state farce. But who could have guessed that in the festive, joyous Moscow of 1826? The death of the hounded and lonely Pushkin was a little more than ten years away.

One hundred seventeen years later, in the fall of 1943, Moscow was a completely different city—not a "porphyry-bearing widow," as Pushkin once called it, but a real capital of a mighty state, albeit without a too close resemblance to the model empire that Nicholas I, the "Don Quixote of autocracy," had imagined. In 1918, after a hiatus of over two hundred years, the government was moved back to the Kremlin by the Bolshevik leader Vladimir Lenin, and his heir, Joseph Stalin, made it the symbol of his power: It was no longer an exotic background for sumptuous coronations, but a brain center of an enormous and dynamic country.

What a leap, and what irony of fate! The Moscow in which Nicholas I received Pushkin appeared festive and filled with myriad lights. Stalin's Moscow of 1943 was a military city—sparsely populated, hungry, dimmed, and grim. But there was something in common between the two Moscows—first of all, in the psychology of the two leaders. Both Nicholas I and Stalin had lived through a terrible crisis: their greatest fright, which they may have never fully gotten over. For Nicholas I, it was the Decembrist rebellion; for Stalin, the real threat of defeat in the war with Adolf Hitler's Germany.

The war had begun on the night of 22 June 1941, when Nazi troops invaded the Soviet Union and in a few days drove the Red Army to the brink of catastrophe. The Germans moved on inexorably over a huge space—from the Baltic Sea to the Black Sea. Stalin was in despair. Rarely losing self-control, in a fit of rage he shouted angrily at his terrified comrades, "Lenin created our state, and we've shitted it away!"[6]

In October the Germans were outside Moscow, and the capital could fall at any moment. On 16 October panic spread through the city, which many years later theater director Yuri Lyubimov described to me this way: "They were burning documents, black snow flew, as in

Mikhail Bulgakov . . . It was a scene out of the Apocalypse."[7] The most important ministries and institutions were hastily evacuated from Moscow, including the Bolshoi Theater; a special plane awaited Stalin to move him to Kuibyshev, deep inland. But Stalin remained in the capital. Like Nicholas I, he knew the importance of personal example.

In the confrontation with the Decembrists, Nicholas I managed to turn the tide in large part due to his cool demeanor. At first stunned in the face of advancing disaster, Stalin also managed to demonstrate the determination and ruthlessness necessary for organizing resistance. Soviet soldiers attacked the enemy with cries of "For the Homeland! For Stalin!" A miracle occurred and the Germans were repelled from Moscow. But the real break in the war took place in early 1943, after the defeat of the Germans at Stalingrad, a strategically important city on the Volga, which Stalin in private conversation to the end of his life insisted on calling by its old name, Tsaritsyn.

The Battle of Stalingrad took on legendary status in the annals of modern military history. After it, as many people who knew Stalin well recalled, the Soviet leader, despite the exhausting stress of running the country (he spent sixteen hours and more at his desk every day), looked rested. Stalin's shoulders straightened, and he smiled and joked more frequently.

Stalin knew that the Soviet Union not only was saved but would become, after the successful end of the war, one of the world's super-powers. The time had come to decide on the appropriate imperial symbols. Uniforms were introduced for railroad workers and lawyers; Soviet diplomats were ordered to wear on solemn occasions black suits with silver shoulder boards and gold trim on lapels and cuffs. People quietly joked in Moscow that soon even poets would be put in uni-form, with one, two, or three lyres on their shoulders to show their rank.

Since the revolution, the anthem of Bolshevik Russia had been the French "Internationale." Now Stalin decided that the Soviet Union needed a new state anthem, more in keeping with the circumstances and the change in political ambitions. A special state commission, headed by Marshal Kliment Voroshilov (who liked music and had a small but pleasant tenor), announced a competition, for which a lot of money was appropriated. Hundreds of proposals were sent by contes-tants, who included the country's best-known poets: Demyan Bedny,

Mikhail Isakovsky, Nikolai Tikhonov, Mikhail Svetlov, and Yevgeny Dolmatovsky. The list of composers had the names of Sergei Prokofiev, Shostakovich, and Aram Khachaturian.

In late autumn 1943, Stalin, who kept a close eye over the proceedings, selected one poem out of all the proposals, written by two young poets—the Russian Sergei Mikhalkov and the Armenian Gabriel Ureklyan (who was published under the pseudonym El-Registan). All the composers were asked to set the words, painstakingly edited by Stalin himself, to music. (Not many people knew then that Stalin, as a sixteen-year-old seminarian, published in the Tiflis newspapers several poems, as naïve as could be expected at his age, but sincere and passionate.)

The final round of the competition for the anthem was held at the Bolshoi Theater, whose musicians by then had returned from evacuation in Kuibyshev. Stalin and other Politburo members were present. Each anthem was heard sung by a chorus (the Red Army Ensemble of Song and Dance under the direction of a Stalin favorite, composer Alexander Alexandrov, who had several titles—professor at the Moscow Conservatory and major general in the army, as well as People's Artist of the USSR), then played by the orchestra of the Bolshoi, and, finally, performed by both chorus with soloists and orchestra. Besides the competing anthems, for the sake of comparison several others were played: the "Internationale," the "Marseillaise," "God Save the King," and—most intriguingly—the strictly banned symbol of pre-revolutionary Russia, "God Save the Tsar," the anthem written in 1833 at the personal request of Nicholas I by Alexei Lvov, a former aide-de-camp of Benckendorff and future general and director of the Court Cappella Choir.

Shostakovich and Khachaturian sat in the empty auditorium; their anthems had made it to the final round. They were tense, and the crimson and gilt of the recently renovated theater (damaged by German bombing at the beginning of the war) did not improve their mood. Shostakovich nervously stared at the restored ceiling, which depicted the nine muses with Apollo soaring in a blue sky. He later recalled that he had thought grimly, "I hope they accept my anthem. It would guarantee that I won't be arrested."[8]

The Bolshoi was truly an imperial theater, erected in 1856 from plans approved by Nicholas I. Stalin loved being there, missing almost no premieres in either opera or ballet. He attended some productions, primarily Russian classics, many times. He avoided appearing in the center box, formerly called the Tsar's Box. Not too many people knew that Stalin sat behind a curtain in box A, to the left, directly above the orchestra pit. That box was armored, in case of an assassination attempt. No one ever knew exactly when Stalin would come to the Bolshoi, but the performers could easily guess: That day General Nikolai Vlasik, the head of Stalin's personal bodyguards, would come to the theater accompanied by dandified aides-de-camp. In preparation for Stalin's visit, he walked around, greeting no one, giving the shivering staff a hard, suspicious look as he checked every nook and cranny of the theater.

During the performance the hall and the wings were filled with bodyguards in civilian dress. The frightened artists threw themselves onstage as if into an icy river. One singer in Tchaikovsky's *Queen of Spades,* aware that Stalin was in attendance, hit a wrong note. Stalin knew *Queen of Spades* well. He called in the Bolshoi director for an explanation. When the man practically crawled into the box, Stalin asked: "Does that singer have any honorary titles?"

"He is a People's Artist, Comrade Stalin."

Stalin shook his head and merely noted, "A generous people we have . . ."[9]

Many Bolshoi singers were Stalin's personal favorites. One was the great bass Maxim Mikhailov, a colorful man, short and stocky, a former church deacon. He was impressive in the role of Ivan Susanin in the then-eponymous opera by Glinka, originally titled *A Life for the Tsar.* They say that Stalin sometimes broke off evening sessions of the Politburo in order to catch Susanin's famous final aria. Mikhailov told conductor Kirill Kondrashin a secret: Sometimes the singer would be summoned in the middle of the night to the Kremlin to keep Stalin company. He would be alone in his office with a bottle of good Georgian wine on the desk. "Well, Maxim, let's sit and be silent a while . . ." Several hours would pass. Toward morning Stalin would say goodbye. "Thank you, Maxim, we had a fine talk."[10]

Among the performers of the contestant anthems were leading singers of the Bolshoi, including Mikhailov. One of them later insisted that the works by Prokofiev, Shostakovich, and Khachaturian did not make a good impression on the commission. In fact, the situation was more complicated than that. Stalin distinguished the anthems by

Shostakovich and Khachaturian right away, giving them the top score of ten. They had each written several versions and even one jointly, on the express orders of the leader, who believed in the efficiency of the collective. Stalin said that only in Shostakovich's and Khachaturian's works did he hear something original; the rest came up with clichéd marches.[11] But Stalin also recognized that originality was not a priority in a national anthem. An anthem, first of all, must be easily remembered and comfortable to sing. In that sense, the solemn "Anthem of the Bolshevik Party," composed by Alexandrov before the war, suited him. Stalin called the song a "dreadnought." By his lights, it should have gone powerfully with the patriotic text by Mikhalkov and El-Registan, which mentioned great Russia, Lenin, and Stalin, "the people's choice."*

Stalin rarely rushed important decisions. He preferred to get a wide spectrum of reactions from people whose professional opinion he respected. After one run-through an announcement was made from the stage: "Shostakovich and Khachaturian, come to the box!" Both were quickly led, accompanied by guards, to Stalin's box.

In the small red room adjacent to the box (the performers called it the "steambath antechamber") stood the leader and at a distance the other members of the Politburo: Molotov, Voroshilov, Mikoyan, Khrushchev, a total of ten to fifteen people. Shostakovich, who knew them from their portraits and had a phenomenal memory, politely greeted each man by his name and patronymic. "Hello, Iosif Vissarionovich! Hello, Vyacheslav Mikhailovich! Hello, Kliment Efremovich! Hello, Anastas Ivanovich! Hello, Nikita Sergeyevich!" This pleased Stalin. "We don't like shy people, but we don't like brash ones, either," he used to say.[13]

They regarded each other with curiosity: the leader, of medium height, broad-shouldered, with a pockmarked face, smoothing his legendary and now graying mustache, and arguably the most prominent "serious" composer of his country, bespectacled, with his eternally youthful forelock and deceptive air of a pupil nervous about rattling off his lesson. Stalin was wearing a new marshal's uniform in pale khaki, with broad red stripes. His ever-present pipe was in his hand.

---

*Interestingly, Stalin crossed out "the people's choice" from the final text—he had never been a candidate in a single national election. He also crossed out the word *griadushchee* (the future), explaining that the peasants were unlikely to understand it.[12]

Stalin spoke to Shostakovich. "Your music is very good, but what can I do, Alexandrov's song is more suitable for an anthem." Then he turned to his comrades: "I think that we should take Alexandrov's music, and as for Shostakovich . . ." Here, Stalin paused; Shostakovich later admitted to a friend that he expected to hear "as for Shostakovich, take him out into the courtyard and have him shot." But the leader completed his sentence differently. "As for Shostakovich, he should be thanked."[14]

Then Stalin turned to Alexandrov, who was also there. "But, Professor, there's something off in the arrangement." Alexandrov began making excuses: Time was short and he had his deputy, Victor Knushevitsky, do the arrangement, and he must have done a shoddy job. Shostakovich unexpectedly exploded, interrupting Alexandrov. "Shame on you, Alexander Vasilyevich! You know perfectly well that Knushevitsky is a master in his field and is a brilliant orchestrator. You are accusing your subordinate unjustly, and behind his back, when he can't respond. Shame!"

Silence reigned. Everyone froze, awaiting Stalin's reaction to this extraordinary behavior. Stalin puffed on his pipe and looked back and forth with interest between Shostakovich and the abashed Alexandrov—and said, at last, "Really, Professor, this isn't very nice . . ."[15]

Shostakovich had achieved his goal: Knushevitsky was spared being fired, or perhaps even arrested. Molotov asked Shostakovich, "Did Knushevitsky orchestrate your anthem, too?" The firm reply was that a composer should orchestrate his own works. After the musicians left the room, Stalin said to Molotov, "That Shostakovich seems to be a decent man."[16] Bearing in mind the difference in eras, temperaments, and situations, this could be considered the equivalent of Nicholas I declaring Pushkin "the wisest man in Russia."

A state resolution proclaimed Alexandrov's song the national anthem of the Soviet Union. It was played for the first time on Moscow radio on 1 January 1944. On New Year's Eve, Shostakovich, who knew that he was under the constant surveillance of the ubiquitous "competent organs," and suspecting that his mail was being read, wrote to a friend in Tashkent, weighing every word. And yet he was unable to hide his sadness behind the picket fence of overly "correct," clichéd phrases: "It is the last day of 1943, 4 p.m. A blizzard is howling outside my window. 1944 is coming. A year of happiness, a year of joy, a year of victory. This year will bring us much joy. Freedom-loving people will at last throw off the yoke of Hitlerism, and peace shall reign throughout the world, and once again we will live peaceful lives, under the sun of the Stalin constitution. I am certain of this and therefore feel a great joy. We are temporarily separated now; I miss you so much, otherwise we could take joy together in the glorious victories of the Red Army headed by the great military leader Comrade Stalin."[17]

On the next day the artist and photographer Alexander Rodchenko, mourning the end of avant-garde art in Russia (of which he had been one of the leaders), wrote in his secret Moscow diary:

> Today they played the new anthem by the composer Alexandrov. Very interesting . . . There are no others.
>
> After all, they can't give it to Shostakovich or Prokofiev.
>
> Besides which, it's "truly" Russian . . .
>
> The empire of false realism and pilfering . . .
>
> They say that authorities focus in art on realism, on the Wanderers, on Russian art.
>
> What is to be done?
>
> I'm sewing a shroud for the death of art, mine and everyone's . . . on the left . . .
>
> Lord and people of the future, forgive me!
>
> For not living at the right time.
>
> I won't anymore . . .
>
> It was very boring living here.
>
> Why did we live, always waiting, waiting and believing . . .
>
> What we made, nobody needed.[18]

As early as 1936 the amazing resemblance between Stalin's behavior as a ruler and Nicholas I's was noted by Georgii Fedotov, one of the most astute observers of Stalinism, in his essay in a Parisian Russian émigré journal: "Some of his gestures seem directly copied from Nicholas I."[19]

This resemblance, it must be added, was not obvious. Rather, Stalin tried to hide it. His attitude was quite different when it came to such

Russian autocrats as Ivan the Terrible and Peter the Great. The parallels with them were stressed in the Soviet press and art even before the war. There was a sarcastic joke at the time: Leaving a showing of the film *Peter the Great,* released in the late 1930s (and subsequently awarded the Stalin Prize), a boy asks his father, "Daddy, were all the tsars for the Bolsheviks?"

This new political line confused many people, for the attitude toward these two odious monarchs among Russian liberal historians before the revolution and certainly in the early years of Soviet rule were, to put it mildly, not apologistic. For instance, the *Malaya Sovetskaya Entsiklopediia* [Short Soviet Encyclopedia] denounced Peter the Great for his extreme mental unbalance, cruelty, drunkenness, and uncontrolled debauchery. It had no less contempt for Ivan the Terrible. The tone changed sharply when books, plays, and films about these tsars—created on Stalin's direct orders—praised their policies and their personalities. But Nicholas I continued to be treated with deep hostility.

Yet the policies of Nicholas I certainly served as a model for Stalin, and particularly in the sphere that most interests us—culture. Neither Ivan the Terrible nor Peter the Great devoted much attention to questions of literature and the fine arts, but Nicholas I could not allow himself to ignore them (even though, in the phrase of Count Vladimir Sollogub, he "simply did not like people who wrote").[20]

It was in the reign of Nicholas I that three principles were proclaimed for Russian education and culture: orthodoxy, autocracy, and nationality. Count Sergei Uvarov, minister of education under Nicholas I, formulated this triad (a modification of the military motto of the War of 1812—"For Faith, Tsar, and Fatherland!") in 1833. For many years it lay at the basis of all of Russia's cultural life, eliciting a growing resistance in the liberal intelligentsia.*

Stalin, who had always been fascinated by Russian history, had undoubtedly read a lot about this renowned ideological triad. Alexander Pypin, cousin of revolutionary idol Nikolai Chernyshevsky and

---

*By 1841 the popular critic Vissarion Belinsky mocked this formula (not in the press, however, but in an ironic private letter): "Our literature is flourishing, for it is clearly moving away from the fatal influence of the wicked West—becoming so orthodox that it smells of relics and resounds with bell ringing, so autocratic that it consists of nothing but denunciations, and so nationalistic that it can express itself only in profanity."[21]

prolific historian of literature, wrote a lot about the triad in the prerevolutionary years. He even produced a book on it, *Characteristics of Literary Opinion from the 1820s to the 1850s;* published in 1890, by 1909 it had come out in four editions. In it Pypin explained Uvarov's formula as a kind of bureaucratic catechism that regulated all forms of social and cultural life in Russia in the years of Nicholas I. Interestingly, Pypin was most negative about the third dogma—nationality—considering it to be an out-and-out euphemism for retaining the status quo; he saw it as a perverted "official nationality," intended to justify an autocratic regime. The whole theory, wrote Pypin, "boiled down to a panegyric to the present."[22]

But what angered the prerevolutionary liberal had to warm the heart of Stalin when, in the early 1930s, he planned a transition from the former Leninist "proletarian" state to an "all-national" one, under his aegis. Thus the formula of the Nicholas I era was very useful for Stalin.

Of course, as a short and unattractive man (many contemporaries noted Stalin's pockmarked face, sallow complexion, and low brow), the Communist dictator must have envied the tall, well-built, and handsome emperor, though Peter the Great's height did not keep Stalin from admiring that Russian tsar. Many things tied him to Nicholas I— first of all, their absolute conviction, based on personal experience, of their destined role and total irreplaceability as the country's leader.

Hence the desire of both rulers to build the state according to their own design from top to bottom, as an ideally functioning mechanism, with a rigorous hierarchy in all areas, including culture. In the systems of both Nicholas I and Stalin, discipline was a constant goal, and obedience and service the highest qualities. Order had to reign in everything. "We are engineers," Nicholas I liked to say. Stalin once compared writers to "engineers of human souls." Undoubtedly, he saw himself that way, too.

Both Nicholas I and Stalin felt that the Russian people needed a boss, a tsar.* The boss knows better than the rest how to lead his people to the radiant future. But the boss not only demands diligence and hard

---

*Curiously, the aforementioned Belinsky, an iconic figure of "progressive" Russian thought, at one point tended to hold the same idea, insisting that "unquestioning obedience of the tsar's power is not only our benefit and necessity, but the higher poetry of our life, our nationality . . ."[23]

work from his subordinates; he must work himself, setting an example for the others. Nicholas I and Stalin were workaholics, who spent sixteen to eighteen hours a day at their desks. They micromanaged the work of the state apparatus. As lady-in-waiting Alexandra Tyutcheva (daughter of the great poet Fyodor Tyutchev) recalled of Nicholas I, whom she had observed closely, "He believed honestly and sincerely that he was capable of seeing everything with his own eyes and transforming everything with his will." Exactly the same could be said of Stalin.

Both rulers were simple in their personal tastes, but appreciated fully the need for pomp and circumstance to create the image of a great state. Neither Nicholas I nor Stalin spared money for propagandistic aims, even though otherwise they were rather tight-fisted. At a time when black tailcoats were prevalent in Western Europe, Nicholas I devoted special attention to the design of brilliant military outfits. In that, as in many other ways, Stalin was his direct follower.

Nicholas I wanted to erect an iron curtain between Russia and Western Europe. In this he differed strongly from his great-grandfather Peter the Great, although in other ways he spent a lifetime trying to imitate him. Peter had intended to open up Russia rather broadly to Western influence. In one of the first manifestos of Nicholas I after the Decembrist rebellion, the completely opposite goal was formulated: "Purge Holy Russia from the infection brought in from outside." It was recommended that the people have a "domestic, natural, and not foreign upbringing."[24] In that area, Stalin also followed Nicholas I, criticizing Peter the Great for the fact that "too many Germans crawled into Russia" during his reign.[25]

Konstantin Simonov, a writer close to Stalin, recalled how in 1947, in a conversation with writers at the Kremlin, the ruler stressed that the unjustified kowtowing before foreign culture came to Russia with Peter I: " 'First the Germans, then the French, there was veneration of foreigners,' Stalin said, and suddenly, with a sly smile, in a barely audible aside, made a rhyme, *zasrantsy,* chuckled and turned serious again."[26] (*Zasrantsy,* "shitty," rhymes with *inostrantsy,* "foreigners.")

In 1831, Nicholas I decreed that Russian youths could not study abroad. This was in deep contradiction to the ideas of Peter I, who insisted that as many young Russians as possible be educated in Europe. Stalin followed Nicholas I rather than Peter I on this issue, too, even though publicly he presented Peter and Ivan the Terrible as his political predecessors and never mentioned Nicholas I: Why bring attention to an ideological similarity to the infamous executioner of the Decembrists and the purger of revolutionary culture?

And yet, Nicholas's ideological triad of orthodoxy, autocracy, and nationality fit Stalin like a glove, even though he could not use it in its original form. Under Stalin, orthodoxy, which was denounced by the Bolsheviks as the "opium of the masses," was replaced by the new religion—Communist ideology. The cult of autocracy was replaced by one that played the same political and ideological role, the cult of the leader—in this case, Stalin. And the vaguest postulate, nationality, became part of a new, no less vague term, "socialist realism."

Interpretations of socialist realism have appeared in thousands of books and pamphlets and innumerable articles in many languages. All this quasi-scholarly production in Soviet times was just a variation on the original definition, developed with the participation of Stalin, Maxim Gorky, Nikolai Bukharin, and Andrei Zhdanov in 1934 and formulated then in the charter of the Union of Soviet Writers: "Socialist realism, being the basic method of Soviet literature and literary criticism, demands from the artist a truthful, historically concrete depiction of reality in its revolutionary development. At the same time, the truthfulness and historical concreteness of the artistic depiction of reality must coexist with the goal of ideological change and education of the workers in the spirit of socialism."[27]

This comparatively laconic description, bearing the clear imprint of Stalin's bureaucratically tautological style, sounds rather elliptical, nevertheless. I think that the essence of socialist realism was formulated much more frankly and accurately, albeit more cynically, a hundred years earlier by Nicholas's chief of gendarmes, Benckendorff: "Russia's past was amazing, its present more than magnificent, and as for its future, it is better than what the most heated imagination can picture; that is the point of view from which Russian history must be examined and written."[28]

The resemblance between the cultural ideas and issues of the eras of Nicholas I and Stalin is rather striking. But of the most personal interest for Stalin was the relationship between the emperor and Pushkin. Stalin's literary tastes were formed primarily during his years at the Tiflis seminary in the late nineteenth century. This was the period when the tsarist government cemented its view of Pushkin as the greatest national poet. His works were studied at every educational institution in the land. Pushkin's centenary in 1899 was celebrated with great extravagance. The jubilee was marked, as the newspapers noted, "on a vast expanse from the Pacific Ocean to the Baltic Sea and from the Arctic Ocean to the borders of Afghanistan," with innumerable lectures, symposia, concerts, and plays (and even free chocolate bars with the poet's picture on the wrapping handed out to schoolchildren). The Russian Orthodox Church joined in; there were services honoring the birthday everywhere, including the Tiflis seminary.

Stalin adored Pushkin from his adolescence, according to recollections. In that period, the poet's works were studied primarily through the prism of Nicholas's triad of orthodoxy, autocracy, and nationality; a special emphasis was laid on the relationship between poet and tsar. Nicholas I's words about the "wisest man in Russia" were repeated frequently, and Pushkin's gratitude for the tsar's mercy toward him was stressed.

Stalin had already read Marx's *Das Kapital* by then and, considering himself a Socialist, headed the underground Marxist group of students at the seminary. As a revolutionary, Stalin was skeptical about the official legend of the good relations between poet and tsar. But he had to appreciate Nicholas's strategy in dealing with Pushkin. As was written at the time, "cunning conquered wisdom": The emperor charmed the poet and prompted him to create works from which the government could reap substantial ideological and propagandistic benefit.

At Nicholas I's special request, Pushkin wrote a long secret memorandum, "On National Education," as well as studies of the Pugachev rebellion in 1773 and of Peter I. These were intended first of all for the emperor's eyes, and the tsar read attentively, pencil in hand; in the margins of "On National Education" he made thirty-five question marks and one exclamation point.[29] In his memorandum, Pushkin proposed the abolition of corporal punishment for students; he maintained that republican ideas must also be studied in Russian educational institutions, which was anathema to the tsar. Next to this remark, Nicholas I put five question marks, but still asked Count Benckendorff to extend to Pushkin "his highest appreciation."

But while attempts at direct recruitment of the poet failed, his work did perform a service for the emperor. I am referring to several of

Pushkin's poems that helped, in one way or another, to create what might be called the cult of personality of Nicholas I, who came to the throne unexpectedly in 1825 after his older brother Konstantin's renunciation of the title; he was little known to the general public. The propaganda machine was set into motion, comparing Russia's new ruler with his ancestor Peter the Great. Pushkin joined this campaign with a poem, published with the tsar's permission in 1826, called "Stanzas," in which he drew parallels between Peter I and Nicholas I and called on the latter to be merciful to the rebel Decembrists:

> In hope of glory and good
> I gaze forward without fear:
> The start of Peter's glorious days
> Were darkened by rebellions and executions.
>
> But with truth he attracted hearts,
> But with science he quelled mores . . .

And so on. This publication impaired the reputation of the poet. The idol of enlightened Russian society, he was now accused by some of his closest friends of selling out. Rumors were spread that "Stanzas" was written on Nicholas I's orders right in his Kremlin office, in fifteen minutes, and that Pushkin was now spying on the political opponents of the government.

Pushkin felt profoundly insulted, but did not retreat from his position. His response to the attacks from the "left" was the poem "To My Friends" ("No, I'm not a flatterer, when / I write free praise of the tsar . . ."), in which Pushkin insisted on his role as liberal advisor to Nicholas I:

> Woe to the country, where slave and flatterer
> Are the only ones close to the throne,
> And the singer chosen by heaven
> Is silent, eyes downcast.

After this poem was also presented to the emperor, Benckendorff informed Pushkin that "His Majesty is completely pleased by it, but he does not wish it to be printed." He said, "Celà peut courire, mais pas être imprimé" (It can circulate, but may not be printed).[30] In this manner, Pushkin's work was given official permission to be in that era's *samizdat* (Soviet "self-publishing"—that is, circulation of typed manuscripts banned by the censors).

Pushkin's poems dedicated to Nicholas I were endlessly reprinted in prerevolutionary Russia, and Stalin knew them well, of course. But he must have also memorized two nationalistic works by Pushkin that were part of the Tiflis seminary's curriculum: "To the Slanderers of Russia" and "Anniversary of Borodino." The seminary laid particular stress on them. They were a response by Pushkin to the anti-Russian uprising of 1830–31 in Poland. He completed them just as the Russian troops, who cruelly suppressed the Polish insurrection, entered Warsaw, and read them immediately to Nicholas I and his family. On the monarch's orders, both works were included in a special brochure, *The Taking of Warsaw,* instantly published by the military printing house.

It was important for Nicholas I to prepare public opinion for a possible confrontation with the West, which was very hostile to the Russian military action. That is why the tsar so greatly appreciated the propaganda value of Pushkin's nationalist emotion:

> *Or is the Russian tsar's word now powerless?*
> *Or is it now for us to argue again with Europe?*
> *Or has the Russian forgotten how to be victorious?*
> *Or is there not enough of us? Or from Perm to Tauris,*
> *From the cold cliffs of Finland to fiery Colchis,*
> *From the stunned Kremlin*
> *To the walls of immovable China,*
> *Steel bristling and sparkling,*
> *Will not the Russian land arise?*

These verses of Pushkin's produced a lively polemic (which, for obvious reasons, was not reflected in the press) in Russian society. One friend wrote to Pushkin in delight: "At last, you are a national poet; you have at last discovered your calling." Another, on the contrary, scolded him severely: "This is very important in the state sense, but there isn't a penny's worth of poetry in it . . . What does it matter what politics can and must do? It needs executioners, but you're not going to sing their praises."[31] It's very unlikely that anyone, including Pushkin himself, guessed then that those verses would be used for propaganda a hundred years later. But that is exactly what happened: On Stalin's orders the quoted lines were reprinted widely during the war with Hitler (without the mention of the tsar).

But Stalin realized the huge propaganda potential of Pushkin even before the war, when he turned the centenary celebrations of his death in 1837 into a political show of unprecedented scope. The poet's works were published in special editions of approximately twenty million copies. The newspapers were filled with editorials and features about Pushkin that passed for important political news, their contents dictated by the Kremlin. Factories, kolkhozes (collective farms), schools, and army bases organized rallies, readings, lectures, concerts, and exhibits dedicated to the poet. Stalin used Pushkin's name to achieve several highly ambitious goals. His stories and poems became the foundation of the "socialist education" program for the masses. Under the banner "Pushkin in every family!" Pushkin was translated into the many languages of the other republics composing the Soviet Union, including Azeri, Kazakh, and Tajik.

His life was used as a model for the "new Soviet man." Here Stalin accepted Nikolai Gogol's remark about Pushkin being "a Russian developed as he might appear two hundred years from now." But just as with Stalin's notorious Five-Year Plans for the country's economic development, the second of which concluded ahead of time in 1937, the ruler decided to accelerate the process of bringing up "new Pushkins": He wanted them to appear now.

Stalin's propaganda always preferred positive examples to negative ones. The enemy should never take center stage—that is why Stalin never held exhibits like Hitler's show of "degenerate art" in 1937. The positive, pure image of the patriot Pushkin created by Stalin's mass media was to help quash the pathetic image of the routed opposition—all those Zinovievs, Kamenevs, and others—making them look like degenerate traitors and lackeys of Western imperialism. Stalin condemned them to execution, but more importantly, to total oblivion and erasure from the national memory, while Pushkin would be remembered forever. As the poet Nikolai Tikhonov predicted at a celebration of Pushkin at the Bolshoi Theater: "And when we finally win throughout the world, and all the nations bring to the feast of friendship the happy names of their poets and writers of genius, we will recall you, Pushkin, first at our universal triumph!"

In the Soviet paradigm, Pushkin's fate also served as a constant reminder of how difficult and oppressive life had been in tsarist times, in all spheres, including culture. Pushkin had been persecuted, exiled, humiliated, and finally killed in a duel at the young age of thirty-seven, to the tittering of the court and the sufferance of the tsar. And he was killed by a "shitty foreigner" to boot.

Stalin usually prepared and executed his propaganda plans methodically and rationally, but he did not turn off his emotions completely. Undoubtedly, he sincerely loved Pushkin and considered him a model of the people's poet. It is unlikely that Stalin would have consciously "competed" with Pushkin as a creative figure or writer. But as the new ruler of Russia, he surely compared himself to Nicholas I and judged himself superior. No matter what Stalin felt about the emperor and his cultural program, he accepted the received wisdom among the radical intelligentsia that the emperor was to blame for Pushkin's death. It became the official line under Stalin. If the great poet had lived in Stalin's Russia, he would not have let him die.

This powerful emotion colored Stalin's attitude toward the contemporary cultural figures he also considered the masters of their art: the writer Maxim Gorky and the theater directors Konstantin Stanislavsky and Vladimir Nemirovich-Danchenko of Moscow Art Theater fame. Stalin respected and loved them in his own way, and he even feared Gorky a bit. In any case, he wanted to become their patron, a strict but just advisor, or a friend even—the kind he would have been to Pushkin had he been Stalin's contemporary. The people intuitively felt the intimacy of the leader's feelings for the poet, as reflected in a joke of that era about the competition for a monument to Pushkin. The third-prize winner depicted Pushkin reading Pushkin; the second-prize winner, Stalin reading Pushkin; in first place was Pushkin reading Stalin.

The jubilee bacchanalia organized by Stalin for Pushkin caught up thirty-year-old Shostakovich. There was no avoiding it: Pushkin's name was on everyone's lips; people swore by him, and with his aid attacked enemies and defended themselves. Cultural figures appealed to him for inspiration, even when their work was in a completely different manner. The poet Boris Pasternak, for example, in 1922 liked to stun his anti-Soviet acquaintances by announcing that "Peter and Pushkin were Communists."[32] Ten years later, Pasternak published his para- phrase of Pushkin's "Stanzas" of 1826, which, as we remember, had been addressed to Nicholas I with an appeal for the tsar's mercy for the rebels. In his poem, Pasternak, in a clear reference to Pushkin, addressed Stalin with a similar request:

> *A century is not yesterday,*
> *And the same strength lies in temptation*
> *In the hope for glory and good*
> *To look at things without fear.*

In Stalin's repressive times, this public gesture looked rather bold and was remembered by many: It was not appropriate to speak to Stalin this way, even in verse. Here Pasternak used Pushkin as the model for a political dialogue in verse with the tsar.

Andrei Platonov, a writer whom Joseph Brodsky considered on a par with James Joyce, Robert Musil, and Franz Kafka, wrote in an article: "Pushkin's risk was particularly great: as we know, he spent his life walking 'the path of troubles,' and almost constantly felt himself on the verge of being sent to prison or hard labor. The sorrow of the coming loneliness, oblivion, and deprivation of the ability to write poisoned Pushkin's heart."[33] And he quoted Pushkin's poem "Premonition":

> *Once again clouds above me*
> *Have gathered in silence;*
> *Envious fate threatens*
> *Me with disaster again . . .*

Platonov knew what he was writing about: In 1931, Stalin covered the margins of a literary magazine with Platonov's *Vprok* [Profit] with notations such as "fool," "toothless punster," and "scoundrel." The writer could no longer publish his best works. Platonov was thrown out of literary life, and he died in 1951, not yet fifty-two years old, of the tuberculosis he caught from his son returned from exile: a huge loss that went unnoticed in the leaden twilight of the Stalin era.

Shostakovich had entered Pushkin's world in childhood and always considered him one of his favorite poets. This was inevitable, since, as Andrei Bitov noted, "It is not so much that Pushkin is our national poet, as that our attitude toward Pushkin has become a kind of national trait." But for Shostakovich, who absorbed musical impressions with heightened sensitivity from childhood, appreciation of Pushkin also came through music. For instance, Tchaikovsky's operas *Eugene Onegin* and *The Queen of Spades* and Mussorgsky's *Boris Godunov* are based on subjects from Pushkin. Many of Pushkin's poems were introduced to Shostakovich through the famed songs by Glinka, Dargomyzhsky, Rimsky-Korsakov, and Rachmaninoff. Thirteen-year-old Mitya Shostakovich's first opera was based on Pushkin's long poem *The Gypsies;* he later burned it in a fit of disillusionment (as he called it), regretting it in hindsight. Only a few numbers from it survive.

Shostakovich turned to Pushkin's poetry again seventeen years later, in 1936, a year that proved tragic for him and for so many Soviet people. Stalin had seen and taken a strong dislike to Shostakovich's opera *Lady Macbeth of Mtsensk.* This opera and Shostakovich's ballet *The Limpid Stream,* both produced at the Bolshoi Theater in Moscow, were banned, and Shostakovich was ostracized as part of a large-scale campaign against "formalism" in Soviet art. Many of his friends deserted him. He feared for his life, the future of his works, and the fate of his family. But he did not stop composing music: That was Shostakovich.

On 1 August 1936 he began a cycle of songs set to Pushkin's poetry. The first poem to catch his attention was "The Demons," one of the poet's most turbulent works. Shostakovich was attracted by the image of the mad demonic dance, which carried a metaphoric similarity to the situation around his disgraced opera:

> *Endless, ugly,*
> *In the murky play of the moon*
> *Various demons swirled . . .*

But Shostakovich interrupted work on this song; apparently the negative emotions were too strong, and he was looking for a positive lesson and ray of hope in Pushkin. Therefore he set "Renaissance" to music— Pushkin's mini-parable about an ancient painting, "the creation of a genius," disfigured by barbarians; many years later it "appears with its previous beauty" to an awed audience. The parallel with Stalin, who "scribbles meaninglessly" (from the poem) his barbaric orders right on the genius's painting, is obvious here.

Just as obvious are the contemporary allusions and autobiographical parallels in the third piece of the cycle, "Premonition," the poem that Platonov cited in his article on Pushkin:

> *Will I maintain disdain for my fate?*
> *Will I bring to it*
> *Inexorability and patience*
> *Of my proud youth?*

But, as often with Shostakovich, personal and political tragedies resulted in music of amazing artistic strength, with raw passion only intermittently breaking through to the surface. *Four Romances to the Words of A. Pushkin* is a masterpiece of Shostakovich's vocal writing, underappreciated to this day. Interestingly, even some of his friends found "something loutish" in this cycle. But it was certainly not because of these private reactions that Shostakovich postponed the premiere of this opus for four and a half years, waiting for the storm clouds over his head to pass. In 1936, the public performance of a work with such provocative texts (albeit by Pushkin) could have cost Shostakovich dearly. Nothing was expected from him but self-flagellation—that was the cruel ritual of the era.

After the political scandal with Shostakovich's opera and ballet on the stages of the Bolshoi Theater and its annex, Stalin decided to bring order to his court theater. He installed an artistic director for the entire Bolshoi Theater—both opera and ballet—a post for a little "musical Stalin" that, ironically, was given to the conductor Samuil Samosud, transferred in 1936 to Moscow from Leningrad, and an old friend and admirer of Shostakovich. In 1930 he was the first to conduct Shostakovich's avant-garde opera *The Nose,* and in 1934 he premiered *Lady Macbeth.* But Stalin did not bear a grudge against Samosud for that. Always practical, the leader appreciated Samosud's talent and energy and assigned him a great task: to make the Bolshoi the leading musical theater not only of the Soviet Union but of the world.

Stalin was a consistent adherent of the carrot-and-stick policy. He used to say, "I don't believe too much in conscience. Where there is no real self-interest, there will never be real success." In 1937, the Bolshoi, the country's premier artistic collective, was awarded the highest prize—the Order of Lenin. Samosud and a select group of artists were also given Orders of Lenin and the recently established title of People's Artists of the Soviet Union. Almost one hundred other members of the troupe received other awards. This was considered a great honor, and all the presentations were made with enormous pomp, as if it were a day of national rejoicing.

Pravda of 4 June 1937 published a directive article, ostensibly by Samosud, describing plans for the new productions of Glinka's *Ivan Susanin* and Mussorgsky's *Boris Godunov*. A close reading of the article easily reveals Stalin's advice and the conductor's reactions (it must have been taken down and only minimally cleaned up for publication). The text falls into two stylistically contrasting layers: Stalin's authoritative formulations and Samosud's hurried, respectful agreement.

Stalin: "We understand the opera *Ivan Susanin* as a profoundly patriotic national drama, its blade pointed against the enemies of the great Russian people." Samosud: "The Bolshoi Theater will do everything to clean up the text correspondingly, bringing it closer to Glinka's music and the actual historical truth."

Stalin: "In our opinion, the old productions of *Boris Godunov* on opera stages also showed the Russian people incorrectly. It was usually shown as being oppressed. The main plotline of the opera was considered to be Boris's personal drama. That is wrong." Samosud is, naturally, in complete agreement: "In our production the role of the people in the development of events will be increased significantly, the folk scenes shown vividly and three-dimensionally."

The fact of such a conversation between Stalin and Samosud is confirmed in a recently published letter from Shostakovich to the poet Yevgeny Yevtushenko. The letter was written in 1962, and Shostakovich was not willing, for obvious reasons, to mention Stalin openly then; therefore, he quite transparently calls him "the Coryphaeus of Science," as the servile Soviet press called Stalin during his lifetime. According to Shostakovich (who heard it from Samosud himself), the ruler told the conductor, "There is no need to produce the opera *Boris Godunov*. Pushkin, and Mussorgsky, perverted the image of the outstanding state figure Boris Godunov. He is shown in the opera as a namby-pamby nothing. Because he killed some kid, he suffered torments of conscience, even though he, Boris Godunov, as a leading figure, knew perfectly well that this act was necessary in order to bring Russia onto the path of progress and true humanism." Shostakovich sarcastically adds, "S. A. Samosud reacted with delight to the ruler's extraordinary wisdom."[34]

Shostakovich did not mention, however, that Samosud managed to persuade Stalin of the need for a new production of *Boris*. The conductor was certain that he could "rehabilitate" both Mussorgsky and Pushkin. This was not an easy task. The opera and the tragedy were very different works, but both had a complicated and difficult history.

Pushkin finished his *Boris Godunov* in late autumn 1825, not long before the Decembrist uprising. Using Shakespeare's historical plays as a model, and using the materials from *The History of the Russian State* by Nikolai Karamzin, whom he revered, Pushkin narrated the story of how the ambitious boyar Boris Godunov bypassed more important claimants and ascended the Russian throne in 1598. But all efforts by Godunov to win the people's trust were in vain: Rumor persistently blamed him in the death of the young Tsarevich Dmitri, son of Ivan the Terrible, who had been an obstacle on Godunov's path to the throne.* In addition, starvation and epidemics swept through Moscow; the people were agitated. And here appeared a pretender who claimed to be the miraculously saved Tsarevich Dmitri. In fact, he was Grigory Otrepyev, a young monk who had broken his vows. Gathering under his banner all those who were unhappy with Tsar Boris and obtaining the support of Poland, the Pretender moved on Moscow. In a few brilliant strokes Pushkin draws a picture of the instant disintegration of Godunov's power and might in 1605: Everyone condemns him; no one believes him; torn by pangs of conscience, he dies. The False Dmitri triumphs.

Following Shakespeare, Pushkin combined the lofty and tragic with the comic and coarse; the action unfolds swiftly and intensely, without the slightest slip into sentimentality. This was a revolution for Russian drama, and Pushkin reported delightedly to his friend Prince Petr Vyazemsky that he had completed the final copy of his play. "I reread it out loud, alone, and clapped hands and exclaimed, 'Why, that Pushkin,

---

*Pushkin, following Karamzin and oral tradition, considered Godunov a murderer; modern historians cast doubt on this version.

that son of a bitch, is good!' " Pushkin took the clean copy with him to Moscow when he was summoned there in 1826 by the just-crowned Nicholas I. He presented it to him for his royal approval. At first Nicholas I suggested redoing the play as a "historical novella or novel, like Walter Scott," but then acquiesced: In 1831, *Boris Godunov* was published at last, even though it was not staged until thirty-three years after Pushkin's death, in the fall of 1870.

The St. Petersburg press and audiences received the premiere of Pushkin's tragedy very coolly. This must have influenced the decision of the opera committee of the Imperial Maryinsky Theater when it rejected that same fall the opera *Boris Godunov* by the young composer Modest Mussorgsky. Mussorgsky took the rejection very hard, but his friends persuaded him to make some substantial changes. A new version appeared, and with it, an eternal problem for opera theaters all over the world: which version (or their combination) to prefer? And in which orchestration, the author's own or some later, posthumous arrangement, two of the most illustrious being Rimsky-Korsakov's and Shostakovich's?

Despite all of this, *Boris Godunov* remains one of the most famous and cherished of Russian operas. Even in Russia (not to mention in the West) it is produced incomparably more frequently than Pushkin's tragedy. Mussorgsky is a more passionate and romantic author than Pushkin. His opera is more like Dostoevsky in sound. In part this is due to the nature of the operatic genre: Music and singing enlarge the character, setting him on romantic "stilts." This is all the more inevitable in the swirling, unruly space of Mussorgsky's proto-expressionist music.

Shostakovich considered Mussorgsky his favorite composer throughout his life. He studied his *Boris* thoroughly when he was a student. In the late 1920s the opera was at the center of a stormy public discussion after its new productions in Moscow and Leningrad. The Bolsheviks always regarded *Boris Godunov* as a revolutionary opera. The first Bolshevik People's Commissar of Education, Anatoli Lunacharsky, saw in Mussorgsky's work a reflection of the mood of "angry populism, welcoming rebellion." Mussorgsky was considered to be much more radical politically than Pushkin, who ended his tragedy with the symbolic note: "The people are silent." In Mussorgsky, the people are the main protagonist of *Boris Godunov,* even though the composer does not make them pretty, instead portraying them, according to

Lunacharsky, as "neglected, browbeaten, cowardly, cruel, and weak—a mob, how it could be and must be in conditions of an anti-people regime, for centuries shackling any vitality of democracy."[35]

It was the Pushkin-Mussorgsky *Boris Godunov,* not just Pushkin's, that often served as a mirror for Russia in moments of social upheaval. Passions always flared over this opera, and no one remained indifferent to it. Young Shostakovich very quickly developed his own attitude toward the work.

In an introduction to his *History of the Russian State,* the monarchist Karamzin wrote, "The history of the nation belongs to the Tsar." Pushkin did not agree: "The history of the people belongs to the Poet." This was a very daring and even provocative statement of Russia of that period, and subsequent ones. Pushkin placed himself between two hostile camps. Karamzin's opponents from the revolutionary camp maintained that the history of a nation belonged to the people—that is, it is formed and defined by them. Later this would become the dogma of the Russian populists and, after them, the Marxists. Pushkin's position was prophetic. He maintained that history belongs to those who interpret it—a point of view that became influential in the late twentieth century.

Pushkin realized his idea of the poet's central role in the interpretation of national history in *Boris Godunov.* He introduced an autobiographical image of the Poet, so complex and multifaceted that the author had to divide his various functions among several characters.

His most obvious personification is the chronicler, the monk Pimen, whose name became a common term for historians in Russia. Pushkin did not idealize his hero, however. He knew that real chroniclers were not objective describers floating above events they related; after all, he was one himself.* His chronicler (and poet) performs the functions of witness and judge. The tsar may think that he is above the law because he is at the pinnacle of power. But Pushkin reminds the autocrat:

> *And yet the hermit in his dark cell*
> *Is writing a terrible denunciation of you:*

---

*Historians confirm that the pens of ancient Russian chroniclers "were directed by political passions and worldly interests."[36]

> *And you will not escape earthly judgment,*
> *No more than God's Judgment.*

Another character in his play with whom Pushkin definitely identi-
fied was the *yurodivy,* or holy fool. This is substantiated in the already
cited letter from Pushkin to Prince Vyazemsky: "Zhukovsky says that
the tsar will forgive me for the tragedy—unlikely, my dear. Even
though it is written in a good spirit, I simply couldn't hide all of my
ears beneath the Holy Fool's cap. They stick out!"

Pushkin's holy fool is an image of himself, like the chronicler. Both
characters are typical of medieval Russia. The chronicler culture
existed throughout Europe, but in Russia the chronicles were particularly politicized and therefore influential. The same holds true for the
holy fools: they were widespread in Europe, too, but only in Russia did
their confrontations with the powers-that-be have such public resonance. In that sense, we can speak of the unique significance of the figures of the chronicler monk and *yurodivy* in Russian history and
culture. It is no accident that Pushkin chose them as his alter egos in
Boris Godunov: Through them he dares to tell the truth to the tsar's
face. Thus an influential cultural paradigm was established.

One of the most important themes in Pushkin's tragedy is the
immorality, criminality, and doomed nature of power won through
bloodshed. Pushkin's holy fool reminds us: "No, no! you cannot pray for
King Herod—the Mother of God forbids it." Tsar Boris's entourage
scolds the holy fool for his frank words: "Get away, fool! Grab the fool!"
But Pushkin's tsar stops them: "Leave him. Pray for me, poor Nikolka."

This heartrending exchange corresponds to historical accounts of
the relations between tsars and holy fools and to Pushkin's ideas of the
dialogue between poet and authority. Where the poet did not want to
(or could not) play the role of the measured and majestic Pimen, he
could choose the mask of the mad, and therefore untouchable, holy
fool. Both characters spoke directly to God and therefore had the right
to judge tsars. And according to Pushkin, the tsars understood that.

But even those two masks were not enough for Pushkin to present
the complex functions that in his opinion the poet had to perform in
society. The poet not only describes and thereby formulates a nation's
history; he not only tells the truth to tsars. He can, if circumstances

demand it, appear in the role of active participant in events, as a protagonist of the drama. Hence Pushkin's attention and paradoxical sympathy for the Pretender—a daring adventurer who wanted to take fate by the horns.

Pretenders appear frequently in Russian history. Legends of "switched tsars" and "savior tsars" traveled among the serfs and were powerful enough to propel the False Dmitri to the throne in 1605 and energize the later movements of the Russian peasant leaders Stepan Razin ("Tsarevich Alexei") in 1671 and Emelyan Pugachev ("Emperor Peter III") in 1773.[37] Pushkin clearly admires his Pretender, his courage, cleverness, and confidence. Pushkin's Pretender often uses the word "fate," one of the poet's favorite words. The Pretender shapes his own fate, his own biography: This is a direct parallel with the romantic idea of the "poet's biography" as it began to form in Pushkin's day.

Pushkin allows the Pretender to express some of his most deeply felt thoughts: "I believe in the prophecy of poets," he says. Sometimes it seems that Pushkin treats the Pretender like an unreasonable younger brother. For example, here is a description of the Pretender given by the Boyar Pushkin, a character in the play (and this is another of the author's knowing smiles): "He is as feckless as a stupid child; he is protected, of course, by Providence." (This calls to mind Pushkin's renowned line: "Poetry, may God forgive me, must be a bit stupid.")

The young Shostakovich undoubtedly absorbed the content and issues of *Boris Godunov* through Mussorgsky's opera and not through the Pushkin tragedy, which Mussorgsky had changed substantially for the operatic stage (prompting severe criticism from contemporaries). For our purposes, Mussorgsky's handling of the three characters who represent the Poet for Pushkin is important. They are all elevated and enlarged; the author's gaze, and therefore the audience's, is focused on them more. The chronicler Pimen's role as exposer and judge is moved to the forefront. It is he (and not the Patriarch, as in the Pushkin play) who with his tale of the miracles connected to the murdered tsarevich strikes the final, fatal blow for Boris. Even the Pretender is ennobled in Mussorgsky's version: he shares a radiant, elevated musical leitmotif with the tsarevich. This glowing theme appears almost forty times in the opera, lending the image of the Pretender a positive musical halo. Mussorgsky makes the Pretender really the tsarevich's reincarnation. This is a significant artistic and ideological shift.

The holy fool's meaning also grew immeasurably in the opera. For Mussorgsky the holy fool is the torn conscience and sobbing voice of all the people. That is why he ends the opera with the holy fool's lament, prophesying the arrival of a terrible, dark time:

> *Sorrow, sorrow to Russia!*
> *Weep, weep, Russian people,*
> *Hungry people!*

The words of this simple refrain (one of the greatest pages in Russian music) were written by Mussorgsky. This was not without reason: even Mussorgsky's closest friends frequently called him "idiot" or "*yurodivy*." His identification with the holy fool in *Boris* was even greater than Pushkin's. This prompted me once to call Mussorgsky the first great Russian holy fool–composer.

I then considered Shostakovich to be the second.[38] I had weighty reasons for doing so. Like Mussorgsky, Shostakovich had friends who angrily called him a holy fool. According to Nikolai Rimsky-Korsakov, who knew him well, Mussorgsky's eccentric behavior was influenced by, "on the one hand, his prideful self-opinion and conviction that the path he had chosen in art was the only true one; on the other—total downfall, alcoholism and the consequently always foggy head."[39] Shostakovich's complicated behavior was on the one hand more natural and on the other more "artificial" than Mussorgsky's. Shostakovich had good examples in that regard.

Among his comrades in the "left front of art" in Leningrad in the late 1920s and early 1930s, we see a group for whom *épatage* and eccentricity were an important part of the artistic program. They were the OBERIU (*Ob'edinenie real'nogo iskusstva*, Association of Real Art), Russian Dadaists and early representatives of the literary absurd. The old world had been blown up by war and revolution and its ideals and values discarded. The OBERIUts perceived the new order of things through the prism of the grotesque. Their leader, Daniil Yuvachev, who took the pseudonym Daniil Kharms (an amalgam of the English words "charm" and "harm"), declared, "I am interested only in 'nonsense'; only in what has no practical meaning. I am interested in life only in its ridiculous manifestations. Heroism, pathos, bravery, morality, hygiene, morals, piety, and risk—are words and feelings I detest. But I fully understand and respect: delight and awe, inspiration and despair, passion and restraint, debauchery and chastity, sorrow and grief, joy and laughter."⁴⁰

The moralizing tone of the manifesto is notable. Kharms presents himself here as a modern paradoxical prophet—that is, in the role of a "new holy fool." He toed the same line in his life, creating an image of the eccentric and oddball that was totally unthinkable in Soviet Leningrad. Kharms could be seen on the city streets wearing a light jacket and no shirt, military jodhpurs, and slippers with no socks. A large pectoral cross and a butterfly net completed the outfit. According to a girlfriend, Kharms would stroll around Leningrad calmly and with dignity, so that while passersby did not laugh, some little old lady was bound to exclaim, "What a silly fool!"

The authorities reacted more nervously. The Komsomol (Young Communist League) newspaper attacked Kharms after he climbed up on a chair at a literary soiree at the Higher Course of Art History and announced, brandishing a stick, "I don't read in stables or brothels!" This typical *yurodivy* statement was taken for an attack on the honor of the Soviet educational institution. But the OBERIUts persisted, and came to a party at a dormitory of Leningrad University with a poster "We Are Not Pies!" and called the students gathered there "savages." This time the officious newspaper burst out with what amounted to a political denunciation: "Their departure from life, their meaningless poetry, their irrational juggling is a protest against the dictatorship of the proletariat. Their poetry is therefore counterrevolutionary. This is the poetry of people who are alien to us, the poetry of the class enemy."⁴¹ Soon afterward the leading OBERIUts were arrested.

Making his innovative works available to the wider public, Shostakovich, like the OBERIUts, was playing with fire. His first opera, *The Nose,* was called "an anarchist's hand bomb" by the Soviet press. The establishment perceived many of Shostakovich's early works as "musical hooliganism." And finally, in 1936, the Party newspaper *Pravda,* in an editorial called "Muddle Instead of Music," carried out a sentence that was to be final (and not subject to appeal): "This is music intentionally made inside out . . . This is leftist muddle." As will be shown, these angry opinions belonged personally to Stalin, the country's main cultural arbiter.

Stalin's reaction—"inside out"—is the typical reaction of an incensed ruler to the behavior of a holy fool. The notorious "muddle"

comes from that, too—the revelations of the *yurodivy* were traditionally seen as irrational and "muddled." *Pravda* indignantly described
Shostakovich's music as "fitful and epileptic," an "intentionally disso-
nant, muddled flow of sounds," in which the composer "mixed up all
the sounds." In exactly the same way—as deliberately ugly, febrile, and
fitful—contemporaries described the actions of legendary *yurodivye* of
the past. The coincidences in the vocabulary of invective are astonishing and telling.

For all that, Shostakovich's quotidian mask was not as vividly
provocative as that of his fellow-thinking OBERIUts. Shostakovich, on
the contrary, tended toward the maximal simplification of his person
and behavior, as did his other Leningrad friend the writer Mikhail
Zoshchenko, who ironically described his satirical writing style in this
way: "I write very compactly. My sentences are short. Accessible to the
poor."

The deliberately impoverished, "naked" language (comparable to the
nakedness of the *yurodivy* as an important distinguishing mark—the
legendary *yurodivy* Basil the Blessed, who denounced Ivan the Terrible,
was also known as Basil the Naked) was the result of long efforts on
Zoshchenko's part to find a new and effective manner for his creative
preaching needs. Today, there is no doubt that Zoshchenko was a
preacher, moralizer, and teacher of life. There is something else of
interest: His stylized writing manner gradually extended to his behavior.

This process of simplification can be traced through Zoshchenko's
private letters, which over time began to resemble excerpts from his
"naked" prose. Zoshchenko himself maintained that these were conscious and tormented efforts to find a mask in literature appropriate to
his goals in art and in life: "I was born in a family of the intelligentsia. I
was not, essentially, a new man and new writer. Whatever my innovation was in literature, it was totally of my own invention . . . The language that I took and which, at first, seemed funny and intentionally
mangled to the critics, was, in fact, extremely simple and natural."

The *yurodivye* were known for their mumbled speech, short, nervous, stuttered phrases with repeated words. In Pushkin's *Boris Godunov,*
the holy fool insists: "Give, give, give me a kopeck." That was
Shostakovich all over: Anyone who had ever spoken to him knew his
manner of getting "hung up" on a word or phrase, repeating it over and
over. Psychologists have noted that this is characteristic of children's

creativity, a comparison that suited Shostakovich. His good friend the writer Marietta Shaginyan described the thirty-four-year-old Shostakovich in a letter to Zoshchenko: "The impression was of a very irresponsible, frail, fragile, curled up like a snail, endlessly candid and pure child. It's simply incredible that he's survived."[42]

The impression of fragility and frailness that Shostakovich projected in those years (and later) is very telling—we will see that psychologically, and especially creatively, it was quite deceptive. It was that outward infantilism of Shostakovich's behavior that led the wise Shaginyan (as I knew her in the early seventies) to wonder how he had survived the meat grinder of the Stalin terror after the frontal attack on him in *Pravda* in 1936. But such infantilism can serve as a secure defensive armor, as was noted by the cynical Erasmus of Rotterdam in his *In Praise of Folly:* "Children are loved, kissed, and petted; even a foreign enemy is ready to come to their aid."

"He is endowed with a kind of eternal childhood," Anna Akhmatova said of Pasternak. This "eternal childhood" is apparently one of the necessary components of the image of the poet. Pasternak used to recount that when they wanted to arrest him in the years of the Great Terror, Stalin himself objected: "Don't touch that cloud-dweller, that unworldly one."[43] For Stalin—and for Pushkin—holy fool and poet (actually, any creator, "cloud-dweller") were equivalent concepts.

One more important circumstance. In the Russian religious and cultural tradition, which Stalin, as a former seminarian, knew well, the tsar and the holy fool were tied by an invisible but sturdy thread. Stalin, who considered himself a Russian tsar, felt that connection acutely. It was a combination of emotion and calculation. In initiating and exploiting his contacts with the "new *yurodivye*" in culture, Stalin realized some of his deepest psychological impulses. But most importantly he bore the experience of rulers like Ivan the Terrible in mind. Like him, Stalin was an autocrat who still did not dare to ignore public opinion, knowing its power. Stalin did not want to repeat the fatal mistake of the real Boris Godunov, who had underestimated its strength and as a result was swept from the throne by a wave of popular discontent exploited by the Pretender Dmitri.

That is why the episodes of contact between Stalin and Mikhail Bulgakov or Pasternak, which instantly took on mythical status among the Soviet intelligentsia, are so characteristic. I will describe these meetings later. Here I want to mention the legend connecting Stalin with Maria Yudina, the celebrated Russian musical *yurodivaya*.★ Yudina was perhaps the most eccentric figure in the history of Russian music. She was born in 1899 to a Jewish family, but adopted Christianity as a young woman and remained an exaltedly devout Russian Orthodox to her death. This was sufficiently dramatic in itself, but in the officially atheistic Soviet Union it threatened to disrupt Yudina's biography totally.

After graduating from the piano class of Professor Leonid Nikolayev (also Shostakovich's teacher) at the Petrograd Conservatory in 1921, Yudina immediately became one of the most illustrious performers of the time. When she came out onstage in her usual outfit—a long black pyramidal dress with free bat-wing sleeves and a large cross on her chest—sat at the piano, took a pose of intense concentration, and then, after lifting her hands to the sky, suddenly dropped them onto the keyboard, the audience froze, stunned by the squall of powerful sound; they said that Yudina played with the strength of ten men. Her repertoire was highly unusual: from Bach and Beethoven, skipping the popular music of Chopin, Liszt, Tchaikovsky, and Rachmaninoff, Yudina moved on to Stravinsky, Hindemith, and Shostakovich. In her last years she performed the avant-garde works of Pierre Boulez and Karlheinz Stockhausen.

Her audiences received Yudina's musical interpretations as frenzied sermons, but sometimes the music alone was not enough for her, and she would interrupt the concert to address the audience with readings of poems by the then-banned Pasternak or former OBERIUt Nikolai Zabolotsky. This agitated her audiences even more, but it seriously complicated her relations with the authorities. She was banned from performing for extended periods and fired from her teaching jobs, yet Yudina stood fast. Only physically could she be broken and destroyed, but the authorities never wanted to arrest the celebrated pianist.

It was said that her protection came from Stalin's tolerant attitude toward Yudina. He considered her a holy fool. The legend has it that when Stalin heard Yudina playing a Mozart concerto on the radio, he demanded a record of that performance for himself. No one had the

★I first heard this legend from Shostakovich in the early 1970s, after I had met Yudina in 1970.

nerve to tell him that it had been a live performance that was not recorded. Yudina was urgently called to the studio where the pianist spent a night of intense work with an orchestra and a relay of conductors to make a record that was then brought to Stalin. It was a unique edition of one copy.

When he got the record, Stalin rewarded Yudina with a large sum of money. She thanked him by letter, telling him that she was donating the money to her church—and adding that she would pray to God to forgive Stalin for his grave sins. A letter like that was tantamount to suicide, but no repressions followed. It was reported that when Stalin died, that recording of Mozart was on the turntable next to his bed.

What is important about this story is not whether it is authentic or apocryphal, but the very fact of its rather wide circulation in the milieu of the intelligentsia. Even the skeptical Shostakovich insisted it was true. He, too, considered Yudina a holy fool: He recalled how she gave away the last of her money to the needy; and how once when they were allowed to go to Leipzig in 1950, she set off to St. Thomas Church, where Bach was buried, barefoot, like a true pilgrim, scraping her feet raw on the way. (This eccentric behavior, naturally, was immediately reported to Stalin.)

So, for Shostakovich the possibility of a dialogue between tsar and *yurodivy* was real and important. His public humiliation, the threat of arrest, the betrayal of friends made him consider a new life and work strategy. He adapted the trinity formula of the creative and personal behavior of the Russian poet first proposed by Pushkin and then taken up and developed by Mussorgsky. He is the chronicler Pimen, judging tsars from the point of view of history itself. He is the holy fool, the personification of the people's conscience. He is also the Pretender, not satisfied to merely witness, who tries to insert himself into the historical process as an active participant.

Shostakovich was moving toward adopting all three roles anyway; the crisis of 1936 only precipitated the process. In this life play, Stalin was given the role of the tsar; he knew that and tried to play the part with Shakespearean (or Pushkinian) gusto. How they—the poet and the tsar of the new era—matured to perform these roles and then began to live their parts (almost as prescribed by Stanislavsky's method) is the subject of this book.

Chapter I   Mirages and Temptations

In July of 1906, St. Petersburg, the capital of the Russian Empire, was declared to be in a state of "high security alert." The government was finishing off the 1905 revolution. Tsar Nicholas II was forced to agree to the convocation of the first Russian parliament, called the Duma, but in the summer he issued a decree on courts-martial, and the police corps in St. Petersburg was significantly reinforced.

Kronstadt, the naval base near St. Petersburg, one of the biggest in the world, was also on military alert. Mounted Cossack patrols roamed the Kronstadt streets at night. Local jails were overloaded with sailors arrested for participation in the revolution. In July 1906 the Kronstadt sailors rebelled once again, but they were surrounded and forced to surrender. More than three thousand people were arrested then, and thirty-six sailors were court-martialed and sentenced to death.

On the night of 24 September, they came for the condemned men, who were told that on the request of their defense, they would be shot instead of hanged. The entire jail watched at the windows as the manacled men were pushed into big black horse-drawn carriages, surrounded by gendarmes. In anger and impotence, the prisoners sang a revolutionary funeral march:

> *Tormented by hardship of prison,*
> *You died a glorious death . . .*

In the struggle for the people
You laid down your head honestly.

The gendarmes ran and shouted: "Stop singing!" And from the prison came another popular protest song:

Rage, tyrants, mock us,
Threaten us with jail and manacles!
We are free in spirit, even if our bodies are not,
Shame, shame, and death to you, tyrants!

And on 25 September, in a family that knew and often sang those popular revolutionary songs, Dmitri Shostakovich was born. A half-century later, marking his birthday, Shostakovich decided to write a symphony that would use the revolutionary melodies that he remembered from childhood. He finished the symphony—the Eleventh—in 1957 and gave it an official name, "1905," referring to the first Russian revolution. And in fact, outwardly, the symphony's four movements correspond to the tragedy of 9 January 1905, when on Palace Square in St. Petersburg troops shot at a peaceful demonstration of workers who had come to the Winter Palace to ask the tsar to ease their economic hardship and introduce some form of popular representation.

But Shostakovich's son-in-law, Yevgeny Chukovsky, recalled that originally the title sheet of the Eleventh Symphony read "1906," that is, the year of the composer's birth. This allows us to hear the symphony differently: as a monument and requiem for himself and his generation. Shostakovich's generation had to undergo unprecedented trials: It lost fathers in the maelstrom of the First World War and the Civil War; it lived through the shocks of two revolutions, the horrors of forced collectivization, and the Stalin terror; and it underwent the Second World War and bore the brunt of the postwar collapse. This generation was spared yet another bloodbath only by the death of Stalin in 1953.

Aleksandr Solzhenitsyn once said that the years between 1914 and 1956 were a period of "the collapse of our national consciousness." In 1956, Russia began awakening from a long sleep. In February, at the Twentieth Congress of the Communist Party of the USSR, its new leader, Nikita Khrushchev, gave a secret speech that exposed Stalin's crimes and started dismantling the "cult of personality." This was a revelation for the Soviet people. Then came the news about anti-Communist demonstrations in Poland and an uprising in Hungary. At night, many people pressed their ears to radios, trying to hear newscasts on the Voice of America or the BBC that managed to get past the Soviet jamming.

Shostakovich's friend Flora Litvinova recalled how in those days Shostakovich questioned her impatiently: "Have you heard anything on the BBC? How's Budapest? How's Poland? The empire is falling apart, ripping at the seams. It's always that way. You have to keep your fist clenched, and if you weaken a little, the empire cracks. Only he knew how to do it."[1] Shostakovich meant Stalin. It was clear that an era was coming to an end. This is when Shostakovich decided to sum it up in a symphony with an autobiographical subtext.

"You have to use the brief period of thaw," he explained to Litvinova. "History shows that there will be frosts again, and heavy ones at that."[2]

Paradoxically, the idea of a symphony about the fate of his generation was not in contradiction to its publicly stated revolutionary theme. The Revolution of 1905, unlike the subsequent ones of 1917, had not lost its romantic aura in the eyes of later generations. The poet Osip Mandelstam drew an unexpected parallel between the revolution and the legendary events of the Patriotic War of 1812 against Napoleon, as it was interpreted and described by Leo Tolstoy: "The boys of 1905 went to the revolution with the same feelings as Nikolenka Rostov went into the Hussars: it was a question of love and honor. Both thought it impossible to live without the warmth of the glory of their times, and both felt it impossible to breathe without valor. 'War and peace' continued, but the glory had moved."[3]

This romantic spirit of struggle for a just cause, a spirit of valor and courage, imbues such different but equally ambitious works about the Revolution of 1905 as Sergei Eisenstein's film *Battleship Potemkin* and Boris Pasternak's narrative poems "1905" and "Lieutenant Schmidt." The same romantic halo envelops Shostakovich's Eleventh Symphony.

The surface of the symphony is a pastiche of quotations from well-known revolutionary songs. Underneath come the other hidden hints: the "Mussorgskian" mourning for the heartbreaking lot of the Russian people, and curses for its oppressors. This could be hinted at even in the censored Soviet press, and Lev Lebedinsky, then Shostakovich's friend, used in describing the symphony in a brochure the charged words about the "tragedy of an enslaved people."[4]

Naturally, the parallels with contemporary events (the revolution of 1956 in Hungary) could not be made overtly. But some brave listeners permitted themselves to comment aloud the way one elderly woman in Leningrad did after the premiere: "Those aren't guns firing, those are tanks roaring and squashing people."[5] When Lebedinsky told Shostakovich about her reaction, he was pleased. "That means she heard it, and yet the musicians don't."[6]

And still, there is one more component to the symphony, perhaps the most complex, profound, and intriguing, without which it would not have been written: the autobiographical. Shostakovich considered himself a Petersburger all his life, even after moving to Moscow, and the Eleventh Symphony presents a heady portrait of the city, mixing feelings of horror and awe.

The Eleventh Symphony has two climaxes: the execution scene in the second movement, "January 9," and the finale ("Tocsin"), where the music "depicts" an extraordinary wave of popular wrath seemingly sweeping away the oppressors. One might think, where is the auto-biography here? After all, Shostakovich did not take part in any of the Russian revolutions, did not face bullets, nor with gun in hand take revenge on his oppressors Stalin and Zhdanov. But there was a reason why so many of his friends frequently spoke of uncommon impres-sionability and sensitivity as his important character traits. All informa-tion was digested instantly and not only intellectually, but on a directly emotional basis.

One of Shostakovich's lovers, the writer Galina Serebryakova, spent seventeen years incarcerated after her arrest as the wife of an "enemy of the people" in 1936 and was freed only after Stalin's death. When Khrushchev began his anti-Stalin campaign, Serebryakova was among the speakers at one of the meetings at the Kremlin arranged for the Soviet elite. In front of Khrushchev and other Party leaders, she started to talk about standing in front of an execution squad and about being tortured in prison—and she unbuttoned her blouse to show the scars. Someone in the audience fainted. When Serebryakova finished speak-ing, she was approached by Shostakovich, whom she had not seen in twenty years. It was he who had fainted.

Serebryakova's ordeal was not the only one to affect Shostakovich.

After Stalin's death, a thin stream of people released from prisons and camps and returned from exile began to trickle back to the cities. Their official rehabilitation sometimes took years, even decades. Shostakovich helped actively: he pleaded with high-placed officials and signed innumerable requests to expedite the return of Stalin's victims to society, which meant acquiring work and residence permits.

The granddaughter of the great director Vsevolod Meyerhold, who had been shot in 1940, came to Shostakovich for such a letter. Meyerhold had been cruelly beaten with a rubber hose during interrogations by the NKVD,★ so that the sixty-six-year-old screamed and cried in pain as he tried to avoid the blows. When the granddaughter informed Shostakovich of Meyerhold's fate, he grabbed his head and wept. At their next meeting, when he gave her his letter in support of Meyerhold, he would not let her leave for a long time, repeating in a sad and hopeless tone, "Don't go, I'm afraid."[7] The military prosecutor who was in charge of Meyerhold's rehabilitation case subsequently recalled that during an account of the director's death, Shostakovich also fainted—"they barely carried him out of my office."[8]

Shostakovich's deep empathy with suffering enabled him to chronicle events that he had not experienced—torture, execution, life in the prisons and the camps—and to depict them so vividly. Music is the art of emotion, and attempts in the last century to discredit this old truth now appear old-fashioned. His emotional response to Serebryakova's account of her near-execution may be heard in the second movement of his Eleventh Symphony. The torment of the beaten Meyerhold, crumpled on the floor of his prison cell, was re-created by Shostakovich as autobiographical in the amazing seventh movement of the Fourteenth Symphony, to the poem by Guillaume Apollinaire "In the Santé Prison":

★The secret police organization most commonly known as the KGB was founded after the revolution in 1917 as the All-Russian Extraordinary Commission for Combating Counter-Revolution and Sabotage (the Cheka; the policemen were called Chekists). Over the years, it was reorganized into various directorates and ministries and went by many names and acronyms. In 1922 it became the State Political Directorate (GPU) and later Unified State Political Directorate (OGPU). In the period of Stalinist terror, it was known as the People's Commissariat for Internal Affairs (NKVD) from 1934 until after World War II, when it became the Committee for State Security (KGB). After the collapse of the Soviet Union in 1991, the Russian intelligence organization became known as the Federal Security Service (FSB). People still call its workers Chekists. [Trans.]

They stripped me bare
When they led me into the prison;
Knocked down by fate from around the corner,
I was plunged into the darkness.

The same "aesthetic of participation" sets in motion the finale of the Eleventh. It is an orgy of revenge, a whirlwind of revolutionary songs that starts as a deafening burst of brass. They play the melody of a popular protest song, whose refrain is "Death to you, tyrants."★ Other subversive melodies follow in quick succession, hard on one another's heels, producing the palpable effect of an enraged mob running through the streets and overflowing onto the squares of the imperial capital. Shostakovich learned how to produce these effects in music while working on film scores. Film introduced the previously unknown illusion of being present and participating. The invention of montage compressed action, making it dynamic. Shostakovich uses montage in the finale of the Eleventh, thus reinforcing the feverish rhythm of the music.

For Shostakovich, this was a bold step. Among musicians, this usage was met with equal distrust and suspicion on opposite aesthetic poles. The official music critics complained that in Shostakovich's interpretation, the revolutionary songs take on "a distortedly expressionistic form." In "progressive" circles, people pursed their lips: Quoting popular tunes in a modern symphony seemed unacceptably vulgar. Popular success actually interfered with an objective appreciation of the work, and a certain courage was required to rise above ideological prejudices. Thus, Anna Akhmatova, who at that time was lukewarm about Pasternak's newly circulating "dissident" novel *Doctor Zhivago,* was delighted by Shostakovich's symphony. "The songs fly through the terrible black sky like angels, like birds, like white clouds!"[10]†

★While he was composing the symphony, Shostakovich wrote to a friend, "Everyone who ever loved me has my love. To everyone who did me harm, I send my curses."[9]

†In a comparable situation, five years later, Yudina wrote, in a typically exalted manner, to Petr Suvchinsky, a skeptical adept of the musical avant-garde in Paris, defending Shostakovich's Thirteenth ("Babi Yar") Symphony. "There is truth in the absolute newness of language, as in all your Boulezes and so on, and there is truth in the archaic raiments of the Higher values of human life."[11]

Marietta Shaginyan, a writer of Akhmatova's generation who lived for many years in Leningrad, reviewing the premiere of the Eleventh Symphony in 1957, also stressed its autobiographical nature and drew a cautious parallel with the experiences of the Stalin years: "Memory brings you old St. Petersburg, a snowy early morning, empty squares, and—long-buried in the depths of the experienced but awakened again by the magic of art—the feeling of alienation and fear."[12] Old-timers heard in the symphony a vivid musical portrait of St. Petersburg. The city was depicted in sound as it had settled in the collective memory of the prerevolutionary generations—as the imperial capital of Russia, and as the cradle of rebellion and popular outrage, that is, with the qualities that had long been hushed up by Stalinist propaganda. But it had also been the city that took the cruelest blows of the Great Terror.

For young people all these nuances and hints were then barely perceptible. Akhmatova and Shaginyan, along with Shostakovich, were concerned about the nation's historical memory. The Eleventh Symphony was turning into a palimpsest that would be hard for new generations to read. For an adequate understanding of this work, the listener not only had to know the facts of Russian history, but had to sense them emotionally. Those sensations had been wiped out during the long years of Stalin's rule—and, it seemed, permanently.

Stalin knew how to exorcise a nation's historical memory. He had a brilliant teacher, Lenin. The two men, who equally influenced the fate of Russia in the twentieth century, met for the first time in December 1905 in the Finnish city of Tammerfors. This notable encounter took place at an illegal conference of the radical faction of the social democratic party of Russia, the Bolsheviks. The thirty-five-year-old Lenin was the undisputed leader of the Bolsheviks, while the twenty-six-year-old Stalin was merely a rank-and-file delegate, representing the Caucasus Party organization. For Stalin this meeting was a lesson for life. He expected to see a regal and impressive giant, in Stalin's words, "a mountain eagle." And before him stood a man of less than medium height, seemingly unattractive, with an obvious desire, as Stalin recalled, "to remain unnoticed or, at least, not to attract attention or stress his high position."[13]

There is every reason to believe that it was then that Stalin understood what was possible. He—also short, unattractive, and lacking the gift of oratory—could nevertheless become a great revolutionary leader someday. In order to do that he had to adopt Lenin's ability to argue his position simply and clearly, and also learn Lenin's ruthlessness toward his opponents. Stalin mastered these qualities rather quickly, being a phenomenally gifted political student. But there was one trait in Lenin's ideology that Stalin had trouble mastering, even though he tried. It was Lenin's "hatred for whining intellectuals," as Stalin characterized it. It is well known that, being a political pragmatist, Lenin despised "the puny intelligentsia, the lackeys of capital, who consider themselves the nation's brain." "In fact they're not a brain, but shit," he would add mockingly. The paradox is that Lenin came from the intelligentsia, a specifically Russian social class.

The uniqueness of that class, created by the reforms of Peter the Great in the late seventeenth and early eighteenth centuries and consisting of an ever-expanding circle of more or less educated people who had chosen an "intellectual profession," lay in its commitment to social engagement as a sacred mission.

The Russian *intelligent* felt that he belonged to an order of knights that defended the people from the authorities' knout and arbitrary rule. This idea became particularly popular in the 1860s, when the Russian intelligentsia, disillusioned by the fact that the emancipation of the serfs and other reforms "from above" had not dramatically improved the situation of the oppressed masses, sharply radicalized. Its new idol was the zealous columnist and novelist Nikolai Chernyshevsky, son of a priest from provincial Saratov, who first was imprisoned for his antigovernment articles in the Fortress of Saints Peter and Paul and then sent to Siberia, where he spent over two decades in prison, in the mines, and in exile, acquiring the halo of martyrdom.

Upon reading Chernyshevsky's novel *What Is to Be Done?* (1863), written in the Peter and Paul Fortress, Lenin said, "It plowed me up deeply." The novel became the catechism of the radical intelligentsia; Nikolai Ishutin, a leading revolutionary of the era, maintained that "the three greatest people in history are Jesus Christ, Apostle Paul, and Nikolai Chernyshevsky." His characters, those fanatics of revolution, served as models for Lenin and Stalin. But Chernyshevsky also had enormous influence on Russian Marxists with his philosophy of culture, which one of his followers summarized this way: "Chernyshevsky knocked all edifices of Russian aesthetics from the pedestal and tried to prove that life was higher than art and that art was only trying to imitate it."[14]

Chernyshevsky's slogan "Beauty is life" became the aesthetic mantra for several generations of revolution-minded Russian intellectuals; his conclusion about the aims and goals of art, fully mastered by Stalin, was the foundation of the future Communist leader's ideas about socialist art: "Re-creation of life is the general, characteristic sign of art that comprises its essence; often works of art have another meaning—an explanation of life; often they also mean a verdict on life."[15]

Chernyshevsky held an important place in the world of Dmitri Shostakovich's family. Shostakovich's paternal grandmother, Varvara Shaposhnikova, accepted *What Is to Be Done?* as her textbook for living; following the principles outlined in the novel, she organized a sewing workshop that functioned as a commune. Shaposhnikova's entire family was tied to Chernyshevsky in one way or another: her younger brother, Gavrila, studied with Chernyshevsky in the Saratov high school and called him "such a paragon of intellect, broad and profound knowledge, humaneness, that almost every one of his students burned with the persistent desire to study and study in order to with time serve his neighbor."[16]

Shostakovich's grandfather Boleslav Shostakovich, the son of an exiled Polish revolutionary, was involved in Chernyshevsky's failed attempt to escape from Siberian exile. Boleslav was also close to the underground circle of the already mentioned Ishutin, decimated by the gendarmes after Dmitri Karakozov's failed assassination attempt on Tsar Alexander II in 1866. Boleslav and his wife were exiled to Siberia, where in 1875 their son, Dmitri, the future composer's father, was born. Even though Boleslav Shostakovich ended up as a banker, heading the Irkutsk division of the Siberian Merchant Bank, the family never hid its revolutionary past; they continued to honor the moral ideals of the Russian intelligentsia: public service; concern for the people's welfare; honesty, decency, and modesty.

Nicholas I knew many of the Decembrist rebels personally and had seen or heard of the others. For all their political differences, they were basically of the same circle—and that mattered, manifesting itself in thousands of details that are now difficult for us to see and understand. The same held for the relations in the milieu of the Russian revolutionary intelligentsia in the late nineteenth and early twentieth centuries. Naturally, it was a much broader and more democratic circle with more fluid divisions. But within the framework of this circle, too, the fate of its members intersected in astonishing patterns.

In 1864, Shostakovich's grandfather organized the escape from a Moscow prison of the Polish revolutionary Jaroslav Dombrowski, later a hero of the Paris Commune. Lenin adored Dombrowski. Shostakovich's grandmother's family were friends with Lenin's parents, the Ulyanovs; according to family legend, there was some genealogical connection between the Shostakoviches and the Ulyanovs. In Siberian exile, Shostakovich's grandfather met Leonid Krasin, who later became a Bolshevik people's commissar and colleague and friend of Stalin. Krasin's brother Boris became an influential Soviet music official and extended his patronage to the young composer Shostakovich. Another important "shield" for Shostakovich in the late 1920s and early 1930s was the chief of the Secret Operative Directorate of the Leningrad OGPU, and an amateur violinist, Vyacheslav Dombrovsky.

Stalin never met Shostakovich's father, who was only a few years older. But undoubtedly they moved in the same circles, however large and diffuse. Stalin and the Shostakovich family had common friends, acquaintances, and political idols. More important for us is the striking similarity in their education and aesthetic ideals.

In the second half of the nineteenth century, the Russian Empire had annexed in one way or another enormous territory (including the Baltic states, part of Poland, the Transcaucasus, and Central Asia) and existed as a multiethnic state with conflicting goals: The official policy of Russification was mitigated by the traditional Russian religious and cultural tolerance. Bringing "foreigners" into Russian culture was encouraged, and if they converted to Russian Orthodoxy, no particular career obstacles were erected.

By this time Russia had formed a certain consensus on national education. The state and the Church, which had earlier held the works of the great Russian writers of the nineteenth century in some suspicion, were gradually recognizing their role in the formation of a national consciousness. The works of Pushkin, Lermontov, Gogol, Nekrasov, Turgenev, Dostoevsky, and Leo Tolstoy were included everywhere in school curricula, in primers and textbooks, numerous readers and anthologies. The revolutionary intelligentsia added its own, unofficial curriculum, which included Vissarion Belinsky, Dmitri Pisarev, Nikolai Chernyshevsky, and Nikolai Dobrolubov (it should be noted that they were all celebrated anti-establishment literary critics and opinion makers). Of contemporary writers, Maxim Gorky and Anton Chekhov were held in highest esteem. The satirist Mikhail Saltykov-Shchedrin occupied a special place in this pantheon.

Love for these authors united a large stratum of the Russian intelligentsia. Not knowing them was considered improper. Their works were not merely read, but studied as "textbooks for living," in the Chernyshevskian sense. The result was the creation of an unprecedented single cultural field, a common referential system of cultural values. Lenin, Stalin, and Shostakovich knew Pushkin, Gogol, and Saltykov-Shchedrin and quoted their works from memory. The favorite writer of all three was Chekhov.

The young Lenin was profoundly impressed by Chekhov's novella *Ward Six,* published in 1892; he wrote: "I was terrified, I couldn't stay in my room, I got up and left. I had the feeling that I was locked up in ward No. 6."[17] Shostakovich toward the end of his life maintained that he read *Ward Six* as "memoirs about myself." Chekhov's misogynistic short story "The Darling" was cherished by both Stalin and Shostakovich: They both knew it almost by heart and recited pages of it with pleasure.

Stalin's receptivity to Russian culture was defined in great part by his outsider status. He was twice an outsider: as the son of a poor shoemaker and as a man whose native tongue was Georgian. The introduction of Russian as the teaching language at the provincial seminary in Gori, where young Stalin (still called Soso Dzhugashvili then) started his education, was decreed and enforced from above. The transition from Georgian to Russian was difficult for Stalin. But he mastered it and used it as his primary language, even though he spoke Russian with a pronounced Georgian accent all his life.

As a cultural neophyte, Stalin retained a certain respect for "higher" culture and its creators. Lenin lacked this piety completely. Take, for example, the polar attitudes held by Lenin and Stalin toward opera and ballet. Attending opera and ballet at the Bolshoi Theater was one of Stalin's greatest pleasures. When he was head of the Soviet state, Lenin persistently tried to shut down the Bolshoi (and the Maryinsky while he was at it) in 1921–22. He felt that state money should not be spent on the maintenance of this "piece of purely bourgeois culture," as he called it.

Lenin didn't much like dramatic theater, either, not even the democratic Moscow Art Theater founded by Stanislavsky and Nemirovich-Danchenko. (The contrast with Stalin's tastes is striking here, too.) According to Nadezhda Krupskaya, Lenin's wife, he was bored at the theater, grew irritable, and couldn't stand it for long. "Usually we'd go to the theater and leave after the first act."[18] When, in 1921, People's Commissar of Education Lunacharsky appealed to Lenin with a desperate letter asking for money for the Art Theater, which was on the brink of shutting down, the leader replied with a rude telephone cable: "Suggest laying all theaters in a coffin. The People's Commissar of Education should be teaching literacy, not dealing with theaters."[19]

Stalin, who emulated Lenin in every way, also tried to master his cultural pragmatism. Certainly Lenin's 1905 article "Party Organization and Party Literature" had a profound impact on Stalin. The article became Holy Writ for the Communists even though it was obviously written in haste and very carelessly. In it, Lenin demands that literature be fully subordinated to political goals, becoming the "gear and screw" of the revolutionary propaganda mechanism. (All culture was implied, but Lenin spoke only of literature, yet again demonstrating his total failure to recognize other forms of art.) Stalin must have liked the comparison of literature with the gear and screw of a huge political apparatus; the thread extends from here to his later notorious definition of writers as "engineers of human souls."

Lenin also attacked the influence of the market on culture: "The freedom of the bourgeois writer, artist, or actress is merely a masked (or hypocritically being masked) dependence on money bags, bribes, and maintenance support." The symbolist poet Valery Bryusov countered Lenin in the pages of the elitist journal *Vesy:* "Yes, we are free!" Bryusov was disingenuous. His sophisticated magazine had fewer than a thousand subscribers and depended totally on the subsidies of Moscow millionaire Sergei Polyakov. But Bryusov preferred not to reveal that, instead taking his usual pose as refined aesthete: "To demand that all art serve social movements is tantamount to demanding that the entire textile industry only manufacture fabric for red flags."[20] But even Bryusov, the son of a Russian merchant, understood that special demands are made of culture in Russia: "Where social life is hemmed in, works of art are often used as a devious way to disseminate social ideas or as secret weapons in the struggle of social groups. Where there is freedom of speech, oral and written, there is no longer need for that."[21]

Bryusov could not have known that even a hundred years later his ideal situation for Russia would still not be reality. But he, as an educated man, knew the dramatic and often fatal Russian history of relations within the triangle of regime–intelligentsia–the people. In Russia, most of the intelligentsia were traditionally in implacable opposition to the regime. This began under Nicholas I, who called intellectuals "frock-coat-wearing scoundrels" and threatened to "drive all those philosophers to consumption." The intellectuals, naturally, responded in kind; and the people, as Pushkin has it in the final stage direction of *Boris Godunov,* "were silent."

The conflict only expanded under the subsequent autocratic rulers of the Romanov dynasty: Alexander II, Alexander III, and Nicholas II. Increasing in strength, the intelligentsia wanted to participate in governing, but tsarism was unwilling to share power. The policy of the monarchy toward the intelligentsia varied from direct repressions to imposed concessions; but those two forces, fatally opposed, never did extend a hand to each other.

They did come together, paradoxically, only in their attitude toward the people, seeing it as a mysterious and baffling force with mystical qualities. The tsars and the intelligentsia interpreted those traits differently: looking down from above, as obedience, patience, piety, and faith in the tsar; looking up, as a rebel spirit, a desire for freedom and knowledge, and an instinctive yearning for justice and life on a communal basis. But those above and below felt that the cultural development of the people must be executed and controlled by the state and not by market mechanisms.

It was this distrust—or, more strongly put, fear and revulsion—of market relations in culture that led a significant part of the Russian intelligentsia to support the Bolsheviks after the October Revolution of 1917. Russia's new rulers needed "specialists," and these specialists were thrilled to have at long last the opportunity to enlighten the people with the state's help. A temporary peace between regime and intelligentsia had finally arrived. Among the intellectuals who did not pick up arms to fight the Bolsheviks, or emigrate from the country, or boycott the Communist regime, waiting it out in unheated Petrograd apartments, but who instead went to serve in the new Soviet institutions, was the Shostakovich family.

The Shostakoviches were unlikely to mourn the fallen autocracy. And it was not so much because of their revolutionary past as from their solid convictions as intelligentsia. This held in particular for culture. It is impossible to exaggerate the role of Klavdia Lukashevich, Dmitri Shostakovich's godmother, a prolific and popular children's writer before the revolution. She was related to the democrat poet Liodor Palmin, who in his poem commemorating the poet Nikolai Nekrasov (an idol of Lenin and Stalin) exclaimed:

> *When you embodied in sobbing sounds*
> *The widow's pleas, the cry of the sick orphan,*
> *Or the torments overseen in the dark of hovels—*
> *Then we wept with you.*

These were the emotions and ideas that had a powerful influence on the young Shostakovich. The work of Lukashevich herself was very revealing in that sense. In her parents' house she heard and met such icons of Russian cultural radicalism as Dmitri Pisarev and Nekrasov himself. When in 1871 her mother went to work for the people, under the influence of revolutionary propaganda, young Lukashevich was left with her sisters in her father's care and began earning money at the age of twelve, giving private lessons and transcribing. These could have been the root of her active feminism at the turn of the century. Publishing her first work at the age of twenty, Lukashevich overwhelmed children's literature of the period—she wrote no less than two hundred books of stories, plays, calendars, textbooks, and anthologies. They were all best-sellers, going into ten or more editions. Many of these books were among the first things Mitya Shostakovich read. My personal library holds several rare issues of the children's reader compiled by Klavdia Lukashevich called *Seyatel'* [Sower] from the years 1913 and 1914.

What can be found in this reader? What fed little Mitya's imagination? Naturally, Pushkin, Lermontov, and Gogol. But also a lot by Nekrasov and other democratic writers. And what seems quite astonishing now, Chekhov and Leo Tolstoy, who were controversial in those years. (The latter had just been excommunicated, in 1901, from the Orthodox Church by the Holy Synod.) The liberal strain of these readers is indisputable.

But Lukashevich was not thrilled by the Bolshevik revolution, even though she did not emigrate. At first the People's Commissar of Education, Lunacharsky, brought her in to work on the creation of Soviet children's literature, and in those hungry years she was given a special food parcel as part of her pay. But when she rejected the authorities' proposal to rewrite all her old works to meet the new ideological demands, her food rations were rescinded and her books thrown out of state libraries. Lukashevich resisted, and the authorities practically ceased publishing her works; she lived the last years of her life in extreme poverty, but still did not collaborate with the Soviet cultural apparatus, and she died in the provinces in 1931.

The story of Klavdia Lukashevich demonstrates the political position of the Shostakoviches. She was a close family friend. It's unlikely that the uncompromising Lukashevich would remain friendly with the Shostakoviches if their political orientation had been blatantly pro-Soviet. This is just not the way friendships were maintained in the highly politicized Russian intelligentsia milieu, then or now. Lukashevich spoke movingly at the funeral of Shostakovich's father in 1922, mourning "the thinning ranks of our intelligentsia." That meant that she still deemed Shostakovich part of that chivalrous order, of which she considered herself a member.

Also helping to clarify the important but muddled issue of the Shostakovich family's political sympathies in the initial postrevolutionary years is the intriguing story of his earliest surviving opus, the so-called "Funeral March in Memory of the Victims of the Revolution." This piece for piano appears under that title in all catalogues of Shostakovich's work. In Soviet literature about Shostakovich it is always mentioned as an example of the young composer's vivid pro-Bolshevik feelings. However, in a recently published letter to his mother's sister, his aunt Nadezhda Kokoulina, dated April 1918, eleven-year-old Mitya Shostakovich calls his work "Funeral March in Memory of Shingarev and Kokoshkin," which dramatically changes the political context and hue of this opus.[22]

The murder of two leaders of the centrist Constitutional-Democratic Party (Cadets), Andrei Shingarev and Fyodor Kokoshkin, torn to pieces in a prison hospital by a band of revolutionary sailors and Red Army soldiers, was one of the symbolic episodes on the path of consolidation of power by the Bolsheviks after the October rebellion. This violent lynching occurred in January 1918, when the Bolsheviks illegally broke up the Constituent Assembly, in which they were in the minority. The collapse of the assembly, which was planning to vote on a new constitution for Russia, and the murder of the arrested Cadets horrified the democratic intelligentsia: As the celebrated bass Fyodor Chaliapin recalled, this was "the first terrible shock." Boris Eikhenbaum, the noted literary historian, wrote to a friend, "I was completely horrified by the murder of Shingarev and Kokoshkin. This was, in my opinion, an indisputable sign that the revolution was decaying and perishing morally."[23]

In an article completed after the death of Shingarev and Kokoshkin, "The Intelligentsia and Revolution," Alexander Blok observed, "The best people even say, 'There was no revolution'; those who were beside themselves with hatred for 'tsarism' are prepared to throw themselves into its embrace, in order to forget what is happening now."[24] But at that very time, he himself wrote his celebrated narrative poem *The Twelve,* the heroes of which are part of a Red Army patrol roaming the hushed and frightened Petrograd. The poem was adored by both the Bolsheviks and their enemies; some saw in it a satire of the revolution, others its glorification. Blok's Red Army soldiers were called by some "the apostles of the revolution." But others saw in them common thieves and murderers.

The undistinguished little piece by the boy Shostakovich, begotten by the same tragic incident as *The Twelve,* naturally cannot compare in any way with Blok's great poem. If not for Shostakovich's later achievements, this modest attempt would be forgotten. But it is important to note two things. First, the topical nature of Russian culture: Despite the doubts and fears of proponents of "pure art," it was still not ashamed to respond instantly to current political events; as the slogan used to say, "In the papers in the morning, in verse in the evening." And second: Many works prompted by current events turned out to be significant, open to many interpretations from the start, often of a contradictory nature. These were not one-day wonders to catch the current fashion, but serious, inherently ambivalent reactions in the tradition of the "chronicler" impulse. Blok created an immortal example of such a multilayered work at the end of his life. Paradoxically, Shostakovich began his creative life, in which his major and important works would be interpreted in mutually exclusive ways, with his march. Intuitively and spontaneously he created the paradigm for his future work.

Boris Lossky (son of the prominent Kantian philosopher Nikolai Lossky) was a classmate of Shostakovich, and he recalled the assembly at their Stoyunina Gymnasium in Petrograd in January 1918 for teachers and students, with a memorial service and speeches eulogizing Shingarev and Kokoshkin. Mitya Shostakovich played his "Funeral March" there. Protest meetings against the Bolsheviks were still possible in those days. One took place at the Tenishevsky Hall, where along with other well-known poets (Dmitri Merezhkovsky, Zinaida Hippius, and Fedor Sologub) Anna Akhmatova read her works. When Blok's name was mentioned onstage, the audience shouted, "Traitor!" Zinaida Hippius wrote in her diary disgustedly, "I have no doubt that were the Bolsheviks to last a year (?!), almost all our whiny intelligentsia, especially the literary ones, would crawl to them in one way or another. And you couldn't even blame all of them in that case. There is so much plain poverty."[25]

Lossky, who was friends with Shostakovich, maintained categorically that "Mitya, like most children of the intelligentsia then, showed no sympathy for the government ideology."[26] His words are authenticated by a fact that has not been noticed until now. In the fall of 1922, on Lenin's personal orders, the Lossky family, along with a group of other prominent anti-Communist intellectuals (including Nikolai Berdyaev, Semen Frank, Fedor Stepun, and Pitirim Sorokin), was exiled from Soviet Russia to the West. Not long before their departure, the Shostakoviches invited the Losskys to dinner. In a situation of total surveillance (as we know now, the GPU followed every step of the families marked for exile), this gesture by the Shostakovich family was quite bold, demonstratively signaling their political sympathies.

What happened, then, between 1922 and March 1927, when Shostakovich accepted a commission for a major symphonic work titled *Dedication to October* from the special Propaganda and Education Department of the Musical Sector of the State Publishing House?

The death of the founder of the Soviet state in 1924 and the gradual strengthening of single rule by Lenin's heir, Stalin; the flowering and start of the decline of Lenin's "new economic policy" (NEP), which had allowed exhausted Russia to come to its senses after the horrors of "military communism" and the Civil War; and most importantly, the realization by the majority of the country, including its educated classes, that the Soviet regime was an unavoidable reality. Those who could and did fight the Communist regime with weapons in their hands died or emigrated; now open political or ideological resistance had become impossible. If a family wanted to live more or less normally, it was only a question of which form of collaboration— voluntary or forced—it would undertake with the new regime.

It should be said right away that among those who actively offered their creativity to the service of the Bolsheviks from the first days of the revolution were many members of the avant-garde, participants in the "Left Front of Art"—the theater director Vsevolod Meyerhold; the composers Arthur Lourié and Nikolai Roslavets; the artists Natan Altman, David Shterenberg, and Casimir Malevich; the cultural theoreticians Osip Brik and Nikolai Punin; the film directors Sergei Eisenstein and Vsevolod Pudovkin; and the poet Vladimir Mayakovsky. Of them, Mayakovsky was probably the most prominent and in many ways a symbolic figure. The Russian futurists he headed openly wanted power over culture on a national level. *Iskusstvo kommuny* [Art of the Commune], a newspaper allotted by the commissar of education to the avant-garde movement, featured articles that covered their central idea in every issue: "Futurism is the new state art."

Naturally, the experimental avant-garde culture could not become mass culture without special conditions being arranged for it. The forced inculcation of futurism from above and the suppression of every form of competition from classical culture was what the Russian avant-garde hoped for and demanded from the Soviet regime. "Blow up, destroy, wipe from the face of the earth all the old artistic forms— how can the new artist, the proletarian artist, the new man not dream of this," Punin wrote in the first issue of *Iskusstvo kommuny*. Mayakovsky's rejection of the past was even more total: " 'Down with *your* love,' 'down with *your* art,' 'down with *your* regime,' 'down with *your* religion.' "[27]

People's Commissar Lunacharsky, who had a great appreciation for Mayakovsky's genius and wanted to tie him more securely to the revolution, treated his aesthetic nihilism lightly. "He thinks that the great corpses with their eternally living works are terribly in the way of the success of his own handiwork . . . He constantly sees himself as the first master on a scorched earth and among people who have forgotten the past: it's easier that way, without competitors."[28] Pragmatic Lenin thought that Lunacharsky was too gentle and tolerant of futurism. Not believing for a second in the revolutionary views of Mayakovsky and his friends, Lenin was scornful of them: "It's a special form of communism. It's hooligan communism." Lenin disliked Mayakovsky's poetry, even the verses that were pro-Soviet: "Nonsense, it's stupid, profound stupidity and pretentiousness."[29]

Nevertheless, the Russian avant-garde artists hoped—not without reason—that the new regime would give them a chance to penetrate into the national consciousness and suppress potential rivals, even through violence if necessary.* For that, Mayakovsky and some of his friends were prepared to serve the state faithfully, agreeing to go far—probably much farther than they had originally planned: to direct collaboration with the secret police, the GPU, so reviled by the intelligentsia.

Things were not limited to executing secret missions and all sorts of "delicate" assignments.[30] Mayakovsky wrote and printed loud poetic panegyrics in honor of the GPU and its founder, Felix Dzerzhinsky. A watershed in this sense was 1927, when lines from his poem "Dzerzhinsky's Soldiers," written to commemorate the tenth anniversary of the VChK-GPU, spread widely across the land, turning into aphorisms that were quoted frequently and not always appositely: "The GPU is the clenched fist of our dictatorship" and "Dzerzhinsky's soldiers protect the Union."

The Soviet regime received these desperate manifestations of the avant-garde loyalty as its due, even increasing its demands. But still, it rewarded Mayakovsky not only by publishing his poems in newspapers with mass circulation and arranging lucrative lecture tours in the Soviet Union, but with the opportunity to travel abroad regularly: Of the eight years (1922–29) that Mayakovsky lived in Moscow, where his home was, he spent three abroad. "I need to travel," he explained. Many intellectuals envied Mayakovsky's income, his unprecedented permit to carry a revolver and drive a Renault, which he brought from France

---

*As Mayakovsky wrote, suggesting new possible targets to the Bolsheviks: "Find a White Guards officer—up against the wall. Have you forgotten Raphael? Forgotten Rastrelli? It's time to riddle the museum walls with bullets."

and which was one of the few private cars in Moscow in that period.[31]

For a certain segment of Soviet artistic youth, Mayakovsky was a tempting role model. The writer Valentin Katayev spoke for the group when he recalled, "For the first time we felt freed of all the weight and prejudice of the old world, from the obligations of family, religion, and even morality; we were intoxicated by the air of freedom: all rights and no obligations. We were not capitalists, or landowners, or manufacturers, or kulaks. We were the children of minor civil servants, teachers, excise clerks, and artisans . . . The revolution opened up unlimited opportunities for us."[32]

Mayakovsky personified those unlimited opportunities: Tall and assertive, he declaimed his loud avant-garde poetry on timely topics in a thundering voice. Two people very removed from prorevolutionary temptation, the pianist Vladimir Horowitz and the choreographer George Balanchine, told me about their youthful infatuation with Mayakovsky's poetry and persona. Young Shostakovich did not escape the "Mayakovsky temptation," either.

In the first half of the 1920s, Shostakovich endured serious trials. In 1922 his father died of pneumonia at the age of forty-six. The family was left without a breadwinner, and his mother and older sister were forced to find work. Mitya took a job as a piano player in a movie theater, accompanying silent films: He began, as he put it, "mechanically depicting 'human passions' on the piano." But they were still very short of money for food and rent.

Shostakovich said that it "ruined his health and shattered his nervous system":[33] he was diagnosed with tuberculosis of the lymph nodes and had to undergo a painful operation. At the same time, in his mother's words, "he was thrown out of the conservatory"; he was not allowed to continue graduate work in the piano class. This was the result of some bureaucratic intrigue. The entire episode, which now seems almost silly, at the time must have been of cataclysmic awfulness for the delicate Shostakovich, a sign of the extreme instability of his musical career.

In 1927, Shostakovich suffered another personal catastrophe. In January, on the recommendation of the influential music critic Boleslav Yavorsky (with whom Mitya, judging from published letters, had a particularly close relationship), Shostakovich was sent to Warsaw as part of an official Soviet "team" to take part in the First International Chopin Piano Competition. The mission's goal went far beyond the musical.

The war between Poland and the Soviet Union had ended only six years earlier. The relations between the two countries were still strained.

The Chopin Competition of 1927 became an important cultural event in Europe. But for the Soviet Union, in view of prevailing politics, the competition's magnitude was extraordinary. Stalin paid particular attention to the international success of young Soviet musicians. We know that he liked opera and ballet, but instrumental music also attracted his attention, as memoirs of contemporaries show. Stalin enjoyed listening to the young pianists and violinists Emil Gilels, Lev Oborin, Yakov Flier, David Oistrakh, and Boris Goldstein. And as usual with Stalin, as he listened he did not forget about political gain.

Stalin—probably first among modern political leaders—understood the propaganda dividends that could come if his country's young musicians began winning international competitions. The Western press was filled with materials about the Bolsheviks as Asiatic barbarians. Russian communism was depicted as the enemy of Europe's humanistic culture. And so Stalin decided: What could be better counterpropaganda than the performances of talented, marvelously trained, and charming Soviet virtuosi, performing classical music brilliantly?

Recently published archival documents verify what several generations of Soviet musicians knew: Performers were allowed abroad only after a thorough security check.[34] The final approval was sometimes given at the highest level, right up to Lenin and Stalin (and later Khrushchev and other Party and state leaders). Bearing in mind the political importance of the trip to Warsaw in 1927 and that it was the first propaganda action of this sort, there is no doubt that Stalin saw and approved the final list of competitors. We may assume that this is how he first learned of the existence of Dmitri Shostakovich.★

The Soviet delegation as a whole was a great success at the Warsaw Competition: contrary to all expectations, Oborin won first prize. As Ilya Ehrenburg wrote, "The diplomats had to fade away and the Poles to admit that a 'Moskal' [Polish slang for Muscovite] played Chopin

---

★Evidence of the great importance of the Chopin Competition for the country's leadership is the fact that before leaving for Warsaw, Shostakovich and his friends Lev Oborin and Yuri Bryushkov showed their programs to the chief of staff of the Red Army, Mikhail Tukhachevsky, a well-known patron of classical music (he was an amateur violinist and even made violins).

better than anyone else." The government newspaper *Izvestiya* printed a caricature by Stalin favorite Boris Efimov depicting the triumphant nineteen-year-old Oborin and the decrepit enemies of the Soviet Union, about to burst with envy and anger, with the ironic caption, "This is the hand of Moscow at work." The raptures of the great Polish composer Karol Szymanowski must have been reported to Stalin: "This cannot be called a success, or even a furor. It was a completely victorious march, a triumph!" But Shostakovich's name was not among the winners; he was awarded only an honorable mention. In his letters home to his mother, Mitya tried to sound upbeat, but this was an incredible humiliation for him. Most importantly, it put an end to his rosy dreams of a brilliant and profitable international career as a pianist. He needed to start thinking about other sources of income.

A significant moment had arrived in the life of young Shostakovich. The fact that after the death of his father, the Shostakovich family lived in great need is well known to his biographers. But their poverty is traditionally regarded as a kind of exotic coloration, almost like an episode in a Hollywood biopic. Malnourishment, the desperate search for work, the constant humiliation and morbid worry about the future are mentioned, but somehow never related to the young Shostakovich's creative work, to his selection of themes and texts for his compositions.

Yet the theme of money is a major one in Shostakovich's thinking. It is an idée fixe—he thinks of money no less frequently than the student Raskolnikov in Dostoevsky's *Crime and Punishment*. Shostakovich writes (in the period that interests us here, 1924–26) to his close friend Lev Oborin, "We need money very, very badly"; "There is no money at all. Total moneylessness"; "Now another misfortune. Yesterday mother was laid off"; "My mood is awful right now . . . can't find work, the darkness is surrounding me, and on top of it all, my neck has started swelling . . . Sometimes, feeling this, I start screaming. Just screaming in fear. All the doubts, all the problems, all the darkness suffocates me"; "I'm living badly in the highest degree. Especially in the material sense . . . Yet you need to eat? Need music paper? And you start running, like a squirrel in a wheel"; "I couldn't send you a letter until now, for lack of funds for the purpose of purchasing a stamp"; "The best thing in the world is money. Without money spiritual peace is impossible. Its absence is a painful blow on my nerves, and I feel very rattled. Awful, awful. Everything is very awful! . . . And when you drop by the union, there's a line of unemployed: looking for work. But there isn't any. All this cries out about the impenetrable darkness that exists in the world. . . . You can hear the howl everywhere: money, work, bread!"[35]

How far was Shostakovich willing to go to get money and feed himself and his family? The answer is: pretty far. He certainly was no Raskolnikov and had no intention of removing people from his path. But the dire circumstances of his life pushed Shostakovich toward something that was equally horrible for a creative person: artistic compromise. He was prepared to become a pretender. " 'When you lose your courage, you lose everything,' the German proverb goes, and I, it seems, will soon lose my courage," he confessed in a letter to Oborin.[36]

If the family's hopes and plans had come to pass and Mitya had become a celebrated pianist, that career, even under strict Soviet control, would have required comparatively few concessions to the regime from him, at least in a purely musical aspect. In the final analysis, he would still have been performing Bach, Beethoven, Liszt, and Chopin, probably with the addition of the mandatory Soviet repertoire. But those dreams burst.

Now work as a composer seemed to be the only possible source of substantial income. This increased greatly the temptations of political conformism: for the only existing source of commissions for symphonies, operas, or ballets in that situation was the Soviet state. And it had always demanded ideological loyalty in return. As Zoshchenko noted wryly as early as 1922, "Actually, being a writer isn't easy. Take, for instance, ideology . . . Nowadays they demand ideology from a writer . . . Really, quite unpleasant for me!"[37]

The Soviet ideological press pushed down with varying force at different periods. Of course, the Communist leaders always regarded the artistic avant-garde with skepticism and distrust, considering it to be petit bourgeois. But to a certain point, they were willing to shut their eyes to the formal experimentation in culture in exchange for the avant-garde artists' political loyalty. That was the essence of the temporary agreement with Mayakovsky and other "left-wingers." Young Shostakovich decided to use the same agreement, once he fully realized that he would be building his musical career as a composer.

By then, Shostakovich had experienced his first creative crisis. His major debut as a composer, at the legendary hall of the Leningrad Philharmonic—the premiere of his First Symphony under the baton of

Nikolai Malko in 1926, when he was nineteen years old—was a happy event. The symphony, simultaneously fresh and masterful, playful and meditative, moderately daring and moderately traditional, pleased everyone. Still, Shostakovich soon decided to update his arsenal as a composer. He simply could not write in the old way. According to him, at some point the creative process came to an abrupt halt: "not a single note." He panicked, bitterly burning many of his early works, including the opera based on Pushkin, *The Gypsies*. He had to think about new paths. The experimental artistic atmosphere of Leningrad in the 1920s was conducive to this; the premieres of the latest theatrical and musical works from Europe were awaited impatiently and discussed passionately. The Western orientation promised an escape from "provincialism," a word that had become a bugbear. German expressionism and constructivism seemed very close; the visits of playwright Ernst Toller and composers Alban Berg and Paul Hindemith were real sensations in the Soviet Union.

In this situation, the "Mayakovsky model" could have seemed most acceptable to Shostakovich. He became infatuated with Mayakovsky's Futurist poetry at the age of thirteen and attended his poetic readings in Petrograd. The poet was a charismatic figure, popular and respected in the milieu that was referential for Shostakovich: the avant-garde creative youth. There was talk everywhere of "technical rearmament" in culture, in analogy to what was going on in industry. Why not combine avant-garde form with Communist content, the way Mayakovsky did, with apparent success? Therefore, when Shostakovich was approached by Lev Shulgin, an orthodox old Bolshevik and the head of the Propaganda Department of the Music Sector of the State Publishing House, with a proposal to write a large symphonic work with a choral finale, called *Dedication to October,* for the tenth anniversary of the October Revolution in 1927, he accepted. Not even the shameful quality of the text sent from Moscow for setting to music stopped him. "I received Bezymensky's verses, which upset me greatly. Very bad poetry. But I've started to write anyway,"[38] Shostakovich wrote to a friend in Moscow, gritting his teeth. He also complained bitterly to Boleslav Yavorsky about "verses that are supposed to inspire me, by virtue of Bezymensky and the Music Sector."[39]

Komsomol poet Alexander Bezymensky was a far cry from Mayakovsky, even though at one time Leon Trotsky, then all-powerful military commissar, attempted to promote him as the "proletarian Mayakovsky." But by 1927, Trotsky had lost the political struggle to Stalin and had been stripped of all his posts. Bezymensky, however, kept a finger to the wind. When in 1929 vigilant comrades saw attacks against Stalin in his satirical play *The Shot* (with music by Shostakovich for the Leningrad premiere), the playwright appealed to the leader himself for protection and received an indulgence from him: *The Shot*, Stalin wrote to Bezymensky, could be considered an example of "revolutionary proletarian art for the present time."[40]

Despite the characteristic stipulation "for the present time," this praise from Stalin was enough to guarantee Bezymensky a peaceful and prosperous life (even though he never received the highest award, the Stalin Prize).* Ironically, it was only toward the end of his life that Bezymensky learned that his poem was once set to music by Shostakovich—so rarely had *Dedication to October* been performed over the years. It was retroactively renamed the Second Symphony (its premiere was conducted by Nikolai Malko, who was so dedicated to the young composer).

Unlike the First Symphony, the Second never became part of the repertoire—and probably never will—even though this one-movement work has quite a few highly impressive pages and episodes. Scriabin-like surges with longing motifs in the brass, typical of the mystical composer, are rather unexpectedly placed next to a complex thirteen-voice polyphonic "German" section that foreshadows the opera *The Nose* and lyric moments characteristic of Shostakovich's later symphonies.

Leafing through the pages of the score of the Second Symphony is like looking over the composer's shoulder without permission as he works his magic over what amounts to test tubes in a chemist's laboratory. What less gifted artists would consider a great success, in context of Shostakovich's later work turns out to be no more than an experiment. The choral finale is particularly problematic. It follows a sensational innovation—the sound of a factory whistle, proposed by Shulgin

---

*In the last years of his life (Bezymensky died in 1973), no one took this once-famous author seriously. There was a mocking description of him: "Hair on end. Teeth bucked. An old asshole with a Komsomol badge." Bezymensky summed himself up in two lines of doggerel that showed at least that he had no illusions about his place in the history of culture: "Big belly, small cock—What remains is a crock."

for *Dedication to October*. Then comes the chorus, singing the "ideolog-ically correct" verses of Bezymensky in a melancholy, almost desultory manner. Some of the lines would have brought out even Mayakovsky's sarcasm: "Oh, Lenin! You forged the will of suffering, you forged the will of callused hands." Shostakovich's own sardonic comment was brief: "Voilà."[41]

The chorus's music lacks the drive and conviction so typical of later Shostakovich. It is obvious that this is a formal, stilted addition to a composition already lacking in constructive unity. Shostakovich informed Yavorsky confidentially, "I'm composing the chorus with great difficulty. The words!!!!"[42] In this particular case, Shostakovich never did manage to inflame his imagination, and thus the final words of the text, its "culmination"—"Here is the banner, here is the name of living generations: October, Commune, and Lenin"—are not even given a melodic line; the chorus simply chants them. The final bars of this work sound like a formulaic apotheosis.

All this confirms the feeling that *Dedication to October* was for Shostakovich just a "work for hire." Understanding this fact allows us to revise the still popular view of young Shostakovich's ideological devel-opment. Some biographers suggest that his Second and then his Third ("First of May") symphonies evince their author's pro-Soviet idealism, which was only later replaced by bitter disillusionment. But the facts do not support this theory. It is clear that the pro-Soviet impetus of Bezy-mensky's text left Shostakovich cold; his subsequent music was rarely this formal.

Bearing in mind what we now know, a different path of Sho-stakovich's political maturation becomes more likely. His family tradi-tionally held liberal convictions. There is nothing to indicate their pro-Bolshevik feelings. On the contrary, the Shostakoviches belonged to that significant part of the Russian intelligentsia that, while not overtly anti-Soviet, wasn't among the fierce loyalists, either.

Occasionally biographers refer to certain pages in Shostakovich's let-ters in the 1920s to Tatyana Glivenko, his adolescent love, as proof of his pro-Communist sympathies. They forget the stringent political control over means of communication, including letters, in Soviet Rus-sia. It is a widespread misconception that the apparatus of political repression was not in place until the 1930s. The full and objective his-tory of Soviet security agencies has not been written, nor is it likely to appear soon, but here are the published data for August 1922: In the course of this single month the workers of the section of political control in the state security agencies read almost half of the 300,000 letters that came to Russia from abroad and all 285,000 letters mailed from Russia to the West.[43] It is not hard to guess that the scope of censorship inside the country was no less impressive. As Russian historians now attest, "By the end of the 1920s the country had a system of total, all-embracing control over the actions and thoughts of scientific and cultural figures, with a special role played by the 'punitive sword of the revolution'—the organs of the VChK-OGPU [forerunners of the KGB]."[44]

The Shostakovich family was aware of political surveillance and denunciation even before the revolution. Caution was in their blood. The "Red Terror" of the early years of the revolution, when long lists of executed "conspirators" were posted on pillars in Petrograd, instilled even greater fear; Shostakovich recalled those proscription lists with horror even decades later. Friends and acquaintances began "disappearing" long before the Great Terror of the 1930s. In 1921, this fate befell Mitya's high-school classmate Pavel Kozlovsky, the son of former tsarist general Alexander Kozlovsky, a leader of the renowned anti-Bolshevik Kronstadt Uprising of 1921. Later, in 1929, Mikhail Kvadri, a close friend of Shostakovich to whom he dedicated his First Symphony, was arrested and shot "for counterrevolutionary activity"; after the execution, the dedication to Kvadri disappeared.

In the secret diary of art critic Nikolai Punin, who lived in the same city with Shostakovich and who rather quickly grasped the punitive nature of the Soviet regime, we can find the following very telling notation made on 18 July 1925:

> The lyceum students were shot. They say 52 people, the rest were exiled, their property, right up to children's toys and winter clothes, confiscated. There is no official announcement of the execution; of course, everyone in the city knows about it, at least in those circles with which I deal: the milieu of the white-collar intelligentsia. They speak of it with horror and disgust, but without surprise or real outrage. They speak as if it could

have been no other way . . . I feel that this will
soon be forgotten . . . A great dullness and extreme weariness.[45]

With this in view, it is not the few profoundly "patriotic" passages in
young Shostakovich's letters that surprise us—letters he had every reason to believe were being read by the authorities—but the multitude of
disrespectful and mocking references to the official ideology that bursts
through. The cult of Lenin, being imposed from above, grew to unbe-
lievable excess after his death in 1924; this makes Mitya's favorite joke
even more risky: He persisted in using "Ilyich" (as the press lovingly
referred to Vladimir Ilyich Lenin) for Petr Ilyich Tchaikovsky. In a letter to Glivenko, Shostakovich wrote indignantly about changing Petrograd to Leningrad, which he sarcastically dubbed St. Leninburg.

In a letter to Yavorsky, Shostakovich belittles the mandatory course
in "Marxist methodology" in music for graduate students at the conservatory and gives a hilarious account of his contemptuous behavior at
the oral exam.[46] In this connection, he writes openly and rather carelessly about his "political unreliability."[47] When I was a student, in the
incomparably less "carnivorous" 1960s, very few people, especially in
the rather conformist musical milieu, would have dared to speak out so
heretically in private correspondence.

In this context, we can safely assume that Shostakovich viewed the
conformist finale of the Second Symphony as a forced compromise.
This is substantiated also by the fact that even before he completed the
"official" symphony, in 1927 Shostakovich began working feverishly on
the opera *The Nose* (after Gogol), the polar opposite in ideology. It
must be stressed here that, unlike *Dedication to October,* this opera was
not commissioned and literally flew out of his pen. Considering its
scope and theme, this was a daring step.

The plot of Gogol's "Nose" made this story the precursor of the
twentieth-century literary absurd. With incomparable aplomb and dispassion, Gogol relates the misadventures of a St. Petersburg official
named Kovalev: His nose mysteriously disappears, only to reappear on
the streets of the capital in the form of a higher-ranking official. After
a number of tragicomic turns, when Kovalev has given up all hope of
getting his nose back, it just as inexplicably reappears on its owner's
face. Gogol concludes this brilliant grotesquerie with an ironic after-

word: "What is even stranger, more inexplicable than the rest—is how authors could select such subjects . . . First of all, there is absolutely no benefit to the homeland; secondly . . . and secondly there is no benefit either."

It is not difficult to imagine how this demonstratively "apolitical" statement suited the composer who had to set to music Bezymensky's "super-ideological" but mediocre text. Yet the opera based on "The Nose" was not simply a breather or release for Shostakovich. It became his first creative and social manifesto. So, contrary to the current stereotype of young Shostakovich as an idealistic fellow traveler who later became disillusioned, his actual ideological trajectory led Shostakovich from democratic non-Communist beliefs to opportunistic early symphonies, zigzagging meanwhile to his first opera, *The Nose*. It was a complex and contradictory journey.

No one has noted until now that *The Nose* is an autobiographical opera. Much has been written about its avant-garde nature (montage construction; atonal fragments; the famous octet of janitors, an absurdist eight-voiced canon; and the bold experiment of an orchestral interlude for percussion only) and its satirical bent (it is full of parodic references to the operas of Tchaikovsky, Mussorgsky, and especially Rimsky-Korsakov). But if *The Nose* consisted of only these two elements, it would have been no more than an amusing one-day wonder, while the opera continues to move and excite us. This is so mostly because the central character of the opera elicits our compassion.

This is not so in Gogol, who narrates his "Nose" with marked dispassion, while Shostakovich turns the noseless Kovalev into a tragic hero, giving him a heartbreaking, passionate aria. As Beranger, the hero of Ionesco's *Rhinoceros,* would later feel, Kovalev wants to be like everyone else, crying, "A man without a nose is God only knows what: not a bird, not a citizen." By a strange whim of fate, he becomes "different," and the nose-bearing establishment punishes him immediately, turning him into a pariah. Kovalev races frantically around town in vain, trying to get his nose back: everywhere he meets with humiliation and shame.

Shostakovich turns Kovalev into an outsider being forced by society into conforming. This is an autobiographical theme, a clear reflection of the situation with the Second Symphony. Shostakovich radically rethinks the concept of the prose work that serves as the basis of his opera, imbuing it with autobiographical significance. (He would do the same with his opera *Lady Macbeth of Mtsensk,* after Nikolai Leskov.) In *The Nose,* Shostakovich gives an outlet to all his phobias, savaging treacherous women (this opera has a very strong misogynistic streak), corrupt police, and especially the conformist masses, depicted as a mad and cruel mob caring only for spectacle, easily manipulated, and ready to destroy all outsiders.

Shostakovich's *Nose* is usually seen to be influenced by another Gogol production of the mid-1920s: *The Inspector General* directed by the avant-garde master Vsevolod Meyerhold. There are many reasons for making this comparison, including Shostakovich's own confession. But we could recall a completely different interpretation of *The Inspector General,* much closer to the artistic and political ideas of the young Shostakovich. This was the controversial anarchist production by the Leningrad Dadaist Igor Terentyev, who died in a Stalin labor camp in 1941.

Using Gogol's play as a starting point, Terentyev (with the help of expressionist artists who were pupils of the great Pavel Filonov) depicted the contemporary world as a madhouse run by rough and cruel overseers. Terentyev thumbed his nose at the Soviet regime, which made the official critics howl for "the liquidation of this dangerous sport." In the end, Terentyev was sent for "re-education" on the construction of the Belomor Canal, where, working as a slave digger, he wrote a kind of a self-epitaph in verse, which Shostakovich could have signed had he found himself in a similarly dreadful situation:

> *Kremlin,*
> *See the dot below?*
> *That's me with a wheelbarrow*
> *Full of the earth of socialism.*

Shostakovich highly regarded Terentyev's theatrical experiments. But there is another important "heretical" influence on *The Nose* as well: Shostakovich made a point of collaborating on the opera libretto with the great writer Yevgeny Zamyatin. Zamyatin had participated in the Revolution of 1905, joining the Bolshevik Party then; but after the Communists came to power, he took a challengingly independent position. In 1920, he wrote his best-known work, the anti-utopian novel *We,* banned by the censors but widely read in manuscript form.

However, in 1921, Zamyatin managed miraculously to publish his now legendary literary manifesto, "I Am Afraid," which ended with an aphorism that cost the author dearly: "I am afraid that Russian literature has only one future: its past."

In 1922, Zamyatin was supposed to be expelled from Soviet Russia with Lossky and other oppositionists, but at the last moment the Bolsheviks changed their mind. Zamyatin visited the Shostakovich family, and naturally, the young composer knew the writer's thoughts: "Real literature can exist only where it is done not by obedient and reliable officials, but by madmen, hermits, heretics, dreamers, rebels, and skeptics."[48] Those words, in essence, could be considered one of the main ideas of the novel *We* (which Zamyatin classified under the genre of "urban myth") and, paradoxically, of Shostakovich's *Nose*. Zamyatin mocked the adaptable writers (chiefly Mayakovsky): "Writer X wrote revolutionary verses—not because he truly loves the proletariat and wants revolution, but because he loves and wants a car and public stature. Writer X in my opinion is a prostitute."[49] We can assume that sensitive Shostakovich took this as referring to himself, too—which is why he accepted Zamyatin's advice on *The Nose*. This opera was supposed to be Shostakovich's anti-sycophantic declaration, his own "I Am Afraid."

Interestingly, the first reviewers of *The Nose,* which was produced in Leningrad in early 1930, grasped this rebellious character of Shostakovich's opera. They were clever people, who wrote sharply and smartly, albeit overusing the prevalent ideologized jargon of the times. One of them called Shostakovich's opera "an anarchist's hand bomb" and another declared that the main point of *The Nose* was the depiction of "the feeling of bewilderment of the bourgeoisie, thrown off its tracks." The critic correctly perceived that Shostakovich was focused on "the spiritual confusion" of his alter ego, Kovalev, heard the resonances of Austro-German expressionism (the obvious parallels with Alban Berg's *Wozzeck* and the plays of Ernst Toller, popular then in Leningrad), and roundly condemned the composer's autobiographical theme: "All this reveals the psychological reaction of the bourgeoisie to modern reality." His conclusion: "One cannot consider all this to be a Soviet opera."[50]

It was said harshly, but it was essentially correct. Shostakovich, who had cardiac pains after these reviews, wrote to the director of this production of *The Nose:* "The articles will do their work and readers won't go to see *The Nose*. It will take me a week 'to get over' this, 2 months to get over the gloating of 'friends and acquaintances' that *The Nose* flopped, and then I'll calm down and start working again, I just don't know on what."[51]

The Nose was shown to Leningrad audiences sixteen times. The opera was disliked not only by the critics, but also by the Party boss of Leningrad, Sergei Kirov, and was taken out of the repertory. For the young composer this was a catastrophe, of course, but for the cultural life of the country as a whole, it was an insignificant fact that went little noticed in the annals of the politico-cultural confrontations of that period. The intelligentsia had no time for *The Nose*. The class was shuddering. The ruthless attack on it had begun back in 1929. Stalin had called it "the year of the great watershed": he announced the start of the brutal collectivization and called for "the liquidation of the kulaks as a class." Religious propaganda was made tantamount to a state crime; the outline was approved for the first Five-Year Plan for economic development; and the "right opposition" headed by Nikolai Bukharin was completely destroyed. Trotsky was exiled abroad. In the course of mass "purges" the dossiers of Party members and government workers were checked for degree of loyalty and potential ties with "hostile elements."

A new wave of firings and arrests took place among Leningrad's white-collar workers and scientists and scholars, where the Shostakovich family had many ties. Culturally, the screws were tightened by the influential Russian Association of Proletarian Writers (RAPP) and its musical "sister," the Russian Association of Proletarian Musicians (RAPM), organizations that had been formed in the early 1920s and were becoming particularly aggressive. Behind them stood the Party and Stalin himself, who had celebrated his fiftieth birthday in 1929 and was by now firmly ensconced in the part of supreme leader. The culmination of these widespread attacks along the entire "ideological front" was the persecution of Zamyatin and another writer, Boris Pilnyak, for bypassing Soviet censorship and publishing their works in the West.

Vicious articles in the leading newspapers and hastily organized meetings of writers that passed resolutions condemning Zamyatin and Pilnyak as "undisguised enemies of the working class," traitors, and saboteurs—these formed the framework of a campaign for rooting out dissidence that would be repeated many times by the state. But in 1929 this was all new. An unprecedented sycophantic unity was being demanded of cultural figures. This led to a shocking abandonment of the traditional norms of behavior among the intelligentsia. As the Leningrad writer Mikhail Chumandrin, one of the furious supporters of the new order of things, wrote: "Denunciations? We are not afraid of words. We care about the act behind the word. To expose an alien, hostile tendency, to reveal the enemy and attack the counterrevolutionary, why, that is the honorable duty performed on behalf of the working class!"[52]

This summary of the atmosphere of 1929 should help us understand why Shostakovich grew so nervous after completing *The Nose*. Already exceedingly vulnerable, he undoubtedly suffered greatly from the rapid changes around him, especially since they touched him personally.★ This can explain (but still not justify) the genesis of Shostakovich's Third Symphony ("The First of May"), written in that black year of 1929, in which, he stated, he tried to express "the festive mood of peaceful construction."[53] Shostakovich could not have been feeling very festive in that period, nor can it be felt in the symphony. But, just as in *Dedication to October*, there are many pages that are fresh, vividly original, and profoundly lyrical in mood. One is the pastoral introduction of two clarinets, unexpectedly (coming from Shostakovich) very "Russian." Or the slow movement: The stupor of a weary, exhausted soul is the proto-image of the stagnant, deadly episodes in Shostakovich's late quartets. Enormously expressive music—but what does it have to do with conveying the "general festive mood of the international solidarity of the proletariat"? (This is how Shostakovich described this work.)

But since he had accepted money from the authorities for the symphony, he had to do the work. That is why the new symphony, the orchestral part of which breaks off on an enigmatic ellipsis, has a choral apotheosis tacked on (like *Dedication to October*), here to poetry by Shostakovich's peer Semyon Kirsanov, yet another Mayakovsky imitator. These politically correct verses were a bit better than Bezymensky's

---

★The arrest and execution in 1929 of Mikhail Kvadri, the dedicatee of the First Symphony, made Shostakovich particularly vulnerable.

text for the Second Symphony, but they had not fanned the composer's imagination, either. The finale is stilted, and one is tempted simply to cut it off with a pair of scissors.

For the young Shostakovich this was, one strongly suspects, another painful compromise while he was struggling for survival. But even after composing two politically expedient symphonies, he remained on the periphery of the national cultural discourse. Still, the story of the politically correct text for his "First of May" symphony had a symbolic subtext that was important for Shostakovich. Kirsanov's poem was a palliative: Shostakovich naturally would have preferred to work with the verse of Mayakovsky himself, who was considered the leading poet of the revolution by many, but far from everyone. Many remembered Lenin's hostility toward Mayakovsky. The influential Party ideologue Nikolai Bukharin backed Boris Pasternak for the position of chief revolutionary poet. Apparently to counter Bukharin, Stalin demonstratively applauded Mayakovsky when the poet read an excerpt of his poem about Lenin at a special evening in memory of the dead leader at the Bolshoi Theater in January 1930.

Despite that success, Mayakovsky felt humiliated and persecuted. In a 1929 poem, "Conversation with Comrade Lenin," he complained: "You get tired of fighting and snarling." He feared that he was written out. In that same fatal year of 1929, when Mayakovsky was allowed to travel (for the last time) to France, he met an old friend there, the émigré artist Yuri Annenkov. The conversation turned to a return to Moscow. Annenkov said that he no longer thought about that: he wanted to remain an artist, and in Bolshevik Russia that was impossible. Mayakovsky, looking grim, replied, "Me, I'm going back . . . since I've already stopped being a poet." And sobbing like a child, he added softly, "Now I'm . . . an official."[54]

Wittingly or not, Mayakovsky recalled the prophetic words of Zamyatin, that real literature was created not by officials but by heretics. At that dreadful moment the poet felt like a pretender rather than a chronicler (which he had never been) or, alas, a *yurodivy* (which he definitely had been in the days of the futurist youth). Having started out a greater rebel than Zamyatin, Mayakovsky ended up barking at him and Pilnyak with the zeal of a toady. He joined the official organization RAPP, abandoning his former avant-garde friends. Many of them perceived this as the ignoble sunset of left-wing art in the Soviet Union.

Like Pushkin's Pretender, Mayakovsky was not completely cynical, and therefore he broke the knot romantically: On 14 April 1930 he shot himself. Alexander Rodchenko, brought in to make posthumous photographs of Mayakovsky, noted in his diary: "He lay in his tiny room, covered by a sheet, turned slightly toward the wall. Turned away slightly from everyone, so terribly quiet, and that stopped time . . . and that deadly silence . . . spoke again and again of the vicious mediocrity, of the vile persecution, of the petit bourgeoisness and treachery, of the envy and stupidity of everyone who performed that contemptible deed . . . Who destroyed that man of genius and created that horrible silence and emptiness?"[55]

Rumors spread through Moscow instantly about the causes of Mayakovsky's suicide: unhappy love, syphilis . . . There really was an unhappy love affair, but there was no syphilis. Of yet another reason—perhaps the most important one—they spoke in whispers, looking over their shoulders. We learned about those conversations comparatively recently, with the publication of the autograph statement of the writer Isaac Babel, made to the NKVD after his arrest in 1939: "Mayakovsky's suicide we explained as the poet's conclusion that it was impossible to work in Soviet conditions."[56]

For Shostakovich, as for the entire creative intelligentsia in the Soviet Union, the suicide came as a shock. Shostakovich, twenty-two years old, had met Mayakovsky early in 1929, when he wrote the music to his comedy *The Bedbug* (staged by Meyerhold), and the poet's unceremonious behavior had repelled him. But Shostakovich, even though he preferred Mayakovsky's earlier works, understood the symbolic significance of that great figure. For Shostakovich, Mayakovsky's fate was a warning. He saw where creative pretension can lead: to poetic impotence, despair, and, as the tragic result, suicide. Shostakovich was horrified. Even though circumstances inexorably pushed him toward compromise with the authorities, toward hackwork and opportunism, he did not want to turn into a pretender. He wanted to survive, but not at any price. He wanted to preserve not only himself, but his gift as well. He had to find a way out of an impossible situation.

Chapter II The Year 1936: Causes
and Consequences

On 18 April 1930, the day after Mayakovsky's funeral (thousands of mourners attended, turning it into a kind of spontaneous political demonstration), the telephone rang in the Moscow apartment of the writer Mikhail Bulgakov. When Bulgakov picked up the telephone, he heard a muffled voice with a marked Georgian accent: It was Stalin himself.

Dramatic circumstances led up to this unexpected call. At the time, Bulgakov was a famous prose writer, but even better known as a playwright: His 1926 play *Days of the Turbins* became the first Soviet work to appear on the country's main stage, Stanislavsky and Nemirovich-Danchenko's Moscow Art Theater. The play, starring the favorite actors of the period, became a sensation: Many saw it as an apology for the social stratum under attack just then—the Russian intelligentsia.

Bulgakov admitted it during an interrogation by the GPU, where he had been summoned on the eve of the dress rehearsal of *Days of the Turbins*. "I am acutely interested in the life of the Russian intelligentsia, I love it, and consider it a very important, albeit weak, stratum in the country."[1] Bulgakov's position was confirmed by a denunciation to the GPU that assessed him as "a typical Russian *intelligent,* unstable, dreamy, and deep in his heart, naturally an 'oppositionist.' "[2]

Audiences saw *Days of the Turbins* as a requiem for the counterrevolutionary White movement. Some wept and fainted seeing White officers sympathetically portrayed on the stage of the Art Theater. Stalin could observe these reactions for himself, because—despite his heavy schedule—he went to every performance of *Days of the Turbins,* as if hypnotized. He even admitted to the actor Nikolai Khmelev, who played the main character, the noble White officer Alexei Turbin, that he dreamed about him: "I can't forget it." (It is intriguing to look now at a photograph of Khmelev in the part: It is an idealized portrait of Stalin in his youth.)

Stalin was drawn to this play. It was a window for him into the world of the contemporary Russian intelligentsia. He could read about the prerevolutionary intelligentsia in Chekhov, but here it was before him, a three-dimensional and vivid depiction of the class that had attracted Stalin from childhood and which he, unlike Lenin, thought it vitally important to bring over to the side of the Soviet regime. Bulgakov persisted in calling the intelligentsia "the best stratum of our country." Apparently, Stalin didn't disagree, at least not at that particular moment.

On the other hand, the ruler did nothing to diminish the abuse dumped on Bulgakov after the premiere. The playwright kept a neat scrapbook (just as Shostakovich later would do) of the 301 reviews of his works over the years in the Soviet press; 298 were negative, all but open political denunciations.

Days of the Turbins, and other plays by Bulgakov, were first permitted by the censors and then banned, and he was no longer published. Feeling badgered and deeply depressed, the author wrote an angry letter on 28 March 1930 "to the Government of the USSR" (that is, to Stalin) with a refusal to repent and write, as they demanded of him, a "Communist play." Instead, he demonstratively demanded permission to go to the West, for he had no future in the Soviet Union except "poverty, the street, and death." That is how his missive ended.[3]

And on 14 April, Mayakovsky shot himself. The connection between that tragedy and Stalin's telephone call to Bulgakov is apparent. Paradoxically, Mayakovsky, of whom Bulgakov had a very low opinion (and who responded in kind), "helped" him by his suicide. Stalin really did not want the leading cultural figures of Russia killing themselves off on his watch.

According to later notes made by the writer's widow, Stalin asked Bulgakov point-blank: "Are you asking to go abroad? What, have you gotten very sick of us?"

The stunned Bulgakov did not answer immediately. "I've been think-ing a lot lately whether a Russian writer can live outside his homeland. And it seems to me that he cannot."

Stalin seemed pleased by what he heard. "You are right. I think so, too. Where do you want to work? At the Art Theater?"

"Yes, I would. But I talked about it and I was refused."

"You go apply there. I have the feeling they will agree. We should meet, to talk together."

"Yes, yes! Iosif Vissarionovich, I really need to talk to you."[4]

Here Stalin unexpectedly cut the conversation short. An experi-enced politician and good psychologist, he knew that he had gotten what he wanted: Bulgakov's move to the West was no longer an issue, and the writer, cheered and confused by the call, would probably not commit suicide.

The very next day Bulgakov was greeted with open arms at the Art Theater and hired as assistant director. Moscow's intelligentsia circles buzzed with this fantastic, Gogolian story. The rumors were summa-rized in a remarkable document—a recently declassified "agent-informer report" addressed to Yakov Agranov, in charge of literature at the GPU.

> The impression is that a dam has broken and suddenly everyone sees the true face of Comrade Stalin. For there has been no name, it seems, more surrounded by anger, hatred, and the opinion that he was a vicious, stupid fanatic who was leading the country to its doom, who was considered the cause of all our woes, problems, ruin and so on, that he was a bloodthirsty creature hidden behind the Kremlin walls.
>
> Now people say:
>
> But Stalin really is a major figure. Simple, accessible . . . And most importantly, they say that Stalin has nothing to do with the ruin. He is pur-suing the correct line, but he is surrounded by scoundrels. Those scoundrels persecuted Bul-gakov, one of the most talented Soviet writers. Various literary bastards were building their

> careers on persecuting Bulgakov, and now Stalin
> has flicked their noses. It must be said that Stalin's
> popularity has risen incredibly. They speak of him
> with warmth and love, retelling the legendary
> story of Bulgakov's letter in every variation.[5]

That brief telephone contact, which reaped such a full harvest of propaganda gains, was the only direct conversation between the ruler and the writer. But they developed a kind of imaginary dialogue that continued for ten years, until Bulgakov's death in 1940. In this dialogue, which became his trademark, Stalin demonstrated his extraordinary ability to play cat-and-mouse and manipulate patiently.

Taking a close look at the ups and downs of Stalin's attitude toward Bulgakov, we must remember one important thing: Even Stalin was not born a Stalinist. That is, he was not from the very start an uncompromising executor of the strict and dogmatic system of cultural norms that later became associated with his name. Stalin changed with age and his views on culture developed accordingly.

Of course, as a true Russian Bolshevik and loyal student of Lenin, Stalin always regarded culture as an instrument of politics. But he hardly appeared in the political arena with a full-blown Machiavellian master plan for culture. The more documents are declassified, the clearer it becomes: Stalin's cultural line underwent significant tactical vacillations. Here, as in other spheres, Stalin remained the great pragmatist. He was also capable (at least up to a certain time) accepting suggestions, advice, and even contradiction.

When in 1922 Leon Trotsky raised the question at the Politburo about young writers, poets, and artists needing "attentive, cautious, and gentle treatment" so as not to repel them from the Soviet regime, Stalin supported the proposal as being "fully timely"[6] and also stressed that "material support right up to subsidies in the guise of one form or another is absolutely necessary."[7] Stalin followed this idea subsequently, too.

Without Stalin's approval, the most liberal Party document on cultural policy in the entire history of the Soviet regime could not have appeared. It was a Politburo resolution passed in 1925, when Stalin was already actively supervising all issues relating to ideology. That resolution, written with the participation of Nikolai Bukharin, supported "free competition of various groups and tendencies" in culture and rejected "attempts of amateurish and incompetent administrative interference in literary affairs." How Stalin understood these ideas is clear from his attitude toward Bulgakov. He kept Bulgakov under his constant scrutiny. Beginning in September 1926, the Politburo, headed by Stalin, had held several special discussions about whether a new play by Bulgakov should be permitted to be produced. This was a question that should have been handled on a much lower level—by the theatrical censor's office, Glavrepertkom. In some cases, Stalin wanted plays banned; in others, permitted. It depended on the particular political and cultural situation.

As a viewer and reader Stalin clearly liked Bulgakov's plays. But as a politician, he naturally could not ignore the fact that most writers and theater figures loyal to the regime had opposed the playwright, violently.

Typical is the aggressive tone of a letter to Stalin in December 1928 from the members of the Proletarian Theater Association. Justifiably pointing out the inconsistencies in the attitude of the high authorities and the censors subordinated to them toward Bulgakov, these writers, "more Catholic than the pope," dared to challenge the ruler himself:

> How are we to understand the de facto "greatest indulgence" for the most reactionary authors (like Bulgakov, who has managed to get four blatantly anti-Soviet plays produced in the three largest theaters in Moscow; and plays that are not outstanding in their artistic qualities, but being middle-level at best)? We can speak of "greatest indulgence" because the organs of proletarian control over the theater are in fact powerless in dealing with such authors as Bulgakov. An example: *Flight,* banned by our censors but still managing to get past that ban while all other authors (including Communists) are subject to the control of the Glavrepertkom. How are we to regard this subdivision of authors into black and white, especially since the "white" ends up in the more beneficial conditions?[8]

Of course, Stalin could merely shush those self-styled "zealots of proletarian purity." But he clearly did not want to. He preferred to create a situation in which the sheep (in this case, Bulgakov) would be whole and the wolves (the proletarian writers) sated.

At one meeting with Communist writers unhappy with his "excessive liberality," Stalin—according to a recently declassified transcript—patiently tried to persuade them of the value for the Soviet regime of the plays of Bulgakov and other talented "fellow travelers of the revolution": "The play *Days of the Turbins* played a big part. Workers go to see this play and say: Aha, no force can overtake the Bolsheviks! This is the general impression from this play that otherwise cannot be called Soviet by any means."[9]

Stalin praised the plays *Armored Train* by Vsevolod Ivanov and *Breakup* by Boris Lavrenev, which brought, in his opinion, much more propaganda value than the works of "a hundred Communist writers who try hard but still nothing comes out: they can't write, it's not art." He even concluded that "I cannot demand of a writer that he must be a Communist and should necessarily promote the Party point of view."[10]

Shostakovich had a mixed reaction to Bulgakov's plays. He shared his theatrical impressions in 1928 in a letter to a friend: "*Armored Train* as spectacle is extremely successful, despite the presence of Kachalov (Arise, people, and for freedom give up your wives and mothers. We'll get our *muzhik* freedom with our mighty brawn. Hey, Pyatrukha! Take a lookie, is that some *bourjuy* hiding under that-there bush?). And all with that phony accent to achieve the *style paysan-russe-revolution*. *Breakup* is such a lousy play that I was embarrassed the whole time. There are moments of true tragedy in *Days of the Turbins,* there was even loud sobbing in the theater. But it was all spoiled by the final act with its official ending."[11] This sarcastic passage (Shostakovich did not even spare Vassily Kachalov, the star of the Art Theater and favorite of the intellectual audiences) ignores the fact that his own recent *Dedication to October* had a finale much more official than that of *Days of the Turbins.*

Things were both easier and harder for Bulgakov than for Shostakovich in those years: easier because he knew for sure that he had been lifted up from the general flow and was under the observation of Stalin; harder—for the same reason. In less than ten years, Shostakovich would find himself in a similar situation.

With his telephone call promising a meeting, Stalin hooked Bulgakov. As Bulgakov recalled, Stalin "led the conversation powerfully, clearly, statesmanlike, and elegantly." In the writer's heart "hope sprang up: just one step left—to see him and learn my fate." The meeting became Bulgakov's idée fixe: "I have a tormenting misery: that my conversation with the general secretary did not take place. It is a horror and a black coffin."[12]

Stalin had calculated well: Not allowed to have a direct talk with him, the writer entered into an imaginary dialogue. From his pen came one work after another with the central theme being the relationship between a persecuted creative genius and a benevolent figure personifying the higher authorities. This includes the historical drama and novel about Molière and, most importantly, Bulgakov's masterpiece, the novel *Master and Margarita,* about the visit of Satan himself and his entourage to Soviet Moscow and his meeting with a writer ("Master") working on a novel about Jesus Christ and Pontius Pilate. Bulgakov never managed to publish *Master and Margarita,* even though the authorities did not keep him from circulating it among friends.* In fact, Bulgakov could not get another line published, and one by one his plays were taken out of production.

Stalin played the role of Nicholas I in his own way, Bolshevik-style, humiliating his authors more than the emperor had done Pushkin. Encouraging signals came to Bulgakov very rarely and always obliquely, through other people, while bans and bellows came frequently and from many sides. That was Stalin's training school for intellectuals.

Bulgakov appealed time and again with requests to be permitted to leave for the West; they were ignored. His wife wrote in her diary: "Nothing can be done. A dead-end situation."[13] Then the writer decided on an all-or-nothing step: he wrote *Batum,* a biographical drama about the early years of Stalin the revolutionary, a play that the Art Theater and Nemirovich-Danchenko had long demanded from him. *Batum* was the culmination of prolonged and tormented meditation on Stalin.

When you read *Batum* now, you can appreciate Bulgakov's mastery

---

*The circle of first readers included Shostakovich, in whose music *Master and Margarita* would be echoed unexpectedly a few years later.

and professionalism. As with Shostakovich's "commissioned" works, this piece is something other authors would have been proud to write. But *Batum* is not equal to Bulgakov's best; the author is obviously trying to avoid hidden traps.

Nevertheless, the Art Theater accepted the play with delight, and the troupe's star Khmelev (the one about whom Stalin dreamed) said that not getting the part of the ruler would be a tragedy and that he had already memorized it. The premiere was to take place on 21 December 1939, the day of Stalin's sixtieth birthday celebrations.

And suddenly the dictator, who naturally had been given *Batum* to read, stopped everything. In a conversation with Nemirovich-Danchenko, Stalin expressed himself briefly and enigmatically—he considered *Batum* a very good play, but it could not be produced. Bulgakov told his wife: "He's signed my death sentence."[14]

And in fact, fatal illness came swiftly. As his wife later recalled, Stalin's refusal to accept the play dedicated to him struck Bulgakov "on the thinnest capillaries—the eyes and kidneys."[15] The ironic bon vivant with fast reactions and quick movements turned almost overnight into an exhausted, yellowish living corpse. The doctors' diagnosis was hypertonic nephrosclerosis.

People around the dying Bulgakov still made an effort. The conductor Samosud, an energetic and unflagging favorite of Stalin, suggested turning *Batum* into an opera libretto—have Shostakovich write the music; only the woman's part had to be developed. And word came "from above" that the writer would be allowed to go to Italy "for his health."

On 10 March 1940, not yet having reached his forty-ninth birthday, Bulgakov died. A while later the telephone rang in his apartment, and a clerk from Stalin's office inquired, "Is it true that Comrade Bulgakov is dead?" Hearing a confirmation, he hung up without a word.

Later Stalin would proudly sum up his relations with writers: "Our strength is that we taught even Bulgakov to work for us."[16] The ruler was certain that he had twisted the writer around his finger the way Nicholas I had Pushkin. And what about Bulgakov? After initial contact and then an imaginary dialogue with Stalin, he created a few great works. But *Batum* was his defeat, both creatively and morally.

However, Bulgakov managed to complete his masterpiece, *Master and Margarita,* and died in his own bed, a death to be envied in those years. Let's not forget that another magnet for ideological attacks in that period, the writer Boris Pilnyak, was executed in 1938 at the age of forty-three.

In the 1920s Pilnyak used to say, "A writer is valuable only when he is outside the system." But in the 1930s he was forced to praise Stalin, "a truly great man, a man of great will, great deeds and words." As it sometimes happened in that crazy lottery that was a personal relationship with Stalin, Zamyatin, who had taken a more principled position, had better luck: After innumerable appeals, the ruler allowed him to go to the West in 1931. But according to Zamyatin, an enormous role in this fortunate turn of events was played by the intervention of Maxim Gorky.

Gorky was very well known in tsarist Russia: a romantic biography (from tramp to writer), a reputation as a rebel, and the halo of success. People turned to look at him in the street and stared at him in theaters and restaurants. Almost a hundred books were published about him in a few years.

Even before the revolution Gorky had ties with the Bolsheviks, who considered him a "talented mouthpiece of the protesting masses." He was highly esteemed by Lenin; Gorky obtained large sums of money for his underground activity. But after the revolution Gorky harshly condemned "the inexpressibly vile" murder of Shingarev and Kokoshkin by the revolutionary mob, and he wrote of the Bolshevik leader that "Lenin is not an omnipotent sorcerer but a cold-blooded magician who spares neither the honor nor the life of the proletariat."[17]

A social activist by nature, Gorky took on saving the Russian intelligentsia, which was under periodic attack from the Bolsheviks. In those cases, as Zamyatin recalled, "the last hope was Gorky; wives and mothers of the arrested appealed to him."[18] In the end, Lenin got so sick of his pleas for the arrested and sentenced that in 1921 he forced the writer to go to Italy, allegedly for his health.

One of the important tasks Stalin set for himself when he came to power was getting Gorky back to his homeland. The dictator fully appreciated, and perhaps exaggerated, the value of the writer as a propaganda weapon: "Gorky influences the consciences and minds of millions of people in our country and abroad."[19]

Using a purely formal excuse—the fortieth anniversary of the publication of Gorky's first short story—Stalin unleashed a waterfall of awards and honors on the "great proletarian writer": He gave him the Order of Lenin, renamed Moscow's main thoroughfare Gorky Street, and gave Gorky's name to the city where he was born, Nizhny Novgorod. When Stalin decreed that the Moscow Art Theater would now be the Gorky Art Theater, an official noted meekly that it was "more Chekhov's theater." "It doesn't matter," Stalin interrupted. "It doesn't matter. He is an ambitious man. We have to tie him with ropes to the Party."[20]

And this when from the purely aesthetic point of view Stalin much preferred Chekhov to Gorky. But he—not for the first nor the last time—overlooked his personal taste for the sake of political gain. Gorky, in turn, had no illusions about the Bolsheviks, but joined in a complicated political game with them anyway. He admitted, "I never bent the truth before, but now with our regime I have to bend the truth, lie, and pretend. I know that it can be no other way."[21] When Zamyatin pointed out the brutality of the Soviet regime, Gorky answered, "*They* have very large goals. And that justifies everything for me."[22]

In the grim European political situation of the early and mid 1930s, Gorky considered fascism and Nazism much greater threats to culture than communism. This conviction was shared by such major Western writers as Romain Rolland, George Bernard Shaw, and Theodore Dreiser. With Gorky's help, Stalin planned on getting the sympathy of world public opinion, whose reactions the dictator constantly monitored, contrary to the general view of Stalin.

In turn, Gorky and his Western friends considered Stalin a counterweight to Hitler's growing international influence. They saw no real alternative to the Soviet regime. Gorky hoped that the Communists would manage, albeit by harsh methods, to modernize Russia, eventually turning it into a cultured and flourishing nation. Mutual political and cultural interests made Stalin and Gorky allies.

In the end, Stalin got what he wanted: Gorky returned to the Soviet Union and took part in managing Soviet literature. Disbanding the Russian Association of Proletarian Writers (RAPP), Stalin put Gorky at the head of the organizing committee to prepare an All-Union Writers' Congress. That congress was supposed to show the world how much Communists cared about culture, and Stalin gave it enormous political significance.

During this period many people considered Gorky to be second to Stalin in power in the Soviet Union. A Russian-language émigré journal, *Sotsialisticheskii Vestnik,* which was very well informed, with underground channels for confidential information from the Soviet "top," reported: "The only person with whom Stalin is now 'friends' . . . is M. Gorky. For a long time now Stalin has stopped visiting everyone. Gorky is the only person for whom he makes an exception."[23]

Zamyatin, who credited Gorky with "the correction of many 'excesses' in the policies of the Soviet government," described those mysterious meetings between ruler and writer (perhaps from Gorky's own words?): "One with his ubiquitous pipe, the other with a cigarette, secluded themselves and, over a bottle of wine, they talked for hours."[24]

Stalin, when he wanted, could be a charming companion: simple, attentive, cheerful, even gentle. Many of his guests, including major Western figures, described him this way: Romain Rolland, H. G. Wells, Emil Ludwig. Lion Feuchtwanger wrote about his conversation with Stalin, "Not always agreeing with me, he was always profound, wise, and thoughtful."

In his personal notebook, under a notation entitled "Strategic Leadership," Stalin reminded himself to "maneuver rationally."[25] This is how he behaved with Gorky, and the writer responded in kind. Typical is a note Stalin made during a Politburo meeting in the mid-1930s: "Resolve Gorky's questions."[26] This desire to meet Gorky halfway whenever possible played a very important role in 1936 in Stalin's tactics toward young Shostakovich.

But before that, on the night of 8 November 1932, a tragedy occurred in Stalin's Kremlin apartment: His young wife, Nadezhda Alliluyeva, shot herself. The death is still a mystery. Rumors raced instantly through Moscow that Stalin had killed Alliluyeva, but there is no real proof of that. It may very well be that he truly loved that modest, amiable, and devoted woman. At her coffin, tears rolled from his eyes (he had never before been seen to weep), and he muttered, "I didn't protect her." A good actor, maybe?

The official announcement of her death did not mention the cause. The newspapers were filled with condolences for Stalin, among which a brief letter stood out for its extraordinary content and sincerity of tone, signed by Boris Pasternak: "I second the feelings of my comrades. On the eve, I was thinking about Stalin profoundly and persistently; as an artist, for the first time. In the morning I read the news. I am as stunned as if I had been there, lived it and saw it."[27]

They say that Stalin was deeply moved by this letter; Ilya Ehrenburg even claimed that it lay under the glass top of Stalin's desk. One thing was clear—without Stalin's sanction, this provocatively "personal" text, highly unusual in a ticklish situation, would not have appeared in the newspapers. Apparently, it was from this moment that Stalin took a serious interest in Pasternak.★

For Pasternak, this was the start of a risky stratagem. He was close enough to Mayakovsky to see what an unquestioning following of the Party line had done to him. Pasternak had always been impressed by Mayakovsky's enormous gift. But he was repulsed by the "gramophone eloquence" of Mayakovsky, who with his followers "thickened the servile note to physical unbearability."[29]

Pasternak disapproved of Mayakovsky's attempt to become the "main poet" of the Soviet state. Mayakovsky's many compromises led to suicide, in Pasternak's opinion. But Mayakovsky's departure from the literary stage changed the stakes for everyone.

> *Wrongly in the days of the great council,*
> *Where places are given to the highest passion,*
> *The place of poet is left vacant:*
> *It is dangerous, if not empty.*

In those verses by Pasternak written in 1931, after Mayakovsky's suicide, and dedicated to Boris Pilnyak, Pasternak seems to consider filling that "dangerous" vacancy. And there is no doubt that some very important people urged him to do it. Among them were Gorky and Nikolai Bukharin.

This was the start of an intricate cultural-political tango. Gorky had disliked Mayakovsky for a long time. In a letter to Bukharin, who

---

★According to Olga Ivinskaya, Pasternak's mistress and the prototype of Lara in the novel *Doctor Zhivago,* there was a meeting between Pasternak and Stalin in late 1924–early 1925. Allegedly Pasternak, together with Sergei Esenin and Mayakovsky, was invited for a talk about translating Georgian poets into Russian. Stalin then told the poets that they should take on the role of "heralds of the era." Pasternak allegedly reported his impressions to Ivinskaya in this way: "Out of the semidarkness came a man who looked like a crab. His entire face was yellow and pockmarked. His mustache bristled. This was a dwarf of a man, unproportionately broad yet reminiscent of twelve-year-old boy in height, but with a big, elderly face."[28]

shared his cultural views, he wrote of the poet's suicide, "A fine time for it! I knew that man and I didn't trust him."

The former "favorite of the Party" (as Lenin had dubbed him) and then leader of the so-called right opposition, Bukharin had lost his major political confrontation with Stalin, but still had significant authority, especially in issues of cultural policy. In that sphere he was more tolerant than the majority of his orthodox Party colleagues. (Remember Bukharin's role in preparing the comparatively liberal Party resolution on literature in 1925.) He shared Gorky's belief that intellectuals had to cease active opposition to the Soviet regime, as the last true bastion of humanism and antifascism in Europe.

Gorky admired Pasternak, thinking that the poet, "like all true artists, is completely independent," and Pasternak responded with like praise. Pasternak also thought that at the moment the Soviet regime could be the embodiment of the ideas of the Decembrists. To his cousin Olga Freidenberg he wrote that "the world has never seen anything more aristocratic or free than this hungry and crude reality of ours, which is still accursed and can elicit groans."[30]

Pasternak's poetry is often described as apolitical and intricate. And yet the 1923 poem "High Illness" depicts Lenin's speech at the Ninth Congress of Soviets, and the 1926 "The Year 1905" and "Lieutenant Schmidt" are fairly straightforward narrative poems about the first Russian revolution.

Pasternak's 1931 poem "A century plus is not yesterday . . . ," a direct paraphrase of Pushkin's "Stanzas" (in which he praised Emperor Nicholas I, comparing him to Peter the Great and calling for his mercy toward the rebel Decembrists), became emblematic for the poet. In his day, Pushkin was severely criticized by his friends for what they considered his too-sycophantic loyalty. But times had changed dramatically: Pasternak's stated desire to be "one with law and order" elicited approval and even delight from his colleagues—for Soviet publications were filled with much more mediocre and obsequious writing. This poem of Pasternak's must be seen as a milestone: He was one of the first poets in the Soviet era to take up Pushkin's model of relations between poet and tsar. Stalin undoubtedly took notice.

It must be said that at the time the situation in Soviet culture was still rather fluid and periodically instilled hopes of a liberal turnaround. The unexpected and decisive breakup by Stalin of the recently powerful and hated RAPP; rumors of the new role and unprecedented influence of Gorky, who was respected by the intelligentsia; Stalin's personal attention toward writers, his meetings with them—all this gave rise to optimism.

Preparations were in full swing for the first All-Union Writers' Congress, which led many, including Pasternak, to expect new, beneficial decisions. In that atmosphere even the presentation of a new aesthetic slogan—"socialist realism"—did not particularly worry cultural figures. After all, did it not mean merely "writing the truth"?★

In the tense and dangerous political situation of the early 1930s, Stalin maneuvered skillfully, intentionally sending contradictory signals to various people and groups, pitting against one another and then bringing together various factions in the Party and in society. He was clearly directing events or manipulating them from behind the scenes.

Acceding to Gorky's persistent requests, Stalin appointed his vanquished political foe Bukharin executive editor of the government newspaper *Izvestiya*. He in turn hired Pasternak, whose acceptance of Soviet ideas he felt was sincere. If Pasternak was complex and vacillating, for Bukharin it was a mark of a truly romantic figure with a Pushkinian aura. He wanted to give Pasternak the opportunity to appeal to the broadest reading public. Mayakovsky, on the other hand, seemed to Bukharin servile, crude, and opportunistic.

Pasternak recognized the role and in 1934 wrote to his father, "I am hastily re-creating myself into a prose writer of the Dickensian variety, and then, if I have the strength, into a poet of the Pushkin sort. Don't think that I'm comparing myself with them. I'm naming them in order to give you an idea of my inner change . . . I've become a particle of my time and state, and its interests have become mine."[31]

Such "statist" sentiments were not the exception in those years; many talented people—not necessarily toadies or careerists—spoke and wrote that way. The constant changes made people's heads spin, and it was not difficult to lose orientation.

Viktor Shklovsky called on writers in 1925: "Change your biography. Use life. Break yourself over your knee." Shklovsky in 1975 regret-

---

★Stalin liked the label "socialist realism" for three reasons: One, it was short—just two words; two, it was understandable; and finally, there was a connection with the great tradition of Russian "critical realism"—Dostoevsky, Tolstoy, and Chekhov.

ted those words and added in justification, "But we were different then."[32] Not everyone. In late 1933, Osip Mandelstam wrote an anti-Stalin lampoon in verse, "We live not feeling the country under our feet," which even his fearless wife, Nadezhda, equated with suicide. When Mandelstam read to Pasternak his description of Stalin from the poem, "His fat fingers, like worms are obese, and his words, like lead weights are true," Pasternak was horrified. "I didn't hear that, you haven't read it to me—because you know, now strange, terrible things have begun happening, people are being picked up; I'm afraid that the walls have ears. Perhaps the park benches can listen, too."[33]

Pasternak felt that writing and especially distributing such works was a pointless risk, for Mandelstam's lampoon was not worthy of his genius: "What you have read to me has nothing to do with literature, with poetry. It is not a literary fact, but an act of suicide, of which I do not approve and in which I do not wish to participate."[34]

But Mandelstam stubbornly continued reading his satire to acquaintances; in the opinion of Nadezhda, his refusal to remain silent was an act of civic courage: "He did not want to depart from life without leaving an unambiguous statement about what was happening before our very eyes."[35] Mandelstam was arrested on the night of 13 May 1934, charged with committing a terrorist act against the ruler—that is how the investigator viewed the poet's anti-Stalin verse. This confirmed his assertion that "only here is poetry respected—they kill over it."

Learning of the arrest, Bukharin rushed a letter in defense of Mandelstam to Stalin, with a postscript, "Pasternak is also concerned." Stalin immediately made an order about Mandelstam: "Isolate, but preserve."[36] And instead of the expected execution, Mandelstam was sent into exile for three years to Cherdyn, a backwater town in the Urals.

What was the cause of Stalin's unexpected "mercy"? The version offered by Emma Gershtein, a close friend of the Mandelstams, seems likely: Stalin, paradoxically, might have admired those madly bold verses—after all, as Nadezhda Mandelstam said, they were "accessible, direct, easy to comprehend," only very remotely reminiscent of the poet's other work, with its intricate imagery, surrealistic metaphors, and an overabundance of metaliterary allusions. In Gershtein's unexpected but convincing supposition, Stalin might have been amused by the satirical description of his entourage:

> *And surrounded by a pack of thin-necked leaders,*
> *He plays with the services of half-humans . . .*[37]

He did not consider them to be real people and he destroyed most of them eventually. Like Nicholas I, Stalin could occasionally appreciate directness.* Mandelstam sensed this and commented that "the poem must have made an impression."[38] He was right.

When told about Mandelstam's suicide attempts in exile, Stalin ordered his punishment reduced. It was the eve of the much-heralded Writers' Congress, and in order to circulate news of his latest act of mercy in Moscow, Stalin used a method that had worked well for him before: He telephoned Pasternak.

This short conversation, which took place in June 1934, generated even more legends than the Bulgakov call because Pasternak chose not to leave a definitive report, causing competing oral accounts to spread. Probably the most accurate retelling comes from a friend of Pasternak who was lunching at the poet's house when, after three o'clock, the telephone gave a long ring; when Pasternak answered, he was given a Kremlin number to call to speak with Stalin. When the suddenly pale Pasternak dialed, he heard, "This is Stalin. Are you interceding on behalf of your friend Mandelstam?"

"We were never actually friends. Rather the reverse. I found it difficult dealing with him. But I've always dreamed about talking to you." According to other versions, Pasternak added, "About life and death."

"We old Bolsheviks never deny our friends. And I have no reason to talk to you about other things."[39]

Here Stalin, as he had in the conversation with Bulgakov, unexpectedly hung up. This was a well-rehearsed move. Stunned and confused, Pasternak immediately redialed, but Stalin did not pick up the phone again.

As with Bulgakov, Stalin won the round with Pasternak: He had achieved his goal and bewildered and confused his interlocutor. We know that Pasternak, like Bulgakov, returned over and over—to the end of his days—to this mysterious dialogue with the ruler, re-evaluating his response. Nadezhda Mandelstam and Anna Akhmatova gave him "a solid B."

---

*Remember the reaction of Pushkin's Tsar Boris to an insulting remark by the *yurodivy*: "Leave him. Pray for me."

Osip Mandelstam, who learned from Pasternak that Stalin wanted to know whether Mandelstam was really a "master," joked, "Why is Stalin so afraid of artistic 'mastery'? He thinks we can make shaman magic."[40]

This fascination with "shamanism" (which was characteristic, incidentally, of the real Tsar Boris—rather than Pushkin's fictionalized version—who, historical sources tell us, surrounded himself with witches and healers) clearly shows in Stalin's attitude toward Pasternak. Stalin must have been impressed by the line from Pasternak's letter to him after Alliluyeva's suicide: "I am as stunned as if I had been there, lived it and saw it." Stalin could have had a sense of the poet's mystical presence in the Kremlin as the tragedy unfolded.

Pasternak, as a man with the intuition of genius, naturally felt this rapport that formed between ruler and poet, and he worked to strengthen it. For instance, in 1935 he wrote a letter to Stalin in which he admitted there was "something secret that, beyond all that is comprehensible and shared by everyone, connects me to you."[41]

The poet developed that theme in the poem "The Artist" published in the New Year's 1936 issue of Bukharin's *Izvestiya*. It spoke of a "genius of action" (that is, Stalin) who lived "behind an ancient stone wall" (that is, the Kremlin), in meditation about whom "another poet is absorbed" (that is, Pasternak). Pasternak was proposing a dialogue of equals, based on the mystical tie between tsar and holy fool mythologized by Pushkin. In effect, he was telling Stalin that he could read his secret thoughts.

According to Pasternak, the ruler acts and the poet comprehends and judges. Did Stalin understand this? Probably. Did he like it? Probably not. This poem dedicated to Stalin was never reprinted in the ruler's lifetime, even though it primed the pump for the endless flow of glorification of Stalin in Soviet Russian literature.

And it was not only that Stalin did not appreciate Pasternak's poem. It's quite possible that he did. But for propaganda purposes as he understood them, the poem was useless. For his goals, he needed completely different poetry. In general, Pasternak seemed unsuitable for the role of "beacon" in this exceptionally utilitarian sphere. So Stalin didn't support the idea to make Pasternak the "leading" poet at the first All-Union Writers' Congress.

Opened on 17 August 1934, it was subsequently dubbed the "congress of deceived hopes" by the disillusioned writers. But it started with great pomp in Moscow. For the first three hours Gorky spoke. At Gorky's insistence, Stalin permitted Bukharin to make an important speech about poetry. Pasternak was in the presidium and listened to Bukharin cleverly praise him, simultaneously denigrating the significance of Mayakovsky, whose primitive *agitki* (propaganda pieces) the speaker declared no longer needed by Soviet literature. The latter, he said, demanded "poetic paintings" à la Pasternak.

Bukharin's speech received an ovation. The audience rose, and the terrified Bukharin, as they tell it, whispered to Gorky that the applause was like a death sentence to him. He knew how closely Stalin, who was not in the auditorium, was watching the tiniest details of the congress's work from behind the scenes.

We know now that Stalin received almost daily reports from the NKVD, the secret police, on what writers were saying in the corridors of the congress and what their mood was. He read the anonymous leaflet intercepted by the secret service. It was "an appeal from a group of writers" to the foreign guests at the congress, who included Louis Aragon, André Malraux, and Martin Andersen-Nexø. "For the last seventeen years the country has been in a state that absolutely precludes any possibility of free expression," the leaflet said. "We Russian writers are like prostitutes in a brothel, with the only difference that they sell their bodies and we sell our souls; and as they have no way out of the brothel except a hungry death, neither do we."[42]

Even if that desperate plea had reached the celebrated foreigners, they were unlikely to respond: For them (as for Stalin and Gorky), the congress served as an important statement of a Europe united against fascism. What was a little leaflet compared to that? The Soviet delegates, on the other hand, were very sarcastic. Here is Isaac Babel's characterization of the congress, according to a report from an informer: "We must demonstrate to the world the unanimity of the Union's literary forces. And since all of this is being done artificially, under the stick, the congress is as dead as a tsarist parade, and no one abroad, naturally, believes the parade."[43]

The NKVD reports also stated that many writers were thrilled by Bukharin's "amazing" speech, its "marvelous clarity and boldness." The congress halls were filled with lively debate on Gorky's closing words, in which he reluctantly admitted that the deceased Mayakovsky had been an "influential and original poet," but insisted that his hyperbole had a negative influence on young authors.

We can picture Stalin wincing as he read this: The alliance of the power-loving old man Gorky with the renegade Bukharin was a definite irritant. In counterattack, Stalin chose to use Mayakovsky, so disliked by Bukharin and Gorky. How had Mayakovsky put it? "I want the pen to be made tantamount to a bayonet . . . Stalin to make speeches, from the Politburo, on the work of poems." Stalin, not Bukharin! The fact that the poet had committed suicide was even better in this case: His moods no longer had to be watched, and no new whims or surprises would occur.

The impetus for Stalin's new cultural initiative became a letter to him from Lili Brik, Mayakovsky's mistress for many years. In conversations with me and others, Brik always insisted she had appealed to the top on her own initiative. "They were all enemies of Mayakovsky! All those so-called realists hated him! Well, so I said, 'Comrades, I can't take it anymore. There is only one address where I can write—Stalin.' "[44]

In her subsequently legendary letter, which Brik sent to Stalin in late November 1935, she complained that Mayakovsky's books were no longer reissued, that the poet was clearly underestimated, even though his poems five years after his death were still "absolutely timely and were a most powerful revolutionary weapon."

The way Stalin reacted to this letter makes one think that the whole action had been coordinated and sanctioned from above. The letter was instantly passed to the Kremlin and that very same day Stalin wrote a resolution on it that was soon published in an editorial in *Pravda*: "Mayakovsky was and remains the best and most talented poet of our Soviet era; indifference to his memory and his works is a crime."[45]

This was the first time in the history of the Soviet state that the ruler's personal opinion about a creative figure printed in the press was officially equated with the final truth and was not subject to any disagreement.[46] The results were spectacular: huge printings of Mayakovsky's poems, the creation of his museum, his name given to numerous streets, squares, and schools throughout the country, the instant and irreversible canonization of the poet as a Soviet classic.

Pasternak acerbically commented that "Mayakovsky was forced down on us compulsorily, like potatoes under Catherine the Great.

That was his second death. This one wasn't his fault."[47] But he wrote this more than twenty years later. At the time Pasternak, in a special letter to Stalin, joined in the general delight: "[I] warmly thank you for your recent words about Mayakovsky. They match my personal feelings."[48]

Those who were displeased by this unexpected ascension of Mayakovsky's kept quiet. Stalin only heard a chorus of rapture over his "progressive" cultural tastes. This was a repetition of the situation played out by Nicholas I vis-à-vis Pushkin, with the difference being that the dead Mayakovsky could no longer be a source of unexpected difficulties. From that time on his poetry and image would work for communism.

Thus Stalin established communication with the cream of the Russian elite and concluded several important ideological operations successfully. He outwitted major creative figures and forced them to collaborate. The ruler must have decided that he understood their psychology very well and could subtly and cleverly get them to serve his needs.

That was Stalin's mood as he entered 1936, for he had planned, among other urgent affairs, yet another domestic campaign in culture: the eradication of "formalism," that is, art that was complicated and incomprehensible to the masses, and therefore useless in the construction of Soviet culture.

According to his calculations, this campaign would also go smoothly. But a painful stumble occurred—because of the young composer Dmitri Shostakovich, who had not yet entered the orbit of Stalin's keen attention, and his opera *Lady Macbeth of Mtsensk*.

One of the most mysterious episodes in Shostakovich's work history is his selection of the subject for his second mature opera, after *The Nose*. Unlike Gogol's novella, Nikolai Leskov's sketch "Lady Macbeth of the Mtsensk District," which first appeared in 1865 in Dostoevsky's journal *Epokha*, was certainly not among the recognized or even notable works of Russian literature. For the first sixty-odd years after its publication, the sketch was not discussed. The breakthrough came in 1930, when an illustrated edition of the work was published in Leningrad. The drawings were done by the late Boris Kustodiev, the great Russian artist. It is believed that this edition caught twenty-four-year-old Shostakovich's eye.

His attitude toward Kustodiev was special: As a teenager he first visited the artist's house in 1918 and became almost part of the family. Kustodiev began working on the illustrations for the Leskov sketch in the early 1920s, but it was not published then. The secret was recently revealed: Besides the "legitimate" illustrations, the artist also drew numerous sexually explicit variations that were not intended for publication. After his death, his family, fearing a search, hastily destroyed the drawings.

If we assume that the young Shostakovich saw those immodest illustrations, it makes clearer the genesis of this opera, which has a plotline heavy with sex and eroticism. There is no eroticism in the Leskov original. But Shostakovich, seeing the published Kustodiev illustrations, could have recalled his much franker drawings. They may have ignited his imagination.

Shostakovich's relationship with his future wife, Nina Varzar, an enormously independent, proud, and strong woman, was developing at that time. *Lady Macbeth of Mtsensk,* completed in late 1932, is dedicated to Nina; they had been married seven months earlier.

Galina Serebryakova recalled that in his opera Shostakovich "wanted to re-create the theme of love in a new way, love that recognized no barriers, that risked crime, that was inspired by the devil himself, as in Goethe's *Faust.*"[49] Serebryakova felt that Leskov's heroine (like Nina Varzar?) had overwhelmed Shostakovich with the fury of her passion. Perhaps, but let us take a look at the opera's plot.

In a dull Russian province, in the wealthy merchant Izmailov family, Katerina is bored and frustrated with the husband she does not love. In his absence, she has an affair with a new farmhand, Sergei. Her father-in-law finds out, but Katerina murders him with rat poison. When the husband returns and catches Sergei in Katerina's bedroom, the lovers kill him, too, and hide the body in the cellar.

Katerina and Sergei hurry to wed, but fate catches up to them in the person of a drunken "shabby little peasant," who accidentally finds the body in the cellar. The police arrest the newlyweds: Now they must go to Siberia with a group of convicts. In Siberia, the finale of the melodrama plays out on the shore of a lake. Sergei's affections for Katerina have cooled and he is making passes at a tough convict woman, Sonetka. In desperation Katerina throws herself into the lake, pulling Sonetka after her. The convicts continue their grim path:

Eh, you boundless steppes,
Endless days and nights,
Our thoughts are joyless,
The gendarmes are heartless.

The plot follows Leskov's sketch rather closely, but Shostakovich radically transforms the heroine's character (as he did the hero's in *The Nose*). Leskov had Katerina smother her baby. Shostakovich tossed out that murder, and for good reason: His aim was to justify Katerina's behavior.

In a discussion of the opera, when someone said to Shostakovich, "Your opera shouldn't be called *Lady Macbeth* but *Juliet* or *Desdemona of Mtsensk*," he readily agreed. Katerina's part in the opera is the only one devoid of even a hint of grotesquery or mockery.

Shostakovich subtitled his opera a "tragedy-satire." The tragedy is Katerina, and the satire, everything else. We can safely presume that Katerina in many ways is a portrait of Shostakovich's wife, Nina, as he saw her then. He was courting her while writing the opera. It was by all accounts a stormy affair. Nina, in her early twenties, was strong-willed, well educated, and apparently sexually liberated. This seemed to simultaneously attract and repulse Shostakovich. He was ambivalent about committing himself and even canceled the announced wedding at one point. Shostakovich spoke darkly to his friends about love that knows no rules and is ready to overcome all moral boundaries. Obviously, he associated this kind of intense and uncontrolled love with Nina.

Shostakovich, in a way, repeated the well-known situation involving Tchaikovsky's *Eugene Onegin*. There Tchaikovsky imagined that his fiancée, Antonina Milyukova, was Pushkin's heroine Tatiana. Now Shostakovich consciously rehabilitated Katerina, giving her some of Nina's traits.

There was another important autobiographical element. Shostakovich's musings on Nina's independent character were tinged with the realization of how easily a vivid and outstanding personality could be stifled in Russian conditions. There was a danger of being deformed and eventually destroyed, not only by direct and brutal oppression: The eternal and stupefying Russian boredom could accomplish this just as well. At this time, artistic contacts with the West were being cut off. As Sergei Prokofiev expressed it, Soviet composers were faced with "the real danger of becoming provincialized." Shostakovich expressed this fear of cultural asphyxiation musically in the opera by caricaturing Katerina's entire milieu.

All his later confused explanations for such an unexpected and cardinal transformation of Katerina's image, with references to Alexander Ostrovsky's drama *The Storm,* as interpreted by the critic Dobrolubov ("a ray of light in a dark kingdom"), are merely rationalizations in hindsight for an intuitive and impulsive creative act. Here Shostakovich was covering his tracks.

The opera was a great canvas that captivated listeners with its unusual combination of tragedy and satire, lyrical power and passion, with the vividness of not only the leading parts but the secondary roles, and the brashness of the orchestral writing. The action unfolded swiftly and entertainingly and the music in turn shocked, amused, and brought tears to the audience. Five orchestral interludes served as authorial prefaces and summaries.

All this brashness was quite unusual by Russian operatic standards, as was Shostakovich's penchant for boldly mixing angles and styles. There were elements of realistic musical drama, German expressionism, and Italian verismo. Pure lyricism and savage mockery elbowed each other. A deeply felt utterance would be followed by an outrageous scene, such as the father-in-law's ghost appearing to music parodying the entrance of the statue of the Commandatore in Mozart's *Don Giovanni.* For the average opera-going audience, this was at first baffling but finally exhilarating.

And of course, the blatant eroticism coursing through the music was very apparent. It was particularly noticeable in the context of the long-standing tradition in Russian culture of modesty in the depiction of sex. "The sound of a kiss frightens them more than an exploding shell," the satirists Ilf and Petrov wrote in 1932, summing up the position of the Soviet censors. Did they realize that the sensitive censors were catching signals coming from Stalin?

We know that Stalin was outraged by sexual scenes in literature, theater, and film. Rather crude in his own life and free with swear words in his small circle, the ruler could not stand sex in art. In his regime, naked bodies almost completely disappeared in paintings, not to mention film. The culture bureaucrat in charge of film showings at the Kremlin kept an eye out for "improper" scenes in the Western movies that were shown privately for Stalin and his comrades. He remembered the time when he offered Stalin something risqué, "for relaxation." As soon as Stalin realized what was happening on screen, he banged his fist on the table. "This is not a bordello!" The furious ruler got up and left, followed by the members of the Politburo.[50] Stalin's spontaneous reaction helps us understand the fate of Shostakovich's opera.

The Soviet critics, who first hailed the work, skirted the issue of its eroticism. This is how Shostakovich's friend Valerian Bogdanov-Berezovsky reviewed the opera in an article printed in Bukharin's newspaper, *Izvestiya,* in 1933. "In essence, the opera's plot is very old and simple: love, betrayal, jealousy, death. But the theme is broader and deeper than the plot; it is an unvarnished view of the bestial face of tsarist Russia, a revelation of the brutishness, stinginess, lust, and cruelty of prerevolutionary society."[51]

Sergei Eisenstein, analyzing the opera in 1933 with his students, could be a bit more frank. "The 'biological' love line is expressed with extreme vividness in the music."[52] Even franker was Sergei Prokofiev in private conversation: "This is swinish music—the waves of lust just keep coming and coming!"[53]

Prokofiev's friend and confidant Boris Asafiev developed this viewpoint in print only in 1936, when Shostakovich had fallen into disfavor with the authorities. It was done in Asafiev's usual florid manner, but it sounded at that point like an open denunciation. "I personally was always surprised by the combination in Shostakovich of Mozartian lightness and—in the best sense—feckless lightheartedness and youth with a far from youthful, cruel and crude 'taste' for pathological states instead of revealing humanity."[54] Later Asafiev wrote about the "sensuality that reveals itself with extreme cynicism" in the opera. Shostakovich never forgave Asafiev for those lines.*

---

*Interestingly, of the early reviews, the most prudish complaints about the music of *Lady Macbeth of Mtsensk* came in the American press, when the opera was presented in New York in 1935: "Shostakovich is without doubt the foremost composer of pornographic music in the history of the opera."[55] The critics were particularly outraged by the scene in which Sergei copulates with Katerina to the accompaniment of unambiguously descriptive trombone glissandi: the Americans called this episode "pornophony." The music critic of the *New York Times* was furious: "One simply wonders at the composer's effrontery and his lack of self-criticism."[56]

The opera became an event even before it was completed. An opinion formed almost immediately that in the history of the Russian musical theater, there had been no work since Tchaikovsky's *Queen of Spades* of such scale and depth as *Lady Macbeth*. Some reached even farther back in time, saying that Katerina's role was "one of the strongest women's parts since Verdi's Aida."[57] Concluded ubiquitous Asafiev: "Soviet musical culture in the person of Shostakovich has a phenomenon of a Mozartian order."[58]

It was not surprising that two of the boldest and most enterprising opera collectives in the country grabbed the right for first production: in Leningrad, the Maly Opera Theater, where the conductor was Shostakovich's friend Samosud, and in Moscow, the eponymous Musical Theater directed by the legendary Nemirovich-Danchenko.

Leningrad's production beat Moscow's by two days, but Maxim Gorky attended the Moscow premiere at January 24, 1934. The reception in both cities was overwhelming. The description in *Krasnaya Gazeta* of the Leningrad premiere elicited associations with Bayreuth's Wagnerian ecstasies: "The audience in wondrous agitation rushed to the footlights, to the orchestra: arms raised amid the silver molding of the boxes, faces illuminated by delight, eyes turned to the stage, thousand of hands flying into thrilled applause." The author's young age of twenty-seven was particularly astonishing. "The audience had expected to see a mature man, a new Wagner, who had powerfully organized this storm of sounds, and instead before the viewers came a very young man, even younger looking, almost an adolescent."[59]

The words "Mozart" and "genius" filled the air. This in itself was amazing enough: The Soviet cultural elite in the 1930s was ruthless, and people spent time knocking each other down rather than offering praise. But even more surprisingly, Shostakovich's genius was proclaimed on both the right and the left by leaders of uncompromisingly hostile aesthetic camps: the "realists" Nemirovich-Danchenko and Alexei Tolstoi and the "avant-garde" Meyerhold and Eisenstein.

Even the vigilant and eternally grim Party leaders fell sway to the delight: Shostakovich's opera was approved by People's Commissar of Education Andrei Bubnov, and after the Moscow premiere the theater administration issued a special edict proclaiming that the opera "evinces the start of the brilliant flowering of Soviet operatic creativity on the basis of the historic decision of the Central Committee of the All-Union Communist Party (Bolshevik) of 23 April 1932."★

The unprecedented general approval was intensified by the opera's real success with the public, which is rare for a modern opera. In the Soviet Union, as throughout the world, high praise by the elite did not guarantee mass recognition. For instance, Eisenstein's film *Battleship Potemkin* was a flop in wide release, despite the rave reviews and support from the government. This was not the case with *Lady Macbeth of Mtsensk:* In Leningrad it played fifty times in less than a year "with standing room only with increased prices," as Shostakovich noted with pleasure.

When the opera was produced in 1935 at the Bolshoi Theater Annex, as well as continuing in repertory at Nemirovich-Danchenko's Musical Theater, and the Bolshoi itself premiered Shostakovich's comic ballet *The Limpid Stream* (also a big hit), the composer had his work on view simultaneously in three leading theaters of the capital—an incredible event.

The sensational atmosphere was pumped up by reports of successful productions of *Lady Macbeth* and other Shostakovich works abroad: in England, Sweden, Switzerland, and the United States. The writer Yuri Olesha admitted, "We still want recognition from the West. The great conductor Toscanini performs Shostakovich's symphony. The young Soviet composer is pleased by being recognized by a great Western conductor. The West's recognition of, say, Stravinsky, has a special significance for us. We still have a strange respect for Chaliapin, because he was Russian and became famous in Europe. When our books are translated in the West, it satisfies our vanity."[60]

When Romain Rolland sent his friend Maxim Gorky a letter of praise for *Lady Macbeth,* for Gorky it was an important confirmation of his own first emotional reaction: He had been overwhelmed at the premiere and wiped away tears during the last act, with its hapless convicts.

For Gorky and his ally on the cultural front Bukharin, *Lady Macbeth* was very timely: Here was an outstanding work by a young Soviet composer, based on the Russian classics (Leskov, whom Gorky loved),

---

★This referred to Stalin's decision to dissolve the proletarian "creative" organizations. Thus, the success of Shostakovich's opera was presented as the direct consequence of the ruler's wise cultural policies.

innovative and emotionally captivating, highly esteemed by the elite but accessible to a wider audience, recognized in Moscow and abroad. It served Gorky's aim of uniting Soviet art, so important to him in that period, while at the same time being an excellent product of the new socialist culture to export to the West.

Stalin should have shared Gorky's ideas on this. But he also was facing huge new problems—economic, social, and purely political. Pre-revolutionary Russia had been primarily an agrarian country, with the majority of the population illiterate. The Bolsheviks wanted to improve the situation, but things were moving slowly. Ten years after the revolution, the USSR was nineteenth in literacy in Europe. Yet literate workers were needed to realize Stalin's ambitious program of industrialization.

In the 1930s tens of millions of former peasants filled the cities, and they had to be urbanized quickly. Stalin said, "We are not at all indifferent to the way workers come to our factories and plants, whether they are cultured or uncultured. This is a very serious issue. We cannot develop serious industry without making our population literate." And Stalin must have remembered Lenin's thoughts that "it is insufficient to liquidate illiteracy, we must also build the Soviet economy, and in that case you won't go far with literacy alone. We need an enormous elevation in culture."

The question was a fundamental one: What kind of culture was needed in an enormous country in which even in the late 1930s two-thirds of the population were peasants? A great amount of work lay ahead, and its main objectives had to be selected.

The direction of Stalin's plans becomes clear from a revealing letter dated 26 February 1936 from the Bolshevik writer Alexander Fadeyev to his close friend Esther Shub:

> The country's best people see and feel a huge contradiction between the big and truly human and constantly growing needs of the masses and those products of art, products of the latest, so to speak most "left" sophistication (as a result of the *collapse* of the old), which are frequently praised by fools who are lackeys before that sophistication, but which are capable of satisfying only

people in glasses, with skinny legs and thin blood. Someday—soon—the best people of the country and the Party will have the opportunity (in terms of time) to deal with the affairs of art *on a daily basis*—and then many things will fall into place.[61]

Cultural historians have not paid enough attention to this highly noteworthy document. Fadeyev, a talented writer, one of Stalin's favorites, was also a leading cultural functionary. Stalin spoke with him alone quite a few times, and Fadeyev knew some of the ruler's innermost thoughts and ideas.

"The best people of the country and the Party" is naturally a euphemism for Stalin. The passage about people "in glasses, with skinny legs" is a portrait of a completely recognizable, concrete figure, Shostakovich, and the letter as a whole surely reflects the content of a conversation between Fadeyev and Stalin about a recent event, which had taken place on 26 January 1936. On that day Stalin, accompanied by his closest comrades—Vyacheslav Molotov, Anastas Mikoyan, and Andrei Zhdanov—attended a performance of *Lady Macbeth of Mtsensk* at the Bolshoi Theater Annex.

This was not the first time Stalin had seen a Soviet opera in 1936. On 17 January Stalin and Molotov had heard *The Quiet Don* by a young Leningrad composer, Ivan Dzerzhinsky, based on the popular novel by Mikhail Sholokhov. A few days later the press ran an official communiqué announcing that Stalin and Molotov "noted the significant ideo-political value of the production."[62]

Had Stalin really liked the opera so much? An indirect clue is the fact that when, in 1941, the first Stalin Prizes were announced with great fanfare (works of the last six years were eligible), Dzerzhinsky's opera was not among the honorees, while Sholokhov's novel received a First Class prize.

But Stalin's reserved attitude toward Dzerzhinsky's music did not keep him from supporting the opera as an acceptable "ideo-political" model. How and why did that happen? A possible answer can be found in a newly declassified document. In his report to Stalin of 2 January 1936, Alexander Shcherbakov, one of his closest cultural aides, pleaded: "Today literature needs a militant, concrete slogan that would mobilize writers. Help create that slogan, Comrade Stalin."[63]

Shcherbakov was a devious and experienced courtier, who could divine the ruler's as yet unspoken wishes. Stalin deigned to respond to his plea, sending down the slogan "Simplicity and National Character." That motto, which reflected Stalin's meditations of recent years on the aims of culture, in some measure crystallized the too-vague definition of the "method of socialist realism" presented not long before that at the first Soviet Writers' Congress.

Now "Simplicity and National Character" needed to be illustrated by positive and negative examples from the current cultural scene. As the subsequent ideological campaign made clear, Stalin decided to start with visual art and music, in which he had a personal interest. As the positive cultural example, he chose Dzerzhinsky's opera. As the negative one, Shostakovich's came to hand. Here is how it happened.

Stalin arrived at the performance of *Lady Macbeth of Mtsensk* (his favorite Alexander Melik-Pashaev was conducting) in what must have been a good mood—he enjoyed opera and ballet. His previous attendance at a Soviet opera *(The Quiet Don)* had ended well. A pleasant evening was expected this time, too: After all, Shostakovich's opera was almost unanimously recognized as "a victory of the musical theater" (this was the headline of the full-page article devoted to the opera in the official newspaper *Sovetskoe iskusstvo* [Soviet Art]).

Shostakovich, who was supposed to go to Arkhangelsk to perform his First Piano Concerto at the invitation of the local radio committee, was urgently called to the theater by Yakov Leontyev, the director of the Bolshoi. Leontyev, another experienced courtier, was a friend of Mikhail Bulgakov. A unique document has survived: a written-down humorous "oral story" by Bulgakov about this event, which, we can safely assume, relied on information that came from Leontyev.

Bulgakov gives an ironic description of Shostakovich, "white with fear," rushing to the theater and Stalin and his entourage settling down in the government box. Then: "Melik furiously lifts his baton and the overture begins. In anticipation of a medal, and feeling the eyes of the leaders on him, Melik is in a frenzy, leaping about like an imp, chopping the air with his baton, soundlessly singing along with the orchestra. Sweat pours off him. 'No problem, I'll change shirts in the intermission,' he thinks in ecstasy. After the overture, he sends a sidelong glance at the box, expecting applause—nothing. After the first act—the same thing, no impression at all."[64]

Bulgakov's oral micronovella is of course grotesquely exaggerated. (In particular, *Lady Macbeth* has no overture; the opera begins with a brief introduction to the heroine's first tensely lyrical monologue.) But this written record is of immense value in helping us to understand the atmosphere, especially if we bear in mind how few eyewitness accounts of this event remain.

The important thing is that Bulgakov's information matches that of Shostakovich's close friend Levon Atovmyan, a music bureaucrat. He confirmed that on that fateful day the orchestra went overboard— probably spurred on by the presence of VIP guests.

In addition, the brass instruments (called by the Italian word *banda* by musicians all over the world) had been increased for the occasion, and they played, especially in the orchestral interlude just before Katerina's wedding scene, with excessive volume, as Shostakovich thought. The wind section was right under the government box and Shostakovich, "white as a sheet," in Atovmyan's recollection, was horrified.

After the performance, Shostakovich could not calm down, and as he headed for his concert tour in Arkhangelsk, he questioned Atovmyan irritably. "Tell me, why did they have to overincrease the sound of the banda? What was it, Melik-Pashaev's shashlik temperament, that made him overpepper the intermezzo and that whole scene? The people in the government box must have been deafened by the brass section. I have a feeling that this year, like all leap years, will be a bad one for me."[65]

The highly superstitious Shostakovich (he retained a belief in popular omens throughout his life, just like Pushkin) left for Arkhangelsk "with a sorrowful soul," as he wrote in a letter to his friend Ivan Sollertinsky: He realized that his opera had not pleased the high Party leadership. But even he could not imagine the scope and horrifying effect of the catastrophe that was barreling toward him.

In Arkhangelsk, on a cold wintry day, Shostakovich lined up at a newspaper kiosk. The line was moving slowly, and Shostakovich shivered in the cold. He bought the country's main newspaper, *Pravda* (in those days it was officially called *C.O.*—that is, "Central Organ"), for 28 January 1936, opened it to the third page, and saw an editorial (unsigned) with the headline "Muddle Instead of Music." The parenthetical subtitle read "About the Opera *Lady Macbeth of Mtsensk*." He began reading instantly, without moving away from the kiosk. Sudden horror shook him. Someone in the line cried out, "Hey, brother, got soused first thing in the morning?"[66]

Even now, decades later, it is impossible to read "Muddle Instead of Music" without shuddering. We can understand why Shostakovich felt the earth open beneath his feet. His opera, his beloved creation that had won recognition throughout the world, was unexpectedly subjected to a crude, untrammeled, and illiterate attack. The article has become a classic example of authoritarian cultural criticism. What was the article talking about and what did it threaten—not only to Shostakovich but to all of Soviet culture?

There are two layers in the text of "Muddle Instead of Music." One is the author's impressions of the music of Shostakovich's opera and its production at the Bolshoi Theater Annex. The other layer is theoretical, so to speak. The response to the music is spontaneous and highly emotional. "The listener from the very first minute is stunned by the opera's intentionally unharmonious muddled flow of sounds. Snatches of melody, embryos of musical phrases drown, escape, and once again vanish in rumbling, creaking, and squealing. To follow this 'music' is difficult, to remember it impossible."

Like some Western critics, the author of the article was particularly offended by the opera's erotic episodes. "The music grunts, moans, pants, and gasps, the better to depict the love scenes as naturally as possible. And 'love' is smeared throughout the entire opera in the most vulgar form." These were the most upsetting scenes in the production at the Bolshoi Theater Annex. "The merchant's double bed holds the central place in the setting. All the 'problems' are solved in it." Interestingly, the article's author had read Leskov and did not agree with the interpretation of his work in Shostakovich's opera. "The predatory merchantess, clawing her way to wealth and power by way of murder, is presented as some 'victim' of bourgeois society. Leskov's slice-of-life novella is burdened with a meaning that it does not have."

The theoretical and political aspects of the article were even more important. Shostakovich's opera was accused simultaneously of formalism and naturalism. The use of those terms in the cultural battles of the period was nothing new. "Naturalism" applied to the excessively frank passages, and "formalism" was usually used for complicated works that were too smart by half, in the opinion of the critics. Shostakovich had been forced to fight off accusations of formalism before. In 1935, in Bukharin's *Izvestiya,* he stubbornly and challengingly declared: "These rebukes I never accepted nor do accept in any measure. I was never nor will be a formalist. Labeling any work as being formalist on the basis that the language of that work is complicated, or sometimes not immediately understandable, is intolerably thoughtless."[67]

But now *Pravda* maintained that Shostakovich's "petit bourgeois formalistic contractions" constituted political transgression. "This is music intentionally made inside-out, so that there would be nothing to resemble classical music, nothing in common with symphonic sounds, with simple, accessible musical speech . . . This is leftist muddle instead of natural, human music."

Pravda made it clear that it was upset not only by Shostakovich's opera in itself. "The danger of this tendency in Soviet music is clear. Leftist ugliness in opera is growing from the same source as leftist ugliness in painting, poetry, pedagogy, and science. Petit bourgeois 'innovation' is leading to a gap away from true art, science, from true literature."

The style of the article, humiliating and offensive, was not unheard of; in fact, it was rather the rule for the polemics of those years. What was shocking (and not only for Shostakovich) was *Pravda*'s unexpected interference after more than two years of growing triumph for the opera. And even more substantive was this: In previous discussions of naturalism and formalism, one side could attack while the other actively fought back and even counterattacked. Now the situation had changed sharply. The tone of *Pravda* was peremptory, as it was called then, "directive." This was underlined by the absence of a signature under the article. The presumption was that it represented the opinion not of some single critic or even a group, but of the Party as a whole. This automatically turned any attempt to argue with it into criminally "anti-Soviet" behavior.

Not that long before, Bulgakov, Zamyatin, and Pilnyak were taxed with exclusively political demands, and there was no mention of aesthetics. Now, for the first time, aesthetic "sins" were made tantamount to political ones. This was a new and dangerous development. Many cultural figures, upon reading "Muddle Instead of Music," must have shivered when they reached the warning, "This is playing at things beyond reason that can end very badly."

Who stood behind that vicious threat? Determining the identity of the writer of "Muddle Instead of Music" turned into a cottage industry over the years. Various scholars have various candidates: Some of the names mentioned are journalist David Zaslavsky, music critic Victor Gorodinsky, Isaac Lezhnev—the head of *Pravda*'s literature and arts section—and Platon Kerzhentsev, chairman of the Committee on Arts Affairs, founded in January 1936. Yuri Elagin maintained that the article had been written by Andrei Zhdanov.[68]

But informed contemporaries began saying almost right away that the real author of "Muddle Instead of Music" was Stalin. This is apparent, in particular, in Bulgakov's "oral story" already cited. Using information that came from Stalin's "court" circle, Bulgakov describes in a grotesque but convincing form the "collegial meeting" which presumably took place in the government box after the opera. Bulgakov's Stalin says, "I will not pressure other people's opinions, I will not say that in my opinion it is cacophony, muddle in music, but I will ask the comrades to express their completely independent opinions." Bulgakov follows this with a comic presentation of the sycophantic reactions of Stalin's comrades who were at the opera, and concludes with an announcement that *Pravda* then ran the article "Muddle Instead of Music," in which "the word 'cacophony' appears several times."[69]

Here Bulgakov is mistaken; *Pravda* mentioned "cacophony" only once. But even this error is telling—it conveys the writer's impression about the tautological style of "Muddle." Tautology was one of the most important characteristics of Stalin's manner of expression. He used it like a weapon, fully consciously, as Mikhail Vaiskopf, who studied Stalin's style, wrote: "The method, intended to create a hypnotic effect, came to him easily as a consequence of his limited vocabulary, but with time took on a premeditated development."[70]

The article on Shostakovich's opera in *Pravda* uses the adjective "leftist" *(levatskii, levatskoe)* four times; the author employs variations of "crude" six times and "muddle" or "muddled" five times (including the headline). Shostakovich first pointed out to me that "muddle" had migrated to the article on music straight from material published the day before in *Pravda* on outlines for history textbooks that was signed by Stalin.

Shostakovich had another proof of Stalin's authorship. He maintained that the other alleged authors were all educated people. It was unlikely that they would have written passages about music in which "nothing was in common with symphonic sounds" (what mysterious sounds would they be?) or about the composer's pretensions "to create originality by methods of cheap originalizing." These phrases (and others like them) in "Muddle Instead of Music," in Shostakovich's opinion, had to be Stalin's own words, otherwise they would not have made it onto the printed page—the editor would have crossed them out.

Of course, Stalin may not have written the article by hand, but have dictated it—perhaps by telephone—to one of *Pravda*'s leading journalists and then checked it before it was printed. Dmitri Shepilov, at one time *Pravda*'s editor-in-chief, who had been present at more than one such occasion, described the procedure. According to him, important "directive" articles that for some reason or other were not to be signed by Stalin were dictated by Stalin, slowly, weighing every word. They were taken down either by Stalin's aide or by the paper's editor.

"This work sometimes took many hours," Shepilov recounted, adding, "And sometimes the work began in the daytime and ended only at dawn the next day."[71] Stalin personally determined not only the form of the article—whether it would be a front-page piece or an editorial, whether it would be signed with a pseudonym or attributed to a certain "Observer"—but also the page layout, whether it would be illustrated, and so on. So it does not matter whose hand wrote down "Muddle Instead of Music." Its real author would still be Stalin himself.*

This supposition is supported by the ruler's attitude toward "Muddle Instead of Music." Of all the anonymous directive articles in *Pravda* (and in that year and subsequent ones a large number appeared), this was the closest to his heart, as we will see in the chapter describing the events of 1948. Other articles of this time would appear, serve their function, and vanish in the endless flow of other Party directives. Only "Muddle Instead of Music" continued to be the banner of Soviet culture for long decades, surviving even Stalin.

---

*Mikhail Goldshtein said in his memoirs that in 1962 he asked David Zaslavsky, who had been a leading *Pravda* journalist from 1928 until his death in 1965, if he had been, as many supposed, the true author of "Muddle Instead of Music." According to Goldshtein, Zaslavsky replied, "I was brought a finished article from the Central Committee, which had been checked and approved. I had only to prepare it for publication and smooth out a few mistakes in the Russian and some swear words."[72]

But if the real author of the editorial was the ruler, what had prompted him to attack Shostakovich's opera so harshly? As usual with Stalin, political reasons came first. Still, some personal matters came into play.

Stalin was firmly convinced that an "all people's" culture that had to be accepted and mastered by the masses had to be created and inculcated. This universal "cultural literacy" would transform the country. Stalin understood the importance of culture as an instrument of political upbringing and control. But for all that, his personal tastes in art were not solely pragmatic.

Unlike many other political leaders of the twentieth century, Stalin could be called a culture fan. He calculated that he read an average of five hundred pages a day. Of course, most of that was paperwork. But Stalin read a lot of literature, fiction and nonfiction: attentively, pencil in hand, leaving lively notes in the margins.

His interest in classical music was not feigned. He listened to it frequently and with apparent pleasure. He preferred Russian operas and ballets—Tchaikovsky, Glinka, Borodin, Rimsky-Korsakov, and, to a lesser degree, Mussorgsky. But Stalin's favorites also included Bizet and Verdi.

Take the case of the program for the concert planned for the closing of the Extraordinary Eighth All-Union Congress of Soviets in 1936 (which ratified the draft of the new "Stalin" constitution). When the program of light music was shown to Stalin for his approval, he personally wrote in the finale of Beethoven's Ninth Symphony with its famed "Ode to Joy," replacing some of the lighter fare. It was a political gesture, but an eloquent one. The irony is, of course, obvious.

Stalin enjoyed folk songs, Georgian ("Suliko") and Russian ("A Birch Tree Stood in the Meadow," "I've Traveled the Universe"), and often listened to records of these songs (writing his ratings on the jackets—"excellent," "good," and so on); and he liked to sing in company. He had a high tenor.* This kind of music was on the radio a lot, but the classics were given priority. Stalin kept an eye on that. He liked to stress his interest in classical music. When the celebrated tenor Ivan

---

*Molotov recounts this scene: Stalin, Molotov, and Voroshilov singing church music, accompanied by Zhdanov at the upright piano.[73] In his close circle Stalin and his comrades even sang Russian émigré music banned for many years in the USSR—for example, the "White Guard" songs of Alexander Vertinsky and Petr Leshchenko.

Kozlovsky, a Stalin favorite, sang for the members of the Politburo, they demanded that he sing a merry folk song. Stalin intervened. "Why pressure Comrade Kozlovsky? Let him sing what he wants. And what he wants to sing is Lensky's aria from Tchaikovsky's *Eugene Onegin.*" And the Politburo members had to swallow a classical aria.[74]

Stalin enjoyed listening not only to singers but to instrumentalists: pianists, violinists, and cellists. Among his favorites were young musicians who later became world celebrities—Emil Gilels, David Oistrakh, and, later, Sviatoslav Richter and Mstislav Rostropovich. They all received the Stalin Prize at different times.

I have already mentioned the political underpinning of Stalin's attention to young artists. It is obvious: These musicians demonstrated the "human face" of Soviet socialism to the world. But on the other hand, Stalin's personal interest in this area of culture seems sincere. A connoisseur of craftsmanship in all spheres, the ruler appreciated the high professionalism of Russian musicians.

In 1933, under Stalin's aegis, the All-Union Music Performance Competitions were instituted; many of the winners took their rightful places as leaders of Soviet culture. One of the participants in the first competition was the eleven-year-old violinist Boris (Busya) Goldstein. Stalin was delighted by his playing and invited the wunderkind to the Kremlin, where he was given a large cash prize. Stalin joked, "Well, Busya, now you're a capitalist and probably will become so conceited that you won't want to invite me to visit you." "I would be very happy to invite you to our house," the quick-witted Goldstein replied. "But we live in a small apartment and there wouldn't be any place for you to sit." The next day Busya and his family were given an apartment in a new building in the center of Moscow.[75] As Stalin said in one of his famous speeches of those years, "Life has become better, life has become more fun." The expressionist mode of Shostakovich's *Lady Macbeth of Mtsensk* did not fit into that simple but effective formula. That unrelenting piling up of sex, murder, and horror was alien to Stalin's tastes and led to an outburst of irritation and indignation in the Soviet ruler (as it did in many a conservative lover of classical music all over the world—here Stalin was not the dumb exception, as some people now try to depict him).

But on that memorable January evening in 1936 when Stalin came to a performance of *Lady Macbeth,* he had more important considerations than just enforcing his personal tastes. He took pride in his ability to subordinate his emotions to the tactical needs of the moment. And that moment demanded an active assertion of the new state "Soviet morality": The government was planning to pass laws banning abortion and a new code on family and marriage. In Stalin's opinion, the Soviet family had to be strengthened in every way. On his initiative, divorce became much more difficult. Photographs of Stalin with children in his arms appeared regularly in the press. And suddenly there was an opera saluting "free love" (or, in Stalin's words in "Muddle Instead of Music," "merchant lust"), in which the problem of divorce from a hated husband was resolved simply and brutally: by murder.

All this allowed Stalin to accuse Shostakovich on social issues, formulated in "Muddle Instead of Music" in *Pravda:* The composer had "missed the demands of Soviet culture to banish crudity and wildness from every corner of Soviet life."

Now it is perfectly clear to us that the campaign against "formalism" in culture was planned by Stalin and executed following a definite scheme. This is evinced by the speedy consecutive appearance in *Pravda* of "antiformalistic" editorials: blows against film ("A Crude Scheme Instead of Historical Truth," 13 February), architecture ("Cacophony in Architecture," 20 February), painting ("On Mess-Making Artists," 1 March), and theater ("Outward Brilliance and False Content," 9 March).

What remains astonishing is this: Why did music need to be struck several times in a row, and each time the object of the attack was the same composer—Shostakovich?

After the opera was denounced in *Pravda,* Shostakovich's comic ballet *The Limpid Stream,* running with great success at the Bolshoi Theater, was subjected to harsh criticism ("Ballet Falsehood," 6 February). Until now, little attention was paid to the fact that Shostakovich was "worth" three articles in *Pravda.* The third can also be considered an editorial, since it was published without a signature (13 February), though the "directive" essence of "Clear and Simple Language in Art" was masked by its placement in the "Press Review" section. (Shepilov's account of Stalin's strategy of pushing his point of view through materials in different sections of *Pravda* comes to mind again.)

Three editorials against the same man appeared in the country's main newspaper in the space of two and half weeks. And the man was

not a dangerous political enemy, not a British or French prime minister, but simply a twenty-nine-year-old composer, who was little known
until then by the mass readership of the country. This was obviously a
striking overreaction. Even more important: this, as we will see later,
was perceived by many people as an obvious overreaction. What
brought it on?

This conundrum cannot be solved using only pragmatism and ratio-
nality. We need a psychological key. Not even the most pragmatic and
cool-headed politician can operate like a machine, and the human
emotional element inevitably enters into his decisions. This observation pertains to Stalin as well.

The pendulum of contemporary opinion of Stalin swings too far:
Some demonize his actions, explaining them by almost exclusively
irrational impulses; others declare him to be the embodiment of
absolutely impersonal, evil pragmatism. The truth must be that while
he was a great master of political games and an extraordinary states-
man, Stalin often made mistakes when he trusted his intuition. The
textbook example is the fatal error in evaluating Hitler's intentions in
1941, when he invaded the Soviet Union, surprising Stalin. The result
was military catastrophe in the early months of the war.

It is quite probable that in the case of Shostakovich, Stalin was
blinded by emotion. Not only did the plot and music infuriate him,
and not only did the opera contradict Stalin's cultural direction for that
period, but on top of that, the composer was hailed as a genius, not just
in the Soviet Union, but in the West. This, I believe, was what pushed
Stalin over the top. The prominence of other Soviet cultural figures
was for the most part local, hemmed in by the country's borders and,
consequently, dependent on Stalin's control and manipulation.

The exceptions were very rare: Gorky, naturally. Of course, the West
respected Stanislavsky, but so did Stalin. Sergei Eisenstein had an international reputation, but for good reason, thanks to the film *Battleship
Potemkin,* which Stalin himself rated very highly. And yet he was constantly irritated by Eisenstein and had to rein him in, often in the most
unrestrained and offensive way. Meyerhold's international status served
him badly. And the same held for Shostakovich. Stalin decided that he
knew better, took the bit in his teeth, and raced ahead.

Proof of this is Stalin's reaction to *The Limpid Stream.* Stalin did like
ballet, but he also adored comedy as a genre, laughing until he cried at

screenings of Soviet film comedies that were copies of Hollywood fare. *The Limpid Stream,* choreographed by the brilliant Fedor Lopukhov, was, as everyone who saw the production confirms, first and foremost an entertaining show, in which the vaudeville plot of life on a kolkhoz in the Kuban region served as an excuse for a string of striking dance numbers. The ballet was a success in Leningrad and was quickly followed by a triumph at the Bolshoi Theater in Moscow. Lopukhov was made director of the Bolshoi's ballet troupe—an appointment that had to have Stalin's approval.

The Limpid Stream was sure to please Stalin: a vivid, life-affirming spectacle, with dazzling dancers, sets by one of his favorite artists, Vladimir Dmitriev (who eventually received four Stalin Prizes), and finally, Shostakovich's music, which, in contrast to his music for *Lady Macbeth*, was simple, melodic, and festively orchestrated. In addition, it was a perfect illustration of Stalin's motto about life, which had become better and more fun.

But instead of approval, *Pravda* thundered with "Ballet Falsehood." This editorial, more smoothly written than "Muddle Instead of Music," still betrays the very specific hand (or voice) of Stalin: "The authors of the ballet—the producers and composer—apparently feel that our public is not demanding, that it will accept whatever dexterous and impudent people will feed it"; "Some people in clothing that has nothing in common with the clothes of Kuban Cossacks jump around on stage in a frenzy." Or this typically Stalinist passage about the ballet's music: "In *The Limpid Stream,* however, there is less showing off, fewer strange and wild dissonances than in the opera *Lady Macbeth of Mtsensk.*" But this does not save Shostakovich from Stalin's wrath: "The music is therefore without character. It jangles and expresses nothing." He is wrong whatever he does.

It was quite clear that Stalin had decided ahead of time to beat up the creators of *The Limpid Stream.* He watched the ballet only to find things to pick on. His irritation was so strong that he began to sound like a sarcastic anti-Soviet writer: "According to the ballet's authors, all our difficulties are behind us. On stage everyone is happy, cheerful, and joyous." One would think that this was good and should be praised. Not at all; one can almost see Stalin's forefinger wagging under the noses of the ballet's creators. "Do not turn your art into mockery of the viewers and listeners, do not trivialize life."

One should not give free rein to emotion in politics, even if it is cultural politics. The introduction of the emotional element immediately confuses the situation. It is not surprising, therefore, that these instructions, colored so strongly by Stalin's personal feelings, made the heads of workers of the "cultural front" spin. Depicting life "monotonously, in bestial image" (a quote from "Muddle Instead of Music") was not allowed; that was understandable. But neither was depicting " 'joy' in dancing," as "Ballet Falsehood" so scornfully put it. Then what was allowed? What were the models?

In total bewilderment, the newspaper *Sovetskoe iskusstvo* tried to resolve the ideological brainteaser in the article "Against Falsehood and the Primitive." It explained that *Pravda* was fighting on two fronts— against the formalistic "petit bourgeois innovation" and, simultaneously, "against those who, hiding behind the slogan of simplicity and accessibility, want to impose the primitive in Soviet music and thereby impoverish and enfeeble Soviet art."

The editorial staff at *Sovetskoe iskusstvo* must have been very pleased by their cleverness. But they were slammed for it right away in a third anonymous *Pravda* article ("Clear and Simple Language in Art") on 13 February, cited before. "This is a confused depiction of 'two fronts.' Both our first and second articles were directed *against lies and falsehood alien to Soviet art*—the formalistic trickery in *Lady Macbeth* and the sickly sweetness of *Limpid Stream*. Both works are equally distant from the clear, simple, and truthful language in which Soviet art must speak. Both works treat folk art contemptuously. That is the point, and not the allegedly 'complex' music of the opera and the allegedly 'primitive' music of the ballet. For all its convolutions, the music of *Lady Macbeth* is pathetic, impoverished, in the worst sense of the word primitive in its content."

Then whose work and whose style of expression was Comrade Stalin promoting as a model that all Soviet art should follow henceforth? The presumed answer was simple: It was the style of Stalin himself. This was not spelled out; Stalin did not want to appear ridiculous. But the clues to solving the *Pravda* puzzle were scattered more freely than in a cheap mystery novel.

The frequent juxtapositions of "simplicity and clarity" with "formalism and falsehood" appear throughout the entire text. And the lead article in *Pravda* of 3 March, "A Direct and Simple Answer," at last revealed who was characterized by maximal directness and clarity: "Directness and clarity are the characteristic traits of all statements and speeches of Comrade Stalin."

By then, the other publications had figured it out. *Literaturnaya gazeta* brought to everyone's attention (in an article with the incredibly original title "Simplicity and Clarity") that Stalin's style was a "marvelous and artist-inspiring classic example of simplicity, clarity, and chiseled expression and of splendid and courageous power of truth. This is our good fortune; for us Soviet artists, these are the examples from which we can learn courage, strength, and truth."[76]

Stalin should have been satisfied. The slow-witted journalists had finally realized whom he had meant; all over the country, hastily organized meetings of cultural figures condemned "formalism and falsehood" and praised the articles from *Pravda* for their "wise clarity and simplicity." But not everything was going according to plan. The creative elite had begun to grumble. Stalin learned this from secret reports of the NKVD, some of which have been declassified recently.

Informers reported that leading masters resented the *Pravda* editorials. Many of the dissatisfied had guessed who was behind the articles, and even that did not stop them. Andrei Platonov said, "It's clear that someone of the very high up wandered into the theater, listened without understanding anything about music, and flew into a rage."[77] A friend of Anna Akhmatova, the prominent poet and translator Mikhail Zenkevich, said, "No one imagines that there are music experts at the Central Committee, and if the random opinion of one or another leader is instantly canonized, we'll go to hell in a handbasket." The poet Sergei Gorodetsky complained, "It's obnoxious to write as a law what someone's left leg wants." He was seconded by writer Abram Lezhnev: "The horror of any dictatorship is exactly that the dictator does whatever his left leg wants."

Many others spoke out in a way that should have been particularly offensive for Stalin. According to the reports, the well-informed Isaac Babel commented wryly, "After all, no one took it seriously. The people are silent, but in their hearts, they're laughing quietly." Prokofiev's close friend the musicologist Vladimir Derzhanovsky expressed himself even more clearly, "The people are laughing till they cry, since it turns out that the Party members don't know what to say about composers."

Zenkevich was indignant about "Muddle Instead of Music." "The article is the height of arrogance, it is false through and through, ascribing qualities to Shostakovich that he certainly does not have. Besides which it is clear that the article was written by someone who understands nothing about music." The respected Leningrad writer Vissarion Sayanov had a bone to pick with "Ballet Falsehood," too. "The second article is gentler, but still, the phrase about 'impudent and dexterous people' is very incautious." Viktor Shklovsky added, "Very frivolously written."

Something was happening that today seems extraordinary to us. We are accustomed to thinking of the second half of the 1930s in the Soviet Union as a time of total fear, complete unanimity, and absolute subordination to the dictates of Party and state. When I started studying music in comparatively liberal Riga in the 1950s, the Party resolution of 1948 accusing Shostakovich along with Prokofiev and other leading Soviet composers of formalism was still constantly cited. And I remember no one ever doubted the resolution. I am certain now that many people were seething inside but dared not express themselves. Every word in the Party newspaper was regarded as law in that period—they were used to it and took it for granted.

When I later met some of the people who in 1936 had loudly expressed outrage over *Pravda*'s attacks on Shostakovich—Shklovsky, for instance—none of them ever mentioned with pride that in their day they had denied the right of the Party and Stalin to dictate cultural opinions to them. Even if they had brought it up, young people would not have believed them. But their dissent and protests were preserved for history by the sharp ears and fast hands of the snitches. What a paradox! The only thing keeping us from enjoying the irony of history is the sober realization that in those days such reports were actual "invitations to a beheading."

Stalin had to have been particularly annoyed by the reaction of musicians. Of course, here too, superficially things were going well. The zealous public critics of formalism in general and Shostakovich in particular made up the majority, and among them were many former friends and admirers of the composer. But as Stalin was informed in a secret Party memo: "Direct statements of disagreement with the *Pravda* articles were made at meetings of Leningrad critics and music historians by [Ivan] Sollertinsky and [Alexander] Rabinovich."[78]

The same secret report speculated that in the Shostakovich affair there was "a silent conspiracy of formalists of various tendencies, even those who were hostile to one another." It pointed out that two highly authoritative composers who had never felt any particular warmth for Shostakovich's work—Leningrader Vladimir Shcherbachev and Muscovite Nikolai Myaskovsky—thought it necessary to support the young composer after the *Pravda* articles appeared. According to one report, Myaskovsky explained his new position this way: "I fear that paucity and primitivism might otherwise reign in music today." The report to Stalin indignantly stated that such behavior was "a hidden form of sabotage of Party directives."[79]

There was danger that these sentiments would become widespread—another memo from the NKVD reported that in Leningrad "the mood is very grim in musical circles. Various people—musicians, artists, the public—gather near the Maryinsky Theater and discuss events in agitation."[80]

All this information reaching Stalin underscored one thing: The *Pravda* articles against Shostakovich had been rejected and mocked by the creative intelligentsia. Stalin had to take this development as a personal affront. He had expended so much time and effort on meetings with the cultural elite; you would think he had understood their psychology by now—and suddenly this unpleasant surprise. Of course, he could overlook the opinion of the subjugated "creative masses." But the situation was significantly complicated by Gorky's pro-Shostakovich position, about which Stalin learned in mid-March 1936.

This independent stance of the country's greatest cultural authority was set down in his letter to Stalin, and the draft was recently found in the Gorky Archives. It was written from the Crimea, where Gorky was vacationing and where he met with André Malraux, at that period an eminent figure in the European antifascist cultural front, who was on a brief visit to the Soviet Union.

Gorky wrote to Stalin that Malraux immediately peppered him with questions about Shostakovich. This was intended to remind the ruler that the "progressive circles" in the West held Shostakovich in high esteem and were worried about his fate. Stalin also knew that another great admirer was Gorky's friend and comrade-in-arms Nobel laureate Romain Rolland, who had been received with pomp at the Kremlin not long before that; during the meeting Stalin assured Rolland several times that he was at his "complete disposal." On 29 January 1936, *Pravda* called Rolland, on the occasion of his seventieth birthday, "a great writer" and "great friend" of the Soviet Union. The panegyric was accompanied by a large photograph of the writer on the front page.

Gorky's letter was quite sharp. He rejected "Muddle Instead of Music" resolutely, pretending he had no idea who was behind it. " 'Muddle,' but why? How and in what is that 'muddle' expressed? Here the critics should give a technical assessment of Shostakovich's music. What the article in *Pravda* did is allow a herd of mediocrities and hacks to persecute Shostakovich in every way."[81]

Of course, Gorky was careful not to back Stalin into a corner. So he pretended to think that Stalin's real position was quite different. "In your speeches and also in your articles in *Pravda* last year, you frequently spoke of the necessity of 'caring attitudes toward people.' In the West, this was heard, and it raised and expanded sympathy toward us."

In order to convince Stalin of the need to reverse, Gorky used a powerful argument. Shostakovich, according to the writer, "is highly nervous. The article in *Pravda* struck him like a brick on the head, the fellow is completely depressed." This, coinciding with the NKVD reports that Shostakovich was close to suicide, had to have given Stalin pause.★

Things were obviously slipping out of control. Stalin's ideological initiative, planned as a large-scale but really internal action, unexpect-

---

★Some doubts have been expressed whether the letter was in fact sent and reached Stalin. Paradoxically, in this case it does not matter. Gorky's inner circle was infiltrated by Stalin's informers. The writer's personal secretary did not hide that he worked for the NKVD. Regular reports were sent by the maid, members of Gorky's entourage, many of his friends and visitors: Stalin wanted to know about literally every one of the writer's steps and words. In that "transparent" situation it was enough for Gorky to set his thoughts down on paper for them to be known to Stalin, especially since they were in the form of a letter to the ruler. In addition, Gorky made no secret of his negative attitude toward the attacks on Shostakovich. There is a transcript of a conversation of Gorky's in early spring 1936 with Semyon Tregub, chief of the literature and arts section of the newspaper *Komsomolskaya Pravda*. "Now Shostakovich was whipped. He's a talented man, very talented. I've heard him. He should have been criticized with a greater knowledge of music and with great tact. We are always calling for sensitive treatment of people. It should have been shown here, too."[82] The coincidence of what the writer said to Tregub with what was in Gorky's letter to Stalin is striking. Clearly, Gorky was using Tregub and others like him to signal the Kremlin of his attitude toward the badgering of Shostakovich. These signals were immediately picked up by the NKVD, whose informant named "Osipov" reported that "Gorky is very displeased by the discussion of formalism."[83]

edly took on international resonance. This was very inconvenient: Just then the French Chamber of Deputies was discussing the Franco-Soviet agreement on mutual aid, signed almost a year before but only now coming up for ratification. The right-wing French press was fighting the agreement. In those conditions, every step had to be weighed, and the position of such influential figures as Rolland and Malraux took on even greater significance. Shostakovich's suicide could turn into an international scandal with unpredictable ramifications.

That was when Stalin apparently decided to retreat. It is not hard to guess how unpleasant and humiliating this extraordinary step was for him. Stalin knew how to maneuver when circumstances demanded, and he did it more than once in his political career. But he was a morbidly proud man, and with this unforeseen turnaround, the affair of *Lady Macbeth of Mtsensk* became a serious blow against his cultural authority. In order to compromise and yet not lose face, Stalin needed the help of one man—Shostakovich himself. And he got it.

Chapter III 1936: Facing the Sphinx

Shostakovich's friends, and the composer himself, had no illusions about who was behind the unexpected and brutal attack on *Lady Macbeth of Mtsensk*. They understood quite well that thunder, as Shostakovich's friend Isaak Glikman used to say, quoting Pushkin, "came not from the manure pile but a storm cloud." As he put it, "No one but Stalin could raise a hand against the famous opera and demolish it."[1]

His admirers had been observing the extraordinary explosion of Shostakovich's gift and the almost unanimous recognition of his genius by audiences and the artistic elite. And then—such an unprecedented catastrophe. Now many felt that they saw "a different, ruthless era, the darkness of which would hide the star"[2] of the composer.

Everything seemed to confirm it: articles and meetings attacking Shostakovich for "formalism"; the disappearance of his "sinful" works from the stage and the repertory; and, finally, the ominous political atmosphere—the Soviet media were already equating formalism with counterrevolution.

We can get a feel for the mood in Moscow in those months from a letter to Gorky from the writer Vsevolod Ivanov: "The city is filled with talk about the two enemies of the Soviet regime—imperialism and formalism."[3] Stalin's confidant Ivan Gronsky publicly promised that "all measures of influence up to physical ones will be brought to

bear" against the "formalists," who for him were tantamount to coun-
terrevolutionaries.[4]

His faithful friends were concerned about whether Shostakovich
would bear up under the pressure. But through those terrible days,
Shostakovich, who had always seemed so fragile and nervous, turned
out to be a tough nut. Back from Arkhangelsk, he behaved imper-
turbably, repeating, "In our family, you get upset if you cut a finger, but
when a major misfortune strikes, no one panics."

His friends discovered that the crisis had made a seemingly new man
out of Shostakovich. He explained to one, "Remember that experienc-
ing inside of you all the bad things around you, trying to be maximally
controlled and showing total calm is much harder than screaming,
weeping, and wailing."[5] But very few people guessed just how much
this incident changed Shostakovich's personality and future.

The significance for Shostakovich of the *Lady Macbeth* incident is
impossible to overestimate. It might not be an exaggeration to say that
in some very important way his entire life and work can be divided
into two parts—before and after the fateful *Pravda* editorial. It was said
that decades later, Shostakovich wore a plastic bag with the text of
"Muddle Instead of Music" around his neck, under his shirt, like an
"anti-talisman."[6] The perceptive observer Zoshchenko felt that
Shostakovich never recovered from Stalin's blow in 1936. That is debat-
able. But one thing is clear: The trials of that period produced a
remarkable acceleration in the development of his character and gift.
These experiences led Shostakovich to important conclusions and
decisions.

From Arkhangelsk he telegraphed a Leningrad friend to sign up at
the post office for newspaper clippings mentioning his name. He had
never bothered to collect reviews of his music, but in 1936 he began a
special album, with "Muddle Instead of Music" glued onto the first
page. He methodically added the numerous negative references, some
of which belonged to his recent admirers and even friends, to this
masochistic collection. Bitter misanthropic remarks are not unusual in
the letters of the young Shostakovich; surely, one would not expect a
constant rereading of this newspaper garbage to have improved his
opinion of humanity.

Yet, paradoxically, at that moment Shostakovich feared public support much more than opprobrium. In Arkhangelsk, the audience gave

him a standing ovation at the concert that took place after the *Pravda* attack. The applause was so thunderous that he thought the ceiling had collapsed.

This was obviously a demonstration. Shostakovich's response was amazingly sober. He did not bask in the admiration of the audience, because he knew what Stalin's reaction might be. Shostakovich showed psychological acuity here. Only people close to Stalin knew his morbid reaction to public manifestations. He did not believe in their spontaneity, seeing "conspiracies" everywhere.

Akhmatova always believed that one of the reasons for Stalin's attack on her in 1946 was her success with the public, which stood to applaud the poet at her reading at the Hall of Columns. Stalin's reaction was the infamous line "Who organized the standing up?"[7]

In this situation Shostakovich's greatest fear was that Stalin's hostile attention would be attracted by some demonstrative action at a performance of *The Limpid Stream* at the Bolshoi Theater. So he was almost relieved, as strange as it may seem now, by the publication of "Ballet Falsehood," the *Pravda* article against *The Limpid Stream* that appeared on 6 February 1936. After the article, the ballet vanished from the Bolshoi stage, and with it the possibility for new recriminations.

Another of Shostakovich's quick, intuitive reactions to the new situation was his firm refusal to allow a concert performance of the last act of *Lady Macbeth,* the one that Stalin was too irritated to listen to on his fateful visit to the Bolshoi Theater on 26 January. Shostakovich explained his decision to a friend this way: "The audience, of course, will applaud—it's considered *bon ton* to be in the opposition, and then there'll be another article with a headline like 'Incorrigible Formalist.' "[8]

There must have been hope that once Stalin heard the music, he would change his negative opinion of Shostakovich.* We know that Marshal Mikhail Tukhachevsky, a big admirer and patron of Shostakovich, appealed to Stalin in the composer's defense. Shostakovich, in whose presence the letter was written, never forgot the fear in which the military commander wrote his appeal, continually wiping the sweat from the back of his neck. Shostakovich must have recalled his neck

---

*There is a written note by Nemirovich-Danchenko expressing his conviction that if Stalin had come to see *Lady Macbeth* at his theater, the catastrophe would have been avoided: The director would have been able to persuade him of the composer's genius and defend his work.[9]

when he read a little more than a year later about Tukhachevsky's arrest and execution on Stalin's orders.

Unlike some of his great contemporaries, Shostakovich by then had no illusions about Stalin. In 1936, the writer Kornei Chukovsky noted in his diary the ineradicable impression made on him and Pasternak when they saw Stalin at the Congress of Komsomol. "What happened to the audience! And HE stood there, a bit weary, thoughtful and majestic. I could sense his enormous habit of power, strength, and at the same time something feminine and soft. I looked around: Everyone's face was infatuated, tender, spiritual, or laughing. Seeing him— simply seeing him—was happiness for us all. Demchenko★ kept talking to him about something. And we were all jealous, envious—lucky woman! We perceived his every gesture with awe. I had never thought myself capable of such feelings . . . Pasternak kept whispering rapturous words to me about him . . ."[10]

Compare this exalted response with the parodistic report, so super-formal it could have been copied from a communiqué in *Pravda,* by Shostakovich in a letter to his friend Ivan Sollertinsky about a meeting of Stakhanovite workers in 1935, where he had been invited as a guest. "I saw in the presidium Comrade Stalin, Comrades Molotov, Kaganovich, Voroshilov, Ordzhonikidze, Kalinin, Kosior, Mikoyan, Postyshev, Chubar, Andreyev, and Zhdanov. I heard speeches by Comrades Stalin, Voroshilov, and Shvernik. I was captivated by Voroshilov's speech, but after listening to Stalin, I completely lost all sense of measure and shouted 'Hurrah!' with the rest of the audience and applauded endlessly . . . Of course today is the happiest day of my life: I saw and heard Stalin."[11]

Ilya Ehrenburg was also at the meeting, and in his later, anti-Stalinist memoirs, he described Stalin's effect on the audience as hypnotic. But Shostakovich was clearly not hypnotized. His reaction—written in a markedly bureaucratic style, where the "reported speech" (Mikhail Bakhtin's term) is clearly read as such—was intended to be read by the censors, while Chukovsky's attitude (and Pasternak's, according to Chukovsky) is colored by sincere, albeit undoubtedly exaggerated, emotion. This is supported by Pasternak's poetry addressed to Stalin of that period (see chapter 2).

★Maria Demchenko, Stakhanovite harvester combine operator [Trans.]

Shostakovich could not expect Stalin's wrath to change to mercy upon listening to act 4 of *Lady Macbeth of Mtsensk.* In an opera written more à la Dostoevsky than à la Leskov, the finale was the most Dosto-evskian. Its clear source was Dostoevsky's book about Russian hard labor camps, *Notes from the House of the Dead,* which the composer knew almost by heart. For Shostakovich (and for Dostoevsky), the con-victs were victims first and foremost.

When Shostakovich wrote this music in 1932, he already knew about the arrest and exile of many of his colleagues and friends: the poets Daniil Kharms and Alexander Vvedensky, the director Igor Te-rentyev, and the Jewish artists Boris Erbshtein and Solomon Gershov. But it was in 1934 that Stalin struck severe blows on Leningrad after the mysterious murder in the corridor of Smolny on 1 December 1934 of one of the Party's leaders, Sergei Kirov. Mass arrests, executions, and exiles began immediately in the city—the so-called Kirov flow, which was described in her secret diary by Leningrader Lubov Shaporina, close to Shostakovich's circle: "All these arrests and exiles are inexpli-cable, unjustified. And inevitable, like a natural disaster. No one is safe. Every evening at bedtime I prepare everything I'll need in case of arrest. We are all guilty without guilt. If you are not executed, arrested (or exiled), thank your lucky stars."[12]

After the *Pravda* attack on Shostakovich's opera, much that was too harsh and bold in *Lady Macbeth* and that had been conveniently explained away as "exposing the tsarist regime" suddenly appeared in a completely different light. The horror of life in an enormous country where in an atmosphere of general surveillance and suspicion the police reign supreme, where fate can turn any petty informer into the messenger of dread, and where the humiliation of the human spirit is the only reality, terrible in its ordinariness and constancy—this was now projected onto Soviet reality.

But it was the convict scene that was now totally unacceptable, for Stalin had shut down back in 1935 the Association of Former Political Convicts and Exiled Settlers and had liquidated their publication, *Katorga i ssylka* [*Hard Labor and Exile*]. Hard labor had to be forgotten completely, for the word itself could trigger "incorrect allusions." And the majority of Russian revolutionaries of the pre-Stalin period were to follow into the black hole of oblivion. People were torn out stratum by stratum from life, so as to make life correspond to the new scheme of things. The official history, even of the very recent past, was hastily rewritten.

The intelligentsia, impotent and terrified, observed in horror. Acutely aware of its unprecedented vulnerability, it tried to find a possible strategy of behavior. Nikolai Punin, arrested and then released after his wife, Akhmatova, appealed to Stalin with a desperate letter, wrote in his diary of 1936, "I know that many people are living with the desire to protect themselves from life: Some shrink into invisibility, others not waiting for the blows, strike out first. No one is on good terms with it. I failed with life. The end will be soon. Death is terrifying."[13]

Shostakovich, for all his outward calm, was as tense as strung wire and, many claimed, near suicide. According to the NKVD report that went to Stalin, the composer Yuri Shaporin (Lubou's husband) said so. The memo also stated that Shostakovich's mother had called Zoshchenko and asked in despair, "What will happen to my son now?"[14]

Shostakovich and his family were afraid and expected the worst. A close friend, stressing that Shostakovich had behaved "with extraordinary control and dignity," recalled how "he paced the room with a towel and said he had a cold, hiding his tears. We did not leave him and took turns keeping watch."[15]

It was in this period that Shostakovich fully adapted the Pushkin model of behavior for a Russian poet faced with a direct threat from a tsar. (In that paradigm, as expressed in Pushkin's *Boris Godunov* and then in Mussorgsky's opera, the poet hid behind three masks: chronicler, holy fool, and pretender.) Shostakovich's behavior in 1936 was unexpected, but natural. It came from an intuitive analysis of the situation that is so characteristic of geniuses.

Shostakovich knew he carried the gift of national chronicler: it was a gift, because music is lyric art par excellence; and epic ventures, especially ones socially tinged, are comparatively scarce. Yet in 1934, in his own expression, he "was gestating" an epic symphonic work, feeling out its form and narrative means. This "chronicle" work was his Fourth Symphony.

The meat grinder of the "Kirov flow" also pulverized the last illusions of the Leningrad intelligentsia. The same issue of *Leningradskaya Pravda* of 28 December 1934 in which Shostakovich first announced his work on a new symphony had on the facing page a call, typical of those hysterical days, from the "working masses" to destroy "enemies and wreckers": "Eternal damnation to them, death! . . . They must be wiped from the face of the earth without delay!" The intelligentsia had mastered the same cannibalistic jargon. The annual waves of printed and oral demands to "destroy," "execute," and "eradicate" became a ritual that very few managed to avoid.

Émigré poet Georgi Adamovich would write later in a Paris newspaper with justified sorrow, "Here is a list of people demanding 'ruthless dealing with the vipers': professor so-and-so, poet so-and-so, nationally famous honored actress so-and-so. . . . Are they worse than us, weaker, viler, stupider? No, not in the least. We remember them, we knew them, and if it were not for the revolution, if it had not forced them to turn into zealous Marats, none of us would have ever doubted the rightness of their principles and loftiness of their desires."[16]

Civil discourse in the Soviet Union was irreversibly compromised with the advent of the era of terror. The earlier, still permitted "innocent opposition" (in Lydia Ginzburg's expression) now became unthinkable, and individual reactions were essentially excluded from public discourse. The media presented only clichéd responses, with minuscule deviations, to current events.

In those conditions Shostakovich, who in previous years enjoyed addressing in the press topical cultural issues, took a radical step: He stopped making "serious" public statements. His appearances in the press took on an ever more grotesque character. Finally they turned into totally pro-forma remarks that had practically nothing in common with the real man behind the wall of official words and clichéd phrases.

Shostakovich donned the jester's mask. It was supposed to satisfy the tsar, but potentially could seriously undermine his position in the intellectual milieu. He was in danger of turning in the eyes of the elite from the genius, the Mozart, into a fool, a *yurodivy,* who could be disdained by any "decent" intellectual.

This was an unbearably difficult and humiliating position for him to adopt. In taking it, Shostakovich broke with a long tradition in which a member of the Russian intelligentsia was required to give profound statements on every important issue worrying society. That was how, for instance, Russian musicians (among them Leonid Nikolayev, Shostakovich's future piano professor at the conservatory) behaved during the Revolution of 1905, publishing a bold demand in an opposition newspaper: "When life is bound hand and foot, there can be no free art, for art is only part of life . . . Russia must at last enter onto the path of radical reform."

By the mid-1930s a comparable public gesture in the Soviet Union was impossible, and since there was no opposition press, cultural figures were left with the unappetizing choice of supporting the status quo more eloquently or less. Grotesquely, the cultural elite still cared about the responsibility, seriousness, and stylistic sophistication that went into expressing that "support."

A notable example of this exquisite servility is Yuri Olesha's speech in 1936 at a meeting of writers in Moscow, where the *Pravda* articles against Shostakovich were being discussed. Olesha began by saying that he liked Shostakovich's music and liked him as a person. "This man is very gifted, very detached and reserved. This is obvious in everything. His walk. His manner of smoking. His hunched shoulders. Someone said that Shostakovich was Mozart."[17] But here Olesha makes a pirouette and explains why the *Pravda* articles made it clear to him that Shostakovich was in fact no Mozart. "Externally genius can be expressed in two ways: in radiance, like Mozart, and in disdainful aloofness, like Shostakovich. This scorn for the lowly is the source of some quirks of Shostakovich's music—those muddled and eccentric moments that are born of disdain and are called in *Pravda* muddle and showing off."

But Olesha's most impressive maneuvering is saved for praising the author of the *Pravda* articles. "I thought that Leo Tolstoy himself would have proudly signed those articles."[18]* And then the sophisticated writer makes it absolutely clear exactly with whom that mind-boggling comparison is being made. "A passionate, fierce love of the people, thinking about the suffering of the people that must be stopped, hatred of the wealthy classes and social injustice, scorn for the so-called authorities and for lies—these are the traits that unite the great Russian writer and the leaders of our great homeland." The audience understood Olesha correctly: In the transcript of the meeting "applause" is indicated after those words.

---

*By then Olesha was famous for his novel *Envy*, celebrated for a refined style and sophisticated metaphors; the novel is still considered a masterpiece of Russian twentieth-century prose. Therefore, Olesha's flattery carried special force.

This was the circle of real connoisseurs and gourmets of cultural political acrobatics that Shostakovich was determined to leave forever, taking on instead the demanding and totally nonglamorous role of national chronicler (for which, Shostakovich justifiably believed, he had the creative guts and stamina). For nonmusical discourse, Shostakovich now invariably donned the jester's mask of the holy fool. It was a step for which he would pay dearly.

The poet Nikolai Zabolotsky has a line about a flame flickering in a vessel. Shostakovich felt that fire within him. The question was, Would Stalin, who held life and death for every one of his subjects, destroy the flame along with the vessel?

The preliminary, still uncertain answer to that question came on a specific date: 7 February 1936. On that day Shostakovich was received by then chairman of the Committee on Arts Affairs, Platon Kerzhentsev. That polite and educated (by Bolshevik standards) official, who was author of several learned books on the theater, in this case was merely playing the part of Stalin's emissary, which is clear from his memorandum to the ruler about this conversation, so important for Shostakovich's fate.

In 1826, Nicholas I read Pushkin's *Boris Godunov* and repeated Tsar Boris's gesture defending the unruly Holy Fool from his overzealous courtiers: "Leave him." In 1936, Stalin emulated Nicholas I and "forgave" *his* Holy Fool, Shostakovich. The difference was that the Soviet leader did not deign to meet personally. (Perhaps he did not dare—what if the conversation turned to "symphonic sounds" and sharps and flats? Stalin always liked to appear prepared, competent, and authoritative. He managed it with literature, but with music . . .)

Pushkin's model for the poet/tsar discourse worked again. But just as it had been a century earlier, it was a dangerous strategy. Its success depended on the tsar following a semi-mythical cultural tradition. Stalin did it, but he demanded that Shostakovich take steps to meet him halfway.

Kerzhentsev passed along several questions and proposals clearly received from Stalin. Among them was Stalin's favorite idea (completely alien to Kerzhentsev, as a theoretician of culture) that Shostakovich "on the example of Rimsky-Korsakov travel around the villages of the Soviet Union and record folk songs of Russia, Ukraine, Belorussia, and Georgia and select and harmonize the best one hundred songs." Shostakovich expressed his agreement, but as we shall see he had no intention of going anywhere. (Interestingly, when the same request was made later to composer Aram Khachaturian, he docilely set off on a trip around the villages of Armenia.)

Another of Stalin's proposals to Shostakovich was that "before he writes an opera or ballet, [he] send us the libretto, and during the work process test written fragments before worker and peasant audiences." Here Shostakovich solved the problem simply: Despite the various "creative plans" he publicly announced from time to time, he never in his life wrote another ballet or opera. Therefore, he never offered another libretto for Stalin's approval.★

The most important and treacherous question from Stalin, passed along by Kerzhentsev, was whether "he fully accept[ed] the criticism of his work" in the *Pravda* articles. This was the direct parallel with the question Nicholas I posed to Pushkin in 1826: Had he changed his "rebellious" manner of thinking? The poet then promised the emperor to change, but he did it with visible vacillation. In that situation Pushkin was not risking his life, but Nicholas I was impressed by the poet's sincerity. Pushkin intuited that truth was expected from him rather than servility and he gave the right answer.

Under much more dangerous circumstances, Shostakovich repeated Pushkin's gambit, stating, according to Kerzhentsev's report to Stalin, that in the Party's criticism of his works "he accepts most of it, but he has not fully comprehended it all." In that refusal of total and unquestioning repentance lay an enormous risk: Shostakovich had put his life on the line, and not only his own, but the lives of his family—his wife, Nina, and his unborn daughter, Galina (Nina was six months pregnant then).

The Egyptian Sphinx was the legendary monster that killed travelers who could not answer its riddle. Oedipus was the only one to give the right response. And Shostakovich—after Pushkin—turned out to be an Oedipus, intuiting the right reply for Stalin.

★For Shostakovich, a born musical theater composer, this self-imposed limitation was a painful autoamputation. He had ambitious operatic plans. He had considered writing a trilogy, even a tetralogy, a Russian *Ring of the Nibelung,* in which *Lady Macbeth* would be *Das Rheingold.* Now that project was dead. And when, in 1942, Shostakovich began the opera *The Gamblers* (after Gogol), he dropped it when he realized the danger of the undertaking.

That he had arrived at the answer via a profoundly painful process is clear from a letter he wrote in that period to a friend, the composer Andrei Balanchivadze (brother of choreographer George Balanchine): "In this time I've gone through a lot and rethought a lot. For the time being I've concluded the following: *Lady Macbeth* for all its great inadequacies is for me a work that I could never choke . . . But I believe that you have to have the courage not only to kill your works but to defend them."[19]

Publicly championing *Lady Macbeth* then was "impossible and useless," in his words. But Shostakovich was also concerned about defending a work that was not yet born and on which he had been working since 1934. That was his Fourth Symphony, two movements of which had already been written down. The furor around *Lady Macbeth of Mtsensk* interrupted work; now Shostakovich was eager to complete the symphony. It, too, was his child, which had to enter the world at any cost.

Prince Petr Vyazemsky had said of Pushkin, "When he felt the presence of inspiration, when he started work, he calmed down, matured, was reborn." According to Vyazemsky, for Pushkin his work was "sacred, a font in which wounds were healed . . . and weakened powers restored."[20] Shostakovich experienced similar feelings. In his old age he recalled, "Instead of repenting, I wrote the Fourth Symphony."[21]

But back then, in 1936, Shostakovich told Isaak Glikman, "If they chop off both hands, I'll still write music with the pen between my teeth."[22] A terrifyingly real possibility was a different turn of events—he would keep his hands but lose his head.

But the Stalin Sphinx decided otherwise: For now, Shostakovich kept his life, freedom, and opportunity to compose. This became "widely known in narrow circles" (a biting phrase of those years) soon after Shostakovich's conversation with Kerzhentsev on 7 February. On 9 February, Erwin Sinkó, a Hungarian émigré Communist writer living in Moscow, wrote in his diary that from the moment "Muddle Instead of Music" appeared, it was "tactless"[23] to mention Shostakovich's name. But on 17 February the well-informed Sinkó noted, "Babel told me that Shostakovich wanted to commit suicide. Stalin, however, called him in and consoled him, telling him to pay no attention to what the newspapers write, and that he needed to travel and undertake the study of folk songs."[24]

As we see, the change in tone, in a week's time, is striking. In those days, people stopped talking about those who had been arrested or those about whom it was clear that they would be arrested any day. Apparently that atmosphere had been created around Shostakovich after the *Pravda* articles. It was just as obvious that the situation had changed sharply after the audience with Kerzhentsev.

Babel, at that period close to the higher levels of the NKVD and Gorky, was an authoritative source; we can assume that he was used as an unofficial conduit for passing necessary information into the milieu of the Moscow intelligentsia. It is not important that Shostakovich did not meet with Stalin but with his emissary; what is important is that the conversation was interpreted as a direct dialogue between the ruler and the composer, like the meeting of Nicholas I and Pushkin. It was with that spin that the story was disseminated: Mercy had to flow personally from Stalin and not from some cultural bureaucrat.

We will never learn all the considerations that led Stalin to spare Shostakovich and allow him to continue working. But we can sum up the most obvious reasons. They would include the unexpectedly solid, albeit hidden, resistance in cultural circles to the *Pravda* articles; Maxim Gorky's displeasure; the opinion of Nemirovich-Danchenko and other specialists Stalin respected; the unforeseen interest in "the Shostakovich affair" of Western (especially French) intellectuals and the possibility of international complications; the modest but firm behavior of Shostakovich, who did not act flustered and did not repent or appear in public looking "insulted and injured." It even may have been that Stalin felt he had overdone it in this case and it was to his benefit to play the merciful tsar.

But among the most important causes was another practical reason: Shostakovich's work in the cinema.

When talking about Soviet film we must remember Lenin's famous statement in 1922 that "of all the arts the most important for us is the cinema." It was Stalin who turned the dictum into reality. Soviet film in his regime came into being as an industry, the main goal of which was not making a profit, as in the West, but the ideological upbringing of the masses. In Stalin's concept, the state became the producer. This combined the Party's propaganda needs with the dictator's personal hobby.

Stalin loved the movies, domestic and foreign; he liked the minutiae of film production, talking with actors, screenwriters, and directors. As a result, he took an incredibly active part in the fate of the Soviet film industry: He wrote long-term plans, handed out commissions, read many screenplays closely, and made major editorial changes. Without Stalin's screening and approval, no Soviet film could be distributed.

Even completed films often were reworked and changed on his orders. There were times when a dissatisfied Stalin banned a film made on his own request: This happened in 1946 with part 2 of Eisenstein's *Ivan the Terrible.* And in 1937, a furious Stalin had the emulsion on the film stock of Eisenstein's *Bezhin Meadow* wiped completely. Only fragments of the negatives survived.

As it happened, by the mid-1930s the most important state commissions were executed at Lenfilm Studios in Leningrad. When, in 1935, Stalin first decided to encourage the workers of Soviet film, of the eight directors who got the Lenin Order—the highest given then— five were from Leningrad. Lenfilm as a studio also got the Lenin Order, the first ever given to a cultural organization. It had produced in 1934 Stalin's favorite film, *Chapaev,* about the semi-mythical Red commander of the Civil War, directed by Sergei and Georgi Vasilyev.

Shostakovich's professional contact with film began in 1923 when he worked as a piano player in movie houses, illustrating the "burden of human passions" (his expression) on an out-of-tune upright piano and unwittingly mastering the know-how of influencing a mass audience. He appeared at the Leningrad film studio in 1928: The young avant-garde directors Grigory Kozintsev and Leonid Trauberg hired him to compose the music for their silent film *The New Babylon,* about the legendary days of the Paris Commune. As Kozintsev recalled, Shostakovich had "an almost childlike face. He was dressed the way artists did not dress then: a white silk scarf and soft gray hat; he carried around a big leather briefcase."[25] *The New Babylon* is recognized as a masterpiece of expressionist film and in our day is shown with success around the world, often with a symphony orchestra playing Shostakovich's eccentric score.

When "the Great Silent" began to speak, it produced a seismic shock everywhere—in Hollywood, in film studios in Rome and Berlin. In Soviet film the switch to sound took place in the early 1930s and was also extremely painful.

A veteran of Lenfilm, Sergei Yutkevich, recalled how the sophisticated silent film became, practically overnight, artistically old-fashioned.²⁶ Stalin, appreciating the propaganda potential of sound in film, invested a lot of money in acquiring the new technology. Work came to a boil at Lenfilm: Yesterday's avant-garde directors and virtuosos of montage, Kozintsev and Trauberg, and other Leningrad directors like Yutkevich and Fridrikh Ermler, willy-nilly found themselves among the pioneers of Soviet sound film. They had to reject their own former refined poetics, simplify and coarsen their cinematic language, and switch to the "realistic" narrative technique.

The cultural and psychological trauma that many film directors experienced throughout the world was exacerbated at Lenfilm by the requirement to fulfill the increasingly propagandistic "social commissions" from the Party. One participant recounted: "You had to change yourself. That's why it was so painful for Kozintsev and Trauberg to switch to the prosaic realism of the trilogy about Maxim after making the almost perfect *New Babylon* with its expressionist poetics. Just as hard was the change for Ermler from symbolist *Remnant of the Empire* to *Counterplan* and for Yutkevich from the declarative passion of *Golden Mountains* to *Counterplan*."²⁷

Almost all these new films (which were popular both with mass audiences and the Party leadership) had scores by Shostakovich, who by that time was the favorite composer at Lenfilm. Paradoxically, as his success grew, his enthusiasm and pleasure in the work diminished. The more he did it, the more he considered writing film music merely a major source of income and therefore work that had to be done professionally and on time, but nothing more. Shostakovich once formulated the composer's role in film succinctly: "The music's basic goal is to be in the tempo and rhythm of the picture and to increase the impression it creates."²⁸ He often told his students that one should take movie work only when broke.

But bearing in mind that the supreme filmgoer in the Soviet Union was Stalin, work in movies took on an additional significance, which was unknown, for instance, to the denizens of Hollywood, but was for Shostakovich the most important: a safe-conduct pass. Since Stalin watched all Soviet films, and knew all their main creators by name, there was a chance that he could, if needed, save them from disaster. This was at least a fragile straw to cling to in the atmosphere of general uncertainty and anxiety that reigned among the Soviet cultural elite, where life resembled nothing more than a lottery.

Shostakovich's lucky ticket seems to have been writing music for the movie *Counterplan,* released by Lenfilm in 1932 for the fifteenth anniversary of the October Revolution. Its directors were Fridrikh Ermler and Sergei Yutkevich, who was a friend of Shostakovich and who had worked with him on *Gold Mountains,* one of the first sound films of Soviet cinema. *Counterplan* was about the "response plan" proposed by workers in a turbine plant to speed up delivery of a powerful turbine needed by the state. But the film had its lyrical moments, and one of its highlights is a charming, tender and perky song, "The Morning Greets Us with Coolness," written by Shostakovich. Its catchy melody made it the first Soviet hit song to come from the movies. The whole country, from peasants to government leaders, sang "The Morning Greets Us." The lyrics were written by the then-famous poet Boris Kornilov, who was named by Bukharin two years later at the All-Union Writers' Congress as one of the most promising revolutionary talents.

But by 1935, a memo of the Leningrad NKVD to Zhdanov placed Kornilov in "a counterrevolutionary nationalist group of young writers." It reported, "He is the author of a number of anti-Soviet works, which he reads in public places—the Writers' Club, the House of Writers, as well as in restaurants and bars."[29] In 1936, Kornilov, like Shostakovich, was publicly accused of all sorts of sins. But Stalin spared Shostakovich, while Kornilov was arrested and executed.

Shostakovich, whose daughter Galina had just been born, was horrified that Kornilov's wife, the poet Olga Berggolts, miscarried after being beaten during interrogation by the NKVD. Berggolts survived and during the war years became a celebrated bard of Leningrad's resistance to the Nazi blockade. Her words were carved into the central granite steel of the Piskarev Memorial Cemetery in Leningrad in 1960: "No one is forgotten, and nothing is forgotten." For Leningraders the words were a visual reminder not only of the horrors of the war but (in the years when you could not talk about it aloud) of the Stalin terror. Berggolts's poetry was officially proclaimed the requiem for the victims of the German siege, but it was at the same time a hidden memorial to the victims of the Stalin's terror machine. This profound resemblance to Shostakovich's Seventh Symphony was felt by both the poet and the composer.

Shostakovich's song continued to be performed everywhere, but it no longer bore the lyricist's name. Subsequently the melody won international acclaim: It was sung during World War II by members of the French Resistance; and in the United States, with new words, it was performed as the song "The United Nations." But in 1936 the song may have saved Shostakovich's life.

Here is how it happened.

Stalin liked watching movies at night. It was both relaxation and to some degree a continuation of work. The screenings gave the ruler food for thought. At the same time, Stalin calculated how to use film to inculcate a new ideological point into the mass consciousness.

Films for the dictator and his closest comrades were brought to a special small room at the Kremlin. The screenings were usually attended by the boss of Soviet cinematography, whose duties included making commentaries where needed. In 1936 the job was held by Boris Shumyatsky, an experienced Party fox distinguished by wily resourcefulness, energy, and keen wit.

Shumyatsky was the Muscovite Eisenstein's sworn enemy and a patron of Lenfilm, and therefore tried to promote the work of the Leningrad directors. At that moment, this coincided with Stalin's position, so Shumyatsky felt he was on relatively safe territory here.

Shumyatsky wrote down the comments made by Stalin and his cohorts on Soviet film—not for publication but as guidelines for himself. According to one of these notations, dated 30 January 1936, the conversation touched on "Muddle Instead of Music," which had appeared in *Pravda* just two days earlier. People's Commissar of Defense Kliment Voroshilov asked Shumyatsky what he thought of the editorial. Here Shumyatsky, if his notes can be believed, behaved rather boldly. Agreeing with the directives of *Pravda* (and how could he not?), he at the same time began defending Shostakovich. The most important thing of which he reminded Stalin was that Shostakovich had composed "The Morning Greets Us with Coolness." Stalin, as it turned out, liked the song, which he considered melodic and appealing.

Encouraged, Shumyatsky cautiously suggested to Stalin that Shostakovich "can write good realistic music, but only if he is supervised." This apparently echoed Stalin's own thinking and he reacted approvingly: "That's the point. But no one supervises them." And then he got on his favorite hobbyhorse: "That's why people throw themselves into all kinds of show-off convolutions. And they get praised for it, too—overpraised. But now, when *Pravda* has given an explanation,

all our composers must begin creating music that is clear and understandable, instead of rebuses and riddles which kill the meaning of the
work."[30]

From these words, recorded by Shumyatsky, it's still not clear what
decision Stalin took on Shostakovich's fate. For in the ruler's eyes no
single creative success, even in his beloved cinema, could be an absolute
and final indulgence. The fate of Kornilov, Shostakovich's coauthor of
"Morning," is not the only example. Another tragedy in the cinemato-
graphic world that would touch Shostakovich personally was the arrest
of the artistic director of Lenfilm, Adrian Piotrovsky, a playwright,
translator, critic, screenwriter, and scholar of Hellenism. In 1931,
Shostakovich wrote the music for Piotrovsky's play *Rule, Britannia!* All
the best movies at Lenfilm of the period were made under Piotrovsky's
supervision, including *Chapaev* and other pictures Stalin loved. His sudden fall in 1938 plunged the Leningrad cinema community into confusion. His fate was yet another warning that in Stalin's eyes not a single
subject of his huge empire, whatever his previous achievements, had
permanent immunity.

The struggle for creative and physical survival had to be waged every
day. For the Soviet elite, life in the second half of the 1930s was like
being on a swing—up, down, up, down. And no one knew when it
would be his turn to fly down.★

All this hung over Shostakovich's head like a black cloud when he
sat down to write his Fourth Symphony. He had great hopes for this
composition: Everything in it—concept, language, dimension—was
revolutionary for the Russian symphonic literature. At that time, a lot of
attention was being paid to the problem of the Soviet symphony, and
in 1935 the Composers' Union held a special three-day conference on
the topic, in which Shostakovich participated. It was a reflection of the
Party's "social commission," according to which the new era was to be
depicted in epic forms.

One must not oversimplify the situation, reducing it to Stalin or his
cultural advisors sending down instructions that the creative workers
rushed out to execute. The country was undergoing a gigantic social
upheaval, which changed consciousness and forms of perception and

---

★As Boris Shumyatsky had not known. In early 1938 he was first fired from the post of
head of Soviet cinematography and soon afterward arrested and shot.

created a new audience. Colossal artistic problems were arising, and there were no manuals for solving them. In this situation every honest artist tried to find his or her own path, painfully, stumbling and falling. For many (including Pasternak) the issue arose of "going beyond the limits of the small form that had ceased to satisfy," in the observation of Lydia Ginzburg; poets "were seeking ways, without resorting to plot, to move lyric material great distances."[31]

The young Shostakovich was trying to solve the same problem in his Fourth Symphony. In the West, the symphonic genre was also undergoing a crisis. The last great symphonist was the Austrian Gustav Mahler, who had died in 1911. The European novel was in a similar crisis, being a parallel to the symphony as a genre. Mandelstam felt that the swan song of the European novel was Romain Rolland's *Jean-Christophe*, completed in 1912. (Mandelstam did not know that the novel's hero reflected some traits of Mahler.)

In his later years, Shostakovich admitted that of his fifteen symphonies, "two, I suppose, are completely unsatisfactory—that's the Second and Third."[32] He properly considered his Fourth as a major leap forward. Of course, a lot of it—the length (over an hour of music); the huge orchestra used for gigantic crescendos; a persistent use of "banal" melodic material—comes from Mahler, whose symphonies Shostakovich had studied very closely by then. (During work on the Fourth Symphony, Shostakovich had the score of Mahler's Seventh on his piano, friends recall.)

But nevertheless, from the very first measures, the Fourth Symphony is easily recognized as being Shostakovich's. It is due in part to the close resemblance of the musical material of the symphony and that of *Lady Macbeth*. In particular, one of the repeating leitmotifs of the first movement is the "police" march from the opera. (Alfred Schnittke perceived the first movement as the "drama of the composer's life"; its autobiographical nature is apparent.) Shostakovich leads us by the hand like voyeurs at an amusement park: here are the carousel, and the roller coaster, and the Ferris wheel, and the fun house, and the tunnel of horrors—all under the ever-vigilant eye of the police. "Life's carnival" (in the Bakhtinian sense) remains the central theme of the second movement, too. The final, third, movement, begins with a funeral march.

This "Mahlerian" funeral march becomes the dominant motif of the finale. And no wonder: Shostakovich began writing this movement after the condemning articles in *Pravda*. By then, he had already decided that his public statements would in no way reflect or touch upon his true inner life. All autobiography, all "statements" and "appeals," would go exclusively into music, hiding in it as if under water.

Paradoxically, this creative strategy merely strengthened the symphony's narrative, bringing it closer to a loosely constructed novel—with the difference that in the symphony the presumed "plot" remained hidden.

Mahler wrote that "starting with Beethoven, there is no new music that does not have an internal program. But any music in which the listener must first be informed what emotions it contains, and correspondingly what he is expected to feel is worthless."[33] Shostakovich perhaps wanted to tell the whole world about his emotions, but he could not do it. He could only encrypt them in the hope that the audience would guess his message—if not now, then at least in the future.

He wanted not only to give his audience the general character of emotion—in the finale of the Fourth Symphony it is clearly tragic and cannot be mistaken for anything else—but to be as specific and concrete as possible. So he scattered additional keys to the solution, sometimes so obvious that you wonder how they remained undeciphered for so many years. The resemblance of the funeral march in Shostakovich's finale to the melody in the last song of Mahler's cycle *Songs of a Wayfarer* (1883–84) is apparent. And what is Mahler's song about? "Nun hab' ich ewig Leid und Grämen!" ["Sorrow and grief are now with me forever!"] Any commentary would be superfluous.

At the end of the finale, Shostakovich clearly parodies a festive gathering. He quotes the opening of act 2 of *Oedipus Rex* by Igor Stravinsky, well known to him and other Leningrad musicians. (Boris Asafiev, a great expert on Stravinsky, wrote about this work in detail in 1929.) And here is the corresponding Latin text from that episode: "Gloria! Laudibus regina Iocasta in pestilentibus Thebis." The translation: "Glory! We hail Queen Jocasta in pestilent Thebes." In other words, Shostakovich was unambivalently drawing a parallel between the contemporary Soviet Union and the plague-ridden city from Greek mythology. Stalin's rule in Shostakovich's interpretation is a "feast in the time of the plague" (a reference, perhaps, to Pushkin's famous short play by that name).

There is another transparent musical parallel in the finale of the Fourth, also from Stravinsky: an obvious quotation from the finale of the ballet *The Firebird*. Stravinsky's music is filled with triumph and relief over the death of Kashchei the Immortal, the evil sorcerer from the Russian fairy tale, ruler of the Rotten Kingdom. Shostakovich's music registers as an incantation: "Die, Kashchei-Stalin! Die! Begone, Rotten Kingdom!" This is the first time he formulates the musical characterization of Stalin, which is subsequently more fully developed in his Tenth Symphony.

From this point on, there will be quite a few musical hints embedded in his works. I believe that only a small number have been discovered and the main research in this area lies ahead.

In general, encryption in Soviet culture of that era was apparently used much more frequently than we now imagine. But the keys to many of those "messages in a bottle" are lost now, perhaps forever.

One such incident was described by the son of the Leningrad poet Nikolai Zabolotsky, arrested in 1938. Before his arrest, he let his wife read a poem that spoke of the terrible times in which they lived and the grim prison cells where innocent people were tortured. Then he read her another poem, about nature, completely innocent, in which the first words of every line and the rhymes were the same as in the anti-Soviet poem. They burned the seditious verse, and Zabolotsky said he would be able to restore it when better times came from the lines of the poem about nature.[34] Alas, while Zabolotsky lived the better times never came.

Shostakovich was in a comparable situation. He undoubtedly considered his Fourth Symphony to be a seditious work. He expressed that very clearly with a dramatic decision: Just before its scheduled premiere in December 1936, he canceled the performance.

This extraordinary step was interpreted in different ways. Some people explained it by the resistance of orchestra musicians who did not want to play a "formalist" work; others by the indifference of the conductor; and still others by pressure from above. Probably all three factors were at work to some degree. But for Shostakovich, this was primarily yet another gesture in the continuing role game with Stalin.

He had shown the Fourth Symphony to friends, and one of them asked in fright: What did Shostakovich think the reaction from *Pravda* would be? What was meant, of course, was Stalin's reaction. The composer scowled and jumped up from the piano, saying curtly, "I don't write for *Pravda,* but for myself."[35] Shostakovich regarded the Fourth Symphony, especially the finale, as his "creative reply to unjust criticism." But he could not help fearing Stalin's reaction if that reply became public.*

Later, Shostakovich showed his ability to resist pressure from the authorities, refusing in 1963 to cancel the premiere of his "ideologically immature" Thirteenth Symphony. But the atmosphere in 1936 was just too threatening. In August the newspapers announced the Trial of the Sixteen, in which Grigori Zinoviev, Lev Kamenev, and other leading figures in the Party opposition were charged with "subversive activity" and trying to organize an assassination attempt on Stalin. The subsequently widely used label "enemy of the people" was introduced in this period. To the accompaniment of hysterical newspaper headlines ("Punish the Vile Killers Severely!"—"Squash the Foul Creatures!"—"No Mercy for Enemies of the People!") all sixteen defendants were shot.

With the Trial of the Sixteen a new spiral of repressions against cultural figures ensued. The press carried articles stating that "now the acuteness and importance of the fight against formalism, begun by *Pravda,* is even more clear." Among the arrested was the writer Galina Serebryakova, with whom Shostakovich had had an affair. Even earlier, Elena Konstantinovskaya, a young translator in whom he had been very interested for a while, was imprisoned on a political denunciation. (When I was a student at the Leningrad Conservatory in the 1960s, the still flirtatious and well-groomed Konstantinovskaya taught English there.)

The noose was tightening around the Shostakovich family as well. In the spring of 1936, his older sister Maria's husband, the prominent physicist Vsevolod Frederiks, was arrested for being a "member of a terrorist organization." And at the end of the year, Shostakovich's mother-in-law, Sofya Varzar, was arrested, and all appeals on her behalf were fruitless. The answer was: "The NKVD does not make mistakes."[36]

---

*I suspect that Shostakovich was worried that Asafiev would denounce him to the authorities: He could easily catch the "seditious" quotations in the finale of the Fourth Symphony. This may be the real root of Shostakovich's strong dislike of Asafiev after 1936.

Most important, Shostakovich lost his most powerful defender in the face of Stalin's wrath: In June, Gorky died at the age of sixty-eight of a mysterious disease. People in Moscow immediately began talking of poison. In 1938, at yet another political trial directed by Stalin, the defendants were charged with the murder of Gorky, by then buried in a special niche in the Kremlin wall and proclaimed "the closest and most faithful friend of Comrade Stalin." The true circumstances of Gorky's death (and of Kirov's murder in 1934) are still the subject of fierce debate: Was Stalin behind it?

Obviously, Stalin and Gorky had a complex and ambivalent relationship. Publicly they often expressed admiration of each other, but privately they sometimes displayed quite different emotions. A part of the canon of Soviet culture was Stalin's verdict in 1931 on an early verse fairy tale by Gorky, "The Maiden and Death." Stalin wrote, "This thing is more powerful than Goethe's *Faust* (love conquers death)." The absurdity of Stalin's evaluation, placing Gorky's sentimental doggerel above one of the greatest masterpieces of world literature, is obvious; nevertheless, this judgment was hailed and seriously discussed in numerous Soviet books, articles, and scholarly dissertations. But the writer's friend Vsevolod Ivanov maintained that Gorky had been insulted by Stalin's remark, considering it mocking.[37] And as for Stalin? His true attitude toward his own "historic" statement can be seen in the mock-up of Gorky's book published in 1951, which is in his archives. He struck out the statement three times in blue pencil.[38] At the same time, Stalin crossed out a photograph of him sitting next to Gorky. This is where his true feelings for his "closest friend" were revealed.

Tellingly, Shostakovich immediately understood the grotesque character of Stalin's reaction to "The Maiden and Death." In 1937, he played with the idea of writing a parodic opera *The Maiden and Death,* in which the final chorus would sing Stalin's words. He even noted down a melody a friend offered for this chorus, but things did not progress beyond that. Later Shostakovich realized a similar idea in his parodic cantata *Antiformalist Rayok,* aimed against Stalin and other Soviet leaders.

Seemingly unsuited for life, often appearing naïve in his reactions to daily existence, Shostakovich at the decisive moment in his life displayed an amazing grasp of the new situation in which the creative fate and even the life of any prominent cultural figure came to depend on

Stalin's personal attitude toward him or her. Concrete ideological instructions changed with dizzying speed, often in unpredictable or mysterious directions. Guessing their evolution was difficult; obeying them without losing the remnants of self-respect and creative honesty was impossible. Nor was it appreciated.

The only chance to survive lay in following the unwritten parameters of the cultural discourse offered by Stalin at every new twist in Soviet history. These parameters were often ambivalent, which was part of Stalin's plan. The intentionally vague rules of the game provoked the workers in culture to make new "mistakes," so that the ruler could "correct" them—strictly but fairly, as a father should. That was the meaning of the conversation between Stalin and Shumyatsky about Shostakovich in late January 1936.

It was not necessary to demonstrate total sycophancy; on the contrary, within the framework of the Russian tradition of tsars' condescension toward holy fools, a certain artistic eccentricity was welcome—to a point. But in the end, what was demanded was "transparency" and a stated desire to do "honest" quality work. Like many professional politicians (but not only them), Stalin primarily valued people because they were needed, and that had to be proved over and over.

Comprehension of these new rules was the epiphany that came to Shostakovich in Arkhangelsk on that cold day when he read "Muddle Instead of Music." That is why one of the first things he said to his friends who met him upon his return from Arkhangelsk was the momentous phrase "Don't worry—they won't manage without me." This was a sober and, for the young and vulnerable person he was, a radically new assessment of the situation. It had to be accompanied by a completely new program of physical and creative survival.

Chapter IV   The Tsar's Mercy

I n the dramatic circumstances of 1936, Shostakovich's cancellation of the performance of his Fourth Symphony was a painful but probably saving act. At that moment, Shostakovich had not written a letter of repentance usual for the times or spoken out with ritual "self-criticism." But he had decided upon a much more selfless step in Stalin's eyes: He sacrificed his potentially "formalist" (read: unneeded by the masses) symphony and instead plunged headlong into composing "needed" music for film. Among the pictures was a trilogy about the Bolshevik Maxim, highly regarded by Stalin, which was made by the former avant-garde directors Kozintsev and Trauberg, and the two-part *Great Citizen,* a hagiography of Sergei Kirov (called Petr Shakhov in the film), who had entered the ranks of Communist sainthood after his murder.

The director of the film about Shakhov-Kirov was a colorful figure, former Chekist Fridrikh Ermler, who would show up on the set with a Browning revolver in his back pocket and who on at least one occasion threatened to shoot an actor for insubordination. He sincerely liked Shostakovich, and when he read "Muddle Instead of Music," he sent the composer an encouraging telegram: MY PRAVDA PICKED ON YOUR LADY. DON'T WORRY. THE FUTURE IS OURS.

In planning a film on a ticklish subject, Kirov's murder, Ermler was taking a risk. A high Party official had this to say about the screenplay for *Great Citizen:* "This screenplay teaches how to kill rulers. Only Ermler's rotten soul could have created it."[1] However, Stalin felt differently. "Read Comrade Ermler's screenplay ("Great Citizen"). It is constructed with indisputable political literacy. The literary qualities are also indisputable."[2]

In giving Ermler's film the green light, Stalin demanded that the murder of Shakhov-Kirov not be shown on the screen. The result paradoxically was one of the film's most expressive episodes. Shakhov comes up to the door behind which the killer is waiting for him. And suddenly the camera, as if hurrying to warn the hero of danger, pans in on the door at great speed. But it's too late. The door handle in close-up slowly turns. The next shot is the horrified face of the woman who witnesses the murder.

The audience does not hear a shot: Instead, Shostakovich's music cuts in at extreme volume and the camera moves to Shakhov's funeral. For this scene, Shostakovich wrote a ten-minute funeral march of great power, based on the revolutionary song "You Fell Victim." But in the final version of the film, the episode, taking into account Stalin's directives, was cut by a third. Shostakovich, usually very nervous about any changes of his music, was absolutely calm about this surgical operation: By then he considered himself nothing more than a hired hand in film.

Shostakovich's advice to his students to take up film music only in cases of extreme need has already been cited. The specter of that need (which Shostakovich experienced in his youth) appeared before him once again after the attacks in *Pravda.* In a letter to a friend in late 1936 he touched on this: "While I used to make 10,000–12,000 a month, now I barely made 2,000–3,000. And on the nineteenth of November 250 rubles were transferred to my account in the copyright department. I'm not getting depressed, even though I have to economize in everything. I have to deny myself many things. That doesn't scare me. What scares me is that I have to find commissions. Well, it will work out."[3]

The numbers need some context. For the sake of comparison, in that period a blue-collar worker's average monthly salary was 200–300 rubles; a teacher got 300 rubles, as did a hospital doctor. A professor at the Moscow Conservatory earned 400–500 rubles a month, which was also the salary of musicians in leading Moscow orchestras. But the members of jazz bands brought home 5,000 rubles a month, and music hall stars had astronomical earnings—several tens of thousands a month.

Composers got very good royalties when their works were performed in concerts and theaters; this explains Shostakovich's comparatively high earnings (forty times that of a worker) at a time when his new opera and ballet were regularly performed in several major theaters. But after *Lady Macbeth of Mtsensk* and *The Limpid Stream* vanished from the repertory, his income shrank. Despite what his friends knew to be a modest lifestyle, Shostakovich had no savings. Not only did he support his family and relatives, but many friends depended on his financial help, as well. Besides the other important reasons, the threat of being penniless compelled him to work a lot at Lenfilm.

In the meantime, Shostakovich was slowly and painfully developing musical ideas for the Fifth Symphony, which would be perhaps his most famous and popular opus. It is a breakthrough in every sense. It played a major role in Shostakovich's life and in the history of the symphonic genre in the twentieth century. The wound still ached for the Fourth Symphony, canceled and buried alive, but he was already seeking ways to express in symphonic form the fears, doubts, and desperate hope for survival that raged within him.

Shostakovich spent the spring of 1937 in one of his favorite places, the Crimea, at Gaspra, a sanatorium for scientists and cultural figures. Once upon a time Leo Tolstoy had recuperated here, in what was then the palace of Countess Panina, after a bout of pneumonia. Now the Soviet elite vacationed here: the physicist Abram Ioffe, the ophthalmologist Vladimir Filatov, the film director Yakov Protazanov, the pianist Lev Oborin.

Lydia Ginzburg later wrote that Stalin nourished that kind of people as potentially useful for the regime, but they often were the first to perish because they were closest to hand: "The people who went to the ballet and visited friends, played poker and rested at the dacha were the very ones who received news in the morning about the loss of near and dear, the ones who were chilled by the phone ringing at night, who expected 'night guests' . . . For now still alive, they barricaded themselves with entertainment: If they offer it—take it."[4]

The enormous sanatorium grounds looked like Eden in two colors—pink and white. In the evenings, the guests gathered in the large living room. The weak splash of the Black Sea, blending into the horizon, came through the windows. Shostakovich always refused to play the piano when asked. But one of the guests noted that early in the morning, when the others were still asleep, he "tiptoed carefully into the empty room, opened the lid of the instrument, and played something and wrote it down on music paper."[5]

This was the Fifth Symphony, which was written down very quickly. The first three movements were composed in the Crimea, and the third movement, which he admitted to finding the most satisfactory (it truly can be considered the symphony's emotional and intellectual center), was set down in just three days. That was a record even for Shostakovich, who usually worked on the principle of "harness slowly, ride fast"—that is, he could work out a piece over a relatively long time in his mind and then write it down with incredible speed.

Only the finale was left to do, but in early June Shostakovich went back north. There he showed the new pages of the symphony to conservatory professor Nikolai Zhilyaev, whom he esteemed highly. An eccentric but influential figure, Zhilyaev lived alone in a room piled with books, music, and manuscripts, with two dominant objects: a grand piano and a portrait on the wall of Marshal Mikhail Tukhachevsky, a close friend.

Shostakovich had met Zhilyaev at the marshal's house, and the three men frequently got together. That is why seeing Zhilyaev was so important. It was a courageous step, because he must have already known the news: In late May, Tukhachevsky, Shostakovich's mentor and patron, was arrested on charges of being in a "military-political conspiracy" against Stalin. He was executed soon afterward, and a mass purge of people involved with him in any way began.

Zhilyaev was stunned by the symphony. As Grigory Frid, a young composer who was present, recalled, "Zhilyaev patted Shostakovich on the head with paternal tenderness, repeating almost soundlessly: 'Mitya, Mitya . . .' "[6] Zhilyaev also understood the significance of Shostakovich's evening visit, and he tried to explain to the naïve Frid the true meaning of the music they had just heard, making parallels with Zhilyaev's beloved works of Edgar Allan Poe. "This is the tragedy of conscience!"

Soon after the newspaper announcement of Tukhachevsky's death sentence, Frid visited Zhilyaev once again. They spent the evening in oppressive silence. The Tukhachevsky portrait, which had been on the wall, was now leaning up against the bed so that the marshal's face appeared behind the bars of the headboard.

It was clear that danger was imminent, and even Frid was not surprised when he learned of Zhilyaev's arrest. The professor vanished without a trace.

The execution of Tukhachevsky and other leading Soviet officers involved a dramatic incident into which Pasternak was dragged. It was demanded that he sign a collective letter from writers approving of the death sentence. Pasternak refused. The pressure continued. As the poet later recalled, his pregnant wife fell to his feet, begging him not to destroy her and the child and to sign the ill-fated letter. Pasternak stood his ground and even wrote to Stalin, saying that the ruler could do whatever he wanted with Pasternak's life, but the poet did not consider himself capable of judging the life and death of other people.[7]

After this Pasternak, expecting imminent arrest, said, "I prefer to die with the masses, with the people." But he was not arrested. Instead, he received a newspaper with the published letter from writers in support of the execution of the military men, which included Pasternak's signature. As some people tell it, Pasternak wept in despair, repeating, "They've killed me."[8]

Morally, yes, but not physically: After all, in those days access to participating in such collective letters meant official trust. As Nadezhda Mandelstam wrote, "Whoever breathed that air perished, even if he accidentally saved his life. The dead are dead, but everyone else—the executioners, ideologues, facilitators, praisers, the ones who shut their eyes and washed their hands, and even those who gritted their teeth all night—they were all also victims of the terror."[9]

Mercy and blows rained down simultaneously, as Stalin liked it. On 4 June 1936, Leonid Nikolayev, first among the professors of the Leningrad Conservatory, was awarded the Order of the Red Banner of Labor, an important medal in those days. (The other recipients that day were Oistrakh, Oborin, Gilels, and the wunderkind Busya Goldstein.) The next day, Shostakovich's mother sent Nikolayev a letter of congratulations: "I would have liked to do this in person, but a terrible misfortune is hanging over us, and I just can't think straight."[10]

The misfortune that could not be mentioned in a letter was that Maria Frederiks, Shostakovich's older sister, whose husband had already been arrested, was now being exiled to Central Asia, and Shostakovich's mother-in-law, Sofya, was sent to a concentration camp in Kazakhstan. It was in these circumstances that he returned to Leningrad and completed the Fifth Symphony.

The finale is perhaps the most disturbing and ambivalent music of the twentieth century. Its vivid pictures of a mass procession give rise to heated arguments even today, many decades after its creation. The other movements, especially the first and the third, while emotionally powerful, generated no such controversy. The majority of even contemporary Soviet critics agreed that in this music, as one of them put it in 1938, "the emotional tension is at the limit: another step—and everything will burst into a physiological howl."[11] Another critic wrote then, "The passion of suffering in several places is brought to a naturalistic screaming and howling. In some episodes the music can elicit an almost physical sense of pain."[12]

But in the finale of the Fifth Symphony some Western musicologists to this day, disregarding Shostakovich's own statements, prefer to see not a reflection of the catastrophic situation of the 1930s, but sincere enthusiasm. The real circumstances in which the music was written are completely ignored. Playwright Yevgeny Shvarts, a contemporary of Shostakovich, put it this way: "A friend of mine had a parrot that knew only two words, 'My joy!' He repeated those two words when he was sad and when he was hungry. The cat would be creeping up on him, his feathers would be ruffled in horror, but he would cry out the same words, 'My joy!' " Critics who still insist on the authenticity of the "joyful" emotions in the finale of the Fifth should remember that Shostakovich was no parrot.

The symphony was a complex work, into the fabric of which Shostakovich masterfully wove sophisticated "telling" hints and allusions, as he had in the Fourth. Music scholars have only begun excavation for these hints. For instance, the similarity has been established between the basic theme of the finale of the Fifth and a melody from a later work by Shostakovich—a setting of Robert Burns's poem "MacPherson's Farewell," where the tune is sung to the words "Sae wontonly, sae dauntonly, So rantinly gaed he," as the outlaw hero is led to "the gallers tree." That is, Shostakovich interpreted the "festive" march in the finale as a procession of the condemned to their execution: a shocking and horrifying yet absolutely accurate, almost naturalistic image, if we remember the Great Terror and the mass hysteria of the period. Scholars are finding hidden quotations now in the finale from passages in Berlioz's *Symphonie fantastique* and Richard Strauss's *Till Eulenspiegel*—that also depict the procession to an execution. From this point on in Shostakovich's music, this becomes an idée fixe, and more and more frequently it is associated with the Via Dolorosa, the final path of Jesus Christ.

Some musicians see a hidden parallel to the baroque musical symbol of the cross in a number of his works. In this context, Shostakovich's outburst comparing himself with Christ, recorded in Marietta Shaginyan's 1943 diary, does not seem quite so unexpected.[13] Three images relating to Golgotha—the procession to execution, the mockery of the crowd, self-sacrifice—were first embodied in Shostakovich's work, with such conviction, in the Fifth Symphony. The autobiographical nature of these motifs is self-evident. Shostakovich had experienced the pain of public condemnation, the betrayal of friends, and the jibes of bystanders. After everything that happened to him in 1936, Shostakovich felt martyred.

The Christ complex in the Fifth Symphony is projected on the Pushkin model we have already described. Allusions to the Pushkin-Mussorgsky *Boris Godunov* are scattered throughout. The hope for salvation and a mystical inner emancipation heard in the finale is related to both the Gospels and Pushkin.

This hope is again expressed through a coded musical hint: a self-quotation from a recently written and not yet published song to Pushkin's poem "Renaissance." The symphony has a melodic figure that Shostakovich uses in the song for these lines of Pushkin:

> *Thus vanish the misconceptions*
> *From my tortured soul,*
> *And visions arise in it*
> *Of the early, pure days.*

In this innermost episode of the symphony, Shostakovich seems to be overcoming personal pain. Here is the parallel with Jesus and with Pushkin, when the poet was dying of the wound he received in a duel. Pushkin supposedly did not want to groan out loud, even though he was in terrible physical pain. "It would be ridiculous for this nonsense to overpower me," the poet said. "I do not want it." Shostakovich also used every bit of strength to keep "this nonsense" from overpowering him. As Yevgeny Shvarts, a rather skeptical observer, noted in amazement about the events of 1936, "The nobility of the material from which Shostakovich is created makes one marvel. Real people, whether they want to or not, repay fate with good for evil."[14]

Melding the personal and private with the public, Shostakovich created a unique artistic document of the era. Tchaikovsky once called the symphony "a musical confession of the soul." Shostakovich liked to compare a symphony with a novel. His Fifth was a novel about the dark and confusing 1930s, the likes of which did not appear in the Soviet Union or in the West, for that matter. It was a symphony-novel with several false bottoms. In that way it acquired, in the words of Vladimir Toporov (regarding the works of Akhmatova and Mandelstam, similar in their genesis with Shostakovich's music), "that status of vagueness and significance that deprives the text of finality and completeness of semantic interpretations and, on the contrary, makes it 'open,' existing constantly *in statu nascendi* and therefore capable of capturing the future, of being adapted to potential situations."[15]

The paradox is that the era demanded straightforwardness from artists, but prompted the best of them to create ambivalent images. The audience that gathered at the Leningrad Philharmonic Hall on the night of 21 November 1937 for the premiere of the Fifth Symphony most likely did not appreciate all these artistic subtleties or catch the hidden psychological and political hints. However, there is no doubt that the symphony stunned the public—there are numerous accounts of those who attended. Many wept, a highly unusual reaction to a modern symphony. Intuitively, deeply, the audience understood the symphony's emotional subtext. One person later compared this premiere with the performance of Tchaikovsky's Sixth ("Pathétique") Symphony shortly before the composer's death; another recalled, "During the finale many listeners involuntarily rose in their places."[16]

By the end of the symphony, the entire audience was standing, applauding wildly through their tears. The young conductor Yevgeny Mravinsky, later to be the first and best performer of many of Shostakovich's symphonies, responded to the half-hour ovation by raising the score in both hands high above his head to cries of approval. His gesture was provocative in those days.

The artist Lubov Shaporina, a bold and independent observer, had been at the Philharmonic on that historic evening, and she wrote in her diary that the tumultuous ovations were a demonstration against the official persecution of Shostakovich. "Everyone kept saying the same thing: He responded and he responded well."[17]

This contemporary account was later reiterated by the composer Johann Admoni, who as one of the directors of the Leningrad Philharmonic in 1937 participated directly in organizing the premiere of Shostakovich's new opus. "The success of the Fifth Symphony could be seen as a protest of the intelligentsia that had not yet been destroyed, those who were not yet exiled or executed. The symphony could be interpreted as an expression of his attitude to the horrible reality, and that was more serious than any issues about musical formalism."[18]*

The premiere in Leningrad did not dissipate the tense atmosphere surrounding the symphony. Influential listeners noted in their diaries that the music of the Fifth was "painfully grim" (the composer Vladimir Shcherbachev);[19] the writer Alexander Fadeyev wrote of the allegedly "life-affirming" finale: "The end sounds not like an exit (and certainly not like a triumph or victory) but as a punishment or revenge on someone."[20] Isaak Dunaevsky, a man who always knew which way the wind was blowing, and at the time the chairman of the Leningrad Composers' Union, hastily put together a special memorandum on the Fifth Symphony, warning that "an unhealthy phenomenon of agitation, even psychosis to some degree, which in our conditions can do a disservice to the work and its author,"[21] was building around the symphony.

But suddenly, and unexpectedly, the wind changed direction. This did not occur, as some naïvely believe, on its own, elementally. Someone's powerful hand carefully but persistently moved events in a direction that favored Shostakovich. The first, rather obvious and clear, signal came in a review of the Fifth's premiere, signed by Alexei Tolstoi and printed in the government newspaper *Izvestiya* on 28 December 1937. Tolstoi, the "Red Count," as he was sometimes called, took over the role of "leading writer" of the Soviet Union upon Gorky's death; Stalin par-

---

*I knew Admoni well; he was cautious and circumspect, having spent many years in a Soviet hard labor camp in Kazakhstan on false charges of espionage. Admoni never tossed out antigovernment statements for fun. Therefore, it can be believed that he and many others at the premiere really perceived the Fifth Symphony as protest music.

ticularly liked him, which was well known, and so his review carried great weight. "A major example of realistic art of our era . . . Glory to our era, that it throws out into world such majesty of sounds and thoughts with both hands. Glory to our people, who give birth to such artists."[22]

This article by Tolstoi had great impact and even reached the West, earning a sarcastic retelling by Stravinsky in his famous Harvard lectures of 1939.[23] But few have paid much attention to the unusual gap, even by Soviet standards, between the premiere and the appearance of such an influential, even decisive review—more than a month. Obviously, Stalin was considering the fate of the symphony and its composer.

We know that Shostakovich, despite the public success of his new work (or perhaps because of the "oppositionist" nature of that success), was terribly nervous during that period. Maxim Kostrikin, Shostakovich's uncle and Old Bolshevik, had been arrested, accused of being one of the leaders of the "counterrevolutionary Masonic" organization the Great Brotherhood of Labor, associated with the mystic George Gurdjieff, and then shot.[24]★

Yet Stalin was clearly in no hurry to issue an evaluation of the Fifth Symphony. We can imagine that the ruler was mulling over the information that came to him from different sources. Denunciations, reports, and memoranda about the symphony and various reactions to it flew to Moscow from Leningrad, while top culture bureaucrats were sent from the capital to Leningrad to check out the situation on site. (I met one of those officials, Boris Yarustovsky, in Moscow in the early 1970s, and I can well imagine that huge, loud-voiced man shouting, as the director of the Leningrad Philharmonic recalled, "The symphony's success was scandalously fixed!")[25]

In Leningrad, after the premiere of the Fifth Symphony, a special performance was arranged (on Sunday, by invitation only)—an unheard-of innovation—for the local "Party activists." If Stalin were to decide to reject Shostakovich's work, it could be blamed on the reaction of the Party audience.

★Shostakovich, who was rather cool toward the institution of relatives in general, had a special liking for Kostrikin, a jolly and kind man. When Shostakovich and his wife had a second child in 1938, they named him Maxim in memory of their late uncle.

For Stalin, the opinion of Alexei Tolstoi and other "masters of culture" he esteemed, like Nemirovich-Danchenko, was of course much more important than the reaction of the entire audience at the Leningrad Philharmonic, stuffed with Party functionaries, most of whom were soon to vanish from the political arena anyway. But an even more substantive factor was Shostakovich's behavior in that difficult situation. Having chosen the "Pushkin model," Shostakovich acted in a way that made Stalin trust him—he did not fuss, wriggle, or lie. He went on working. This had to have had a beneficial effect on the final decision.

The publication of Tolstoi's article (albeit tellingly not in *Pravda,* where it would have had an even more effect) was the first clearly positive signal from above. The article legitimized the awed reception given the Fifth Symphony in Leningrad and neutralized the dangerous possibility in those paranoid times of being accused of a "conspiracy." (The Moscow "inspector general" Yarustovsky tended toward that charge at first.) The next important step was the publication, on 25 January 1938, the eve of the long-awaited Moscow premiere of the symphony, of an article by Shostakovich called "My Creative Answer" in *Vechernyaya Moskva,* the official newspaper of the Moscow City Party Committee and the Moscow City Soviet. This is a very unusual and mysterious text—even by the standards of Shostakovich, whose legacy includes many contradictory and evasive statements. It was never seriously analyzed, even though it was in this article that Shostakovich first made the statement, later widely reprinted, that the Fifth Symphony was "a constructive creative answer of a Soviet artist to just criticism."

In the Soviet Union this definition, so clearly related to the Stalinist era, later was avoided in embarrassment. But in the West it took on the status of an official author's subtitle for the Fifth Symphony; and it is still reproduced in innumerable textbooks, dictionaries, reference works, and encyclopedias.

I believe that the true author of that lapidary and memorable formula is none other than Stalin himself: Analysis of the article's text and the circumstances of its appearance lead to that conclusion. For after the criticism in *Pravda,* Shostakovich kept silent for a long time. "My Creative Answer" was his first official statement after "Muddle Instead of Music" and the entire antiformalist campaign. And this most important article literally begins with the formula quoted above, presented as the response of an unnamed listener, which gave him "particular joy," in Shostakovich's words. Even more notable: This anonymous reaction was set in boldface in the newspaper, the way directive Party instructions and slogans were usually printed.

It is impossible that in the paranoid atmosphere of the late 1930s, when covert enemies of all kinds were constantly sought and exposed, the editors of a Party newspaper would have printed the slogan that way if they had not known its true author. Then, later in the article, Shostakovich quotes Alexei Tolstoi's reaction to the symphony. That means that the author of the formula about the "constructive creative response" *wished* to remain unnamed.

The authoritative tone of the statement, its familiar stylistic idiosyncrasies, and the fact that it gave Shostakovich "particular joy" (in those days a ritual reaction to any speech by Stalin) all point to Stalin as its author. As we now know, Stalin often injected into general discourse his opinions and statements in this anonymous way.

The entire article was undoubtedly carefully edited. It is astonishing that Shostakovich does not repent his formalist errors and that the word "formalism" is not mentioned at all—and this in a period when only the indolent had no opinion on formalism. This eloquent silence also needed to be sanctioned from above, especially since this was an article by the main culprit in the recent antiformalist campaign.

Another point, also apparently arranged with the higher-ups, requires attention. Shostakovich says that "Soviet tragedy as a genre has every right to exist." The composer is thus defending his Fifth Symphony. In those days the question of the legitimacy of tragedy in Soviet art was frequently debated. Many of the functionaries felt that under socialism even "the possibility of contradiction and conflict was excluded."[26]

Here too Shostakovich obviously was given the green light. Stalin tended to agree with the supporters of the validity of "Soviet tragedy." After all, some of his favorite films—*Battleship Potemkin* and *Chapaev*—belonged to the genre.

An oxymoron was coined to define this kind of work: "optimistic tragedy." That is how Vsevolod Vishnevsky, one of Stalin's favorite playwrights, titled his 1932 drama about the deaths of a detachment of revolutionary sailors, a work that was enthusiastically supported by military commissar Kliment Voroshilov and other members of the Politburo.

Accepted into the cultural discourse, the term "optimistic tragedy" was first used in relation to Shostakovich's Fifth at the special performance for the Leningrad Party elite. It was done by musicologist Leonid Entelis, who more than once carried out ticklish assignments for the authorities. This was a fig leaf sent down to Shostakovich from higher up. He used the leaf with as much dignity as the complicated situation permitted.

Stalin was expected at the Moscow premiere of the Fifth Symphony, which was a huge and triumphant success like the one in Leningrad. But he did not show up. This did not mean that he could not have heard the work on the radio (it was broadcast several times) or, if he had wished, in a recording made especially for him. In fact, in 1938 a recording of the Fifth was made available to the public.

But in this case, the actual symphony was of secondary importance to Stalin. Much more consequential than "symphonic sounds" (Stalin's expression in the infamous *Pravda* article) was the fact that he and Shostakovich had had, in Mikhail Bakhtin's term, "an ideological conversation on a large scale."[27] Bakhtin's concept is that this kind of dialogue (not necessarily face to face) includes various forms of ideological communication, social acts of purely ceremonial character among them. In this Byzantine dialogue the participating sides send symbolic signals. It was a highly elaborate ritual, realized in a cultural space where the code of behavior was only developing. It was observed accurately that "The life of the Soviet intelligentsia to a great degree was based on 'guesses,' 'subtexts,' 'feelings' of what was permitted and what was banned."[28]

The ruler was not yet old; he had begun planning the celebrations of his sixtieth birthday in 1939 and was capable of significant flexibility in maneuvering. When the crisis in his relations with Shostakovich was repeated ten years later, the rules of the game would be much more rigid.

At the banquet honoring Shostakovich after the premiere, Alexei Tolstoi raised a toast: "To the one of us who can already be called genius!" The toast by the "Soviet classic," expressing slight envy and sincere delight, was well chosen: in the genre of the symphony with its "flickering" message, permitting a saving multitude of interpretations, Shostakovich managed to do what the greatest Russian authors of those years could only dream about—create an emotionally wrenching epic narrative, accessible to a comparatively wide audience, about the fate of the intelligentsia in the Soviet era.

Among those who were enthralled by the idea of writing a big novel about the intelligentsia and the revolution was Pasternak. Working intensely on fragments of prose, he wrote to his parents in 1937: "I want to write a novel again and am writing it gradually. But in poetry I am always master of the situation and know approximately what will come out and when it will come out. Here I can't predict anything, and with prose I never believe in its successful result. It is my damnation, and for that reason I am always drawn more strongly to it."[29] The contours formed very slowly and painfully of what would finally appear as *Dr. Zhivago.*

Pasternak, who loved music (and even tried his hand at composition), compared his work on prose to composing a symphony. But at that moment, a symphony in prose was not working for him, and unashamedly, with his childlike directness, he expressed his "white envy" of the Fifth Symphony: "Just think, he went and said everything, and no one did anything to him for it."[30]

Similar emotions, albeit less kindly, were expressed by Osip Mandelstam. The poet intuitively sensed in Shostakovich a strong rival, since Mandelstam was also enthralled by the idea of a large-scale prose narrative. Nostalgically, he said that the great nineteenth-century novels "were as much events in public life as artistic events. Contemporaries underwent a mass self-recognition, peering into the mirror of the novel . . ."[31]

But Mandelstam's prose masterpieces—*Noise of Time, The Egyptian Stamp,* and *Journey to Armenia*—were greeted by Soviet critics for the most part skeptically, as a kind of "muddle instead of prose." Mandelstam passionately wanted to reach the mass reader, but in response he heard that "the writer is infinitely far from our era. His entire world perception is in the past."[32] He had to seek an outlet for his "populist" emotions in poetry.

In a letter to a friend in 1938, Mandelstam disparagingly compared Shostakovich's Fifth Symphony with Leonid Andreyev's pseudo-symbolist play *Man's Life,* which was popular before the revolution.

Paraphrasing Leo Tolstoy's famous line about Andreyev ("He frightens, but I'm not scared"), Mandelstam called Shostakovich's music "dreary intimidation."[33] His irritation becomes more understandable when in the same letter he declares, "I will continue to fight in poetry for *constructive music.*" Shostakovich's Fifth cannot be considered "constructive" music as the poet understood it at the moment: It is a profoundly tragic work—Mandelstam is right about that. At that moment, the music of the Fifth Symphony kept him from hearing a positive, optimistic note inside himself; hence his dissatisfaction with Shostakovich.

In exile in provincial Voronezh (after Cherdyn) because of his anti-Stalin verse lampoon of 1933, Mandelstam wrote his own Soviet "Stanzas," harking back to Pushkin's "Stanzas" addressed to Nicholas I.

> *I do not want amidst hothouse youths*
> *To spend the last penny of my soul,*
> *But as the peasant joins the kolkhoz,*
> *I join the world—and people are beautiful.*

Mandelstam, for good reason, regarded his Voronezh exile as Stalin's mercy—both he and others had expected the death penalty for his poem against Stalin. And then he began (as did Bulgakov and Pasternak before him) the imaginary conversation "over the barriers," traditional for Russian culture, between holy-fool poet and tsar, the culmination of which was his "Ode to Stalin," written in the early months of 1937 and diametrically opposed to his anti-Stalin satire.

This remarkable poem has elicited the most varied opinions. Some consider it a forced work, his creative and moral capitulation before Stalin. But Joseph Brodsky described it differently: "In my opinion, this may be the grandest poetry that Mandelstam ever wrote. This poem is perhaps one of the most significant events in all twentieth-century Russian literature."[34]

In the "Ode to Stalin," Mandelstam appears as a portraitist, drawing a picture of the ruler; he sets this out in the very first line: "If I were to pick up charcoal . . ." (Brodsky suggested calling it the "Charcoal Ode" by analogy to another work by Mandelstam, his "Slate Ode.") The poet makes a "charcoal sketch" of Stalin's features: the raised, thick eyebrows, attentive eyes, firm mouth, "modeled, complex, steep eyelid." These elements are given in a bold combination of angles, which astonished Brodsky ("the phenomenal aesthetics of this poem: cubist, almost posterlike") and recalled the photomontages of avant-garde artist Alexander Rodchenko.

The unexpectedness of these angles creates an unusual effect—an extreme closeness of the portraitist to his subject, which is strange and disconcerting. In Brodsky's opinion, Mandelstam was consciously using a poetic trick: He insolently violated the "territorial imperative," the distance that should be maintained were the "Charcoal Ode" a traditional court portrait.[35]

A familiar thesis in the Russian avant-garde aesthetics was that a portrait inevitably combines the features of the subject with those of the artist. But for Mandelstam, even more important was Pushkin's idea of the dialogue between holy-fool poet and tsar. This idea was developed in 1935 by Pasternak in a poem addressed to Stalin.

In his time, Pasternak rejected Mandelstam's anti-Stalin lampoon as being far from poetry and unworthy of his genius. Now Mandelstam entered into a professional competition with Pasternak in the genre of odes to Stalin. Mandelstam, in his poem, used brilliantly the fact that he and Stalin were namesakes. He mentions it at least three times, and by the end he manages to create a subconcious feeling of a mysterious resemblance between poet and ruler. Brodsky felt that via the "Charcoal Ode," Mandelstam somehow "inhabited" Stalin. "And that is the most terrifying and stunning part." I tend to accept Brodsky's paradoxical supposition that it was this outwardly apologistic poem that served as the true reason for Mandelstam's arrest on the night of 2 May 1938.[36]

He was first charged with "terrorism," and that carried a death sentence, but Mandelstam was eventually found guilty of "anti-Soviet agitation" ("wrote a harsh counterrevolutionary lampoon against Comrade Stalin and disseminated [it] among his acquaintances by reading it") to five years' imprisonment in a concentration camp. This unexpected reduction of the sentence was possible, of course, only through a direct intervention by Stalin, who clearly continued to vacillate in his attitude toward Mandelstam.

Brodsky made a very subtle analysis of Stalin's psychology, and I think his guess was correct: "Stalin suddenly realized that Mandelstam was not his namesake, but that he was Mandelstam's . . . that's what suddenly struck Stalin. And it served to destroy Mandelstam. Iosif Vissarionovich apparently felt that someone had gotten too close to him."[37]

But the "easy" punishment turned out to be Mandelstam's death sentence: He grew ill on the journey to the camp and died in a transit camp in the Far East in late 1938. The prisoners considered him mad; he kept repeating that Romain Rolland would write to Stalin about him, and Stalin would have him released. Stalin did not. Was he informed of Mandelstam's death? This we will not know with full certainty: too much information in the Soviet Union—a society that seemed overbureaucratized to the extreme—was transmitted orally.

Stalin was an even greater master than Hitler (who left no written orders to destroy European Jews) at covering his tracks. Still, we can safely presume that in the 1930s, when multitudes were subjected to the repressions, the fate of the cultural elite was decided personally by him.

We know that Stalin signed off on albums containing summaries of the political cases, one to a page, of one hundred to two hundred defendants: "Stalin leafed through the album, looking for familiar names. And would put the number one (execution) or two (ten years of imprisonment)."[38] Undoubtedly, decisions about such major figures as Mandelstam, Akhmatova, Zoshchenko, Pasternak, Shostakovich, Platonov, Meyerhold, Eisenstein, and Babel were made personally by Stalin, and they were weighed carefully. Why did some of these people survive and others perish?

Probably millions died in the years of the Great Terror, but for Stalin that was merely a statistic—he fought with entire social groups, not individuals. The destruction of real and potential political rivals and enemies could be explained in most cases by pragmatic (albeit barbaric) considerations. But what were the hidden motives in executing cultural masters? How much was political calculation, how much aesthetic hostility, or personal irritation?

Recalling the era, Ilya Ehrenburg wrote, "Many of my contemporaries ended up under the wheels of time. I survived, not because I was stronger or more perspicacious, but because there are times when a man's fate resembles not a chess game played by all the rules, but a lottery."[39] The comparison to a lottery persists when you analyze a long line of specific examples of Stalin's wrath and mercy.

Think of Andrei Platonov. Stalin's handwritten marginal notes on *Vprok* [Profit], Platonov's 1931 novella about kolkhozes, published in the Moscow journal *Krasnaya Nov'*, have survived: "fool," "bastard," "scoundrel," and so on. Here is Stalin's conclusion, immediately sent to *Krasnaya Nov'*: "A story by an agent of our enemies, written with the goal of destroying the kolkhoz movement." In that same note, Stalin demanded that Platonov be hit so hard that the author would "profit" from the punishment.[40]

Platonov stopped publishing for a while, and the rigid muzzle of censorship was placed on him often afterward, but the writer was never arrested, even though Stalin's hatred and scorn for him—both ideological and personal—are indisputable and documented. But the playwright Vladimir Kirshon and the journalist Mikhail Koltsov—favorites of Stalin's, capable and energetic, ready to carry out the most dangerous assignments for him—were executed.

Obviously, Stalin did not always operate rationally. But it is hard to believe that repression took the form of a lottery, too—still, the wheel of fortune turned with mysterious breakdowns, which sometimes led to absolutely unpredictable results.

An example is the fate of two extraordinary figures, the writer Isaac Babel and the director Vsevolod Meyerhold. Both were arrested in 1939, when the wave of the Great Terror was receding. People's Commissar of Internal Affairs Nikolai Yezhov, whose name was given to that period of mass repressions, *yezhovshchina,* had himself been arrested and replaced. But it was then that Stalin seems to have decided to hold a well-publicized political trial that would expose an "enemy cell" in the field of culture.

Alexander Matskin analyzed Stalin's reasons perceptively: "He was convinced that Trotskyism, like a plague, had infected the Russian artistic intelligentsia, and since there were criminal elements, that meant they must have had a leader . . . And he was shuffling the names like cards: Who fit the bill? Ehrenburg, Eisenstein, Babel, Koltsov, Shostakovich?"[41]

At the Lubyanka NKVD headquarters, the notorious prison in Moscow, both Babel and Meyerhold were interrogated with torture, which by that time was officially permitted and even encouraged: The secret police beat compromising material out of people from the largest possible circle of suspects. Both the writer and the director, broken by

The young Dmitri Shostakovich:
a member of the Russian intelligentsia

Was Tsar Nicholas I (1796–1855) a role model . . . for the Communist dictator Joseph Stalin?

Alexander Pushkin's (1799–1837) play *Boris Godunov* presented the *yurodivy*, the Chronicler, and the Pretender as the poet's alter egos.

Modest Mussorgsky (1839–1881): his opera
Boris Godunov, based on the Pushkin play,
influenced Shostakovich.

Russia's new "holy fools": the pianist Maria Yudina

. . . dadaist writer Daniil Kharms

. . . and twenty-seven-year-old Shostakovich, who also adopted the postures of the Chronicler and the Pretender. Portrait by Nikolai Akimov, 1933.

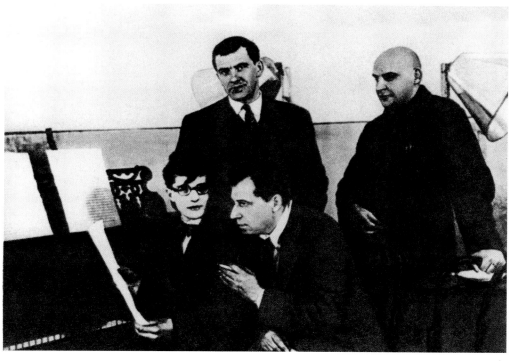

Shostakovich (far left) performs his work for
the theater director Vsevolod Meyerhold (seated), the
poet Vladimir Mayakovsky, and the artist Alexander
Rodchenko (standing, left to right), 1929.

An older Shostakovich in 1933, after completing his opera *Lady Macbeth of Mtsensk*. In 1936, the opera was denounced in *Pravda*'s editorial "Muddle Instead of Music."

Shostakovich with his wife, Nina, to whom *Lady Macbeth of Mtsensk* was dedicated

The set of the original production of
Shostakovich's opera, staged by the great
Vladimir Nemirovich-Danchenko,
Moscow, 1934

Stalin with his favorite cultural
adviser, the writer Maxim Gorky

Mikhail Bulgakov. Stalin loved his play
The Days of the Turbins.

The poet Osip Mandelstam: mug shots
from the files of Stalin's secret police, 1934

The poet Boris Pasternak,
in a portrait by Yuri Annenkov

The poet Anna Akhmatova, in a
portrait by Yuri Annenkov

Stalin with his henchman Andrei Zhdanov
(left) at the funeral of the assassinated
Bolshevik Sergei Kirov, in Leningrad, 1934

Shostakovich with his closest friend, the
music critic Ivan Sollertinsky

The satirical writer Mikhail
Zoshchenko in a 1923 photograph

Shostakovich performing his Piano
Quintet with the Beethoven Quartet.
This composition received the Stalin
Prize in March 1941.

A 1941 propaganda
poster depicting
Leningrad under
German siege

Shostakovich in
July 1941. The image
of the composer in
a firefighter's
uniform was used
for propaganda.

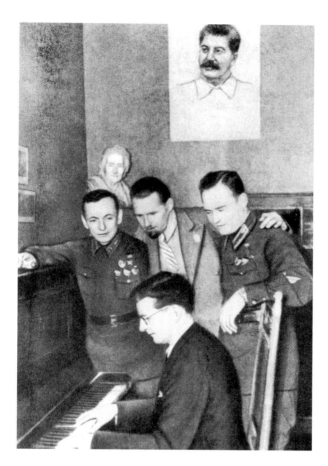

Shostakovich performs
for the military under
the watchful eye of the
Great Leader, as Stalin
liked to be known.

The First Congress of
the Composers' Union
put out a resolution
denouncing
Shostakovich, among
others, Moscow, 1948.

From the left: Sergei Prokofiev, Shostakovich, and Aram Khachaturian were denigrated as the "anti-people formalists."

Vano Muradeli performs his opera *The Great Friendship* for a group especially selected from the "working class," Moscow, 1947. Soon after, Stalin cited it as an example of "formalism."

A defiant Shostakovich in 1948, the year he completed the First Violin Concerto, written, as they say in Russian, "for the drawer"

Shostakovich with the cinematographer
Mikhail Chiaureli while working on the
film *The Fall of Berlin*, 1949

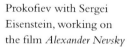

Prokofiev with Sergei
Eisenstein, working on
the film *Alexander Nevsky*

December 15, 1949:
Shostakovich with his
wife, Nina, attending
a premiere of his
oratorio *Song of the
Forests,* for which the
composer received his
fourth Stalin Prize

Shostakovich being awarded the
International Peace Prize by Tikhon
Khrennikov, Moscow, 1954

Д. ШОСТАКОВИЧ
D. SHOSTAKOVICH
Op. 113

**ТРИНАДЦАТАЯ
СИМФОНИЯ**

THIRTEENTH
SYMPHONY

ДЛЯ СОЛИСТА БАСА, ХОРА БАСОВ
И СИМФОНИЧЕСКОГО ОРКЕСТРА

FOR BASS SOLO, BASS CHORUS
AND SYMPHONY ORCHESTRA

Слова Е. ЕВТУШЕНКО
Words by Ye. YEVTUSHENKO

ПАРТИТУРА
SCORE

СОВЕТСКИЙ КОМПОЗИТОР
SOVIET COMPOSER
Москва 1971 Moscow

The title page of the score of
Shostakovich's Thirteenth
Symphony, whose 1963 premiere
aroused the wrath of the authorities.
The inscription reads: *"To dear
Solomon Moiseyevich Volkov with
my very best wishes. D. Shostakovich.
May 3, 1972, Repino."*

Dmitri Shostakovich with
Solomon Volkov, Moscow, 1974

beatings and threats, "confessed" to all sins and gave the interrogators statements against other leading cultural figures.

The expanded "Trotskyite organization of conspirators and saboteurs" was quickly taking shape and included, among others, Ehrenburg, Pasternak, and Shostakovich (named by Meyerhold) and Yuri Olesha and Eisenstein (named by Babel). One would think that inevitably they all would be arrested.

But things went differently. Even though both men renounced their statements, Babel and Meyerhold were shot in early 1940, along with Yezhov. Their bodies were cremated at night, and the ashes—bloody gendarme and creative geniuses together—shoveled into a common grave.

But here is the astonishing fact: None of the "Trotskyite agents" named by them were arrested—not then, not later. Nor was Stalin's idea of a show trial of Trotskyites in culture ever realized.

Why this happened we can only guess. Every scenario sooner or later hits a black wall, the dead end that Stalin's hidden plans remain for us if we do not find a key in the form of documents or reminiscences. Probably this is what Ehrenburg had in mind when he spoke of a lottery.

Shostakovich had to feel this "lottery" underpinning of life with his entire being. Naturally, he could not have known that he was already listed in NKVD transcripts as a "Trotskyite saboteur." Nor did he guess about Babel's statement: "We all had in common holding the humiliated Shostakovich as a genius and compassion for Meyerhold."[42]

In those days, the concept of guilt by association was used loosely: If you knew an enemy of the people, you were one, too. Babel and Shostakovich never had close contact, but he remained friendly with Meyerhold, even though they were not as intimate as they had been in the late 1920s.

When Meyerhold put on Tchaikovsky's opera *Queen of Spades* in Leningrad in 1935, Shostakovich was so impressed that he publicly stated that the production was "a discovery of *The Queen of Spades,* a discovery of Tchaikovsky's score, the first revelation of that tragedy . . . I simply do not know whether there is anything comparable in the directorial art of our Union and the whole world."[43]

Meyerhold repaid the compliment soon after the attacks in *Pravda,* bravely supporting Shostakovich in a sensational lecture in Leningrad, which the composer attended. He heard Meyerhold say, "We hail in him, in Shostakovich, that which was valuable for Pushkin in [the poet Yevgeny] Baratynsky: 'He is original among us—for he thinks.' I hail in Shostakovich that ability to be a thinker in music."[44] In a private letter to Shostakovich dated 13 November 1936, the director was even more sympathetic and tender. "I was very saddened to read your lines about not feeling well. Dear friend! Be brave! Be cheerful! Do not give in to your sadness!"[45]

But a little more than a year later it was Shostakovich's turn to express his sympathy to Meyerhold: His world-famous avant-garde theater was liquidated by a special resolution of the Politburo of the Central Committee for being "alien to Soviet art." Stalin wanted theater to be more naturalistic, and Meyerhold's experiments were of no use to him. The denouement—Meyerhold's arrest—was not far behind.

One of the absurd moments of this tragedy became the final meeting of Shostakovich and Meyerhold in Leningrad in 1939. Shostakovich, who was often totally helpless in daily life, was standing in front of his apartment door, trying to unlock it. Meyerhold appeared, heading up the stairs to visit a neighbor of Shostakovich's one flight up. Seeing the bewildered composer struggling with the lock in vain, Meyerhold helped, and together they managed to open the door. They agreed to meet the next day, but the director was arrested that night. The last close friend Meyerhold saw while still at liberty was Shostakovich.

It was in this tense atmosphere that Shostakovich continued to compose. He had set himself a task of unimaginable complexity—he was going to compete with himself and break his own record. The unprecedented success of his Fifth Symphony went far beyond mere music, turning into a cultural event with world resonance. The symphony was called a Shakespearean tragedy of a new era, and in fact it was. Under the direct impact of its premiere, Bulgakov renewed (and almost completed) work on the final edition of *Master and Margarita,* and we can see a similar connection with the creative breakthroughs of Alexei Tolstoi (he completed his epic novel *The Road to Calvary*) and Sholokhov (the dramatic finale of *The Quiet Don*). As we saw, the Fifth also touched Mandelstam and Pasternak and many others. No other

Russian symphony ever had such a contemporary response, including Tchaikovsky's "Pathétique."

The magic of numbers: Shostakovich's new symphony would be his sixth, eliciting inevitable associations with Tchaikovsky's.* Shostakovich knew that comparisons and parallels with that signal work were unavoidable; it was one of the most tragic pieces in the history of Russian culture. Among Leningrad musicians, including Asafiev, the "Pathétique" was seen as Tchaikovsky's requiem for himself.

It may have been natural for Shostakovich to write a similar requiem at that time, but in Stalin's Soviet Union it could have easily turned into an invitation to a beheading. And Shostakovich had no intention of creating his own musical obituary. Shostakovich tried to throw his persecutors off his track by announcing in two newspapers on the same day (20 September 1938) his plan to write a vocal symphony about Lenin to texts by Mayakovsky and medal-bearing Soviet "folk tellers" Suleiman Stalsky of Dagestan and Dzhambul Dzhabayev of Kazakhstan.

But the new symphony presented by Shostakovich two years after the premiere of the Fifth had nothing to do with Lenin. His old teacher Maximilian Steinberg wrote in his diary about the first movement of the Sixth: "a very good work, although once again gloomy and brooding."[46] But the subsequent development of the music confused most listeners: two fast movements followed and—the symphony ended. No tragic finale that would have suited Tchaikovsky's Sixth.

Many perspicacious musicians got the impression that Shostakovich had thumbed his nose at them. After the symphony's Moscow premiere, the esteemed conservatory professor Alexander Goldenveizer was upset. "The finale is written with extreme brilliance and orchestral mastery. The inner content: a cynical mockery of everything in life. Life as a tavern, hooliganism, mischief, cynical perversion . . ."[47]

In a letter to a friend, Shostakovich summed up the situation rather ironically, albeit not without a certain disappointment. "All (sic!) com-

---

*In writing symphonies, the number nine inevitably makes a composer anxious, evoking thoughts of Beethoven's Ninth: This was something Bruckner, Mahler, and Alfred Schnittke all faced.

posers were outraged by my symphony. What can I do: I obviously didn't please them. However much I try not to be too upset by this, it still bothers me a little. Age, nerves, it all takes its toll."[48]

Behind Shostakovich's irony lay confusion. The creation of the anti-"Pathétique" had been both a provocative conceptual gesture and a not trivial life act in the spirit of Pushkin's Pretender. But what was he going to do next?

Salvation, not for the first time, came from Pushkin and Mussorgsky: The conductor Samuil Samosud asked him to do a new orchestration of *Boris Godunov* for a production at the Bolshoi Theater. This offer Shostakovich accepted gladly; he was quite critical of Rimsky-Korsakov's edition of *Boris,* which at the time was considered a model of orchestration: "Rimsky-Korsakov combed, permed, and poured cologne all over Mussorgsky."[49] But he wasn't very pleased with Mussorgsky's own version, either.

Shostakovich was a genius of orchestra, and when he composed he always heard the full score in his mind. The very process of orchestration was an inalienable part of composing rather than a tiresome chore—unlike Prokofiev, who often assigned his orchestral scores to an assistant. So Shostakovich took on the reorchestration of Mussorgsky's opera with pleasure, like sinking into his beloved warm pine baths at the Gaspra sanatorium in the Crimea (which, in fact, was where he completed work on *Boris*). This creative hiatus can be compared with Pasternak's work at this same time on a new translation of *Hamlet,* which gave him, in his words, "justification for disappearing into Shakespeare. Being in him, that is, at least slow reading, is in itself an incomparable treasure." In those difficult times in the late 1930s, Pasternak wrote to a friend, "I was ashamed that we continue moving, that we talk and smile."[50] His work on translating Shakespeare promised salvation, a way out, and a future.

Shostakovich experienced similar emotions. The immersion in Mussorgsky and Pushkin was a healing experience, as usual: It gave birth to the Piano Quintet, perhaps Shostakovich's most perfect and harmonious creation. The Piano Quintet is usually classified with the neoclassical works. This is partially justified, but the never-ending charm of the quintet lies in the total absence of stylized irony and grotesquerie. Its neoclassical motifs are imbued with a light sadness of the Pushkin manner: "My sorrow is radiant . . ."

The Piano Quintet breathes with the weary wisdom of a person who has just recovered from a severe illness. Here Shostakovich stepped back in time from Mahler to Bach. This was another timely discovery. The Soviet intelligentsia, recently drowning in the horrors of the Terror, wanted to surface for a brief moment to look around and catch its breath. A contemporary recalled that Shostakovich's Piano Quintet appeared like a "precious crystal of timeless truth" amid the gray, depressing life, filled with "the feeling of fear mixed with disbelief for what the newspapers wrote and official propaganda beat into us."[51] Audiences thought of the words of Mitya Karamazov to his brother: "And even underground we will sing the chant!"

The first performance of the Piano Quintet, on 23 November 1940, was given by the Beethoven Quartet with Shostakovich at the piano. Marietta Shaginyan recorded the audience's reaction. "A feeling of enormous pleasure and gratitude was on every face. An elderly man did not notice the tear rolling down his cheek. What had moved him?"[52]

Even the official critics appreciated Shostakovich's work as a great achievement in Soviet music. It suddenly became clear that the Piano Quintet was one of the main contenders for the Stalin Prize, the country's preeminent new award.

The Stalin Prize was announced at the end of 1939, in connection with the ruler's sixtieth birthday. Prizes would be given for outstanding achievement in literature, art, and science. This kind of award was being introduced in the USSR for the first time, and the name stressed its special prestige, which was bolstered by its enormous monetary value. The Stalin Prize First Class was 100,000 rubles. (The average annual salary of engineers, doctors, and teachers was approximately 3,600 rubles.)

The appearance of the Stalin Prize sharply changed Soviet artistic life, injecting the element of direct competition. Stalin wanted that. From the start, he planned to control the awards personally, but for the preparation of short lists, he created a special structure, the Committee on Stalin Prizes. In the area of literature and art, forty people were on the committee, including seven musicians—for the most part respected figures like Goldenveizer, Myaskovsky, Shaporin, and Samosud. Shostakovich was not among them, but passions began boiling over his Piano Quintet (and over other musical works that were potential winners).

In a letter of denunciation to Stalin, an influential musical bureau-crat of the day, Moisei Grinberg, insisted that Shostakovich's quintet should not be given the prize under any circumstances, since it contin-ued "abstract formal seekings of special, new sounds." Instead of Shostakovich, Grinberg promoted Ivan Dzerzhinsky's opera *The Quiet Don*, a presumably clever move, since Stalin supported the work in 1936 and condemned *Lady Macbeth of Mtsensk* for "formalism."[53] (The irony is that publicly Grinberg had supported the Piano Quintet, pub-lishing a positive review of the premiere: as Cicero exclaimed, "O tem-pora, o mores!")

Imagine the shock for Grinberg and his numerous allies when they opened *Pravda* on 16 March 1941 and saw the list of names and pho-tographs of the laureates. Shostakovich's Piano Quintet received the First Class prize, and his portrait was placed ahead of the other win-ners, clearly out of alphabetical order. Dzerzhinsky got nothing.

This decision could have been made only by Stalin. His logic could be explained this way. For Stalin the list of the first laureates had partic-ular significance: The ruler was summing up the results of his cultural policy for the entire period. The list had to be especially complete, and therefore was selected by Stalin with an obvious look over his shoulder at history: With Shostakovich, the other winners of the First Class prize were Mikhail Sholokhov, for his novel *The Quiet Don;* Alexei Tolstoi, for his novel *Peter I;* and Sergei Eisenstein, for his film *Alexander Nevsky.* The other winning composers included Myaskovsky, Sha-porin, and Khachaturian (the latter received a Second Class prize). The absence of Prokofiev's name was striking. He had spoken out harshly against Shostakovich's Piano Quintet. Prokofiev had to wait another two years (as punishment?) for his first Stalin Prize.

Neither Pasternak nor Akhmatova received a Stalin Prize. That did not mean that their candidacies were not submitted. Akhmatova's case is particularly revealing; her example demonstrates how intricate and unpredictable the zigzags of Stalin's cultural policy were. Akhmatova recalled that in 1925 she was stopped from publishing completely, although still consistently attacked in the press. "That continued until 1939, when Stalin asked about me at a reception for writers who had received awards."[54] This was a loud and clear signal, and the literary bureaucrats reacted hastily: At a special closed meeting the Presidium of the Writers' Union passed a resolution "On Helping Akhmatova," which, "taking into account the great contributions of Akhmatova to Russian poetry," established a personal pension for her and appealed to the Leningrad authorities to give her a private apartment.

Alexander Fadeyev, Stalin's most trusted representative in literature, who always responded to the tiniest changes in the ruler's cultural tactics, immediately announced that Akhmatova "was and remains the major poet of the prerevolutionary period."[55] This quotation likely came from Stalin—its similarity is striking to the ruler's statement about Mayakovsky. In 1940, in record time, a collection of Akhmatova's poems was published. But more than that, Sholokhov (deputy chairman of the Committee on Stalin Prizes) and Tolstoi (head of its literature section) immediately proposed Akhmatova's book for the prize.

It seemed that Akhmatova was assured the highest prize. But no—a quick reversal took place. In a special resolution, the Secretariat of the Central Committee of the Party condemned the publication of this collection of "ideologically harmful, religious-mystical poems" and ordered the book's removal from sale.

Of course, there was nothing left to remove from sale: The book sold out instantly, and Pasternak wrote to Akhmatova, "Recently, Andrei Platonov was here and told me that the fistfights for the sold-out edition continue and the price for a used copy has risen to a hundred fifty rubles. It is not surprising that as soon as you showed yourself, you won again."[56]

Akhmatova always thought that Stalin had been offended by one of the old poems in the collection, "Slander" (1922): "And slander accompanied me everywhere." She also blamed literary intrigues, writers' denunciations, and so on.[57] But as we have seen, Stalin could ignore the most convincing denunciations. In this case, though, he must have decided that the unexpected and sensational success of the book had become a form of protest. If they did not fit his current plans, Stalin usually nipped such spontaneous demonstrations in the bud. Tellingly, the punishment for the "guilty" publisher of Akhmatova's book was very light for those times: He got off with a scolding.

Life under Stalin's eye was inconceivably and inexpressibly unpredictable and dangerous. For millions of Soviets, "from Moscow to the very borders, from the southern mountains to the northern seas" (as the popular song put it), Stalin's name was a symbol, inspiring them "to work and perform deeds." For the Soviet cultural super-elite (and how many were there—probably no more than several hundred?) Stalin was a real person, the possible and probable first reader, listener, viewer, and, as in Pushkin's case with Nicholas I, "first censor."

For this comparatively small group of greatly talented people, who knew that Stalin kept them under his personal control, existence was particularly thorny. Dialogue with the ruler was an exhausting duel— without advisors or prompters, often with nothing but intuition as a guide, demanding enormous courage and inner conviction.

Success promised, in Mandelstam's words, "thundering valor of coming ages." Behind failure lay the threat of punishment much more terrible than anything Pushkin and his contemporaries could have imagined.

Chapter V

War: Triumphs and Tribulations

B y politicizing the symphonic genre, Shostakovich breathed new life into it. In that sense alone his Fifth was a breakthrough. But he reached for a new record in the Seventh ("Leningrad") Symphony. Its performances in the years of World War II became, thanks to the unprecedented joint efforts of the Stalinist cultural apparatus and American mass media, the most sensational in the history of the symphony.

With the Seventh Symphony, Shostakovich shattered yet another cliché: "When the cannons speak, the muses are silent." In the West the Seventh was hailed before being thrown from the pedestal. In the Soviet Union, it was invariably listed among the masterpieces and transformed into one of the most potent cultural propaganda symbols of the Great Patriotic War.

This war, which took at least twenty-seven million lives, was a cataclysmic event for the Soviet Union. Its memory is sacred for Russians, and anything related to it still evokes understandably heightened emotional reaction. In particular, this is the reason why the official, ossified interpretation of the Seventh Symphony has not been subject to discussion for several decades. But now, like Shostakovich's other "war" compositions, it is once again in the center of heated arguments.

Sunday, 22 June 1941, when Nazi German troops invaded the Soviet Union, is a day remembered by everyone who lived through it. Olga Freidenberg, Pasternak's cousin, recalled the confusion. "It was terribly unexpected, almost unreal, even though it had been predicted with certainty. The attack was not incredible—who hadn't expected it? And it wasn't the war with Hitler that was incredible: our politics did not inspire trust in anyone. What was incredible was the uproar in our lives."[1]

Shostakovich learned about the start of war at the Leningrad Conservatory, where he had been teaching from 1937, and where he was hearing final examinations; later that day he and a friend were planning to attend two soccer games. He kept the unused tickets (the matches were canceled) for a long time.

Less than a month later, Shostakovich began to write down the first pages of his new Seventh Symphony. I chose the words "write down" rather than "compose" intentionally. As we remember, Shostakovich liked to say, "I think slowly, but I write fast." In practice this meant that he, like Mozart, often wrote down a work that had almost completely been formed in his mind. In these cases, what sounded in Shostakovich's imagination only needed to be transferred to paper. It is important to stress this, because traditionally the idea for the Seventh is dated June 1941, which is an error on several fundamental counts.

Composing a symphony (or a novel) about war is not the same as writing a song on the topic, which only needs an appropriate text. War songs began appearing in great number soon after the start of combat, including ones written by Shostakovich. A true symphony is a huge living organism that requires a certain incubation period.

That the concept and musical text of the Seventh Symphony were maturing in Shostakovich's mind even before the Nazi invasion of the USSR is supported by a growing number of accounts, which naturally could not be made public when the official version was the only acceptable one. For instance, Galina Ustvolskaya, Shostakovich's favorite student, maintains that he told her that the Seventh was almost complete before the war.[2]

Of course, we cannot know which of his preliminary ideas were used in the final version. But the supposition of the existence—at least in his head—of such a preliminary version is confirmed by the fact that the Seventh Symphony was made part of the planned concert season of the Leningrad Philharmonic for 1941–42, announced in the spring of 1941: that is, before the war.[3] Precise and punctual in these matters, Shostakovich would not have permitted such an announcement if he had not been perfectly clear about what the new work would be like by then.

The main argument of the proponents of a "war" origin for the Seventh Symphony is the official "program" of the first movement. This means first of all the "invasion" episode, in which the grotesque march theme, repeated eleven times, grows in intensity (à la Ravel's *Boléro*), creating a picture of evil forces inexorably approaching. The interpretation of this episode as an illustration of the events of the first month of war with Germany won wide popularity in the Soviet Union and in the West, and for a long time seemed absolutely irrefutable.

However, new information on the genesis of the "invasion" episode casts doubt on its traditional interpretation. Musicologist Ludmila Mikheyeva (daughter-in-law of Ivan Sollertinsky, Shostakovich's closest friend) recently revealed that the composer played these variations to his students at the Leningrad Conservatory before the war with Germany began.[4]

It is telling that Shostakovich, in describing the Seventh Symphony, did not speak of the episode or the theme of "invasion"—that word appeared in articles and reviews by numerous commentators. On the contrary, in a highly evasive author's note for the premiere, he stressed: "I did not set myself the goal of a naturalistic depiction of military action (the roar of planes, the crash of tanks, cannon fire), I did not compose so-called battle music. I wanted to convey the content of grim events."[5]

What "grim events" if not the war could be depicted in the work of a Soviet author in 1941? This question would evince either a total ignorance of Soviet history or a willful ignoring of it. The beginning of the war could not erase the bloody memory of the mass purges of recent years.

Shostakovich formulated his position, much later, this way: "Even before the war, in Leningrad there probably wasn't a single family who hadn't lost someone, a father, a brother, or if not a relative, then a close friend. Everyone had someone to cry over, but you had to cry silently, under the blanket, so no one would see. Everyone feared everyone else, and the sorrow oppressed and suffocated us. It suffocated me, too. I had to write about it, I felt that it was my responsibility, my duty. I had to write a requiem for all those who died, who had suffered. I had to describe the horrible extermination machine and express protest against it."[6]

But perhaps this explanation is merely an attempt by Shostakovich to give his work meaning in hindsight that had not been there originally? Eyewitness accounts by Shostakovich's peers, which became known in the era of glasnost, speak to the reverse.

In 1990, in the journal *Novyi mir,* musicologist Lev Lebedinsky, for many years Shostakovich's confidant, affirmed that the Seventh Symphony had been planned before the war: "Back then the famous theme developed in the first movement was defined by Shostakovich as the *Stalin* theme (this was known to Dmitri Dmitrievich's close friends). Right after the start of the war, he called it the *anti-Hitler* theme. Later that 'German' theme Shostakovich called the theme of 'evil,' which was certainly correct, since that theme was as equally anti-Hitler as anti-Stalin, even though in the consciousness of the world musical community only the first of these two definitions became established."[7]*

In 1996, the journal *Znamya* published the memoirs of Shostakovich's friend Flora Litvinova, in which she quoted what she heard him say in 1941, right after he completed his Seventh Symphony: "This is music about terror, slavery, constrained spirits." And she added, "Later, when Dmitri Dmitrievich got used to me and began trusting me, he told me directly that the Seventh as well as the Fifth were not only about fascism but also about our regime, generally about any totalitarianism."[9]

Now we can take a look at the "invasion" episode with different eyes, and ask a "naïve" question: Why does the "invasion" theme begin in the strings very softly, *pianissimo,* and only gradually expand, turning into a howling monster? The Nazis had attacked the Soviet Union with their entire military might; their invasion was, as everyone recalls, an instantaneous shock of enormous power. There is nothing of the sort in Shostakovich's music. If this is an invasion, then it comes from within rather than from outside. It is not a sudden incursion but a gradual takeover, when fear paralyzes the mind.

---

*Astonishingly, composer Arthur Lourié sensed it, living as an émigré beyond the ocean, as he wrote in 1943 in New York: "One could think that his symphony was begun before the German invasion of Russia and then with the events of the war it was shaped and grew."[8] Perhaps Lourié had some information about this from Russia?

At first the "invasion" theme does not sound threatening at all. In fact, Shostakovich quotes here from Franz Lehár's operetta *The Merry Widow* (the entrance song of Graf Danîlo), which was very popular in Russia: "Da geh' ich zu Maxim." As the perceptive Arthur Lourié characterized this "trite, intentionally silly motif": "This tune can be whistled by any Soviet man on the street; there is something of Zoshchenko's characters about it."[10]

Here Lourié's opinion coincides with conductor Yevgeny Mravinsky's. The latter always insisted that when in March 1942 he first heard the Seventh Symphony on the radio, he decided that the "invasion" episode was a generalized image of spreading stupidity and triteness.[11]

Nowadays other recollections of contemporaries read differently. In 1971, in Shostakovich's lifetime and under Soviet censorship, the writer Galina Serebryakova published a book of memoirs. She stressed that the Seventh was not at all a "wartime work": "Hell and heaven, crime and innocence, madness and reason, dark and light—Shostakovich reflected all that in his symphony of genius. It is broader than any one theme, it is an immortal narrative about humanity, like the work of Dante."[12]★

In the Seventh Symphony, as in previous ones, Shostakovich used musical "code"—a method that became second-nature for him. In the second movement a motif appears, first employed in the finale of the Fifth Symphony, which the author most likely considered to be an image of procession to an execution.

Look at how Shostakovich utilized the same motif—in *Six Songs to the Words of English Poets* (1942) and in the Thirteenth ("Babi Yar") Symphony in 1962—in contexts that leave no doubt as to its meaning. Both times the music paints the same grotesque image: the accused heading toward execution with his head held high and even dancing a jig, boldly challenging his executioners.[†] This image is readily deci-

---

★Serebryakova was a former camp inmate. But there was no hope of publishing her memoirs about her camp experience, *Smerch* (published in Paris in the Polish émigré journal *Kultura* in 1967), in the Soviet Union of those days. Nevertheless the writer, wherever she could, made hidden parallels to her experiences in the years of the Great Terror. In the symphony by her long-ago love she must have heard coded reflections of the madness and horror of those days, and she hinted that she perceived the work as a musical depiction of Stalin's circles of hell.

†Arthur Lourié mentions the "March to the Scaffold" from Berlioz's *Symphonie fantastique* in connection with Shostakovich's Seventh.

phered with the help of the verses Shostakovich selected for the vocal cycle, "MacPherson's Farewell" by Robert Burns:

> *Sae rantingly, sae wantonly,*
> *Sae dauntingly gaed he,*
> *He'd played a spring, and danc'd it round*
> *Below the gallers-tree.*

Thus, Shostakovich projects the hidden message of living on the edge. This supports the notion that Shostakovich had started thinking about composing his Seventh Symphony before the war, as a work that, in the words of Arthur Lourié, would be a "musical portrait of our long-suffering Homeland."[13] It was supposed to be something similar to the poem Anna Akhmatova was writing in those same years, *Requiem,* a symbolic image of Russia beleaguered by the Great Terror. Akhmatova wrote *Requiem* for herself and her closest friends, letting them read in secret the verses she had written and then burning the paper so that it would not be seen by informers. This made *Requiem* a profoundly esoteric text, poetry for the initiates. Shostakovich's Seventh Symphony might have had the same fate. But while Shostakovich was deciding how best to transfer his symphony onto music paper, war came to the Soviet Union. That changed the situation instantly and radically.

The Nazi attack paradoxically forced the authorities to look the other way when the creative intelligentsia took liberties. As Ilya Ehrenburg commented, "Usually war brings with it the censor's scissors; here, in the first eighteen months of the war, writers felt much freer than before."[14]

In these new circumstances Shostakovich suddenly had the hope that his message could not only be set down on paper but also brought to a mass audience. He had to find the path from individual feelings to common ones and to express his hidden emotions in a way that would make them accessible to the audience and allow it to experience catharsis.

Here, the model for Shostakovich was Igor Stravinsky's 1930 Symphony of Psalms for chorus and orchestra. As soon as the score of the Symphony of Psalms (for which Stravinsky originally used the Russian text of the Psalms, only later switching to Latin) reached Leningrad,

Shostakovich arranged it for piano for four hands and often played the composition with friends and students. He was deeply impressed.

When he was still thinking about his Seventh Symphony, one of Shostakovich's first impulses was to write it, in imitation of Stravinsky, with a chorus that would use the Psalms of David. In particular, he planned to have a soloist sing excerpts from the Ninth Psalm:

> *Sing praises to the Lord, who dwells in Zion!*
> *Declare His deeds among the people.*
> *When He avenges blood, He remembers them;*
> *He does not forget the cry of the humble.*
> *Have mercy on me, O Lord!*
> *Consider my trouble from those who hate me.*

The motif of individual suffering was interwoven in Shostakovich's mind with the theme of "avenging blood": He hoped that the war would bring purification and retribution, that it would be the "cleansing storm, stream of fresh air, breath of deliverance," about which Pasternak would later write in *Dr. Zhivago*.[15]

The idea of using biblical texts in his work, which he considered from the moment he heard Stravinsky's symphony, was impossible to realize in the prewar years. But the war swept away many ideological barriers. In the face of mortal danger, Stalin even started cozying up to the Russian Orthodox Church. A crafty tactician, Stalin used whatever could unite the nation in its fight against the enemy.

And yet, Shostakovich probably made the right decision in creating the Seventh as a work without text. From the purely artistic angle, this took it out of direct competition with Stravinsky's symphony; and from the ideological, it guaranteed it an uninterrupted life in the Soviet Union—a vital consideration in view of the eventual censoring of some of Shostakovich's fundamental works.

The religious content of the Seventh thus went into the subtext, but it continued to reverberate, eliciting an emotional response from the audience. Akhmatova's husband, Nikolai Punin, a typical member of the St. Petersburg intelligentsia, noted in his diary of the early war months: "If the churches were open and thousands could pray, probably with tears, in the flickering twilight, how much less palpable would be the sere iron milieu in which we now live."[16]

At the first run-throughs of the Seventh, even when Shostakovich showed it to his friends playing it on the piano, listeners wept, a typical reaction. The requiem pages of the first movement made a special impression.

The orchestral performances of the symphony began to resemble religious rites, giving an escape for the hidden thoughts and suffering accumulated over many years. As Punin wrote then, "The greater part of what exists must perish, and that is known to each of us, but each thinks: 'Maybe not me.' The gloomy ones, however, think: 'That's me.' People will die from both groups, but it is absolutely unknown who exactly will die. There is something very comparable to how we lived in the 'Yezhov days'; then everyone thought: 'Maybe it will be me tomorrow, too.' "[17]

Because all these hidden emotions were expressed with such power and passion, the Seventh Symphony turned into a major public event, one that began not on the orders of the authorities, but thanks to the sincere enthusiasm of the intelligentsia. The significance of this spontaneous reaction was first noted by Alexei Tolstoi, who had played such an important role in the life of Shostakovich's Fifth Symphony. Tolstoi apparently truly loved Shostakovich's music (back in 1937 he had publicly proclaimed him a genius). After hearing an orchestra rehearsal of the Seventh in February 1942, the writer, who with Ehrenburg had become a leading national spokesman in the war, immediately published a rave review in *Pravda*. Like all of Tolstoi's reviews, it was eloquently written. He called Shostakovich the "new Dante," but stressed that he was a Russian and that his symphony was a profoundly national work in which the "Russian raging conscience" of its young author spoke out.[18]

In fact, the symphony was indebted to Mahler (the strange second movement), Bach, and the émigré Stravinsky (the majestic Adagio). But this was the right move on Tolstoi's part. Stalin, we know, read *Pravda* closely. He had to have liked Tolstoi's comments about how "Hitler did not scare Shostakovich. Shostakovich is a Russian man, and that means an angry man, and if you get him really angry, he is capable of fantastic feats."* Tolstoi's interpretation of the Seventh Symphony corre-

*In that passage, Tolstoi's conscious or unconscious imitation of Stalin's tautological manner is striking.

sponded with Stalin's support of nationalism and patriotism as the main ideological aces in the war with Germany.

But no less important was this: Stalin knew that without the help of the United States and Britain, the Soviet Union would not win, and therefore he appreciated the importance of propaganda directed at their new allies in the anti–Hitler coalition. Shostakovich was one of the few internationally famous Soviet artists. At that moment, this was more of an advantage in Stalin's eyes, because it made it possible to promote the Seventh Symphony simultaneously in the East and in the West.

As we know, both before and after the war, Stalin was highly suspicious of spontaneous expressions of mass enthusiasm. He saw them—not without reason—as veiled instances of oppositionist feelings. But during the war years, Stalin realized that suppressing enthusiasm "from below" was unwise—and if you can't suppress it, join it. So Stalin gave his approval for a propaganda campaign around the Seventh Symphony. The efficient ideological machine of the totalitarian state swung into full gear in support of Shostakovich's music.

The Seventh was performed all over the Soviet Union: Kuibyshev, Moscow, Novosibirsk, Tashkent, Yerevan . . . The performances were broadcast on the radio, and newspapers and magazines kept writing about Shostakovich's new work. In April 1942, a little more than a month after the symphony's premiere, it received the Stalin Prize First Class, Shostakovich's second such award in two years. Stalin's ideologue Fadeyev brought the leader's thoughts on the matter to the creative intelligentsia: "Let us try to create now, during the war, works that are real, serious, big, but ones that can be used right now as weapons, not set aside for later . . . Make it for now, like the Seventh Symphony."[19]

The symphony continued to have enormous, unprecedented success: People still wept at concerts; listening to the finale, they often stood, and then applauded obliviously. But now the fame of the Seventh was also supported from above by a potent propaganda campaign. The culmination was the celebrated performance of the symphony on 9 August 1942 in Leningrad, while the city was besieged by Hitler's army.

Thousands of pages have been written about the horrors of the blockade of Leningrad, which began in September 1941 and lasted almost nine hundred days, until Soviet troops broke through in January 1944. Eyewitness accounts talk of the heroism of Leningraders who went through inhuman suffering but refused to surrender to the Germans. The winter of 1941–42 was the worst, when hundreds of thousands of people starved to death.

Characteristically, Stalin took care to have the artistic elite evacuated from the city in good time: Shostakovich, Akhmatova, Zoshchenko, and others were brought to Moscow in early autumn by special military transport planes. (Shostakovich took only a few necessary items with him—which included his transcription of Stravinsky's Symphony of Psalms.) But before Shostakovich's departure, the successful propaganda scenario was set into motion.

The German air force had begun dropping incendiary bombs on the city, and the Leningrad Conservatory (like other institutions) had organized a "volunteer" fire department. It consisted of instructors and students who had to be on duty on the roof during air strikes.

The memoirs of "firefighter" composer Dmitri Tolstoi (son of Alexei Tolstoi) dispassionately relate how they set up the show with Shostakovich, specially brought in for this. "They put the fireman's helmet on his head, asked him to go up onto the roof and be photographed there. The whole world knows that picture. And even though Shostakovich's participation in the anti-incendiary-bomb defense took no more than ten minutes, I can attest that no one on the team complained about comparing their service with his. Everyone understood: Shostakovich had to be protected."[20]★

Stalin also understood that. On his personal orders, the military stopped any "volunteer" efforts by celebrities to get to the front: Their lives were controlled only by Stalin himself. Shostakovich's requests to go to the front in any capacity, "even mess cook," were refused. When Alexei Tolstoi begged to be sent to the front, even as a war correspondent, he got an unequivocal reply: "Under no circumstances. There is a direct order from Stalin—protect Tolstoi, do not send him to the front."[22]

It is obvious that neither Tolstoi nor Shostakovich would have made a good soldier. But Stalin, master of the propaganda gesture, knew the invaluable practical benefit that would come from engaging culture in the war effort. The propaganda apparatus created before the

★Gabriel Glikman confirmed in his memoirs that the Shostakovich picture was nothing more than a photo op.[21]

war worked very efficiently. One of its greatest successes was with Shostakovich's Seventh Symphony.

Besieged Leningrad was living hell. Eyewitnesses reported corpses of people who died of hunger and cold lying in doorways and stairwells. "They lay there because people dropped them there, the way newborn infants used to be left. Janitors swept them away in the morning like rubbish. Funerals, graves, coffins were long forgotten. It was a flood of death that could not be managed. Entire families vanished, entire apartments with their collective families. Houses, streets, and neighborhoods vanished."[23]

There was no time for music in that apocalyptic situation, and local radios had switched to round-the-clock political appeals. As one of the managers of Leningrad broadcasting recalled, "Well, we didn't have enough agitators either; there were entire hours of silence, when only the metronome ticked: tick . . . tick . . . tick . . . tick . . . Can you imagine? It was like that all night, and even in the daytime."[24]

This rejection of musical broadcasts, sanctioned from above, in the doom-filled atmosphere of starvation and freezing was suddenly reversed. Fadeyev thought it was on the initiative of Zhdanov, then secretary of the Leningrad Regional Party Committee and City Committee, who allegedly said, "Why are you spreading gloom? Why don't you play something?"[25] But in this case, as in many others, behind the city bureaucrat and future "chief ideologist" of the country, the silhouette of the supreme leader with his pipe was clearly visible. That was his manner of expression, his vocabulary.

The situation changed instantly. Leningrad Radio put together a symphony orchestra again, and its musicians were given additional rations. First they played the traditional repertoire: Beethoven, Tchaikovsky, Rimsky-Korsakov. But in July 1942 the conductor, the experienced and demanding Karl Eliasberg, was given an important propaganda task: prepare a performance of Shostakovich's Seventh. After all, the title page of the score read: "Dedicated to the city of Leningrad." (Hence the symphony's nickname, "Leningrad.")

The score was delivered to Leningrad from Kuibyshev, along with medicine and other valuable cargo, by a special military plane that broke through the blockade ring. When they began learning the Seventh, some of the orchestra musicians protested: They had so little strength, why waste it on such an intricate and not very accessible work? Eliasberg ruthlessly put an end to the growing rebellion by threatening to hold back on the additional rations.[26]

Then, things developed in a fantastic way. The Germans were preparing for the final storm of Leningrad, yet Zhdanov's closest assistant, Alexei Kuznetsov, then in favor with Stalin, took over the premiere of the Seventh. It was decided that the top leaders of the city's defense would attend, and that meant protecting the Philharmonic building from possible enemy fire. On the orders of the commander of the Leningrad front, a carefully planned full-scale military operation was carried out: On the day of the concert, Soviet artillery opened a squall of fire on the Germans, dropping three thousand high-caliber shells on them.

The radio broadcast of the concert was preceded by a brief announcement that said, in particular: "Dmitri Shostakovich has written a symphony that calls for struggle and affirms faith in victory." The propaganda action, planned and executed with flair, energy, and scope, was a triumph. "Never will anyone present forget this concert of August ninth. The motley orchestra, dressed in sweaters and sweatshirts, jackets and Russian-style shirts, played with inspiration and tension. Skeletal Eliasberg floated above them, ready to leap out of his tails, which were as baggy on him as on a scarecrow . . . When they played the finale, the entire audience stood up. You couldn't sit and listen. It was impossible."[27]

In planning the whole show starring Shostakovich's Seventh, Stalin also had correctly counted on international effect. The day after the premiere in Kuibyshev, the story appeared in the London *Times*. The Soviet Union's Western allies thought it very important to humanize the image of the Bolsheviks, who only recently had been described in the popular press as godless villains and barbarians. Now, on the contrary, the public had to be taught that the Russian Communists, together with Britain and the United States, were protecting the high values of European culture from fascism. Shostakovich's symphony, "composed in besieged Leningrad under enemy fire," was perfect for the job.

On 26 May 1942 a treaty was signed in London between Great Britain and the USSR on mutual aid for twenty years; and in late June, coinciding with the anniversary of Hitler's attack on Russia, the Western premiere of the Seventh took place in Royal Albert Hall, the audience packed with men in uniform. It was seen first of all as an important political event.

But the real public-relations effort came when the work was performed in America, where the press sensationalized the story of the symphony's creation and the score's delivery (which smacked of adventure films) by plane from Kuibyshev to Teheran, then by car to Cairo, and then once again by plane through Africa to London and across the Atlantic to New York. The leading conductors fought for the right to stage the first American performance: Serge Koussevitzky in Boston, Leopold Stokowski in Philadelphia, Artur Rodzinski in Cleveland, and Arturo Toscanini in New York. The battle royale, as the press dubbed it, was won by seventy-five-year-old Toscanini, with his reputation as an implacable antifascist.

The culmination of the pre-premiere excitement, which was compared to the anticipation of the New York premiere of Wagner's *Parsifal* in 1903, was the 20 July 1942 issue of *Time* magazine, with its cover portrait of Shostakovich in profile. Wearing the golden fireman's helmet, with burning buildings and flying notes behind him, the composer gazed steadfastly and courageously forward, while the caption proclaimed: "Fireman Shostakovich: Amid bombs bursting in Leningrad, he heard the chords of victory." Bypassing Stravinsky, Prokofiev, and Copland, among many others, Shostakovich became the first composer to appear on the cover of *Time:* an honor coveted by major politicians and newsmakers all over the world.

The American premiere of the symphony, conducted by Toscanini on 19 July 1942, was broadcast nationally; it was followed by hundreds of other performances and innumerable reviews. Never before had a serious musical work had such coverage. But the reaction of Shostakovich's colleagues could be called favorable only by a great stretch of the imagination.

Béla Bartók was so infuriated by what he considered the undeserved success of the Seventh that he sarcastically parodied it in the fourth movement of his new Concerto for Orchestra. The only commentary from Sergei Rachmaninoff, who had listened to the radio broadcast, was, according to legend, a grim "Well, and now let's have some tea." Virgil Thomson, a composer and critic from a very different camp, called the symphony "unoriginal and shallow" and predicted that if

Shostakovich continued writing music in this manner, it might "eventually disqualify him for consideration as a serious composer."[28]

Subsequently, similar voices of condemnation were heard more frequently and loudly in the West, and in the period of the Cold War they predominated. The Seventh Symphony was always a convenient target: a strange, incongruous hybrid of Mahler and Stravinsky, on first hearing too long and too emotionally open; its broad narrative gestures seemed to some connoisseurs to be simultaneously naïve and calculated.★

Disdainful remarks about the Seventh being nothing more than a bombastic accompaniment for a bad war movie could be heard right after the London and New York premieres. But in the cultural and political heat of those days, they had no effect. Thanks to the efficiency of the American public-relations machine, which in this case joined its efforts with the Soviet propaganda apparatus, the Seventh Symphony was turned into a symbol of cooperation and spiritual unity of the Russian and American people in their struggle against the Nazis.

With his Seventh Symphony, Shostakovich made such a high leap in public and political success that no other twentieth-century artist could break the record. He himself failed, even though he clearly tried to do just that with his next symphony. The Eighth was undoubtedly an even more ambitious work than the Seventh.

I have already mentioned the parallels between the Seventh Symphony and Akhmatova's *Requiem*.[†] That symphony also bears a resemblance to the creative evolution of Pasternak in the prewar and war years, with his conscious efforts to reach a broad audience and write about what was important and painful with sincerity and power, using devices significantly simpler and more accessible than in the past.

But the literary parallel for the Eighth is Mandelstam's "Poem About the Unknown Soldier"—the poet's most complex work, written in 1937. As far as we know, Shostakovich did not read the poem, which was unpublished at the time and not widely circulated in *samizdat,* but

---

★From the West, these negative views seeped into the Soviet elite milieu, where they became entrenched. I remember listening to the Seventh in New York in 1994 with the composer Alfred Schnittke, who had come for the American premiere of one of his works. When the performance was over, I saw that Schnittke was astounded by what he had heard. Turning his pale, agitated face to me, he said that he had seriously underestimated the Seventh: "It's a masterpiece."

†I treat these parallels and the role of both works in the dizzying transformation of the St. Petersburg mythos in the twentieth century in my book *St. Petersburg: A Cultural History.*

the resemblance is amazing. He was not alone in thinking about the great war before it began. Images of war's meat grinder inevitably mixed with images of the meat grinder of the Great Terror.

"Poem About the Unknown Soldier" is a visionary, apocalyptic work, in which Mandelstam foresees the annihilation of the world in a coming universal war. The poet regards the terrible battles as if from above, from space. This breath-catching cosmic perspective is present in the Eighth Symphony.

There is information that Shostakovich had given the finale of the Eighth a name: "Through cosmic space the Earth flies toward its doom."[29] The combination of tragic cosmism and Boschian grotesquerie that characterizes "Poem About the Unknown Soldier" distinguishes Shostakovich's symphony as well. (Here one thinks of the paintings by the avant-garde "cosmist" Pavel Filonov, which Shostakovich knew.)

The Seventh Symphony was an attempt to bring to the surface what was covert and hidden. In that sense it continued the line of the Fifth. The predecessor of the Eighth is probably the Sixth Symphony, of which the opposite is true. The same holds for Mandelstam's "Unknown Soldier." Commentators are still looking for the key to this work. They agree only on one thing, that it is about the destruction of our planet through global war—as is, apparently, the Eighth Symphony.

Shostakovich was incredibly lucky. Unlike writers, he managed to appear publicly with a sorrowful message, and the authorities not only pretended that everything was fine, but actually encouraged him. This situation was repeated over and over with Shostakovich, delighting and sometimes infuriating his contemporaries.

Many were already ascribing Shostakovich's "luck" to the polysemous nature of the music. Recalling the premiere of the Eighth Symphony in November 1943, Ehrenburg wrote, "I came home stunned from the performance: suddenly there was the voice of an ancient chorus from Greek tragedy. Music has an enormous advantage: it can, without mentioning anything, say everything."[30]

The intertextual hints in music are not always easily recognized. For instance, the first and last movements of the Eighth cite the theme of Manfred from Tchaikovsky's symphony of that name.

Manfred, composed in 1885, less than sixty years before Shostakovich's Eighth, stood out in Tchaikovsky's work by being his only openly programmatic symphony. Modeled on Berlioz's *Harold in Italy,* it also used a plot from Byron, drawing an ultra-Romantic picture of a cosmic pessimist and dissident. Manfred in Byron (and Tchaikovsky) travels around the world in search of death and leaves life without fear or regret. We cannot say for sure whether Shostakovich was actually toying with the idea of death while at the peak of success, but the autobiographical image he presented then in music was suicidal. This is corroborated not only by these clear quotes from *Manfred* (Tchaikovsky explained this music by saying "there is no limit or end to the boundless despair of Manfred"), but by other musical allusions. In Shostakovich's Eighth Symphony we can hear echoes of the "mortal wound" motif in Wagner's *Parsifal* (fourth movement) and reminders of Sibelius's *Swan of Tuonela,* the symphonic legend of the mythological land of the dead.

This universal despair was perceived by the more sensitive of the early listeners of the Eighth Symphony. Among them was the conductor Nikolai Golovanov, who was stunned after the premiere and muttered, "What lunar craters gave rise to this music, this endless tragedy—the end of the world?"[31] Golovanov and others thought that they had decoded the enigmatic message of Shostakovich's new symphony. The authorities were not thrilled by the music, but they did not ban the Eighth then. That came later, after the war.

"Millions killed cheap / Trampled a path in the void." As in Mandelstam's "Poem About the Unknown Soldier," the theme of death dominated in Shostakovich in this period, for the first—but, as we know, not the last—time in his work. Grim thoughts poured out onto the paper; all that was needed was an excuse. Even a random commission was enough. In order to express solidarity with the Allies, Shostakovich was asked to write a vocal cycle to the poems of English poets. He set six songs to the poetry of Sir Walter Raleigh, Robert Burns, and Shakespeare; Raleigh's "To My Son" and Shakespeare's Sonnet 66, both in Pasternak's translations, stand out.

Even if this is the only instance of Shostakovich and Pasternak collaborating—and they were not friends or even close acquaintances—they spent their lives thinking about each other and watching what the other was doing. Pasternak, with his musical education and frustrated ambitions as a composer, eagerly followed the very public success of the Fifth and Seventh symphonies, especially in the West. In his turn, with good reason, Shostakovich kept handy the 1940 edition (published for Pasternak's fiftieth birthday) of his *Selected Translations*.

The motif of violent death, starting with Pasternak's oblique rendering of Raleigh, continues with a devil-may-care, desperate attitude toward it in "MacPherson's Farewell," Shostakovich's masochistic number to Burns's poem. This leads us to recall the Manfred theme in Shostakovich's Eighth Symphony and also a verse by Akhmatova from her *Requiem*, titled "To Death":

> *You will come anyway—why not now then?*
> *I wait for you—it is very hard.*

And how similar is the sigh or shriek with which Shakespeare's Sonnet 66 begins: "Tired with all these, for restful death I cry." And then:

> *As, to behold desert a beggar born,*
> *And needy nothing trimm'd in jollity,*
> *And purest faith unhappily forsworn,*
> *And gilded honour shamefully misplaced,*
> *And maiden virtue rudely strumpeted,*
> *And right perfection wrongfully disgraced,*
> *And strength by limping sway disabled,*
> *And art made tongue-tied by authority,*
> *And folly doctor-like controlling skill,*
> *And simple truth miscall'd simplicity,*
> *And captive good attending captain ill:*
> > *Tired with all these, from these would I be gone,*
> > *Save that, to die, I leave my love alone.*

Shostakovich's choice of this sonnet speaks volumes. He set it to outwardly restrained music, imbued with quiet desperation, and dedicated it to his closest friend, music critic Ivan Sollertinsky. Four years his senior, Sollertinsky entered Shostakovich's life in 1927, at a moment of crisis (they were introduced by conductor Nikolai Malko, who had conducted the premiere of Shostakovich's First Symphony). Of Polish descent like Shostakovich (which brought them closer), Sollertinsky was the son of a tsarist senator, by nature a skeptic, cynic, and epicurean, with an unquenchable artistic temperament and great enthusiasm.

His legendary erudition, based in great part on his photographic memory (a single glance at a page of the most difficult text in any of the two dozen languages he knew was enough for him to remember it for life), made Sollertinsky an irreplaceable advisor and mentor. The composer could speak frankly to him about everything under the sun, from sex to Schoenberg. I think that it was Sollertinsky who warned Shostakovich about the dangers of being the pretender. Even though he did not have a professional musical education, it was Sollertinsky who introduced Shostakovich to the work of Gustav Mahler (whom the critic adored) and promoted the transition from what he considered the young composer's "primitive" concepts of avant-garde symphonies toward the psychologically multifaceted "Dostoevskian" opera *Lady Macbeth of Mtsensk.*

It was Sollertinsky who immediately declared that *Lady Macbeth* was a Shakespearean opera, comparable to Tchaikovsky's *Queen of Spades* in scope and depth. He paid dearly for that. When Stalin attacked *Lady Macbeth,* everyone who had supported the opera fell under fire. Sollertinsky was particularly unlucky, since he was designated scapegoat. This was a favorite tactic of Stalin's, which he used many times later: the blow fell not only on the author but on friendly critics. Stalin correctly assumed that this way he created a "burned-ground zone" around the people who displeased him.

In 1936, *Pravda* repeatedly called Sollertinsky "defender of bourgeois perversions in music" and "ideologue of the movement that crippled Shostakovich's music." When the chairman of the Committee on Arts Affairs, Platon Kerzhentsev, conveyed Stalin's wishes to Shostakovich in a conversation with him, among them was the demand that he "free himself from the influence of some servile critics, like Sollertinsky, who promote the worst of his writing."[32]

These were harsh and dangerous times. Recently everyone's favorite, who was always asked for advice, support, and new articles, Sollertinsky suddenly found himself isolated. He was no longer published, his telephone stopped ringing, and acquaintances avoided him. Just six weeks before the *Pravda* attack, Shostakovich wrote to Sollertinsky, "I consider you the only musician and, besides that, a personal friend, and in any situation of life I will always and in every way support you."[33] Suddenly, it became seemingly impossible to keep that promise.

Moreover, Shostakovich, with his Russian sense of guilt, considered himself responsible for the plight of his best friend. That they were both prepared for the worst is evident from Shostakovich's later recollection about his prewar conversations with Sollertinsky. "We spoke of the inevitable that awaited us at the end of our lives, that is, about death. We were both afraid of it and did not want it. We loved life, but we knew that sooner or later, we would have to give it up."[34]

The storm, as we know, didn't kill Shostakovich and Sollertinsky. But the fright resulted, unexpectedly, in the critic's contracting diphtheria, very rare in adults, and with grave complications—Sollertinsky lost the use of his legs, then his arms, and then his jaw.

Shostakovich was very concerned for his friend, whose life hung by a thread for several months. But even in the hospital, Sollertinsky behaved like MacPherson before his execution. Looking death in the face, he refused to give up and decided to learn Hungarian while he was paralyzed. His mother brought a dictionary to the hospital, which she set up on a special stand, and at a sign from Sollertinsky turned page after page. Sollertinsky learned Hungarian and was cured.

In this inextinguishable and stubborn will to live and this ability to look danger in the eyes and respond with creativity, Shostakovich resembled Sollertinsky. The roots of their unusual friendship must have been in that similarity. For hypochondriac Shostakovich, the incomparably more life-affirming and optimistic Sollertinsky was always a support and an example—so much so that the news of his friend's sudden death on 11 February 1944 from a heart spasm came as a tremendous shock.

Shostakovich dedicated one of his greatest works to the memory of Sollertinsky—the Second Piano Trio. Here Shostakovich continued an important Russian musical tradition. Tchaikovsky dedicated his melodramatic Piano Trio "to the memory of a great artist" (pianist Nikolai Rubinstein, who died in Paris in March 1881). Its "weeping and funereal color," as Tchaikovsky put it, was undoubtedly tied to an historical cataclysm—the assassination by terrorists of Emperor Alexander II, which Tchaikovsky perceived as a personal catastrophe.

Tchaikovsky set several "genre records": his Piano Trio is monumental in size, character, and narrative devices. Some ten years later, the young Rachmaninoff, who dedicated his Trio Elégiaque to

Tchaikovsky, entered into a musical dialogue (or competition) with the great composer. This was a very ambitious work, which immediately won (as had the Tchaikovsky trio) great popularity. Composed on the cusp of historical eras, it is also imbued with dreadful foreboding.

Neither Tchaikovsky nor especially Rachmaninoff was among Shostakovich's favorite composers, but Shostakovich had an acute "genre memory" and a heightened awareness of his place in the Russian musical tradition. Therefore his Piano Trio was conceived from the start not only as a human but also as an historical document: a memorial work with a palpable social subtext.

At first, work on the trio went badly. When the writing was not going well (and this happened frequently), he despaired, confessing, "When I am not working, I have a constant headache." At such moments, Shostakovich feared that his creative gift had left him forever and that "some spring in my brain has broken."[35]

But when the composing moved into great speed (its last two movements were written in a bit over a week), Shostakovich also panicked, writing to a friend, the composer Vissarion Shebalin, "My 'creative process' reminds me (let me phrase this scientifically) of a too quick session with Onan's sin. It's a not very self-confident effort, with the use of seductive pictures and superhuman labor (as Yavorsky would have said) of all your physical and, most importantly, mental powers. It's exhausting, not very pleasant, and at the end, there's a total lack of certainty that you've spent your time to any benefit. But the filthy habit is strong, and I'm composing too fast yet again."[36]

The finale of the Piano Trio, which overwhelmed Shostakovich, is particularly interesting: It is a tragic dance in the Jewish mode. He was always fascinated by the ability of Jewish folk music to laugh through tears and weep through laughter; after all, he cultivated a conscious dual-level narrative in his own work.

Shostakovich had used Jewish-sounding musical themes before, but Jewish images came to the forefront for the first time in the Piano Trio. This was the period when Shostakovich first heard about the Holocaust, and in my opinion his feelings of guilt for his friend apparently intertwined into a tight knot with similar feelings for an entire people. The Piano Trio's finale became the greatest music ever written about the Holocaust.

There was one more person on Shostakovich's mind, apparently, when he wrote these stunning pages. His twenty-eight-year-old student Veniamin Fleishman was sent to the front as part of the People's Volunteer Corps, and he died near Leningrad in the first months of battle. This was not propaganda play acting at volunteering, into which Shostakovich was drawn in the first days of the war. With his hypertrophic conscience, typical of the Russian intelligentsia, Shostakovich took Fleishman's death as a personal wound; he told me so.

At the time he was composing his Piano Trio, Shostakovich was working on the completion of *Rothschild's Violin,* an opera (based on Chekhov) on a Jewish theme, begun by Fleishman before the war in his composition class at the Leningrad Conservatory, under the direction and with the support of Shostakovich. The immersion in the Jewish culture of Fleishman's opera, the loss of his student, the death of his friend, the war, the news of the Holocaust, and persistent thoughts of his own death created the social background and psychological soil on which grew the trio, one of Shostakovich's most hopeless compositions. The mood is comparable to Marina Tsvetayeva's lines:

> *It's time—it's time—it's time*
> *To return the ticket to the Creator.*

But Tsvetayeva, who returned to the Soviet Union in 1939 after emigrating, could not take the catastrophes that befell her and hanged herself in August 1941 ("To your mad world / There is only one answer—refusal"), while Shostakovich's Piano Trio, which expressed a despair no less than Tsvetayeva's, received the Stalin Prize in 1946.

That was another paradox of the times. The Stalin Prize was the ruler's favorite toy. He would not even think about recusing himself from selecting "the best and most talented." This is evinced by the fact that in 1944 and 1945, when the tension and exhaustion of sleepless nights in the office of the Supreme Commander (as Stalin was called during the war years) reached their apogee, the prizes were not awarded. We must assume that Stalin simply did not have the time or energy to familiarize himself with all the nominated works and did not wish to allow others to make the final decision. But in 1946, after the victory, the Stalin Prizes were given twice: in January for works created in 1943 and 1944 and in June for 1945.

Shostakovich's trio received the Stalin Prize Second Class in January. His Eighth Symphony, also nominated, was rejected. Fadeyev's speech at the meeting of the Stalin Prize Committee, which held preliminary discussions of the nominated works, helps us understand the logic of Stalin's decision making.

A faithful Sancho Panza, Fadeyev, as usual, not only related Stalin's thoughts on the matter, but used his manner of speech to do it. "In such spheres as literature and painting, we can better tell what is formalism, and see it right away. But in the sphere of music we are very meek, and when experts speak, we respectfully stop, not trusting the living voice of the heart, which in this sphere has very great significance." And so, in accordance with the "living voice of the heart," the Eighth Symphony turned out "to make even the elite nervous, elicits the desire to leave, in order to give the nervous system a rest." At the same time, the Piano Trio, on the contrary, "impresses the person who is not very sophisticated in specific questions of music. Simply a person with a living soul, this work captivates him."[37]

But in 1946, the Supreme Listener "with a living soul," while "captivated" by Shostakovich's Piano Trio, gave it only a Second Class prize.★ At that time, Stalin's preference went to another composer—Sergei Prokofiev, who that year was awarded the Stalin Prize First Class three times: for the Fifth Symphony and Eighth Piano Sonata; for the ballet *Cinderella;* and, finally, for the score for Sergei Eisenstein's film *Ivan the Terrible, Part 1.*

Prokofiev spent ten long years getting to this unprecedented success, beginning with his return to Moscow in 1936 from émigré life in Paris. The fate of other émigrés who came back to the Soviet Union varied: Alexei Tolstoi, for example, was raised to the peak of the socialist Olympus and flourished, while Tsvetayeva, whose husband was executed and daughter arrested, was driven to suicide.

At first things were not catastrophic for Prokofiev, but not brilliant, either. Soon after his arrival in Moscow, he began work on the *Cantata for the Twenty-fifth Anniversary of the October Revolution,* commissioned by

---

★The very fact that the Piano Trio got the award—as did Shostakovich's Piano Quintet before that—is astonishing in the context of Stalin's culture: in complexity and sophistication these works compare to the most hermetic works of Mandelstam, Tsvetayeva, or Pasternak.

the government in 1935, for which he planned to use texts from the works of Lenin.

The times were anxious. The discussion of formalism in connection with the *Pravda* article "Muddle Instead of Music" had just taken place, and the political atmosphere was stormy. Thus, Prokofiev's idea was greeted with great distrust: What if there were dangerous underwater rocks? Instead of quotes from Lenin, the cultural authorities suggested Prokofiev use verse by Soviet poets. He went upstairs—via Marshal Tukhachevsky, who was still in favor then, he reached Stalin's close comrade-in-arms Vyacheslav Molotov. After a consultation, apparently with Stalin, Molotov allowed the newborn Soviet citizen to work with the sacred texts.

It seemed like a victory. But here Prokofiev went too far (perhaps in a fit of gratitude) and included in his final version of the cantata two fragments from Stalin's speeches. This was a terrible mistake. Stalin was profoundly suspicious of artistic depictions of himself and always gave a personal yes or no in every case. Understandably, each decision was the result of a mix of political and emotional reasons. Sometimes he banned a work that he personally liked but which he considered politically unfeasible to make public. This was the case in 1939 with Bulgakov's play *Batum,* about the ruler's early years. On the other hand, clearly mediocre works that nevertheless promoted the image of the wise leader were broadly disseminated.

There was a method in Stalin's selections. In keeping with his character and personality, Stalin wanted to control everything possible and impossible. Therefore, films with a depiction of the leader, once approved by Stalin, could be distributed widely, since they were merely exact copies of an approved original. Thus, Sergei Yutkevich's film about the revolution, *Man with a Rifle* (score by Shostakovich), with actor Mikhail Gelovani playing Stalin, came out unhindered in 1938 and subsequently received the Stalin Prize. A play in a theater was a different thing, because the actor re-created his role every night and therefore was outside constant control. Any unpleasant surprise could occur in live theater, as Stalin once encountered.

The director Yuri Lyubimov told me this story, acting out the parts. In January 1938, for the fourteenth anniversary of Lenin's death, the Vakhtangov Theater put on a special performance of the last act of its stage version of *Man with a Rifle* for the government memorial ceremony at the Bolshoi Theater. Here Lenin was played by the leading actor Boris Shchukin and Stalin by the head of the theater, Ruben Simonov. They were supposed to come out on the stage together, greeting Red Army soldiers on their way to storming the Winter Palace.

Simonov, who was supposed to play Stalin in front of the real Stalin, developed a nervous stomach: he couldn't hold down food for several days before the performance. The real panic hit the actor on stage, when he saw Stalin in the box; as Lyubimov told it, Simonov "opened his mouth, but there was no sound."[38] He had to retreat from the stage.

The ruler reacted instantly to the fiasco: Culture officials were purged, and the order given that such incidents not only were "unacceptable in the capital's theaters, but opened the path to liberties in the depiction and interpretation of the image of Comrade Stalin I. V. by theaters of the provinces."[39] But the "guilty" actor was not punished; moreover, the leader bestowed the Stalin Prize on him on three occasions.

What Stalin feared most was appearing ridiculous. And this possibility existed with Prokofiev's cantata, for the work was going to be very experimental. It called for five hundred musicians: two choruses, four instrumental ensembles (besides the symphonic, there were a military brass band, a bayan orchestra, and a special sound-effects ensemble for the battle scenes). The words of Lenin and Stalin were to be sung not by soloists but by the chorus—another potentially silly moment.★ This all worked against Prokofiev. Therefore, when he presented his cantata to the bureaucrats in the summer of 1937, their reaction was predictable. "How could you, Sergei Sergeyevich, take texts that have become the property of the people and set them to such difficult music?"[40]

Prokofiev's work disappeared for almost thirty years. But in 1966, when it was first performed in Moscow (with Kirill Kondrashin conducting), the episodes with Stalin were omitted—they were still too hot. Interestingly, they remain so in post-Soviet times: The performance of the cantata in New York in 1996 (conducted by Valery

---

★As a connoisseur of Russian classical opera, Stalin might have recalled a scene in Glinka's opera *Ruslan and Ludmila,* where an offstage bass chorus sings the words for the head of a decapitated giant that rises in the middle of the stage; the head is usually made of papier-mâché and often produces a comic effect.

Gergiev) threw some American musicologists into paroxysms of righteous wrath, accusing the performers of propagandizing Stalinism.

But back in the dangerous year of 1937, Prokofiev, although not repressed, ended up (undoubtedly on Stalin's orders) on a gray, rather than black, list. A recognized master, a potential trump card in relations with foreigners and the White émigrés, he was nevertheless given a backseat.

Prokofiev's great revolutionary opera, *Semyon Kotko* (in my opinion, his most organic operatic work), was presented by the Composers' Union for the Stalin Prize in 1940 but did not get it. Even his *Alexander Nevsky* cantata, which he put together from his own music for the Stalin Prize–winning Eisenstein film, was overlooked by the ruler. In view of Shostakovich's two Stalin Prizes First Class for the Piano Quintet and Seventh Symphony, this looked like an intentional humiliation—and undoubtedly was perceived as such by the ambitious Prokofiev.

This had an effect on the already complicated relationship between Prokofiev and Shostakovich, whom Stalin thus forced, in quite a Machiavellian manner, to vie for the unofficial position of top Soviet composer. (Stalin pitted people together this way in other areas of culture, too: literature, theater, film.)

At first Shostakovich treated Prokofiev, who was fifteen years older, as an esteemed master. Prokofiev was self-confident and sarcastic. When he came from Paris to the Soviet Union in 1927 as a celebrated guest star, his attitude toward the young Shostakovich was condescending. "He's talented, but not always principled . . . He doesn't have a strong melodic gift."[41] Berthe Malko, widow of the conductor Nikolai Malko, reported Prokofiev's much later private opinions of Shostakovich's work as a whole ("our little Mahler") and his opera *Lady Macbeth* in particular ("The waves of lust keep coming and coming").[42]

According to the composer Dmitri Tolstoi, when Prokofiev and Shostakovich began meeting more frequently, they discovered "a complete incompatibility of character and taste. There was a clash of the unceremonious directness of one with the morbid vulnerability of the other."[43]

In 1934 Alexei Tolstoi invited Prokofiev and Shostakovich to lunch at his house, along with a large group of the Leningrad cultural elite. After coffee, the host asked Prokofiev to play the Scherzo and Gavotte from his "Classical" Symphony. Prokofiev was a magnificent pianist. The guests were thrilled, especially Shostakovich, who exclaimed, "It's wonderful! Just delightful!" Then, Shostakovich played his First Piano Concerto. Now it was Prokofiev's turn to express his opinion. "Well, what can I say?" he began (as Dmitri Tolstoi told it), crossing his legs and draping his arm over the back of his chair. "This work seemed immature to me, rather formless. As for the material, the concerto seems stylistically too motley to me. And not in a very good taste."

After those remarks, Tolstoi said, Shostakovich ran out of the house, crying, "Prokofiev is a bastard and scoundrel! He no longer exists for me!"[44] As Tolstoi has it, for a time Shostakovich would not allow Prokofiev's name to be mentioned in his presence. Eventually, superficial decorum was re-established, but the deep crack in the relationship of the two great composers remained.

Delicate and shy, Shostakovich, who frequently overpraised even mediocre works by colleagues, now felt he could write to his former idol about his *Alexander Nevsky* cantata, a candidate for the Stalin Prize, the following: "On the whole, I did not like this work. I think that it violates some artistic norms. There is too much physically loud, illustrative music. In particular, I felt that many of the movements ended right at the start."[45] All the softening phrases in Shostakovich's letter, along the lines that he would be "immeasurably pleased if this work were to receive the Stalin Prize," were of small consolation—especially since *Nevsky* did not receive the prize and Shostakovich's Piano Quintet (about which Prokofiev spoke rather sourly) did.

The public verbal sparring between the two composers continued in the war years. With the unprecedented success of his rival's Seventh Symphony, Prokofiev had to have a growing sense of being a loser. So when, in 1943, his splendid Seventh Piano Sonata at last won a Stalin Prize Second Class, this gave an opportunity for his closest friend, composer Nikolai Myaskovsky, to proclaim, "I congratulate you with hellish warmth. Most importantly, you've broken through the conspiracy of silence and neglect."[46] But Prokofiev's complete "rehabilitation" in Stalin's eyes is tied to his work on Eisenstein's film *Ivan the Terrible*.

This project was very close to the ruler's heart. Stalin loved the sixteenth-century tsar Ivan IV, who ruled Russia for half a century and who earned the sobriquet "Terrible" (more properly translated "Awesome"): He considered him along with Peter the Great and Nicholas I to be his predecessor in the work of building a great empire. Stalin was particularly attracted to the six or seven years in Ivan's reign when he utilized the *oprichniki,* a kind of Praetorian Guard he had created to fight the boyar nobility that was hostile to him.

Russia historians, beginning with Karamzin, have long argued over the reasons and wisdom of the Oprichnina Terror unleashed by Ivan IV, which destroyed thousands of actual or imagined opponents to his autocracy. The liberals traditionally condemned Ivan the Terrible for his cruelty and arbitrariness, describing him as a maniac and psychopath; more conservative writers justified him as a wise and far-seeing ruler.

In the early years of the Soviet regime, the view of Ivan the Terrible (and all other Russian tsars) was highly negative. But by the start of the 1940s, Stalin gave orders "on the necessity of restoring the true historical image of Ivan IV in Russia history." According to Stalin, "Tsar Ivan was a great and wise ruler," and his *oprichniki,* who just recently had been described as a band of robbers, murderers, and rapists, were characterized by the ruler as a "progressive army."[47] When these new views were brought to the attention of "creative workers," Ivan suddenly became an enormously attractive figure, and they began not only writing new historical research about him, but also novels and tragedies.

One of these engaged authors was Stalin favorite Alexei Tolstoi, who announced in a letter to the ruler that he saw in Ivan "the concentration of all unique features of the Russian character; from him, as from a source, flow streams and broad rivers of Russian literature. What can the Germans offer in the sixteenth century?—the classic bourgeois Martin Luther?"[48]

It was obvious that Ivan had to be embodied in Stalin's favorite medium—film. For that, Stalin saw no more suitable director than Sergei Eisenstein, whose work he followed from his earliest silent movies—*Strike* (1925) and especially *Battleship Potemkin* (1926), the first major international success of young Soviet art.

With that bold revolutionary film about the legendary rebel ship in turbulent 1905, commissioned by the state, Eisenstein won his pass into the elite club of the Western avant-garde, and *Battleship Potemkin* became part of the worldview of several generations of leftist Western film lovers and a constant presence in critics' lists of the best films of all time.

That this success was no accident Eisenstein proved with his next work, *October,* filmed for the tenth anniversary of the October Revolution in 1927 under the direct control of Stalin. Soon afterward, the director and the ruler met, after which Eisenstein became one of the dictator's favored artists.

To some degree, the relations between Stalin and Eisenstein can be considered paradigmatic of the era. For Stalin, Eisenstein was perhaps the most important representative of the new Soviet culture that was supposed to flourish under the wise supervision of the great leader. Unlike Gorky, Alexei Tolstoi, or even Mayakovsky, Eisenstein as a cinema director began not only after the revolution but after Lenin's death, which in the eyes of future cultural historians would have made him a creature of Stalin himself.

Eisenstein worked in the most popularly appealing of media, imbuing it with revolutionary propaganda content and yet receiving recognition both in the Soviet Union and in Western circles that was impressive to Stalin. This made him a constant presence in Stalin's far-reaching cultural plans. In his turn, Eisenstein, as a worker in the film industry, needed the massive support of the regime for his self-expression. He could not write poems or prose for the desk drawer or stack rejected drawings and canvases under his bed. In a situation where only the state could be the sponsor of his films, entering into open conflict with Stalin would have meant creative suicide.

The dilemma was an outgrowth of Eisenstein's complicated relations with his father, who in the filmmaker's recollection was the "household tyrant."[49] Eisenstein's father became the "prototype of all social tyranny," to which he had to submit, pretending to be "model boy Seryozha" but inwardly rebelling against it with all his being. This conflict—recorded in Eisenstein's terribly frank memoirs, bordering on stream-of-consciousness—was at the creative root of some of the most striking scenes in his films. The director's father, former chief architect of Riga (I often passed his pompous buildings in the modern style when I was a child), left with the White Army and died as an émigré in Berlin.

Eisenstein also lost another father and teacher in the director Meyerhold. He called Meyerhold his "spiritual father," adding, "I never, of course, adored or idolized anyone as I did my teacher." In 1946, when

Eisenstein was writing these words, the expression of such emotions was bold: mentioning executed Meyerhold in positive terms was categorically banned, and it seemed that this situation would never change. Eisenstein wrote hopelessly that the arrest and execution of Meyerhold "wiped away forever the traces of our greatest master of theater from the pages of the history of our theater art."[50]

A terrible word, "forever." Eisenstein—not without reason—feared a similar fate for himself. Was that why he took the desperate risk of preserving his executed teacher's archive at his dacha outside Moscow, thereby saving these priceless materials for future generations?

Throughout almost his entire life as a filmmaker, he balanced on the edge of a knife. The first version of *October* had as a positive character Leon Trotsky, who soon became a political exile. Stalin, who never let Eisenstein out of range of his close scrutiny, personally gave him commission upon commission, rewarding him generously, but also cruelly punishing him, supporting but also lambasting, praising but picking on him—in other words, he behaved in a manner comparable to that of the other two fathers (real and spiritual) in Eisenstein's life. And when Eisenstein, paraphrasing Pushkin, wrote that Meyerhold "was an amazing man, the living denial of the idea that genius and villainy could not coexist in a single man,"[51] did he have Stalin in mind as well?

Sending Eisenstein abroad in 1929, first to Europe and then to Hollywood, Stalin's parting words were, "Study sound cinema thoroughly. It is very important for us."[52] But when Eisenstein stayed on longer in America, Stalin immediately suspected him of "desertion" and ties with Enemy Number One of the Soviet Union, Trotsky. These suspicions were fed by numerous denunciations, written about the director not only by Soviets, but by American Soviet sympathizers. In one, Edmund Stevens, a Moscow correspondent for American newspapers, informed the NKVD that Eisenstein, while in the USA, "repeatedly expressed sympathy for Trotsky."[53]

When, in 1939, the writer Isaac Babel was arrested on Stalin's order, this statement, among others, was beaten out of him during interrogations: "Conversations with Eisenstein in 1936–1937—their main point was that Eisenstein, with a tendency to mysticism and trickery, to bare formalism, needed to find content in which these negative qualities would not be weakened, but reinforced instead. Stubbornly, with a loss of time and significant finances, work continued on the flawed *Bezhin Meadow,* where the death of Pioneer Pavlik Morozov took on the character of a religious, mystical action produced with Catholic pomp."[54]

Babel himself had taken part in the filming of *Bezhin Meadow* as one of the screenwriters. The true story of the young activist's death at the hands of his "retrograde" father was interpreted by Eisenstein and Babel as a biblical drama. This was the story of Abraham, who sacrificed his son, Isaac—yet one more version of a crucial theme for the director.

Eisenstein was not permitted to complete the film: Stalin, seeing some of the rushes, was infuriated by its "anti-artistic nature and blatant political failure," as it was formulated in a special resolution of the Politburo of 5 March 1937, banning *Bezhin Meadow.* On Stalin's orders, the emulsion was wiped from the film stock; only a few shots were accidentally saved (from which thirty years later a small photo film was made that lets us see Eisenstein's intentions). Immediately a collection of articles appeared on the mistakes of that unseen film, where Eisenstein was forced to admit "the profound need to overcome completely my worldview errors, the need for a radical perestroika and mastery of Bolshevism."[55]

In May 1937 the Politburo once again discussed the question of Eisenstein; the draft resolution read: "Consider it impossible to use S. Eisenstein as a director in cinema." Once accepted, this resolution would not only have made him persona non grata in his field, but signal his imminent physical destruction.

But Stalin's decision was different. Eisenstein was made an offer he could not refuse: create a film about the thirteenth-century Novgorodian prince Alexander Nevsky, whom the Soviet dictator decided for political reasons to include in the pantheon of "progressive" Russian historical figures. Prince Alexander, canonized by the Russian Orthodox Church, won a battle against the Teutonic Knights and was therefore useful to Stalin, who was preparing for war with Nazi Germany, as an example of a fearless warrior and patriot.

Eisenstein's film about this unlikely new Soviet hero had a clear plot with a love element and a central character "without fear or reproach" and was filmed in the manner of a grand opera. This differed significantly from the director's earlier revolutionary works. The operatic quality of the film was strengthened by the use of the music written for the film by Prokofiev, whom Eisenstein may have found through their mutual friend Meyerhold. (Meyerhold had tried to persuade Prokofiev back in 1925 to write music for *Battleship Potemkin*.)

Eisenstein and Prokofiev became friends, as they were of similar nature: Both were ambitious, businesslike, energetic, rather ironic, and with a marked rational attitude toward creativity. The director thought the composer was wonderful: "In the crystal purity of his imagery, only Stendhal is equal to Prokofiev."[56] Prokofiev, in his turn, complimented Eisenstein as "not only a brilliant director, but a very subtle musician."

This mutual admiration gave us *Alexander Nevsky:* a textbook example of the intertwining of music and image in film. Stalin was very pleased, although after a zigzag in foreign policy leading to the treaty of nonaggression between the USSR and Germany in 1939, the movie was taken out of the theaters; for the same reason, Prokofiev's opera *Semyon Kotko* was considered inappropriate. But during the war years, *Alexander Nevsky,* with its stirring chorus "Rise up, Russian people, for the glorious battle, the fatal battle!" once again was one of the most popular patriotic works of art.

Having proven themselves as a team, Eisenstein and Prokofiev were sent by Stalin to produce *Ivan the Terrible,* which began filming very far from the front, in Kazakhstan, in 1943. Eisenstein planned an enormous epic in three parts and got the ruler's approval for it. Despite the difficult war situation, Stalin (who once said, "A good movie is worth several divisions")[57] spared no money on the production of *Ivan the Terrible,* because he expected a propaganda masterpiece in the spirit of *Alexander Nevsky.*

However, Eisenstein had his own ideas, which were deeply hidden for the time being. The first image of the new film that came to him was Tsar Ivan repenting in the cathedral in front of a fresco of Judgment Day. Originally Eisenstein had planned to end *Alexander Nevsky* with the hero's death, but Stalin objected: "Such a good prince cannot die!"[58] The political agenda was more important than art. And now the director planned to get revenge.

That Eisenstein had Stalin in mind when he thought about Ivan the Terrible is not in dispute. (Some scholars believe that certain of Meyerhold's traits were also reflected in the image of the tsar.) Eisenstein was planning to present a detailed analysis of the tyrant's psychology. Before him, only Pasternak and Mandelstam, in their poetry addressed to

Stalin in the 1930s, tried (in Brodsky's phrase) to "violate the territorial imperative" of the ruler.

Mandelstam's "Ode to Stalin" is a stunning work, in which the poet looked the ruler right in the eyes, perhaps even into his soul, but its scope is limited by its size and genre. This work (like the similar Pasternak poem "The Artist") is accessible to a comparatively small audience capable of unraveling the poet's convoluted imagery. Eisenstein was aiming for a film epic, with an audience in the millions, and he knew who would be the first (and final) censor of his work: its hero.

Eisenstein's daring was staggering. He first shows Tsar Ivan, in Part 1, as a young idealist, leading the state with a firm hand to his goal: unity and might. But are all means acceptable for achieving the end? Eisenstein poses Pushkin's question. Later, he has the tyrant whisper as he clutches his head in horror and sorrow: "By what right do you judge, Tsar Ivan? By what right do you raise the punitive sword?" This is no longer a character out of Pushkin; he belongs to Dostoevsky. In his 1943 letter to writer Yuri Tynyanov (also a great master of historical narrative with hidden allusions), Eisenstein wrote about his interpretation of Tsar Ivan: "One as the only one and one as the lonely one . . ."[59]

The film's central episode is the dance of the *oprichniki* from Part 2, filmed in color, even though the film was in black and white. This scene, accompanied by Prokofiev's forceful music, burst onto the screen like fireworks: red shirts and black caftans, sky-blue ceiling, gold icons. The mad, swirling whirlwind of evil and destruction is unleashed by the tsar, but he sits in the middle of this terrifying sandstorm of hatred, completely alone, the film double of the guilt-ridden Boris Godunov of Pushkin and Mussorgsky. When a friend of Eisenstein's pointed out the resemblance, the director laughed and then crossed himself, saying, "God, it is obvious? What happiness, what happiness!" And he confirmed that he made the film with the Russian notion of guilty conscience in mind: "Violence can be explained, can be legalized, but it cannot be justified. You need redemption if you're human."[60]

When Eisenstein screened the almost completed Part 2 of *Ivan the Terrible* to his colleagues, they were horrified: There were too many open parallels with contemporary events. But as director Mikhail Romm recalled, "No one dared tell him that in Ivan the Terrible there was an acutely perceived hint of Stalin . . . and in the *oprichniki,* of his minions. There was much more that we felt and did not dare say. But from Eisenstein's boldness, the gleam in his eye, in his challenging skeptical smile we sensed that he was acting consciously and that he had decided to go for broke. It was frightening."[61]

The film bureaucrats were afraid to release Part 1 of *Ivan the Terrible* and even more so of proposing it for the Stalin Prize. They referred to Stalin's own rule forbidding the submission of unfinished works for the prize. But the ruler, having seen Part 1, made an exception for Eisenstein. Not only was it released, but it got the Stalin Prize First Class. For Eisenstein and Prokofiev this was the moment of Stalin's highest approval and recognition.

On 2 February 1946 a ball was held at Dom Kino, the Cinema Center, in honor of the prizewinners, and Eisenstein danced the night away with the famous actress Vera Maretskaya. Many noted the demonstrative wildness of the dance, but no one guessed that for Eisenstein this was MacPherson's dance. Part 2 was just completed and about to be delivered to Stalin for viewing, and Eisenstein was almost positive what the reaction would be. The director was taken from the dance floor straight to the hospital with a heart attack.

Eisenstein was quite right that his interpretation of Tsar Ivan as a character out of Dostoevsky would infuriate Stalin. "Ivan the Terrible was a man with will, with character, and Eisenstein made him some kind of weak Hamlet." The evil dance of the *oprichniki,* men so dear to Stalin's heart, also made him incensed. "He depicted the *oprichniki* as if they were scum, degenerates, like the American Ku Klux Klan."[62] Stalin's opinion of Part 2 of *Ivan the Terrible* was, "This is not a film, it's a nightmare! . . . Disgusting thing!"[63] Eisenstein's film was immediately banned "for its nonartistry and anti-historicism."

Eisenstein survived the heart attack. Through the efforts of the actor Nikolai Cherkasov, a Stalin favorite, who played both Nevsky and Ivan, they were even granted an audience at the Kremlin, where Stalin, Zhdanov, and Molotov instructed Eisenstein and Cherkasov on how "to fix" the film.[64]

Stalin began the conversation in irritation, listing yet again his serious objections. Zhdanov was the yes man: "Eisenstein's Ivan the Terrible turned out to be a neurotic." The ruler insisted on telling Eisenstein the film's political message: "Ivan the Terrible was very cruel. You can show how cruel he was, but you must show why he had to be cruel." Molotov also reiterated Stalin's line: The depiction of repressions is acceptable and even necessary, but their higher reason must be explained.

Eisenstein and Cherkasov did not try to argue—that was their agreed-upon tactic. The cunning actor finally eased the situation by asking Stalin for permission to smoke. The tyrant grew more cheerful and said playfully, "There doesn't seem to be a ban. Maybe we should vote on it?" He offered Cherkasov one of his favorite cigarettes, a Gertsegovina-Flor. When the Kremlin chimes rang midnight, the meeting ended on a more tolerant note than the one on which it had begun. In parting, Stalin even asked after Eisenstein's health and said, "With God's help!" The next day Cherkasov read in the newspapers about the decree awarding him the title of People's Artist of the Soviet Union.

Even as he left the Kremlin, Eisenstein knew that he would not redo his work to fit Stalin's instructions (although he could not have guessed that he would be dead in less than a year, at the age of fifty, from another heart attack in February 1948, and that Part 2 would miraculously appear in theaters just as he had made it, but not until 1958). Eisenstein kept putting off the start of new shooting, telling close friends that he could not and would not change the image of Ivan that had formed in his mind. "I do not have the right to distort historical truth or to retreat from my creative credo."[65]

This must have been a position Eisenstein developed during the war years. It is expressed pithily in one of his drawings, dated 1 January 1944, which was exhibited in New York in 2000. In his expressive manner (he was a master draughtsman) Eisenstein depicted a figure similar to Rodin's Thinker, tied hand and foot, but nevertheless expressing challenge and insubordination, with a brief caption: "A Free Man."

This paradoxical sense of inner freedom was shared then with Eisenstein by many Soviet cultural figures, who were bound hand and foot as he was. Secret reports that went to Stalin in 1943–44 were recently declassified.[66] The informers related that Viktor Shklovsky (who seemed to me in the 1970s a man frightened forever) said things like, "And really, what is there to fear? It will never be worse that the situation in which literature is now." The writer Konstantin Fedin, who was perceived by younger generations mostly as a literary bureaucrat (he was head of the Writers' Union of the USSR between 1959 and

1977), sounded like a dissident in the war years. "How can there be talk of realism when the writer is forced to depict the desired rather than the existent? All talk of realism in such a situation is hypocrisy or demagoguery. The sad fate of literary realism under all forms of dictatorship is the same."

Stalin, reading these reports, must have considered all such remarks heresy. But he would have grown even more wary when he heard the Soviet intelligentsia not only complaining about the situation in culture but also hoping for political changes. Zoshchenko spoke about it rather carefully: "Creativity must be free, while here everything is regulated, ordered, under pressure . . . We have to wait it out. Soon after the war, the situation in literature will change."

Kornei Chukovsky sounded more definite. "With the fall of Nazi despotism, the world of democracy will come face to face with Soviet despotism. We will wait." Wait for what? This was spelled out in the reported daydreams of Yakov Golosovker, who would later write the influential *Dostoevsky and Kant*. "Hitler will be vanquished and the Allies will be able, perhaps, to put pressure on us and obtain a minimum of freedom."

Another writer, P. A. Kuzko, dotted the i's. "The people have found themselves leaders besides Stalin—Zhukov, Rokossovsky, and others. These leaders are beating the Germans and after the victory they will demand their place under the sun . . . One of these popular generals will become dictator or demand changes in the way the country is run . . . The soldiers returning from war will see that agriculture cannot be revived under collectivization and they will overthrow the Soviet regime."

These clearly oppositionist opinions, reported by secret agents, were undoubtedly fragments of a larger mosaic for Stalin. It included the appearance of an entire group of "politically dangerous" art works. Besides Eisenstein's film, Stalin was angered and upset by the movies and screenplays of Vsevolod Pudovkin and Alexander Dovzhenko; the poetry of Ilya Selvinsky, Nikolai Aseyev, and Kornei Chukovsky; the plays of Leonid Leonov and Vsevolod Vishnevsky; and the prose of Konstantin Fedin and Mikhail Zoshchenko.

Among musical works, the ruler's disapproval would certainly be elicited by Shostakovich's new symphony, the Ninth. He completed it in August 1945, literally on the eve of the victorious conclusion of

World War II for the USSR and its allies (Germany capitulated on 8 May and Japan on 2 September). The Soviet Union, through extraordinary sacrifice, not only had repelled Hitler's attack, but had established its influence over enormous new territories in Europe and Asia and enjoyed unprecedented authority.

Stalin, without a doubt, attributed this to his wise leadership. He had reason to consider himself a master of the universe. Now he wanted to see this new role and majesty sung in great works worthy of his genius.

Shostakovich was among the people for whom Stalin had great hopes. Two of his symphonies—the Seventh and the Eighth—were among the most successful works of the war years, and both were highly appreciated not only in the Soviet Union but in the West. Everyone was certain that Shostakovich would create a symphonic "war" trilogy, completing it, in honor of the victory, with a particularly significant and solemn opus—probably with a chorus and solo singers. As composer Marian Koval wrote, "Shostakovich's creativity was at that period the center of attention of the Soviet musical community. How could we not expect an inspired symphony about the victory from Shostakovich?"[67]

This expectation was increased by numerological circumstances as well. For it was Beethoven's Ninth, with its famous final "Ode to Joy" with chorus and soloists, that was traditionally considered the pinnacle of the world's symphonic repertoire and the greatest humanistic manifesto in music. It was assumed that Shostakovich, who in those years was compared to Beethoven even in the West (by conductor Serge Koussevitzky, for one), would write something like a "Soviet Ninth."

As Koval described it, "A group of composers and musicologists gathered around the radio at the Composers' Union. With impatience and agitation they awaited the start of the symphony's broadcast." But when the airing of the unexpectedly short (it lasted only twenty-two minutes) Ninth Symphony, which had neither chorus nor solo singers, ended, Koval said, "the listeners parted, feeling very uncomfortable, as if embarrassed by the musical mischief Shostakovich had committed and displayed—committed, alas, not by a youth but a forty-year-old man, and at a time like that!"[68]

Musical mischief? I suspect that would have been the very mildest description to come to Stalin's mind after hearing Shostakovich's Ninth Symphony. The composition did not have a hint of solemnity or anthemlike inspiration, but it had more than enough of irony. In Koval's nasty (and openly denunciatory) observation, "Old man Haydn and a regular American sergeant unsuccessfully made up to look like Charlie Chaplin, with every possible grimace and whimsical gesture galloped through the symphony's first movement." For a time like that, the music was most unsuitable.

From Stalin's point of view, Shostakovich's Ninth Symphony turned out to be an "anti-people" work, because he demonstratively refused to take part in the officially sanctioned "national joy." But in contradicting the official nationalism (as it was understood by Nicholas I), Shostakovich remained true to another, authentic national tradition described by Mikhail Bakhtin: "The people never share completely in the spirit of reigning truth. If the nation is threatened by danger, they do their duty and save the nation, but they never take seriously the patriotic slogans of the class state, their heroism retains its sober mockery of the pathos of the reigning authority and the reigning truth."[69]

In his Ninth, Shostakovich spoke out as the intuitive populist he always was. His symphony expressed the hidden emotions of the "lower classes." The vitality of Shostakovich's "sober mockery," as Bakhtin would have it, in the chaotic postwar years was remembered by the composer Sergei Slonimsky: "And we, adolescents then, instantly felt the actual appropriateness and necessity of that music in those days. Subconsciously we perceived the polemical meaning of the Ninth, its timely mockery of all sorts of hypocrisy, pseudo-monumentality, and bombastic grandiloquence."[70]

Many musical signs and authorial hints allow us to relate the Ninth Symphony to Bulgakov's *Master and Margarita*—more precisely, with the Moscow part of the novel. (Remember, Shostakovich was present at Bulgakov's home readings of chapters from *Master and Margarita* before the war.) But this subtle and skillful music, full of tragedy, lyricism, irony, and grotesquerie, must have seemed at the time not only irresponsible mischief but a direct challenge to Stalin.

Even more importantly, Shostakovich's demonstrative act of creative insubordination, acting in his *yurodivy* role from *Boris Godunov,* was viewed by Stalin now as part of a general growing resistance among the Soviet intelligentsia. What Stalin perceived as a highly dangerous process had begun during the war, when the authorities had to tolerate contacts with the Western allies. The example of the West was giving rise to dreams of democratic abatements in creative circles. Stalin saw a growing opposition to his leadership.

The cultural elite had to be shown its place, firmly and harshly. After watching Part 2 of *Ivan the Terrible,* the enraged Stalin promised, "We didn't have time for this during the war, but now we'll take care of you all properly."[71]

The execution of this threat was not long in coming.

Chapter VI   1948: "Look Over Here,
Look Over There,
the Enemy Is Everywhere!"

One day in August 1946, Anna Akhmatova dropped by the Leningrad Writers' Union. She thought the staff was in the grip of a flu epidemic: the women were blowing their noses and everyone's eyes were red. Many of them recoiled from her. As Akhmatova recalled later, on her way home she ran into Mikhail Zoshchenko. "I saw him running toward me from the other side of the street. He kissed both my hands and asked, 'Well, and what now, Anna Andreyevna? Bear it?' I had heard that he was having problems at home. I replied: 'Bear it, Mishenka, bear it!' And went on . . . I knew nothing then."[1]

What she did not know (or pretended not to know) was what all of literary Leningrad already knew. On 14 August the Organizational Bureau of the Central Committee of the All-Union Communist Party passed a special resolution, published a week later in *Pravda*, where Zoshchenko was denounced as a "scoundrel of literature." He was accused of "unworthy behavior" during the war, expressed in the publication of a "vile" novella. In the same resolution Akhmatova's poetry was dubbed "alien to our people."[2]

The resolution, in the words of Ilya Ehrenburg, "determined the fate of our literature for eight years."[3] Lydia Chukovskaya, a writer who was very close to Akhmatova, maintained with certainty that the resolution's author was Stalin himself, judging by the style: "His most august mustache protruded from every paragraph."[4] This guess by contemporaries has been confirmed now, after the publication of the transcript of the meeting of the Orgburo of 9 August 1946, when Stalin was present.

The supreme meeting went over the "errors" of Akhmatova and Zoshchenko, with Stalin leading the discussion. He shrugged off Akhmatova disdainfully, stating that all she had was an "old name," and concentrated his fury on Zoshchenko. "The whole war passed, all the people shed blood, and he didn't give a single line. He writes nonsense, it's a mockery." Angrily, Stalin concluded, "We did not build the Soviet system for people to be taught trifles."[5]

Bringing Stalin's thoughts to the intelligentsia and the people, with commentary, was entrusted to Andrei Zhdanov, the Politburo member then in charge of ideology. His speeches on the issue, edited into a brochure with a huge printing that year, were widely circulated and became a mantra of Soviet ideology.[6] Its weight was so great that despite its gradually fading direct influence, it was not formally disavowed until late 1988, at the height of the Gorbachev perestroika. Zhdanov's visible presence in the ideological campaigns of the postwar years gave the whole period the name *zhdanovshchina* (just as the peak of the Great Terror was known as *yezhovshchina,* after the people's commissar of internal affairs, Yezhov).

The term *zhdanovshchina* was accepted even in the West. Yet Zhdanov—indisputably a major and evil figure—was no more in charge of Soviet ideology than the mediocre Yezhov was in charge of the purges of the 1930s. They were both puppets in the hands of Stalin, like many others of his numerous "comrades-in-arms." Therefore the term *zhdanovshchina* can only be used conditionally.*

Zoshchenko and Akhmatova wondered to the end of their days why they were targeted by Stalin for attack (neither doubted for a minute that it had been Stalin's decision). Zoshchenko, who had never written a single line about Stalin, thought that the ruler had recognized himself in an unpleasant and boorish character in one of his stories. He also thought (with reason) that Stalin was annoyed by the numerous reprints of Zoshchenko's satirical pieces in the Russian émigré press in the West.

Stalin was never a great admirer of Zoshchenko, and his displeasure with the writer grew with the years. Zoshchenko, with his attention to

---

*It was noted fairly that "following this logic, the period before 1941 should be called *andreyevshchina,* 1941–1945, *shcherbakovshchina,* and after 1948, *malenkovshchina.*"[7]

"low" life, clearly did not fit Stalin's cultural program. Additionally, the author's parodic and angular manner of writing, with its repetitive narrative and limited vocabulary, sometimes amazingly resembled the style of the ruler's articles and speeches. It could not be said aloud, of course. But Stalin's attitude toward Zoshchenko was not mitigated by this circumstance.

With Akhmatova, there was some reason to suppose that Stalin was well-disposed toward her: In 1935, after her appeal to the dictator, her husband and son were instantly released from prison, and in 1940, at a "hint" from Stalin, her first collection of poetry was published since 1923. In 1942, during the war with Hitler, Akhmatova's patriotic poem "Courage" was printed in *Pravda*. But in 1946, when she appeared at a large poetry evening in Moscow and the audience greeted her with a standing ovation, she—like Shostakovich in his time—felt high anxiety rather than pleasure.

But Akhmatova always considered the main cause for Stalin's wrath the visits to her Leningrad apartment in the fall of 1945 of Isaiah Berlin, who worked in the British Embassy in Moscow. Stalin suspected Berlin, as all other foreign diplomats, of espionage. In 1952, Isaiah's uncle, Dr. L. B. Berlin, who worked at the Clinic of Nutrition at the Academy of Medical Sciences, was arrested on the charge of passing secret information to England through his nephew.[8]

Clearly, Isaiah Berlin was constantly under tight surveillance. In that sense, his meetings with Akhmatova were sheer madness, on his part and hers. Stalin was particularly incensed that on his second visit, the thirty-six-year-old Berlin spent the night at fifty-six-year-old Akhmatova's.

The ruler's disposition toward the poet was based in great part on his perception of her as an ascetic hermit. (In Akhmatova's words, Stalin periodically inquired, "Well, and how's our nun doing?") Learning of Berlin's nocturnal visit, Stalin's honorable feelings were insulted, Akhmatova said. "So our nun receives foreign spies!"[9]

Akhmatova, with her acute sense of the symbolic role of the disgraced poet in Russian society, even felt that Stalin miscalculated when he drew attention to her among the liberal part of the Soviet intelligentsia. In those terrible days, she told a friend, "He's getting the reverse result—they feel sorry for me, commiserate, faint from despair, read me, even those who had never read me before. Why did he have to turn me into a martyr? He should have made me a bitch—given me a dacha, a car, showered me with food parcels, and secretly banned my publication! No one would have known, and I would have been hated for my material well-being."[10]

The paradox was that personally Akhmatova and Zoshchenko interested Stalin very little. As usual, his priorities were ideological and political.

The period from 1946 until Stalin's death in 1953 is sometimes considered the most mysterious in Soviet history. The mystery is the result, in part, of an insufficiency or even total lack of written directives on several important issues of domestic and foreign policy of the period. According to the memoirs of Malenkov and Khrushchev, Stalin began relying more and more on oral directives, trying to avoid recording his orders on paper. In addition, many key archives were substantially cleaned up after his death by his political heirs.

This leads us to yet another reason why this period of time seems mysterious to many. Stalin's death abruptly ended a historical era. We may never learn what Stalin's true long-term plans were, for the simple reason that he did not have time to execute them.

And yet, let us try to outline Stalin's main ideological and cultural policies in the postwar years. The main task was obviously to retain unlimited power in his hands and to suppress any real or potential opposition. Stalin, as we know, tried to discipline the creative intelligentsia, which had gotten out of hand during the war. He thought the main reason for this cultural degeneration was the influence of Western ideas that penetrated the Soviet Union in the war years. The dictator decided to show the intelligentsia definitively that "their sense of Soviet patriotism is not adequately developed. They bow without justification before foreign culture . . . this point has to be hammered for many years, for about ten years this theme will have to be hammered."[11]

This long-range program to root out the harmful Western influences was realized in Stalin's favorite manner: in several directions at once, with unexpected blows from different sides (while playing convoluted, intra-Party games with the bureaucracy at the same time).

In May 1945, at a grand war victory reception at the Kremlin, Stalin raised a special toast "to the health of the Russian people, because they are the most outstanding nation of all nations that are part of the

Soviet Union." This was a continuation of Stalin's "patriotic" line, begun at least ten years earlier.

Within the framework of the Stalinist policy, Russophile moods among the leaders of the Party, the army, and culture were tacitly endorsed. But on the other hand, the ruler watched vigilantly to keep Russian nationalist emotions under control. With that aim in mind, Stalin periodically pitted his subordinates, those who had a tendency toward nationalism and those who were more orthodox Marxists, against one another.

None of these bureaucrats was certain which ideological line the leader would approve in any specific case. This turned every cultural dispute into a battle of gladiators.

Stalin planned the intra-Party intrigues several steps ahead. Take, for example, the campaign against Akhmatova and Zoshchenko. It seemed that Zhdanov was given a starring role. But in promoting Zhdanov, Stalin was digging his grave at the same time. It was no accident that the objects of attack were Leningrad authors, even though Stalin had many problems with Moscow writers as well. This way, the blame fell on Zhdanov, who had been the boss of Leningrad for ten years since 1934 (after the murder of Kirov).

This was confirmed by further developments. Less than two years later, Zhdanov lost his post as ideology chief and soon afterward died unexpectedly (officially, of a heart attack); and just a few months after that, Stalin began the so-called Leningrad affair, rounding up most of Zhdanov's friends and cronies in the top echelons of government and Party. If Zhdanov had still been alive, he might have suffered the same fate.

But for the time being Zhdanov was on top and appeared as the central figure in yet another ideological battle of the period: the attack on Soviet composers. This campaign is a classic example of postwar cultural operations carried out under Stalin's direction. Political and ideological goals, intra-Party intrigues, Stalin's personal tastes and prejudices did combine into one filthy knot. The result was a powerful cultural trauma, the consequences of which are still felt today, more than a half-century later, in the musical life of Russia and other countries that were part of the Soviet Union or in the zone of Soviet domination in 1948.

How it began was recounted not long before his death by Dmitri

Shepilov, a curious and mysterious figure. (He died in 1995 on the eve of his ninetieth birthday.) Charming and imposing, Shepilov loved classical music, especially opera (he could sing Tchaikovsky's *Queen of Spades* by heart in its entirety). In the postwar years he was a Party functionary in charge of propaganda. In this period he was clearly a favorite of Stalin, who valued his erudition and hard work.

Shepilov was a flexible apparatchik who could painlessly maneuver depending on ideological changes at the top. As Shepilov recalled, at a Politburo meeting Stalin asked him a question: "Why don't we have Soviet opera? There are all sorts of Italian, German, and good Russian ones, but why aren't there any Soviet ones?" When Shepilov meekly tried to remind him of Ivan Dzerzhinsky's *The Quiet Don* (supported by Stalin in 1936) and Tikhon Khrennikov's *Into the Storm* (in which Lenin made his first appearance in the genre), the ruler waved him away with the words "We must work on this."[12]

The command for a new ideological campaign was given. As usual, a negative example had to be found. It became the opera *The Great Friendship* by thirty-nine-year-old composer Vano Muradeli, one of the leaders of the Organizational Committee of the Composers' Union.

The Great Friendship was going to be produced in 1947 in almost twenty theaters around the country, including the Bolshoi. This politically correct work was devoted to an important political theme: the struggle for Soviet rule in the Northern Caucasus during the Civil War. At that time, Muradeli's opera was considered a sure candidate for the Stalin Prize. But sophisticated Party bureaucrats, sensing which way the wind was blowing, prepared a memorandum, just in case, addressed to Zhdanov and suggesting the ban of *The Great Friendship* and confiscation of the printed score. Why? "The authors show that the leading revolutionary force is not the Russian people but the mountain dwellers (Lezghins, Ossetians)."

Then came complicated bureaucratic zigzags, typical of late Stalinism. The memorandum on banning *The Great Friendship* was temporarily stuck. In the meantime Shepilov, who was apparently assigned the expansion of the field of attack, prepared another memorandum, "On the Failures of Development of Soviet Music." It also noted that Muradeli's opera "has serious political errors." But Shepilov's main complaint was about Shostakovich and Prokofiev, whose recent works (Shostakovich's Eighth and Ninth symphonies and Prokofiev's opera

War and Peace) were "devoid of clear social content and by their nature profoundly subjective." Switching to the language of direct political denunciation, Shepilov wrote that Prokofiev and Shostakovich "consciously use intentionally complex, abstract forms of nontextual music, allowing them to be 'free' of concrete examples of Soviet reality."[13] That was a daring statement: The two Stalin laureates were accused of hidden dissidence.

Such a pronouncement could not appear in an official (albeit internal) document without a nudge from above. Shepilov deftly added Stalin's favorite idea about the need to concentrate on opera. "It is known that opera and other democratic genres always held a leading position in Russian music." Shostakovich and Prokofiev were behaving as outright saboteurs: "After the failure of Lady Macbeth, Shostakovich has stopped working in opera; Prokofiev has written six symphonies, many sonatas, a few unsuccessful songs, and only one opera, War and Peace, if we do not count the clearly unsuccessful work Semyon Kotko."[14]

The scene was now set for the ruler's intervention. On 5 January 1948, Stalin, accompanied by other Politburo members, heard Muradeli's Great Friendship at a closed performance at the Bolshoi Theater, and he savaged it.

It is important to note here that unlike the incident with Lady Macbeth in 1936, Stalin's reaction was no improvisation. He rarely repeated a mistake. He remembered that back then he was forced to make a compromise with Shostakovich. This time he wanted to prepare his blow without haste. He had dealt with literature (Akhmatova and Zoshchenko), film (Eisenstein and other directors), and dramatic theater. Now he turned to music.

Lydia Ginzburg recalled that the sense of the inexorability of the blow made the Soviet intelligentsia feel more doomed than ever. "It came from the repetition (repetition had not been expected), the horror of the familiar and therefore unchanging model. Someone said then, 'It used to be a lottery, now it's a queue.' "[15]

The day after Stalin saw Muradeli's opera, Zhdanov held a special meeting at the Bolshoi. Muradeli and his librettist, the directors of the theater, and the production team that worked on The Great Friendship, as well as Shepilov and a few other leading cultural bureaucrats, were present.

There is a transcript of that meeting; it is fascinating reading, reveal-ing the hidden mechanism of a looming punitive action.[16] Most of those present were blundering in the dark: They knew that Stalin was angry, but they had no idea what exactly had prompted the supreme wrath. As the director of the Bolshoi Theater put it, "We thought that Muradeli's opera was just what was needed."* Stalin's favorite bass, Maxim Mikhailov, once a deacon, blathered total nonsense at the meet-ing. "This is a great event for us, like Easter for believers. Yesterday we went to the theater as if to the radiant Easter Eve service, with holy trembling."

The transcript makes clear that only three people knew what they were talking about—Zhdanov, Shepilov, and Muradeli. This is surpris-ing at first—but only at first.

One would expect the composer of a work that outraged Stalin so much that he left the theater before it ended to be in a state of shock, confusion, and prostration the next day. Nothing of the sort. Muradeli seems to be following a script, eloquently and almost triumphantly: "I would like this criticism to be heard by all our composers and musicol-ogists, because this criticism makes a historic turn in the direction of development of Soviet music . . . We must help all Soviet composers re-examine their creative views."

A close reading of the transcript strengthens the impression that Stalin's allegedly spontaneous negative reaction to *The Great Friendship* was no surprise to the composer and that he had been warned how the charade would be played out. For a person caught unawares by the tyrant's anger, Muradeli said amazing things, addressing Zhdanov him-self, at the meeting at the Bolshoi: "I considered it wrong to develop the line of Dzerzhinsky, whom we know from the operas *The Quiet Don* and *Virgin Soil Upturned*. This is not the line in Soviet musical art that we need—it is simplicity that never rises to profundity." That is, looking straight into the eyes of Comrade Stalin's ideological deputy, the com-poser who had gotten into such trouble the night before has the gall to contradict well-known statements of Comrade Stalin. For back in 1936, through the newspaper *Pravda*, the ruler spoke of the "significant ideological-political value" of the production of *The Quiet Don*.

---

*In a conversation with me many years later, conductor Kirill Kondrashin, who was at the first performance of this opera at the Bolshoi, said that *The Great Friendship* was "rather professional music."[17]

Muradeli was not a great composer, but neither was he a fool or a suicide.★ That meant that in talking about the "historic turn" and criticizing *The Quiet Don,* Muradeli was not sharing his spontaneous thoughts. His speech was not improvised. Everything points to his being instructed before the meeting. Only Comrade Stalin himself could permit an unpunished disavowal of the precepts of Comrade Stalin.

The ruler had set into motion a favorite tactic: He used Muradeli as a decoy and provocateur. This is confirmed by the step the composer took at this meeting. Unexpectedly for all (besides Zhdanov and Shepilov, of course), Muradeli named the person most responsible for the catastrophe that befell his opera *The Great Friendship:* It was Shostakovich—or, more precisely, Shostakovich's opera *Lady Macbeth of Mtsensk.* "I did not like that opera; there was no human singing, no human feelings in it. But everyone around me praised the opera, said it was a work of genius, and called me backward."

The Party, he continued, gives the ideological and political direction to art; it instructs what music must be created for the people. But composers are kept from executing these instructions by villainous critics and other rotten professionals, who, "if the composer wants to use the heritage of the classics, or folk music, they say to him: It's nice, but it's traditionalism, it's not contemporary. Our young people are being brought up in that incorrect spirit. Young people are afraid of being considered old-fashioned or behind the times."

"So, your soul is stifled? You can't write what you want?" Zhdanov interrupted here, completing the nightmarish picture of modernists and Westernizers, headed by Shostakovich, sabotaging the Party's instructions. This was beginning to resemble a real conspiracy (Stalin's favorite idea). And the conspirators had to be treated harshly, according to Zhdanov: "The turn has to be made so that all the old and obsolete is ruthlessly cast off. That is exactly how the turn was made in literature, film, and theater."

In music the real and powerful start for this Stalinist "turn" was made at the urgently convened meeting at the Central Committee of the Party, held on 10, 12, and 13 January 1948. Over seventy leading Soviet musicians were brought there, including Myaskovsky, Prokofiev,

★In the Khrushchev years, Muradeli became head of the Moscow Composers' Union. He died in 1970 while holding the rather important post of secretary of the board of the Composers' Union of the USSR.

Shostakovich, Khachaturian, Kabalevsky, Shaporin, and Shebalin. The thirty-four-year-old Tikhon Khrennikov was also invited. The composer of *Into the Storm*, Khrennikov had already received the Stalin Prize twice, and the ruler had long-range plans for him.

Zhdanov opened the conference.[18] He had been instructed by Stalin beforehand, as Zhdanov's daybook for early 1948, where Stalin's orders are written down, makes clear. The most eloquent one is "Remind them of *Lady Macbeth of Mtsensk.*"[19] What was meant, of course, was "Muddle Instead of Music." Stalin kept the memory alive of his unappreciated child for twelve years, hurt that it did not receive an enthusiastic reception. Gorky harshly lectured Stalin over that article, and the intelligentsia, reports told Stalin, mocked it in private conversations. Now Stalin was going to get revenge for that humiliation.

There was no need to explain that to Zhdanov twice. Beginning with a review of the shortcomings of Muradeli's opera ("a muddled collection of screeching sound combinations"—is the style familiar?) and expressing dissatisfaction that when "in the course of the action the lezghinka is danced, the melody does not resemble any known popular lezghinka melodies" (and who was the Soviet expert on the lezghinka, a Georgian folk dance?), Zhdanov moved on to the main point: "The shortcomings of the opera by Comrade Muradeli are very similar to the shortcomings that distinguished the opera by Comrade Shostakovich, *Lady Macbeth of Mtsensk.*"

That there wasn't the slightest resemblance between the two operas was obvious to all the musicians present and probably to Zhdanov, too (he, they say, was a tolerable pianist). But insisting on "the amazing resemblance of those errors" allowed him to drag out "Muddle Instead of Music," from which Zhdanov read enormous chunks to the audience.

And he gave them a more obvious hint about its authorship. "The article appeared on orders of the Central Committee and expressed the CC's opinion about Shostakovich's opera." Any lingering doubts about the article's provenance had to vanish. The article took on inviolable status and once again became a manual for action. For, as Zhdanov stressed, "now it is clear that the direction in music condemned back then still lives, and not only lives, but sets the tone for Soviet music."

Interestingly, the other "authority" Zhdanov felt obliged to quote was none other than the guilty Muradeli. Repeating Muradeli's revelations at the meeting at the Bolshoi, Zhdanov admitted that "his speech was one of the impetuses for calling this conference."⋆ Now Zhdanov was provocatively suggesting that the gathered musicians start a discussion on the points Muradeli made: Maybe he was wrong and was painting too dark a picture? And maybe the Central Committee (that is, Stalin) was wrong in "defending the realistic direction and classical legacy in music"? Let those present speak openly on that.

Clearly this was an invitation into a death trap. Did Stalin think that the musicians brought to the Central Committee—experienced people who lived through the Great Terror—would rush into this trap and seriously start debating his instructions? Or was he hoping to see the opposite: fear-maddened celebrities ratting on one another? In any case, Stalin was to be disappointed: Neither happened. No one, naturally, put his head in the noose by arguing openly with Zhdanov. But there was no fight among spiders in a jar, either.

Myaskovsky and Prokofiev said nothing. Shostakovich made do with vague generalities (from a crib sheet prepared for him by his friend the musicologist Lev Lebedinsky). Shebalin, who was director of the Moscow Conservatory then, instead of berating his colleagues, complained that the conservatory roof was leaking and needed repairs. This caused Zhdanov to say in irritation that "there is a hole not only in the conservatory roof, which is easily fixed—a much greater hole has formed in the foundation of Soviet music."

Khrennikov spoke out aggressively, but at the time he had no special authority in the composers' milieu. The tone Zhdanov wanted was also taken up by composer Vladimir Zakharov, who explained that from the point of view of the people, Shostakovich's Eighth Symphony was not a piece of music at all but something that had nothing to do with art. Zakharov tried to hit Shostakovich below the belt, announcing that when workers in besieged Leningrad were starving to death at their lathes during the war, they asked that records with folk songs be played for them and not Shostakovich's Seventh Symphony. But Zakharov was a songwriter, known for his Neanderthal views, so his speech came as no surprise.

To save the situation, Zhdanov had to appear again on the third and

---

⋆Tellingly, this phrase, which revealed too much of the secret mechanism of the intrigue, was crossed out by Zhdanov when he prepared his speech for publication.

concluding day. He expressed extreme dissatisfaction about the attempts of previous speakers "to soften the sharpness of the situation." Demonstrating his knowledge of musical terminology, Zhdanov said that "the game is often played with a mute," while "we have a very acute even though seemingly covert battle between two directions in Soviet music." According to Stalin via Zhdanov, one direction was realistic, developing in a profound organic connection with the people; the other was formalist, based on the refusal to serve the people "so as to serve the profoundly individualistic feelings of a small group of select aesthetes."

Thus, Stalin's old ideas circa 1936 were forcefully reiterated. Only now, Zhdanov was Stalin's spokesman. He announced that the representatives of the formalist direction wrote music that was "crude, graceless, and vulgar," resembling, in Zhdanov's elegant definition, "either a dentist's drill or a musical gas chamber."

We need to pause longer on the thesis of "gracefulness" as the new important trait of socialist music. It was unexpected, to say the least, for the gathered musicians. The very word "graceful" had not been used as a serious aesthetic criterion in Russian cultural discourse for many decades now, and it had to reek of mothballs for the audience. Nevertheless, Zhdanov got hung up on the word, which suggests that it came from Stalin's oral instructions.

Zhdanov, sensing the growing disbelief in the room, was forced to give euphemistically the provenance of the latest aesthetic term. "You might be surprised that the Central Committee of Bolsheviks is demanding beauty and gracefulness from music. What a new misfortune! No, this was not a mistake, we declare that we are for beautiful, graceful music."

Another sure quote from Stalin's oral instructions (as substantiated by Zhdanov's notebook) is the demand to condemn the formalist direction as a "Herostratian attempt to destroy the temple of art created by the great masters of musical culture." Zhdanov's explanation of a ticklish issue had to have come from Stalin: how it happened that these Herostratuses had been given Stalin Prizes. "The formalistic direction in music was condemned by the Party twelve years ago. In the last period, the government bestowed the Stalin Prize on many of you, including those who sinned in formalism. That you were rewarded was a great advance. We did not consider then that your works were free of shortcomings, but we tolerated it, expecting our composers to find the strength to choose the right road. But now anyone can see that the Party's intervention is necessary."

The need for this rather "commercial" argument ("We paid you and you stuck us with rotten goods") was brought on, in part, by the presence of Prokofiev in the audience, dressed with a smattering of the *yurodivy* style that was not his wont. He wore enormous felt boots, and on his ordinary jacket dangled five Stalin laureate medals in artistic disarray. One of the legends arising from this conference involves Prokofiev, and Western scholars were first rather skeptical about it: Allegedly he behaved provocatively during Zhdanov's speech, openly paying no attention to him. Now we know that something like that did happen, as is often the case with legends. It is confirmed by the recollections of several eyewitnesses, particularly Khrennikov.[20] During Zhdanov's speech, Prokofiev started a loud conversation with the man on his left.★

Prokofiev was consciously creating a scandal. In front of him sat Matvei Shkiryatov, one of Stalin's cruelest henchmen, and at that time one of the bosses at the Commission of Party Control. It was known that when Shkiryatov carried out a purge in the Party, he personally interrogated especially important prisoners in "his" prison. So this Shkiryatov, the mention of whose name made people blanch, tried several times to get Prokofiev to behave himself. The composer first pointedly ignored him and then made a scene, shouting, "I am a Stalin Prize laureate, and who are you to tell me how to behave?" (The medals on his jacket came in handy here.) The row took on so much heat that Zhdanov had to stop his speech for a while.

Another story about the conference made the rounds: Allegedly Zhdanov, wanting to show Shostakovich and Prokofiev what real music sounded like, sat down at the piano and played something. Ehrenburg wrote about it in his memoirs, published in 1965. The writer got a furious letter from Shostakovich: "Zhdanov did not sit down at the piano, but lectured composers by method of his eloquence . . . The stories about Zhdanov playing the piano were spread by toadies. I myself had occasion to witness 'the creation of a legend':

★Ilya Ehrenburg, quoting Prokofiev, said that the composer had "dozed off" and upon awakening started asking loudly who the speaker was.

'What an amazing man Andrei Alexandrovich is! In berating the formalists, showing them for what they really were, he sat down at the piano and played melodic and graceful music and then for comparison played something out of Prokofiev or Shostakovich. Those two simply didn't know where to hide from the shame and humiliation. Ah, what a man!' "[21]★

With piano or without, one of the main reasons for convening the conference at the Central Committee, we now can see, was to compile a definitive list of musicians subject to punishment. Naturally, Stalin could have drawn up such a list himself, which he ended up doing. But he apparently preferred it to come about with musicians themselves identifying the "guilty." In this way, Stalin wanted to avoid repeating the mistakes of the antiformalist campaign of 1936.

That is why Zhdanov, having listed the leading "formalists," openly called on the audience to denounce others: "Whom would you like to add to these comrades?" Nothing came of this "democratic witch hunt." A sole anonymous voice called out: "Shaporin!" But no one else added his voice to that of the decoy.

Shostakovich called the debates after Zhdanov's speech "shameful and vile" immediately afterward in conversation with a friend. Shepilov, who watched Shostakovich closely, saw that the composer was "very traumatized by the course of events and was walking around with a bloodied soul."[23] Shepilov left a telling description of Shostakovich's behavior at this Party trial (which he himself helped organize): "Pale, brows tightly compressed, and a wise, piercing gaze from his gray, sharp, and excited eyes, hidden by the thick glass of his spectacles. Periodically convulsions coursed across his face and body, as if he touched an electric wire. He seemed to be playing a part, but that was only the visible facade."[24]

The perceptive Stalinist bureaucrat had guessed correctly: Behind Shostakovich's tight facade there was incredible creative will and stubbornness. He had responded to the attack in 1936 by sitting down to finish his grandiose Fourth Symphony. Back then the composer had formulated his life credo: "If they chop off both my hands, I'll still

---

★Khrennikov, who considered Zhdanov an outstanding figure, in this case supported Shostakovich: Zhdanov could not have sat down at the piano for the simple reason that the conference room of the Central Committee, where the meeting took place, "never had musical instruments."[22]

write music with the pen between my teeth."[25] In 1948, music writing became again his salvation and his reply.

For Shostakovich, that was a typical reaction to pressure. Khacha-turian told me more than once how he envied his colleague's extraor-dinary ability to respond to persecution by composing new, inspired music. "That is why he is a genius and we are merely talents," Khacha-turian concluded.[26]

Returning home after Zhdanov's attack, Shostakovich finished a new powerful work: the First Violin Concerto. He had begun writing it down in the last months of 1947 and had started it, probably, even earlier (in 1942 his friend Shebalin's violin concerto had made a strong impression on him).

For Shostakovich, the violin was a speaking instrument, and he endowed its song with oratorical eloquence. Beginning with the Fourth Symphony, the great majority of his major opuses are more or less "autobiographical." The violin concerto is also clearly autobio-graphical, and the voice of the violin makes the narrative subtext of the composition particularly poignant.

Despite the fact that Shostakovich's Ninth Symphony of 1945 undoubtedly disappointed and insulted Stalin, who did not get the apotheosis he was expecting, the ruler did not show his displeasure right away, waiting instead for a convenient time. In May 1946 he even, in his customary manner, rewarded Shostakovich.

On Stalin's orders, the composer was called by Lavrenty Beria—in those days the dictator's right hand—and informed that he was being given a large apartment in Moscow, a winterized dacha, an automobile, and sixty thousand rubles. Surprised by the unexpectedly generous gifts, Shostakovich started to beg off, especially from the money, saying he could get by and that he was used to earning his own. Beria (a Georgian like Stalin) saw a violation of Caucasian etiquette in the refusal, and grew angry. "But it's a gift! If Stalin gave me his old suit, I wouldn't refuse it, I would thank him!"[27]

In that situation, saying no became dangerous, and Shostakovich was forced to accept the royal largesse, even though he always was wary of such double-edged gifts. Beria practically dictated a thank-you note for Shostakovich to write: "Lavrenty Pavlovich told me that you are very sympathetic to my situation. Everything is going marvelously. In June I will receive a six-room apartment. In July a dacha in Kratovo, and besides that I will get 60,000 rubles for furnishing them. All this has made me extremely happy."[28]

Of the letters of gratitude known to us from other Soviet cultural figures, Shostakovich's letter to Stalin is the most strikingly businesslike: It resembles a receipt.* Shostakovich liked to say that he followed the rule "Don't be particularly happy about anything, don't be particularly saddened by anything." His psyche operated like supersensitive radar; life in the circle of Stalin's attention made the composer particularly nervous, expecting a blow at any moment.

As a friend of Shostakovich's recalled, the composer grew pensive on New Year's Eve 1947 and said, "I'm afraid of this leap year, I feel a storm brewing."[29] His intuition was right this time, too.

This is why there is nothing surprising in the coincidence of the emotional subtext of the First Violin Concerto with the dramatic atmosphere of the early months of 1948. Shostakovich's opus was created under the clear influence of Alban Berg's Violin Concerto. The Viennese composer layered his works with musical allusions and quotations. For Shostakovich (he worshiped Berg, who reacted kindly to the young Leningrader's First Symphony), the great Austrian's method was just what he needed.

And so in the concerto's second movement we catch the clear proto-image of the most important of all of Shostakovich's musical symbols: his signature D-Es-C-H (the German letters for the pitches D–E-flat–C–B, which create the composer's initials in German: D. Sch.). And once again, as in the Piano Trio, a Jewish dance bursts in on almost hysterical tones (a "bloody *freilekhs,*" as a Russian writer put it).[30]

The third movement Shostakovich wrote down during the days of the Zhdanov conference: in form it is a passacaglia, a slow dance beloved by Bach and Handel for its gloomy solemnity. Shostakovich uses that ancient construction to create something like an orator's tribune. From it he gives a fiery speech—but to whom? Could it be to Stalin himself?

There are musical clues to suggest that: the movement begins with the "Stalin" tune from the Seventh Symphony, and the French horns

---

*Stalin's dacha made Shostakovich uncomfortable; after the ruler's death, the composer bought another dacha as soon as he could and returned this one to the state. Because this was such an unusual step, it created suspicion in the authorities: Why would someone who had every right to sell a dacha just give it back for free? "There is something behind it."

intone a rhythmic figure from the famous "fate motif" from Beethoven's Fifth Symphony. "So pocht das Schicksal an die Pforte" (Thus fate knocks at the door), said Beethoven of this theme, and Shostakovich—as he said, completely consciously—joined that reminiscence with a reminder of Stalin: a more than eloquent clue.

The stunning cadenza—the violin monologue—makes us recall a line from Akhmatova's *Requiem,* "the exhausted mouth with which a nation of a hundred million screams," and then dissolves in the feverish carnival dance of the finale.

Shostakovich interprets the carnival in the First Violin Concerto in the spirit of Mikhail Bakhtin's idea of the "national culture of laughter." Bakhtin spoke of the "carnival worldview," which frees one of fear. Shostakovich frequently associated freedom from fear in his works with the condemned man's dance. For him this was an autobiographical emotion of such power that he returned to it in his music over and over. Such is the whirlwind burlesque finale of the First Violin Concerto, which demands superhuman efforts from the performer. The concerto is one of the pinnacles of the violin repertoire, but adequate interpretations are rare—if for no other reason than its incredible physical demands.

The ties between Shostakovich's music and Bakhtin's philosophy of culture are clear; they are gradually becoming the object of more attentive scholarship.* Bakhtin's thoughts on "carnival forms" in culture, which "have become powerful means of artistic mastery of life, have become a special language, the words and forms of which possess the exclusive power of symbolic generalization,"[31] apply to many of Shostakovich's works. Bakhtin found the presence of the Russian carnival tradition not only in his beloved Dostoevsky, but in Gogol, and even in Pushkin (whose *Boris Godunov* Bakhtin considered one of the most "carnivalized" works).

The images of Shostakovich the *yurodivy* and Shostakovich the *skomorokh* fit into Bakhtin's paradigm. The *skomorokhi* were the central figures of the Russian carnival culture. They were medieval wandering minstrels (although some settled at the courts of nobles)—mummers, musicians, jesters. Their descendants lived into the early twentieth cen-

---

*Ivan Sollertinsky, the composer's closest friend, was part of Bakhtin's circle. There is no doubt that Sollertinsky, a proselytizer by nature, discussed Bakhtin's ideas with Shostakovich.

tury, and young Mitya Shostakovich could have seen on Mars Field in Petrograd a performance by one of these sideshow entertainers in the genre of the *rayok*.

In the strict sense of the word, a *rayok* is what is called a peep show in the West: a box into which people look through a special magnifying glass at shifting pictures, often of an improper nature. In Russia the box was called *rayok* [from *rai,* or paradise] because one of the most popular picture series was the story of the fall of Adam and Eve. The commentary or patter accompanying the risqué pictures for the audience, with up-to-date and sometimes dangerously political jokes, came from the fairground *rayoshnik skomorokh*. This fairground genre fascinated the young Shostakovich; in 1925 he wrote to a friend, "Lately I've been studying the history of the *rayoshnik,* and therefore I sometimes speak in *rayoshnik* slang."[32]

Did Shostakovich recall this infatuation of his youth in 1948 when, under the impression of the Zhdanov conference and the pogrom that followed, he came up with one of the most caustic satires in the history of music—his *Antiformalist Rayok*? Probably. But for him, a man who always considered the cultural tradition and who was sensitive to intertexts, even more important was the fact that the Russian composer he most esteemed, Mussorgsky, had written a work called *Rayok* in 1870.

Mussorgsky's *Rayok* is a brilliant musical lampoon in which the composer sarcastically mocked (just like a fairground *skomorokh*) his enemies—musicologists, critics, and composers. Shostakovich borrowed from Mussorgsky some devices—the free form, the sassy fairground-like text (his friend Lev Lebedinsky helped him compose it), and the use of parodic quotations. But Shostakovich chose much more important figures as the object of his satire: Stalin and Zhdanov.

In *Antiformalist Rayok,* Shostakovich presented the Soviet leaders under rather transparent names: Comrades Edinitsyn (One) and Dvoikin (Two), speaking at a meeting at the Palace of Culture with a condemnation of formalist music by anti-people composers.* Edinitsyn sings his text to the music of the Georgian folk song "Suliko." In the Soviet Union, every man, woman, and child knew that "Suliko" was Stalin's favorite song, so that clue was easy. Dvoikin, singing a

---

*There is also a Comrade Troikin (Three), who can be seen as a caricature of Dmitri Shepilov, one of the organizers of the Zhdanov conference.

waltz, demanded from music, like Zhdanov, that it be "beautiful and graceful" and compared the works of formalists to dentists' drills and musical gas chambers. A master of ceremonies represents a sycophantic audience, delightedly thanking the beloved and great Edinitsyn for his paternal concern and Dvoikin for his truly scholarly speech: "What analysis! What depth!" And when, to the music of rollicking cancan from Robert Planquette's operetta *Les Cloches de Corneville,* Stalin calls on them to fight bourgeois ideas and orders those infected by them into hard labor camps, the chorus picks up on those orders with cheerful readiness: "Look over here, look over there, the enemy is everywhere!"

The trick lies in the mocking brilliance with which Shostakovich wrote the piece. At first, *Rayok* resembles a high-school skit, but it is really a little gem. The vocal lines are supple and bright, the rhythm bouncy, the orchestration biting, and it all rolls along in a snappy manner toward the vicious apotheosis of the finale. There are always calls for an encore when it is performed in concerts. I attended several performances of *Antiformalist Rayok* in the West. Even though it was sung in Russian and the audience did not understand most of the verbal and musical allusions and hints sprinkled throughout the text, the hall resounded with laughter.

Andrei Sinyavsky, sent to a hard labor camp in 1965 for "anti-Soviet" writing, recalled that one of the inmates said to him enviously, "For you writers, even dying is useful."[33] He meant that even a negative experience can be used and transformed in literature.

This is what Shostakovich did. Covered in official shit from head to toe, he managed to transform it into the gold of music—the First Violin Concerto and *Antiformalist Rayok*. How different these works are—a tragic canvas in one, fairground jesting in the other. But both works are written with force, drive, and exuberance.

They are united by yet another trait of Shostakovich's. Even though both works were created for the desk drawer, without hope of being performed any time soon—the first because of its tragic content and the other because it was an outrageously daring anti-Stalin satire—he cared about the future audience. He made sure the music would be exciting and entertaining.

This endearing quality in Shostakovich, his constant attention to audience perception, the desire to hold its interest to the end of the work, often irritates commentators. They are unhappy: If the finale of the Fifth Symphony is tragic, then why is it written so that the audience is delighted after the performance? The cancan finale of *Antiformalist Rayok* is so exciting for the same reason: Shostakovich, like a real *skomorokh* or *yurodivy*, is trying to overcome the forces of evil through a show-stopping creative act. Tragic music does not have to be dragging or boring. The same holds for satire: It can be not only caustic and edifying, it can be entertaining as well.

A comparison of the fate of Mussorgsky's and Shostakovich's *Rayok*s is telling. Mussorgsky, a brilliant pianist, demonstrated his satire right and left to the great pleasure of his listeners, and, as critic Vladimir Stasov recalled, "even those mocked laughed so hard they had tears in their eyes." Published a little more than a year later, Mussorgsky's piece quickly sold out. But in time its performances grew rare: in order to get total pleasure from Mussorgsky's *Rayok,* one has to know the history of Russian music well.

Shostakovich, unlike Mussorgsky, wrote his *Rayok* in total secrecy; that is understandable, in view of the objects of his satire and the situation in the Soviet Union. For this reason there are many mysteries about the creation of *Antiformalist Rayok* that are unlikely to be resolved completely. This is a typical work of the catacomb culture, crafted underground, secretly, in spurts, under threat of severe punishment. The world first learned of its existence from my preface to Shostakovich's memoirs, published in the West in 1979, after his death, and the premiere of *Antiformalist Rayok* did not take place until 1989. But since then, it continues to be regularly performed and recorded, and it might turn out to be one of the enduring musical works in the satirical mode. As Pasternak wrote, "Across here moved the riddle's mysterious fingernail." Works marked in this way are often treated well by history.

In *Rayok,* Shostakovich described in a concise and caustic way the cultural crackdown organized by Stalin in 1948. After the Zhdanov conference, *Pravda* carried on 11 February a resolution of the Party's Central Committee "On the Opera *The Great Friendship* by V. Muradeli." It was a classic Stalinist document, summing up the views and instructions of the ruler on the current cultural situation. Insiders found nothing new in it, with the exception of the final list of composers considered part of the "formalist, anti-people direction." Listed were Dmitri Shostakovich, Sergei Prokofiev, Aram Khachaturian, Vissarion Shebalin, Gavriil Popov, and Nikolai Myaskovsky—in that order, having nothing to do with the alphabet.★

In the Soviet period the ritual significance of such lists was enormous: in the absence of any other information, they gave the clearest indication of someone's place in the social hierarchy. We know that Stalin paid a great deal of attention to such things. Now declassified secret preliminary memoranda show that the list of "formalists" was being tweaked until the very last minute: The first position was held by Prokofiev, then by Myaskovsky. Shostakovich's name at the top of the final list reflected Stalin's opinion about the composer's degree of responsibility, in the words of the resolution, in "disseminating among figures of Soviet musical culture tendencies alien to it, leading to a dead end in the development of music, to the liquidation of musical art."[34]

Shostakovich learned all this, as was recently made known, from the horse's mouth. On 11 February he had a call from Stalin's secretary, Alexander Poskrebyshev, and was summoned to the Kremlin. Stalin ordered Poskrebyshev to read the text of the Party resolution personally to Shostakovich.[35] This action on Stalin's part had dual significance. On one hand, it signaled the dictator's special attention. On the other, it smacked of a sadistic spanking where "they beat you and don't let you cry." Stalin probably wanted to hear from Poskrebyshev how Shostakovich took his spanking.

Shostakovich naturally took it as a terrible humiliation. He later recalled that while Poskrebyshev read him the resolution, he could not look him in the face and instead studied the tips of Stalin's secretary's yellow leather shoes.[†]

★On the night of 10 February Sergei Eisenstein died of a heart attack at his desk. He was under pressure to redo Part 2 of his film on Ivan the Terrible with music by Prokofiev. Was there a connection? Had Eisenstein learned that the article was going to appear in *Pravda* ahead of time? We can only guess.

†This unpleasant story has a rather comic epilogue. In 1956, after Stalin's death, Shostakovich went to a VIP pharmacy to pick up medicine for his sister. Standing in line, he heard a familiar voice: "Dmitri Dmitrievich, have you forgotten old friends?" The man's face was not familiar, but he instantly recognized his yellow shoes: Yes, still wearing the same footwear (foreign leather must be very sturdy) was Poskrebyshev. Poskrebyshev told Shostakovich that he too had been a victim of the cult of personality: Not long before Stalin's death he was fired and almost arrested, and now he was in well-deserved retirement.

"Orgmeasures" followed the promulgation of the resolution instantly. Shostakovich was fired from the Moscow and Leningrad conservatories. Some of his major works (like the music of other "formalists") disappeared from the repertoire. Stalin decided to force the long-delayed formation (sixteen years, since 1932) of the Composers' Union: the First Congress took place in April and was opened by its general secretary (a title proposed by Stalin)—Tikhon Khrennikov.

Young Khrennikov executed his assignment—bringing about a cultural "perestroika"—with enthusiasm, shouting at the frightened audience, "Enough symphony diaries, pseudo-philosophizing symphonies, hiding boring intellectual navel-gazing beneath a veneer of profound thought! . . . Our audiences are tired of modernist cacophony! It's time to turn our music back on the path of clarity and realistic simplicity! . . . We will not permit further destruction of the marvelous temple of music created by the composer geniuses of the past!"[36]

That the addressees of this speech were forced to repent publicly did not surprise anyone anymore. Muradeli, however, played the clown. He began with a loud statement: "Comrades! I am not quite in agreement with the resolution of the Central Committee of our Party." Here, as Dmitri Tolstoi, a delegate to the congress, recalled, a tense silence fell over the room. But then Muradeli continued. "The Party did not hit me hard enough! I should have been punished more severely and harder!" Everyone sighed in relief.[37] Things were back in place.

Myaskovsky, one of the composers accused of "boring intellectual navel-gazing," cautiously noted in his diary, "An interesting resolution of the CC ACP(b) in connection with Muradeli's opera. Positively true, negatively inaccurate. I'm afraid that it will cause more harm than good for Soviet music. All the mediocrities were thrilled and activated."[38]★

Alas, Myaskovsky's diary entry merely hinted at the scope of cultural damage. A wave of public gatherings, organized from above and widely reported in the mass media, rolled across the country. In accordance with the prepared rituals, they hailed the "historic resolution" and viciously attacked the "anti-people formalists."

★Even twenty-five years later, in 1973, the last two lines seemed too explosive to Soviet censors, who cut them out in the published version.

It turned into a powerful anti-intellectual campaign. Carefully vetted "representatives of the people" were given the opportunity to lecture and teach common sense to world-acclaimed composers. Typical was a letter published in a newspaper (and servilely reprinted by the magazine *Sovetskaya muzyka*) from Comrade A. Zagoruiko, foreman of a foundry in a machine-building plant in the town of Nalchik. "The resolution is correct, it will bring music closer to the people . . . Some Soviet composers, for whom the people created all the conditions they need to work, write music that you can't even listen to. No rhyme or reason—just a wild whirlwind of sounds."[39]

It looked as if the entire country, from Comrade Stalin to Comrade Zagoruiko, spoke in one voice, and no independent opinion was allowed in the witch-hunt atmosphere. All the more amazing to read the diary entries made then by Mark Shcheglov, a twenty-two-year-old Moscow student and Komsomol member. "The impression from the newspaper reviews is this: For many years people put up with, listened, and performed the music of Shostakovich, Prokofiev, Khachaturian, and others and did not condemn it (at least not so openly and so harshly) only because it appeared that the central, authoritative circles sympathized with it. Everyone was afraid to reveal his lack of understanding of the latest music, because in fact that was something to hide. Now, everyone has suddenly realized that it was all 'false shame,' and almost with delight they inform the world that they've had a headache a long time from the music of Shostakovich and so on."[40]

The young idealist Shcheglov was trying to understand what had happened. He knew that there were a lot of people who did not like or understand not only Shostakovich and Prokofiev but also Glinka, Mussorgsky, even Tchaikovsky, and preferred a Russian folk choir or just pop songs to all those symphonies. Did that mean that serious music had to vanish, making room for the mass genres? Shcheglov concluded: "You can't force Shostakovich to write only versions of folk songs. Even without our interference he wrote not only complex operas, but mass songs and things that were completely accessible to the average listener. I feel bad for Shostakovich."[41]

The terrible truth is that not many people felt that way in those days. Even in musical circles Shostakovich could count on only a dozen or so of his close friends. Yevgeny Shvarts recalled the attitude toward

Shostakovich of professionals he liked to call "musicals beetles." "As soon as beetles crawl together, their conversation fatally turns to Shostakovich. They discuss his attitude toward women, his gait, face, trousers, socks. They don't bother talking about his music—they're so sure that it's worthless. But the beetles can't crawl away from the author of that music. He lives remotely, but still in their milieu, by his very existence confirming certain laws that threaten the beetles."[42]

Shvarts maintained that those musician "beetles" were afraid of Shostakovich and that their wives also hated him. For them, according to Shvarts, he was a biological anomaly, and they perceived him the way Salieri did Mozart in Pushkin's short play about the two composers.

> *I am selected*
> *To stop him—if not, we all are doomed,*
> *All of us, priests and servants of music.*

This almost messianic envy and hatred showed in the characteristic gesture of Vladimir Zakharov, one of the new leaders of the Composers' Union, when at a meeting he banged his fist on the table and shouted, "Comrades! Remember! We've finished with Shostakovich once and for all!"[43]

In those days, Zakharov was not the only one who thought so. Another favorite, Marian Koval, wrote mockingly that "infatuated high-school-coed musicologists" and Western "fame merchants" elevated Shostakovich to the ranks of "classic" and "genius of world music culture." "That was enough to turn his head!" Koval exclaimed, adding in a lecturing tone that such "toadying panegyrics . . . turned Shostakovich away from a profound meditation and comprehension of the articles in *Pravda*." As a result, in Koval's opinion, the unrepentant Shostakovich "continued to disdain the musical language of his people, the Russian folk song, and preferred cosmopolitism."[44]

These accusations were aesthetic only in appearance; they were in fact political charges. At that time in the country the slightest, even imagined deviation from the Party line could lead to total destruction, in keeping with the infamous camp instruction when inmates were being convoyed: "A step to the right, a step to the left is considered escape." Pasternak, who continued to measure Shostakovich's life against his own, inscribed a book to him and called on him to be brave, "and may your great future protect you from afar."★45

But Shostakovich, while putting up a brave front in public (in a letter he even quoted Chekhov's classic phrase "We will still see the sky in diamonds"), was in fact close to despair. During the 1936 crisis he had been twelve years younger, and now he was losing both moral and physical strength. "I have very frequent headaches, and besides which I am almost constantly nauseated, or as the folk say, murky . . . In the last week, or little longer, I have aged significantly, and that aging process is continuing with extreme speed. Physical aging, unfortunately, is reflected in the loss of spiritual youth, too."46

As his friends reported, he expected arrest and thought once again of suicide, remembering Pushkin's line "Long ago, a weary slave, I planned my escape." But he did not know that Stalin had other plans for him.

★Pasternak himself was accused in 1948 of his work "bringing great harm to Soviet poetry."

Chapter VII Final Convulsions and
Death of the Tsar

A joke became popular in the late 1940s among Soviet intellectuals. Armenian Radio is asked: "Is World War III imminent?" The radio replies: "There will be no war, but the struggle for peace will leave nothing standing."

Shostakovich had to have thought of this anecdote when in March 1949, Minister of Foreign Affairs Vyacheslav Molotov, then considered second in rank in the USSR, summoned him. He suggested the composer join a high-ranking delegation to New York for the Cultural and Scientific Conference for World Peace and so take an active part in the "struggle for peace." Shostakovich refused, even though he had long wanted to visit America. He explained to Molotov that he was in poor health (which was true).

On 16 March, Shostakovich's phone rang and he was told to hold on for Comrade Stalin. At first, the composer thought it was a prank. But then he realized no one would dare pull a stunt like that. And the voice he remembered from their personal meeting (in 1943 at the Bolshoi Theater during the discussion of the new state anthem) came on the line, asking why Shostakovich was refusing such a responsible assignment.[1]

Shostakovich had already proven that he could handle himself in a dialogue with the ruler. He did not lose his presence of mind this time, either (he must have prepared himself for this), and replied that he would not go to America because his music and that of his colleagues had not been performed for more than a year; it was effectively banned in the Soviet Union.

And something unheard of occurred: Stalin, who had intended to corner the composer, lost his presence of mind. He pretended ignorance and extreme surprise: "What do you mean, they don't play it? Why don't they play it? For what reason don't they play it?"

Shostakovich explained that there was an order from Glavrepertkom—that is, the censors. And here, Stalin made the first concession. "No, we did not give such an order. I'll have to correct the comrades from Glavrepertkom." And he changed the subject: "And what's this about your health?"

Shostakovich told the pure truth. "I'm nauseated." This was a second surprise for Stalin. We must assume that he was taken aback, but he gave no sign, preferring to take Shostakovich's words literally rather than metaphorically. "Why are you nauseated? From what? You will have an examination."

An entire medical brigade was called from the "Kremlevka," the special hospital for the government and Soviet elite. The Kremlin doctors confirmed that he was indeed not well. Shostakovich called about that to Stalin's secretary Poskrebyshev. But the secretary must have had his orders from the Boss: Poskrebyshev told the composer that he would tell Stalin nothing. He had to go to America, and he had to write a letter of thanks to the ruler—there was no point in arguing. The dictator had already amply demonstrated his benevolence: The order from Glavrepertkom banning the performance of an entire series of works by "formalist" composers—Shostakovich, Prokofiev, Khachaturian, Shebalin, Myaskovsky, and others—had been rescinded.

This story, which was first revealed by Shostakovich in his memoirs, was corroborated by documents published recently.[2] And these documents attest that Stalin's reaction was lightning-fast. Right after his conversation with Shostakovich, that same day, the memorandum from the deputy chairman of the Committee on the Arts under the aegis of the Council of Ministers of the USSR was on his desk, as requested. In it, the terrified functionary, with no idea of which way the wind was suddenly blowing, gave a complete list of Shostakovich's banned works, adding, just in case, that "his best works: The Piano Quintet, First,

Fifth, Seventh Symphonies, and music for film and songs are performed in concerts."

He had labored in vain. The messenger is always punished. The very next day the bureaucrats were slammed by the following directive of the Council of Ministers of the USSR: "Moscow, Kremlin. 1. Recognize as illegal order No. 17 of Glavrepertkom Committee on the Arts under the aegis of the Council of Ministers USSR of 14 February 1948 banning the performance of and removing from the repertory several works by Soviet composers and rescind it. 2. Reprimand Glavrepertkom for publishing illegal order." It was signed: "Chairman of the Council of Ministers of the USSR J. Stalin."[3]

Compare this story with Stalin's telephone calls to Bulgakov (1930) and Pasternak (1934). The honesty, courage, and inner strength of Bulgakov and Pasternak are not in question. They both have a much stronger "anti-Stalinist" image in our time than Shostakovich, for Bulgakov and Pasternak were never laureates of the Stalin Prize. But for them the telephone conversation with the ruler, however brief, became an event of enormous importance, and they returned to the dialogue with Stalin over and over, year after year. For Bulgakov and Pasternak (who called Stalin a "giant of the pre-Christian era"), the ruler was a larger-than-life figure.

Nothing of the sort happened with Shostakovich, even though Stalin must have hoped for that effect. Shostakovich, with his sarcastic worldview, harbored no romantic illusions about the ruler. It's quite possible that the perceptive Stalin was aware of it.

Shostakovich also, unlike Bulgakov and Pasternak, was not a natural interlocutor. The two writers—each in his own way—were born bards and talkers. Shostakovich, on the contrary, was often so withdrawn in dealing with people (especially ones he knew little), so isolated and nervous, that it made him "a man hard for others to bear,"[4] in Yevgeny Shvarts's opinion.

Marietta Shaginyan, who knew the composer well, observed that Shostakovich sometimes resembled a space alien with "some kind of electrical charge, giving up a lot of bioenergy from his entire being. He always spoke with great tension and effort. The first time he came to my room, which was divided in half by a large and solid screen, very steady, no sooner had he crossed the threshold when that steady screen fell down as if it had been blown by the wind. My whole family was as nervous as I was. It was always hard to start talking to him. And you had to understand how to start correctly in order to make the conversation work."[5] That was always my impression of Shostakovich, too.

Stalin's main psychological weapon in conversation was his enigmatic, laconic style. But in Shostakovich he found someone who could be even more laconic and enigmatic.

Shostakovich liked to tell a story about his meeting with Vladimir Mayakovsky in 1929. Upon greeting the budding composer, the eminent poet condescendingly extended only two fingers for him to shake. Shostakovich, staying calm, extended only one in response. "And so our fingers collided."[6]

Something similar occurred in the conversation between Shostakovich and Stalin. Despite the fact that the positions of the two sides were clearly unequal (as the writer Viktor Shklovsky said of a comparable situation, "On their side is the army and the navy, on mine, only my writing pen"), the dialogue between the ruler and the composer ended in a mutual compromise. Stalin had to rescind the order he had inspired, which he did very rarely and with extreme reluctance. In turn, Shostakovich had to go to New York to the peace conference.

At the time, Stalin saw the conference as an important foreign policy action. On his orders, "the struggle for peace" was made the leading slogan; consequently, the priority became the formation of a viable peace movement. Much money and effort went into it.

The idea of a struggle for peace looked completely honorable; as one of the more active participants, Ilya Ehrenburg, recalled, "The cause was pure: try to persuade everyone that a third world war would destroy civilization."[7] Ehrenburg, of course, was prevaricating: Politics is rarely—if ever—that "pure."

The New York conference confirmed this. It took place 25–27 March at the Waldorf-Astoria Hotel and was therefore dubbed the Waldorf Conference. Almost three thousand delegates attended, primarily Americans of liberal and left-wing orientation, supporters of the former vice-president and presidential candidate in the 1948 elections, Henry Wallace.

The Soviet delegation included the writers Alexander Fadeyev and Petr Pavlenko and the filmmakers Sergei Gerasimov and Mikhail Chiaureli—all Stalin laureates. But no one knew them in the United States; for Americans the only star was Shostakovich, who was met at the airport in New York by a huge crowd of fans.

This is another case where a parallel can be made with Pasternak. In 1935, Stalin forced Pasternak to go to Paris for the antifascist International Congress of Writers in Defense of Culture. The poet refused, pleading ill health (like Shostakovich). But Stalin (via Poskrebyshev) let him know that this was an order that had to be followed.

Like Shostakovich, Pasternak obeyed, even though he felt profoundly humiliated. At the Paris congress he was presented to the audience by André Malraux as "one of the greatest poets of our times," and he made a brief and very muddled speech, but he was greeted with a long ovation.[8] In the opinion of Ehrenburg, who was in charge of the Soviet delegation, the French, who knew almost nothing about Pasternak's work, were amazed by his appearance, so appropriate for the image of a romantic poet.

Shostakovich, populist at heart, still could make an impression of eliteness, especially on strangers. But his work, unlike Pasternak's, by then was well known to American intellectuals. Additionally, Shostakovich had been lucky in America—which was also important—in terms of his political reputation.

The attitude toward the Soviet Union had changed several times in the United States. In the 1930s it was rather hostile, and so when Shostakovich was attacked by *Pravda* in 1936, the fame of the composer, already known in the West, only increased. The sharp turnaround during World War II, when the Soviet Union became an ally of the Western democracies, made his reputation legendary. And then, the postwar turn toward the Cold War, when everything Soviet was once again regarded with suspicion in the United States, at first did not affect Shostakovich because of the "antiformalist" Party resolution of 1948.

But in 1949, America's love affair with Shostakovich came to a sudden and brutal end. The cause was the composer's participation in the Waldorf Conference, which was a signal cultural event of the early Cold War.

The conference gave Stalin the opportunity to directly test the attitude of Americans toward the Soviet Union. The suspicious ruler did not trust the reports of professional diplomats, paradoxically preferring to hear the impressions of creative people, who had a broader world-view and greater psychological insight. In 1946 he had sent Ilya Ehrenburg and Konstantin Simonov to America on a similar assignment. At the Waldorf Conference, the informants were Fadeyev and Pavlenko, also writers, but more active politically. Stalin listened to their opinions attentively. (We now know that Pavlenko's denunciation of Mandelstam in 1938 played a fatal role in the poet's life.)

Shostakovich (like Pasternak in 1935) was included in the delegation as a bolster of its respectability. But it was the composer, finding himself the center of attention, who paid the greatest price.

Many well-known leftist Americans took part in the conference—Arthur Miller, Norman Mailer, Lillian Hellman, Dashiell Hammett, and Clifford Odets. The music panel included Leonard Bernstein and its chairman was Olin Downes, music critic of the *New York Times*. But their ideological opponents were not sleeping. A small group of anti-Communist American liberals formed an ad hoc committee called Americans for Intellectual Freedom, supported by the CIA, to disrupt the conference.

The leader of the anti-Soviet group, which included Mary McCarthy, Dwight Macdonald, Arthur Schlesinger, and other New York intellectuals, was the philosopher Sidney Hook. The counterattack on the musical front was organized by Nicolas Nabokov, cousin of the great writer, a composer with good official connections.

Nabokov went to the music panel, where Shostakovich, feeling like a fish out of water, began reading in a nervous, trembling voice a Kremlin-written ritual condemnation of the "clique of war mongers" planning aggression against the Soviet Union. When Shostakovich's speech was finished for him by his American translator, Nabokov jumped up to ask a question. "Is Shostakovich personally in agreement with the attacks that appeared in *Pravda* on the music of Western composers Stravinsky, Schoenberg, and Hindemith?"[9]

Shostakovich rose to reply, he was handed a microphone, and with his eyes lowered, burning with shame, he muttered that yes, he fully agreed with *Pravda*. Nabokov, as he remembered it, was thrilled. "I knew in advance what his reply would have to be, and I also knew that his reply would expose him as being not a free agent . . . Yet this was in my opinion the only legitimate way to expose the internal mores of Russian communism."[10]

What a sad sight: two Russians, two composers, brought together by the cold war in a ruthless duel. We can understand the miserable Shostakovich, shoved into this ring by Stalin's orders. We can understand Nabokov, too, in his desire to strike a blow at Communist ideology, hitting hard at the closest target, not even thinking that the target was a great composer. In addition, it was Nabokov, his compatriot, who understood just how humiliating his ambivalent role at the Waldorf Conference was for Shostakovich. We can also remember that at that moment only one of them was under real pressure, with his life in danger, and that was Shostakovich.★

The attacks by Nabokov and his friends pretty much torpedoed the Waldorf Conference and with it Shostakovich's American reputation. From that moment, regardless of his true emotions and convictions, he was increasingly perceived in the West as a mouthpiece of Communist ideology and his music as Soviet propaganda. This was the inexorable logic of the cold war. The hostile reaction to Shostakovich's music prevailed, with small fluctuations, for thirty years.

The year 1949 was tense: the cold war threatened to turn into a hot one. Mainland China became Communist; Communists fought in Greece and Vietnam. Even though the foundations of NATO were laid, Italy and France were shaken by powerful anti-American demonstrations.

Stalin, who had given up on actively influencing American public opinion after the failure of the Waldorf Conference, still planned to tear Western Europe away from the United States; his hope was that "the struggle for peace in some countries will develop into the struggle for socialism."[12] The French newspaper *Le Monde* wrote that in "the struggle for peace" the Communists had "found a slogan everyone could understand." The so-called Stockholm Declaration to ban the atom bomb, initiated by the Communists, collected hundreds of millions of signatures all over the world. Many prominent Western figures joined the movement: the Dean of Canterbury, Hewlett Johnson; Queen Elisabeth of Belgium; Nobel laureate Frédéric Joliot-Curie. One of the most prominent peaceniks was Pablo Picasso, whose litho-

---

★To the end of his life Shostakovich remembered those excruciating days in New York with revulsion and fear. Interestingly, in 1967 he told Nabokov about Stalin's order and that the text he read in New York had been written for him by "competent organs."[11]

graph of a dove became the symbol of the movement and one of the cultural-political icons of the twentieth century.

This aspect of Picasso's life is still treated in the West as if it were a bit of inexplicable eccentricity on the part of the genius. Nevertheless, the majority of memoirists confirm that Picasso took his duties in the peace movement seriously. As Ehrenburg wrote, Picasso readily participated in congresses and conferences, never refused to appear, attentively listened to orators (wearing earphones for synchronous interpretation) praising Stalin and denouncing American imperialism. He once explained to Ehrenburg, "Communism for me is tightly related to my entire life as an artist."[13]

Compare this to Shostakovich's behavior. The composer also took part in Stalin's "struggle for peace," but, unlike Picasso, he did it under the unrelenting pressure of the Soviet authorities and with great reluctance.

According to Ehrenburg, at a session of the Second World Congress for Peace in Warsaw in 1959, an angry-looking Shostakovich complained to him about having to listen to all that nonsense. The composer cheered up when he found a way out of his predicament—he unplugged his earphones. "Now I can't hear anything. It's wonderful!" Ehrenburg recalled that Shostakovich resembled a child who had outsmarted his mentors.[14]★

It is not surprising that Shostakovich was disgusted by the Western supporters of Stalin and Stalinism, speaking with particular disdain of Picasso (in a private conversation with Flora Litvinova): "You understand that I'm in a prison and that I fear for my children and myself, but he—he's free, he doesn't have to lie!" And he continued, "Who's forcing him to speak? All of them, Hewlett Johnson, Joliot-Curie, Picasso, they're vipers. They live in a world where maybe it's not so easy to live, but you can tell the truth and work and do what you think best. And he does that peace dove!"[15]

The reason for this outburst is clear. Picasso got away with everything—receiving the International Stalin Prize "for strengthening

---

★In 1964, when Shostakovich was still alive, Ehrenburg submitted these reminiscences to the most liberal Soviet magazine of the time, *Novyi Mir,* and even there, the deputy editor-in-chief was shocked by the description of the composer's behavior. "Shostakovich looks so indifferent to the work of peace that he turns off the earphones during the congress!" This episode was not published then.

peace" (in the artist's biographies today it is cravenly called the Lenin Prize) in 1950, and drawing the idealized portrait of Stalin that appeared after his death in the memorial issue of the French Communist weekly *Lettres françaises.* James Lord, a young officer with anti-Communist sentiments in the U.S. military intelligence in France, was present when Picasso demanded from the poet Paul Eluard, a big shot in the peace movement, that the Stalin Prize go to him, since he deserved it more than anyone else. In his memoirs, Lord explained that he did not understand then why the artist wanted the Communist award. But what is telling is that Lord, as he recalls it, was not in the least put off by Picasso trying to get a prize from Stalin: for Lord, Picasso was a modernist god.[16]

In the middle of the twentieth century, modernism was the reigning orthodoxy. Its influential supporters found numerous arguments to justify Picasso's Stalinism and Ezra Pound's fascism. Shostakovich was working in a more conservative idiom then, and therefore he could not count on such protection. This is one of the explanations of why his compromise compositions of the late 1940s and early 1950s have been so furiously derided (to this day)—such works as the oratorio *Song of the Forests* and the cantata *The Sun Shines Over Our Motherland,* and his music for films praising Stalin, like *The Fall of Berlin* and *Unforgettable 1919.*

These works had no more severe critic than their composer. For instance, Shostakovich openly said that he considered *Song of the Forests* a shameful work.[17]★ For *Song of the Forests* and the music for *The Fall of Berlin* the composer received his fourth Stalin Prize, and the new leadership of the Composers' Union got the opportunity to note with approval, "In praising the heroic labor of the Soviet people, D. Shostakovich in the oratorio *Song of the Forests* glorifies Comrade Stalin, the genius creator of the great plan to transform nature."[18]

In fact, Shostakovich's opus least of all "glorified Comrade Stalin"— in complete accordance with its title, it deals with reforestation. The fierce battles of World War II deforested huge tracts of the Soviet Union, and the concern for increasing forest land was a major issue. "Let's dress the homeland in forests!" This appeal is the central musical

★This can be compared again to Picasso, who never disavowed his anti-American work *Massacre in Korea* (1951), which, even in the opinion of his admirers, was pure propaganda.

idea of the oratorio, and Stalin only gets a few pro forma phrases. Their complete superfluousness was demonstrated when after the ruler's death *Song of the Forests* continued to be performed successfully with the lines relating to Stalin removed.

Before the premiere of *Song of the Forests* in 1949 a friend of Shostakovich's said to him, "It would be so good if instead of Stalin you had, say, the queen of the Netherlands—she's a big fan of reforestation, I hear." The composer cried out, "That would be wonderful! I take responsibility for the music, but as for the words . . ."[19]

In essence, that is what happened. *Song of the Forests,* while neither one of the best nor one of the most popular of Shostakovich's works, continues to be performed and recorded even in our day—primarily as an attractive musical pastiche, with reminiscences of Glinka, Tchaikovsky (the boys' chorus from *The Queen of Spades*), and even Shostakovich's beloved Mussorgsky. There is also a direct influence (for some reason not noted before) of Gustav Mahler's *Das Lied von der Erde* [*Song of the Earth*], particularly its contemplative third and fourth movements. Shostakovich hints at it in the obvious resemblance of titles. The propaganda aspect of *Song of the Forests* is rather superficial. But it satisfied the authorities.

In general, those years saw a growing number of ideological events in the Soviet Union being conducted pro forma. For new generations, the Communist ideology was turning into a collection of slogans memorized to show loyalty to the regime. Even Stalin realized it. According to Dmitri Shepilov, Stalin once said to him in irritation, "We studied *Das Kapital.* Memorized Lenin. We took notes, made summaries . . . And the young cadres? They don't even know Marx and Lenin. They study from crib sheets and quotations."[20]

Stalin was particularly angered in this regard by the intelligentsia. So he ordered a new mandatory brainwashing of writers, actors, musicians, and others all over the country. Everyone, even those with high titles and awards, was forced to study, like schoolchildren, the ABC's of Marxism-Leninism and the works of Comrade Stalin, to make summaries and pass tests.

But even this, despite Stalin's intentions, turned into empty formality. For many years afterward, people laughed as they recalled those tests on Marxism-Leninism. Mark Reizen, the renowned bass of the Bolshoi

Opera and a Stalin favorite, was asked by the examining instructor to explain the difference between bourgeois and socialist revolution. He replied, after a pause for thought, this way: "That one I know . . . Ask me another one."[21]

For his Marxist-Leninist education, Shostakovich had a special tutor come to his house. That must have been sanctioned at the top and done, we assume, out of Stalin's increased interest in the indoctrination of music's leading "formalist." Obviously Stalin thought that without a profound mastery of Communist wisdom the stubborn composer would not be re-educated properly. The personal instructor discovered an important and unusual lapse on the part of his student the first time he entered Shostakovich's study: The obligatory and ubiquitous portrait of Stalin was absent from the walls and desk. Shostakovich was chided; like a good student, he promised to correct the error of his ways. But a portrait of Stalin never did appear in his apartment.

Shostakovich told his friend Lev Lebedinsky about another conversation with the instructor. The latter started asking about Stalin's telephone call in 1949, noting, "Just think who talked to you! The master of half the world! Of course, you too are a famous man, but compared to him, who are you?"

"A worm," replied Shostakovich.

"Exactly, a worm!" the instructor agreed.[22]

Not a musician, he did not get the caustic sarcasm of Shostakovich's response, with its allusion to the satirical song by Alexander Dargomyzhsky, "The Worm," to the poem by Pierre-Jean de Béranger, and its refrain:

> *For I am but a worm compared to him,*
> *Compared to him, such a man,*
> *His Excellency!*

As Lebedinsky recalled it, Shostakovich told him the story without smiling, as if deep in thought about something unpleasant. "What are you thinking about?" Lebedinsky asked.

"About how ninety percent of our country's population is made up of fools like him."[23]

For a lifelong populist, this was a tragic conclusion, born, we must assume, of incredible exhaustion and enervation from the never-ending pressure.*

Yet at that time the composer had "in the desk drawer" one of his most populist works, written in 1948—the song cycle *From Jewish Folk Poetry.*

The fate and the place of this opus in Shostakovich's creative legacy are extraordinary. The Jewish cycle is one of the most important ways that Shostakovich addressed the theme of the "little man," central in Russian classical culture, in Gogol, Dostoevsky, Mussorgsky. None of these three could be called philo-Semites by any means, and therefore Shostakovich's decision to create such a populist composition based on Jewish material seems particularly daring. This unusual choice inevitably put Shostakovich on a collision course with the growing government-sanctioned anti-Semitism in the Soviet Union.

The relations between Jews, subjects of the tsarist empire, and the government were always more or less problematic. The majority were required to live in the "pale of settlement," that is, in small towns and villages. There were quotas for Jews in higher educational institutions. From time to time waves of bloody pogroms rolled over the country, which led to the emigration of over two million Jews to the United States in the late 1800s.

The situation changed when the Bolsheviks came to power in 1917: Jews were given equal rights with the rest of the population, anti-Semitism was officially forbidden, and even though Zionist activity was prohibited, Yiddish literature and theater were supported. There were quite a few Jews among the original Bolshevik leaders—including Trotsky, Zinoviev, and Kamenev. But by 1926 Stalin "freed them of their responsibilities as members of the Politburo," which led to the popular joke: "What is the difference between Stalin and Moses? Moses led the Jews out of Egypt, and Stalin led them out of the Politburo." Lazar Kaganovich was brought in as the government's token Jew.

Historians are still debating whether Stalin was a convinced anti-Semite, and if so, from what point: childhood (as some maintain) or later—at the seminary or even during the years of underground Marx-

---

*Comparable emotions oppressed Pushkin in 1828, a dreary year for him, when he addressed the "mob" surrounding him and exclaimed in disgust and anger:
     The voice of the lyre will not animate you!
     You disgust my soul like coffins.

ist work. I tend to agree with the opinion of those who point out the pragmatic and opportunistic character of Stalin's views in this area.[24]

For instance, in 1936, *Pravda* printed Stalin's article "On Anti-Semitism" (his reply to a question from a Jewish journalist from the United States): "National and racial chauvinism is a relic of human-hating mores characteristic of the cannibalistic period. Anti-Semitism, as the extreme form of racial chauvinism, is the most dangerous relic of cannibalism."[25] It is hard to imagine Hitler or any other ideological anti-Semite signing such a statement.

On the other hand, when in the late 1930s Stalin started to renew his ideological arsenal and began inculcating a more nationalistic state policy, it produced a return of popular anti-Semitism. (This was immediately reported to the dictator by Nadezhda Krupskaya, Lenin's widow, who was very sensitive to this sort of thing. "The kids have a new swear word—'kike.' ")[26]

During the war with Hitler, a new wave of chauvinism and anti-Semitism was gathering strength. While still covert, it was manifested in various apparat games, especially in the fields of ideology and culture. In 1942, a secret memorandum appeared written by the Directorate of Propaganda and Agitation of the Party Central Committee "On the Selection and Promotion of Cadres in Art," which expressed anxiety over the fact that in culture, the trendsetters were "non-Russian people (primarily Jews)." A special stress was made on the situation in music—at the Bolshoi Theater and the Leningrad and Moscow Conservatories, where, according to the Party functionaries, everything "is almost completely in the hands of non-Russian people."[27]

Undoubtedly this document reflected the views of the Party leadership; many job dismissals were made soon after. Among those who signed petitions to support fired Jewish musicians was Shostakovich.

In intelligentsia families, like Shostakovich's, anti-Semitism was never approved. But when he was young, anti-Semitic remarks were easy to hear in his circle. I remember the shock I felt when I was going through the archive of the late Leningrad musicologist and composer Valerian Bogdanov-Berezovsky, whom I had known as the perfect gentleman, and came across diary entries of the early 1920s mentioning a conversation with young Shostakovich on the topic of the "Jewish takeover" in the arts. (These notes have been subsequently published in part.)[28]

It is impossible to suspect the mature Shostakovich of anti-Jewish sentiments; there are numerous accounts of his implacable attitude toward anti-Semitism. As Lebedinsky recalled, for Shostakovich the term "anti-Semite" was equivalent to a swear word or the definition of "nonhuman."[29]

The earliest date for Shostakovich's public defense of Jews would probably be 27 November 1938, the day he spoke at a rally at the Leningrad Philharmonic, protesting against Jewish pogroms in Germany. But it is important as well that in 1933, Shostakovich included a Jewish musical theme in his First Piano Concerto. The coincidence in time with the rise to power in Germany of Hitler with his anti-Jewish program is unlikely to be accidental.

Since then, the number of fundamental works in which Shostakovich used Jewish motifs grew, especially in the war years. Take the Second Piano Trio or the Second String Quartet. No non-Jewish composer of Shostakovich's rank before or after him was as taken by Jewish images. Professor Timothy Jackson speaks of Shostakovich's identification with Jews that went far beyond traditional philo-Semitism.[30]

For Shostakovich, the Jew, always persecuted, turned into a symbolic figure that personified alienation. Regarding the fate of Jews, Shostakovich saw in it a bit of his own and of many other Russian cultural figures. He could have signed under Marina Tsvetayeva's lines in "Poem of the End," written in 1924 in exile in Czechoslovakia:

> *In this most Christian of worlds*
> *Poets are kikes!*

This sense of rejection and the perception of his own life as a Via Dolorosa that came to Shostakovich with the first round of Stalin's persecution in 1936 grew much stronger during the period of the Zhdanov pogrom of 1948—that was one of the sources of the "bloody *freilekhs*" in the finale of the First Violin Concerto, which he was composing then. And from here also came an impetus for the vocal cycle *From Jewish Folk Poetry,* which Shostakovich began soon afterward.

But besides that, a dramatic event that took place on 12 January 1948 hung over both these Jewish works. On that day in Minsk, the great Jewish actor Solomon Mikhoels, who had come to the capital of

Belorussia on business for the Stalin Prize Committee, of which he headed the theater section, was killed by a heavy truck. The hit, which occurred without witnesses and was pronounced an accident by the authorities, was in fact a killing planned by and executed on Stalin's orders, as is now known.[31] Despite the official funeral with pomp and circumstance (comparable to Gorky's funeral in 1936), the emotional graveside speeches and lengthy obituaries, some of the titans of culture under Stalin's vigilant eye felt a chill run up their spines. Returning from Mikhoels's funeral, Eisenstein whispered to a friend, "I'm next."[32]

We can imagine the thoughts that tormented Shostakovich then. He learned of Mikhoels's death on 13 January and that same day went to the deceased's apartment to express his condolences to the family (Mikhoels was among Shostakovich's ardent admirers). He arrived there after an exhausting and humiliating day spent at the Zhdanov Conference at the Central Committee: It was on 13 January that Zhdanov in his concluding speech put Shostakovich at the top of the black list of "anti-people, formalist" composers.

At the Mikhoels apartment Shostakovich embraced the actor's daughter and then said, "I envy him . . ."[33] At that moment, instant death seemed a release.

In Zhdanov's speech there was a threat directed at so-called cosmopolites. That euphemism was gradually becoming a code word for Jews. The intellectuals repeated a sarcastic ditty at the time:

> *If you don't want to be known as an anti-Semite*
> *Be sure to call a kike "cosmopolite."*

The murder of Mikhoels marked the start of a much more active campaign to marginalize Jews in the Soviet Union, which grew inexorably right up to Stalin's death in March 1953. The campaign kept moving into new areas—Jewish theaters and publications were shut down and all kinds of Jewish organizations and associations were disbanded. These actions were accompanied by arrests among the various circles of the Jewish intelligentsia.

Today it is sometimes mistakenly thought that Stalin's policy met no resistance inside the Soviet Union. In fact, many members of the Soviet cultural elite protested this anti-Semitic turn. For example, the renowned microbiologist, laureate of the Stalin Prize, ninety-year-old

Nikolai Gamaleia (Ukrainian by birth) wrote a letter to Stalin protesting that "something bad is happening in our country at the present time toward Jews." Gamaleia boldly wrote, "Judging by absolutely indisputable and obvious signs, the reappearance of anti-Semitism is coming not from below, not from the masses, among whom there is no hostility toward the Jewish people, but it is being directed from above by someone's invisible hand. Anti-Semitism is coming from some high-placed persons who have taken up posts in the leading Party organs."[34]

Naturally, this letter to Stalin did not get a response. Shostakovich, unlike Gamaleia, had no doubts about who was behind the anti-Semitic campaign. "Cosmopolites, Jews, they're all to blame for the fact that we are slaves," he said with bitter irony to Flora Litvinova. "Anti-Semitism is a struggle against culture and reason."[35] He did not bother writing letters to Stalin; instead he wrote his Jewish cycle.

This work was Shostakovich's guerilla attack in defense of the persecuted, even though it was impossible to have it performed then. (The premiere took place only in 1955, after Stalin's death.) It is full of warm compassion for the Jewish lot in the past and the present. This music carries not only pain and despair, but real tenderness—an emotion not so often found in Shostakovich's works.

The first three songs of the cycle (with vivid echoes of Mahler's songs from *Des Knaben Wunderhorn*) are lullabies; this was impossible to imagine in Shostakovich before. And they are so different: "Cry for a Dead Infant" is a graveside wail ("Moishele is in the grave, the grave"); then a tender and touching scene, "Fussing Mother and Aunt"; and finally, the resignation of a mother by her child's bed in the face of triumphant brute force ("Your father is in chains in Siberia . . . I bear the need").

The theme of poverty and need is very strong in the Jewish cycle. Here, we can presume, are reflected the author's own worries: it was at this time that Shostakovich was fired from work at the Moscow and Leningrad Conservatories and the list of his permitted works was sharply reduced. The fear of ending up without a piece of bread was something he had felt since his youth, and it erupted in the Jewish cycle in "Song About Need": "Oy, wife, borrow a piece of hard bread for the children." And the culmination of the opus, the song "Winter," is about the final despair where there is no strength left to resist the blows of ruthless fate:

The cold and the wind are back,
There is no strength to bear it in silence.
Shout then, weep then, children,
The winter is back again.

This is also profoundly personal: the composer's constant fear for his family—his wife, Nina, daughter, Galina, and son, Maxim—if he were unable to feed them or if something even worse happened to him and he ended up in chains in Siberia. This was a possibility to take seriously, for the tragic end of Mikhoels served as a terrible warning.

After all, Mikhoels belonged to the golden circle of Soviet cultural figures: He was awarded the title of People's Artist of the USSR and in 1946 received the Stalin Prize. Most importantly, Stalin had promoted him to an important political position—in 1941, after the start of the war with Nazi Germany, Mikhoels was made chairman of the Jewish Anti-Fascist Committee. One of its goals was to get support from the Western Jewish community for the Soviet Union and to raise money in the United States for the Soviet war effort. For that, Mikhoels was sent to America in 1943, where he met with Albert Einstein, his old friend Marc Chagall, and Charlie Chaplin, among other luminaries, and spoke at rallies and conferences in support of the Soviet Union's role in the war against the Nazis. On that trip, Mikhoels raised millions of dollars for his country.

But the word "gratitude" did not exist in Stalin's political vocabulary. In Stalin's eyes, a person's value was measured only in his usefulness that minute. After the victorious end of the war, there was no more need for the Jewish Anti-Fascist Committee, and Stalin became very suspicious of the connections with Western Jews that Mikhoels and his colleagues had developed. He saw in them proof of a conspiracy of world Jewry against the Soviet Union. Mikhoels was the first prominent victim of this paranoia.

There are various, often contradictory, testimonies about Stalin's physical and psychological state in the final period of his life. Most agree that the ruler's health was beginning to give out: he was feeling his age and the major strain of the war years. This must have frightened Stalin: He realized that he was not immortal. In impotent fury the ruler sought someone to blame for his deterioration, and found them: his doctors, many of whom were Jewish.

Stalin always prided himself on his perceptiveness, his ability to find the hidden springs of events. He put two and two together: his failing health and the imagined "international Zionist conspiracy" again the Soviet Union. Thus was born the case of the Saboteur Doctors, whose arrest was announced to the country on 13 January 1953.

With dread, the intelligentsia read the special report in the newspapers written in Stalin's style and vocabulary: "It has been established that these killer doctors, having become monsters of the human race, having trampled upon the sacred banner of science and defiled the honor of practitioners, were hired agents of foreign intelligence."[36]

A new wave of anti-Semitism rolled across the country, but this time not only Jews felt threatened. Long experience prompted many to think that the country was on the brink of a mass purge that would be similar to the Great Terror before the war.

As in the era of the Great Terror, no former contributions or medals guaranteed security. This meant everyone from the top down. Stalin accused his closest top aides; one he called a British spy, another, an American spy. In culture, even the once prestigious title of laureate of the Stalin Prize offered no protection. This had been demonstrated by the murder of Mikhoels. Another signal was the unprecedented resolution of the Politburo annulling the Stalin Prize once given to composer Gherman Zhukovsky: His opera, *From the Heart,* for unknown reasons, upset the ailing ruler.[37] That meant this punishment could be meted out to any laureate, with the resultant consequences.

How would this growing tension and anticipation have ended if Stalin had lived another year or two? Any answer has to be hypothetical. Fate intervened. In late February 1953, Stalin had a stroke, and on 5 March (according to the official communiqué, even though not all historians accept this date), Stalin died. He was seventy-three.

Ehrenburg recalled the shock of the news. "We had long ago forgotten that Stalin was a man. He had become an omnipotent and mysterious god. And now the god had died of hemorrhage in the brain. It seemed incredible."[38] This reaction is very reminiscent of the emotions contemporaries felt upon the death of Nicholas I, almost a hundred years earlier, in February 1855; as one of them wrote in a diary: "I always thought, and I was not alone, that Emperor Nicholas would outlive us, and our children, and probably our grandchildren."[39] The feeling of horror that enveloped many intellectuals in those days is captured in the diary entry of avant-garde artist Nadezhda Udaltsova on 6 March 1953: "There are no words. There is nothing."[40] Understandably, panic hit the political elite; Shepilov recalled feeling "as if something had broken in the main mechanism of the giant machine of the state." Apocalyptic feelings spread among the people.

But not everyone reacted that way. The poet Joseph Brodsky told me how, when he was twelve, the students were gathered in the auditorium of his school in Leningrad on 6 March and the teacher gave them an emotional speech. "She climbed up onto the stage and started talking, but at a certain point she broke off and shrieked in a heart-rending voice: 'On your knees! On your knees!' Then all hell broke loose! All around me everyone was howling, and I was supposed to be howling, too, apparently, but—at the time to my shame, but now, I think, to my credit—I wasn't. It all seemed so barbaric to me. Everyone around me was standing there sniffing. Some were even sobbing, and a few were really seriously weeping. They let us go home early that day, and again, strangely, my parents were waiting for me at home. My mother was in the kitchen. We lived in a communal apartment. In the kitchen, the pots, the neighbor women—and everyone weeping. Even my mother was weeping. I went back to our room somewhat amazed. Then suddenly my father winked at me, and I realized that there really was no reason for me to get particularly upset over Stalin's death."

There is no doubt that Shostakovich, upon hearing of Stalin's death, felt an instant sense of profound relief, but there was no euphoria—this is confirmed by reminiscences of the composer's friends and children. Shostakovich, like many other Soviet intellectuals, had reason to think that the screws would be tightened even more, as a preventive measure. An additional blow came with the news of Prokofiev's death, the same day as Stalin's, also from a brain hemorrhage, just a month short of his sixty-second birthday.[41] Shostakovich and Prokofiev of course had a complex, sometimes strained relationship. Yet the "antiformalist" campaign of 1948, with both composers as its victims, had brought them closer together again and they had made peace. Shostakovich felt that they were in the same boat.

In the last years of Stalin's life Prokofiev and Shostakovich received new rewards from the dictator: Prokofiev in 1951 got his sixth Stalin Prize, for the oratorio *On Guard for Peace,* and Shostakovich in 1952 got his fifth, for a cycle of choruses about the Revolution of 1905. But both knew by now that these prizes were not guarantees of safety and Stalin could send a new bolt of lightning at them at any time.

That is why Prokofiev was so tense when he heard the official bulletins about the dictator's fatal illness. Anticipation of Stalin's end is considered to have hastened Prokofiev's death. Paradoxically, the anniversary of the death of the tyrant and the death of the composer would be marked together, a constant reminder of the bizarre, intertwining, mutual influence and mutual repulsion of politics and art.

At Prokofiev's bier, in the shabby semi-basement of the House of Composers, Shostakovich was more humble and respectful than ever. He kissed the deceased's hand and said, "I am proud that I had the fortune to live and work next to such a great musician as Sergei Sergeyevich Prokofiev."⁴² There were not many flowers at Prokofiev's coffin—they were all taken for the Hall of Columns in the House of Unions, for the bier holding Stalin's corpse.

On 7 March, a cold and gloomy day, the funeral procession with Prokofiev's body started for the cemetery, and in the small group was Shostakovich. They went down almost empty streets, going around the huge rivers of people struggling in the opposite direction to pay their respects to the ruler. I doubt that the obvious symbolism escaped Shostakovich. What was he thinking in those hours? He must have been torn by contradictory emotions.

Shostakovich realized that Prokofiev's life had concluded on a sad note; he died a humiliated and broken man, who thought, perhaps unjustly, that his battle with Stalin had ended in compromise that bordered on defeat. That feeling, without any doubt, was familiar to Shostakovich. But he was still not old (he was forty-six), was comparatively healthy, and despite everything, filled with musical ideas and a desire to work. And now, with Stalin's death, fate had given Shostakovich a chance at revenge.

Epilogue   In the Shadow of Stalin

The faster the twentieth century moves away from us, the clearer it becomes how pivotal a moment of the entire era was Stalin's death, particularly for the Soviet empire. Americans in company often recall where each one was when the news of President John F. Kennedy's death was announced. For Soviet people of a certain age such a fateful day was 5 March 1953. Regardless of individual attitudes toward the omnipotent dictator, the populace of the huge state froze in expectation. Everyone knew that an era had come to a close. But what would the future bring? No one knew that, and everyone—some with fear and some with hope—stared at the vague outlines of tomorrow.

The feelings of the Soviet Union's ruling elite after Stalin's death was best expressed in private conversation by one of the tyrant's heirs, Nikita Khrushchev: "Before we used to live behind Stalin's broad back. We left everything to Stalin. We knew that Stalin would make the right decisions. And we lived tranquilly. And now there is no one to count on. We have to decide everything ourselves."[1]

No matter what we feel about him, Stalin was one of the political giants of the century. Even dead, he continued to cast a huge shadow. And all subsequent leaders of the Soviet Union, from Khrushchev to Gorbachev, had to live in that shadow. They all defined their image and their political programs in the framework of the Stalin paradigm. Stalin's image remained the measure of all things right up until the collapse of the Soviet empire in 1991, and perhaps beyond that.

Even among the Soviet intelligentsia many strong and sober minds could not resist Stalin's spell. The eternal skeptic Ilya Ehrenburg admitted, "I did not like Stalin, but I believed in him for a long time, and I feared him . . . I tied the future of the country with what was daily called for twenty years 'the wisdom of the genius ruler.' "[2]

Even dead, Stalin continued to have an effect on the fate of many major cultural figures. The most dramatic example is the suicide in 1956 of Alexander Fadeyev, who had led the "literary front" for many years under Stalin. Fadeyev's early novel *The Rout* (1927) reveals a literary gift that later was sacrificed to cultural politics. The horrible tension of daily communication with Stalin Fadeyev discharged in his legendary drinking benders, which sometimes lasted several weeks. Reportedly, after one such incident, when Fadeyev—with a brick-red face from the drinking—showed up to see Stalin, the ruler carefully asked, "And how long does this usually last with you, Comrade Fadeyev?"

"Unfortunately, three weeks—that's the illness."

"Could it be shortened a bit, fitting into two weeks? Think about that, Comrade Fadeyev!"[3]

But Fadeyev continued drinking his way, and Stalin accepted it, since he valued the gifted writer and extraordinary organizer.

But everything changed for Fadeyev when Khrushchev came to power. That stocky, bald man with the misleading air of a simpleton had craftily outwitted the other pretenders to leadership of the country—first of all, the chief of the secret police, Lavrenty Beria (whom Khrushchev eventually had shot), Georgi Malenkov, and Vyacheslav Molotov—and took charge of the Soviet Union, taking a few rather bold actions to dismantle the Stalin myth.

The most dramatic was Khrushchev's "secret speech" about the mistakes and crimes of Stalin in February 1956 at a closed session of the Twentieth Party Congress. At that time it seemed like a truly seismic shift, seriously influencing the further development of events in the twentieth century. Khrushchev's anti-Stalin speech was a sensation throughout the world and of course in the Soviet Union, where many claimed that it had opened their eyes to the terrible excesses of the recently idolized leader.

Shostakovich, as we know, had not been that naïve. The news of Stalin's crimes came as no surprise to him, but we remember how he was profoundly traumatized by the frank accounts of friends back from incarceration.

Fadeyev heard those stories, too. But unlike Shostakovich, Fadeyev had a direct role in the repressions that were now officially declared illegal. Like other leaders of the "creative unions" organized on Stalin's orders, he had been forced to accede to the arrest of his colleagues more than once. This sincerely tormented Fadeyev; in his suicide note addressed to the Central Committee of the Communist Party, he was very frank: "I see no possibility of going on, since art, to which I had given my life, has been destroyed by the self-confident ignorant leadership of the Party and now cannot be corrected. The best writers, in numbers that the tsarist satraps could not even dream, were physically destroyed or died thanks to the criminal connivance of the powers-that-be."[4]

Fadeyev did not mention that he had been among those powers-that-be—at least up until Stalin's recent death. Khrushchev was not as forgiving toward him as Stalin had been. He pushed Fadeyev away, and the writer felt he was suddenly in a vacuum.

Ehrenburg explained what happened to Fadeyev this way: "While the severe winter was strong, he held on, but as soon as people smiled, he began thinking of what he had experienced and what he had not written: It was all exposed somehow; and then the motor started balking."[5] Fadeyev dismissed Khrushchev and his new team as "smug nouveaux riches" and predicted that "you can expect even worse from them than the satrap Stalin. He at least was educated, and these men are ignoramuses."[6]

For Fadeyev (as for many former associates of Stalin) the comparison with the late ruler was definitely not in Khrushchev's favor. The world without Stalin seemed devoid of meaning and focus. This is what led Fadeyev to suicide. A friend found Fadeyev on his bed, dressed only in his underwear, his face contorted in terrible pain and a revolver in his dangling hand. The bullet, shot into the heart with anatomical accuracy, went out his back, and he bled onto the bed, soaking the mattress. A picture of Stalin was on the bedside table.

Learning of Fadeyev's suicide, Khrushchev roared, "He was shooting at the Party, not himself!"[7] The denunciatory suicide note was classified for thirty-four years.

"Oh how heavy is the clasp of his stone hand!" exclaims Don Juan in Pushkin's *Stone Guest,* a bold variation on the Don Juan theme. Another of the dictator's posthumous victims, the satirist Mikhail Zoshchenko, felt the fatal clasp of Stalin's stone hand in a different way than Fadeyev.

The special Party resolution that had humiliated Zoshchenko and Anna Akhmatova in 1946, instigated by Stalin, remained in force under Khrushchev. In 1954, more than a year after Stalin's death, a new and distressing confrontation occurred for Zoshchenko. The authorities called him and Akhmatova to meet with a group of English students visiting Moscow. The guests wanted to know how the two writers now felt about the resolution of 1946. Akhmatova rose and replied briefly that she considered it absolutely correct. Zoshchenko began telling the English students with complete seriousness that he considered the resolution unfair and had written a letter about it to Comrade Stalin, who never replied.

Zoshchenko later explained that he could not leave the English guests with the impression that he agreed with being called a scoundrel, hooligan, and slanderer in the resolution and with the accusation of cowardice: "Probably the English would have laughed at a writer who was willing to swallow any rebuke . . . I fought at the front twice, I had five combat medals in the war with the Germans, and I was a volunteer in the Red Army. How could I accept that I am coward? . . . I never was a nonpatriot of my country. I could not agree with that! What do you want from me? That I admit that I'm a sneak, cheat, and coward?"[8]

Zoshchenko paid dearly for this attempt to explain and justify himself before foreigners. Khrushchev was furious, and a new round of persecution began. At a Party meeting of Leningrad writers, indignant speakers declared that Zoshchenko had drawn no conclusions from Stalin's resolution: "The recent facts show that M. Zoshchenko has been hiding his true attitude toward that resolution and continues to defend his rotten position."[9]

Completely badgered, Zoshchenko's mind gave out: he stopped eating almost completely (out of fear of poisoning); he had to use a cane as he shuffled, emaciated, exhausted, as Chukovsky recorded in his diary, "with deadened eyes, a martyred expression, isolated from the world, trampled . . . Now he was just a corpse, hammered into a coffin."[10]

Zoshchenko died soon after, and he was buried hastily. The writer's friends bitterly drew parallels with Pushkin's secret funeral one hundred twenty years earlier. Shostakovich came to the cemetery. When he visited Zoshchenko's grave again ten years later, he said to a friend, "I'm glad he outlived his executioners—Stalin and Zhdanov."[11]

But what bitter thoughts must have buffeted Shostakovich at the grave of one of his favorite writers! Stalin had delivered a blow from which Zoshchenko never recovered. The long arm reached Zoshchenko's throat even after the ruler's death. Shostakovich had pity for Zoshchenko and he was depressed by the satirist's creative destruction in the final years of his life.

Before his death, Zoshchenko confessed that in the last fifteen years he had been irrevocably terrified, "and a writer with a terrified soul has lost his qualification." Shostakovich feared that sort of "loss of qualification" all his life and made every effort to avoid it. Shostakovich also saw Zoshchenko's tragedy in the fact that after the resolution of 1946, while he continued to write (and mostly failed to get anything printed), he never created anything comparable to his masterpieces. Literary people sympathized with Zoshchenko—some sincerely, some condescendingly.

Shostakovich did not wish to be treated with condescension. The composer had always prided himself on being able to continue working after suffering the most terrible blows, and creating masterpieces—the Fifth Symphony in 1937 and in 1948 the Jewish song cycle and the First Violin Concerto, in which Shostakovich carried on an imaginary musical argument with Stalin. Right after Stalin's death that argument was continued in Shostakovich's Tenth Symphony, arguably his most perfect work.

The Tenth Symphony has a clear "subplot": confrontation between artist and tyrant. The wild, frightening Scherzo (the second movement), which overwhelms the listener, is a musical portrait of Stalin. Shostakovich himself told me this, and later it was confirmed by Maxim, his son.[12] But the main evidence that this interpretation is not his later invention can be found, as usual, in the music of Shostakovich, the great master of hidden motifs and quotations and juxtapositions of rhythmic figures. The "Stalin" part of the Tenth Symphony is based in great part on Shostakovich's music for the film *Fall of Berlin* (1950), in which the ruler was a prominent character.

The composer-as-hero is described in the symphony even more clearly: he is represented here by Shostakovich's musical signature—the theme D-Es-C-H, which had appeared in the composer's earlier work only in hints. In the Tenth Symphony, this musical author's monogram does not simply float to the surface; it literally fills the work, becoming its central theme. And Shostakovich pits it (in the finale) against the "Stalin" theme when that reappears on the horizon. This is a direct duel in which the Shostakovich theme wins. The theme D-Es-C-H, executed with maniacal stubbornness by various instruments—first the French horns and trumpets, then strings and woodwinds, and finally the kettledrums—concludes the symphony, as if the composer is repeating the assertion: "And I'm alive!" (Recall Shostakovich's remark at Zoshchenko's grave.)

Naturally, if Shostakovich's Tenth Symphony were merely a musical illustration of the idea that tyrants are mortal and art eternal or that culture can be a shield in the struggle with evil and violence, then the work would not have been worth the paper it was written on. The Tenth is first and foremost infinitely changeable, flexible, multifaceted music; with room for a smile, and sorrow, and pure enchantment. The solo song of the French horn in the third movement is lovely, repeated like a mysterious echo twelve times. It has now been determined that the five notes of the motif contain the name of Elmira Nazirova, the young woman Shostakovich was attracted to at the time.[13]*

Then again, how much of this latent content was perceived by its first audience at the premiere conducted by Yevgeny Mravinsky in Leningrad in December 1953? I doubt that they could decipher all the musical signs and symbols—even many years later, Soviet musicologists who knew the meaning of Shostakovich's "musical signature" still continued to insist with a stubbornness worthy of better application that "this monogram theme should not be endowed with autobiographical significance."[14] But the general emotional meaning and subtext of the Tenth was immediately obvious to many. That is clear even from the reviews of the premiere that appeared in the official press: The sym-

---

*The number of such solved clues will continue growing as his music is studied. We can draw a parallel with the musical legacy of Alban Berg (1885–1935). The intimate secrets embedded in the tightly woven scores of his Lyric Suite for string quartet and Violin Concerto were uncovered by painstaking musicologists only many years after the composer's death.

phony was characterized as "the tragedy of a lone individual seeing no relief to his suffering and doubts" and as "a sensation of pain and suffering sometimes bordering on the hysterical."[15] Yuli Kremlev, an orthodox but astute critic, went further than the rest, in 1957 writing in *Sovetskaya Muzyka:* "The music of the Tenth Symphony with its psychic depression and affectedness is a truthful document of the age."[16]

Yet again, it was Shostakovich who did it. In 1937, his Fifth Symphony was the only publicly aired narrative of the Great Terror. The Seventh and Eighth symphonies conveyed the fullest picture of the horror, despair, and ambivalence of the transition from the prewar to the war era. And now, the Tenth Symphony became the first work to reflect profoundly the change from the harsh Stalin winter to the uncertain "thaw" (as this brief period of Khrushchev's liberalism would be known, thanks to Ehrenburg). All these symphonies were true novels of their time, which combined an epic grasp of historical events from a bird's-eye view with the most subtle psychological insights.

As we have seen, Shostakovich's creative path was attentively and even a bit enviously observed by a celebrated compatriot who had his own deeply felt ideas of what the great contemporary novel of the times should be—Boris Pasternak. He had a musical education, was a fair pianist, and tried to compose music in his youth, dreaming seriously of a career as a composer. Even though for Pasternak great music ended with Scriabin, he grasped what Shostakovich was doing. In his youth, Pasternak told a friend that "a book is a cubic chunk of burning, smoking conscience."[17] This definition is astonishingly appropriate for Shostakovich's works—and Pasternak had to feel that. In addition, the poet must have been impressed by the evolution of Shostakovich's style toward greater simplicity and clarity, while still retaining the multilayered emotional content—the path of Pushkin.

Pasternak was developing in the same direction: beginning as a poet of exceptional metaphorical complexity, he gradually started wanting to write so that "everyone could understand." His dream was to create a book "that would relate to everyone." A comparable work during the war years was undoubtedly Shostakovich's Seventh Symphony. Pasternak's attempt in that vein did not succeed. In 1943 he started writing a long poem about the war called *Dawn,* hoping that it would be published in *Pravda* (which he had been promised). But in the end, *Pravda* ran only an excerpt, and the disillusioned Pasternak stopped working on the narrative poem. As consolation, *Pravda* asked him to translate *Childhood of the Ruler,* a poem about Stalin by Georgian poet Georgi Leonidze, but an affronted Pasternak proved obstinate and refused.

The poet was punished for that: He was crossed off the list of candidates for that year's Stalin Prize, where he had been placed for his translations of *Hamlet* and *Romeo and Juliet.* But the translations were noted in the elite British circles, where a small but influential band of Pasternak's admirers had formed in the late 1920s. These British intellectuals began writing about Pasternak and translating his poetry and prose into English.

For Pasternak that was a breath of fresh air in a stuffy room. He explained to a female friend that those Western ties "turned out to be more numerous, more direct and simpler than I had imagined even in my most daring dreams. This has simplified and lightened in a miraculous way my inner life, structure of thought, activity, and goals, and has also severely complicated my outer life."[18] The Soviet authorities watched suspiciously over Pasternak's unauthorized success in the West. They were particularly upset by the unofficial news in 1947 that the poet had been nominated for the Nobel Prize.

Clouds began to gather over Pasternak. His mistress, Olga Ivinskaya, was arrested. But he could no longer be turned from his chosen new path, where the potential audience in the West was as important as—or perhaps even more important than—the audience inside the Soviet Union. As he later commented, "This was a turnaround, this was a decision taken, this was the desire to start telling everything."[19]

In the winter of 1945–46, Pasternak announced, "I am old, I may die soon, and I can't keep putting off the free expression of my true thoughts," and began writing *Dr. Zhivago,* a panoramic novel about the Russian intelligentsia. He regarded it as his most important work.

Pasternak made sure that the manuscript of the first chapters of *Dr. Zhivago* reached his admirers in England, who were not to publish it yet; this showed who was primary in the author's consideration. He wrote intensely but slowly until the end of 1955.

There is a curious passage in a letter Pasternak wrote in 1953, after Stalin's death and not long before the premiere of the Tenth Symphony. "Music is the most widespread form of avoiding any answers to

the age, heaven, and future, the most popular method of spiritual mask-
ing, thanks to the preciousness of sound, with the aid of which even
materialized ordinariness makes itself heard."[20] For Shostakovich and
numerous listeners, his Tenth was that "answer to the age, heaven, and
future" that Pasternak wrote about, but we can understand his irritation
and impatience. I consider the Tenth Symphony a more perfect work
than *Dr. Zhivago*.★ But from an ideological and moral point of view, *Dr.
Zhivago,* with its Christian underpinning, was a colossal breakthrough.
The author's freedom from Marxist cant, after decades of relentless
brainwashing that made it the only possible paradigm for even the most
talented Soviet cultural figures, was astonishing.

Also unprecedented was Pasternak's orientation toward a Western
audience, which led to *Dr. Zhivago*'s publication first in Italy, then in
France, England, the United States, and Germany. Party censorship had
made it impossible to publish in the USSR. In 1958, a year after *Dr.
Zhivago* appeared in the West, where the novel was a literary and political sensation, Pasternak at last received the Nobel Prize. Pasternak
replied by telegram to the Nobel committee: "Infinitely grateful,
touched, proud, surprised, embarrassed."

Pasternak was the first Soviet writer to become a Nobel laureate, but
the reaction of the authorities (and many colleagues who were literally
mad with envy) was furious. A persecution campaign was sanctioned
from above, in the course of which an article in *Pravda,* "Noise of
Reactionary Propaganda Around a Literary Weed," appeared under the
byline of David Zaslavsky, the same journalist Stalin allegedly used in
1936 in the attack against Shostakovich in *Pravda*.[22]

I remember these events very clearly. It felt as if the Stalinist days had
returned, and sanctions developed along the iron scenario created by
Stalin: Pasternak was berated at meetings, he was expelled from the
Writers' Union, and the newspapers printed hastily organized wrathful
"responses from the workers," the most depressing of which for the
intelligentsia was from Filipp Vasiltsov, the machinist from Stalingrad:
"The frog croaks . . . I haven't read Pasternak, but I know: In literature
it's better without frogs."[23]

★Anna Akhmatova called the novel a "failure of genius," adding that Pasternak succeeded only in his nature descriptions, while the characters were rather cardboard: "I don't
recognize any of these people, and I should have."[21]

Shostakovich watched the "Pasternak affair" unfurl with heavy heart: it was too much like the campaigns against him in 1936 and 1948. He was in a politically delicate situation.

Khrushchev, who had not wanted to hear a word about rescinding the Party resolution of 1946 against Akhmatova and Zoshchenko, suddenly agreed in May 1958 to disavow the ten-year-old "Zhdanov resolution" against Shostakovich, Prokofiev, and other composers. It was done cautiously, with conditions, but at the time it was perceived as a major step away from Stalinist cultural dogmas.[24] Shostakovich in private conversation reacted rather ironically to what he called "the historic resolution correcting the historic resolution." But he had to realize that this was an important friendly gesture from Khrushchev. After a brief hiatus, all the reins of power in the Soviet Union were back in one pair of hands. Khrushchev had turned rather quickly into a new dictator who decided everything personally. He also tried to rule culture, imitating Stalin.

Khrushchev was a clever and crafty politician. His outward spontaneity was in great part a mask hiding a calculating mind. Khrushchev could not use mass terror as the main lever for running the nation. But Stalin had done that already: The huge country was cowed for a long time.

Thus, as Stalin's heir, Khrushchev had enough room to maneuver. In culture he used the carrot and the stick. Who got what depended on the tactical needs of the moment and least of all on Khrushchev's personal taste or preference (as it also had been under Stalin). We can be sure that Khrushchev, unlike Stalin, never listened to an entire symphony by Shostakovich, much less one of his operas. As for Pasternak, Khrushchev later admitted that he had not read his poetry or *Dr. Zhivago*. But in 1958 the political cards required Shostakovich to get a carrot (rather wilted), and Pasternak, the stick.

In Khrushchev's memoirs there is this passage about *Dr. Zhivago:* "I regret that this work was not printed, because you cannot use administrative methods, that is, like the police, to sentence the creative intelligentsia."[25] But this was Khrushchev the pensioner speaking. When he was leader of the Soviet Union he behaved very differently. Pasternak was in danger of arrest, and the authorities were planning to expel him from the country. Under terrible pressure, the writer publicly refused the Nobel Prize and sent letters of repentance to Khrushchev and *Pravda;* in the latter he basically disavowed his novel.

This was unbearable humiliation, since Pasternak continued to consider *Dr. Zhivago* the most important work of his life. But even this rather courageous man, who had gathered his considerable strength and boldly crossed the border of fear, was in the end broken by the still powerful repressive apparatus of the post-Stalinist Soviet Union. This was the intended result, and Khrushchev's later hypocritical regret did not change a thing.

At the Twentieth Party Congress Khrushchev loosened the reins, "eased up," in Shostakovich's words, but quickly corrected that by sending tanks into Hungary. The Soviet intelligentsia had to be shown that it was dealing with a powerful and determined boss. Starting in 1957, Khrushchev conducted a series of meetings with cultural figures, in which he lectured writers, poets, and artists, yelled at them, stamped his feet and swore, working himself up into a frenzy. He wanted to show his actual, potential, and imaginary opponents what he could be like—and he succeeded.

The Pasternak affair was only one example of many, but perhaps the most symbolic of the Khrushchev era, and therefore, the one that got the most publicity. It forced Shostakovich to make several far-reaching conclusions.

One was the gut feeling that under Khrushchev, too, the inviolability of the creative personality remained a fiction. The paradox lay in the fact that while the possibility of physical destruction had lessened significantly, the sense of personal contact with the ruler had been lost. Khrushchev was much less intrigued by the phenomenon of genius and he was much harder to reach, as Pasternak complained: "For even the terrible and cruel Stalin did not consider it beneath his dignity to fulfill my requests about prisoners and to call me about this on the telephone."[26]

Khrushchev had nothing to discuss with Pasternak by telephone. The poet summed up his situation under the new regime this way: "Compared to the movement of the eyebrows of the supreme power, I am a bug that can be squashed and no one would utter a sound."[27] Undoubtedly, Shostakovich's impressions were the same: not only would no one utter a sound, but many of his colleagues would gladly join in the sanctioned persecution. This was another sad observation that Shostakovich made during the Nobel scandal, which confirmed his own bitter experience.

At least twice—in 1936 and 1948—Shostakovich faced the betrayal of friends and admirers. Pasternak went through it in 1958. His former colleagues chorused accusations of "vile treachery." Students of the Literary Institute went to an anti-Pasternak rally with a poster reading "Down with the Judas!" and announced their intention to break the windows in his house. Shostakovich surely recalled the "outraged populace" breaking windows at his dacha when the authorities accused the composer of formalism.

And Shostakovich came to one more painful conclusion after the persecution of Pasternak: Recognition in the West was ephemeral—at least at that time, with the situation being what it was in the Soviet Union. Pasternak, when he was writing *Dr. Zhivago,* had a Western audience in mind as well as Soviet readers. At that time the very thought was revolutionary, much less getting the manuscript out to the West. "The psychological wall between us and the West was solid, built to last—but Pasternak broke through it with one blow,"[28] Veniamin Kaverin later said. But for many observers the success of the attempt seemed much more problematic, for in the end, the authorities forced Pasternak to denounce his work. And on the day before his death, in late May 1960, Pasternak complained bitterly to his son that he was tormented by the knowledge of the "ambivalence of world fame when at the same time there is total obscurity at home."[29]

Some intellectuals, both in the Soviet Union and beyond its borders, had the impression that the West used the Pasternak affair for political goals, helping to turn it into one of the most publicized skirmishes of the cultural cold war. Even Pasternak's death from lung cancer, which his friends and family attributed to the enormous stress the poet suffered during the uproar, was interpreted in this context as a political incident.

The Soviet authorities tried to play down Pasternak's funeral (as had the tsar with Pushkin's burial). They were resisted by a group of young people and some writers who tried to give the funeral an adversarial character. The Western media played a big role in that. At Pasternak's grave close to two thousand people gathered with crowds of Western reporters, cameras whirring and clicking; the KGB recorded the event for its own uses. It was turned into a noisy political show. The echoes of the event can be heard in a number of Shostakovich's most important post-Stalin works.

The many years of interaction between the work of Pasternak and Shostakovich have not been paid enough attention by scholars. They both considered themselves part of the Pushkin tradition, pondering the urgent issues of the artist's role in Russia. For both the law "Render unto Caesar the things that are Caesar's" was a fact of life (Shostakovich even had a postcard of Titian's *Coin of Caesar* on his bookshelf). But what was their common strategy of creative survival led Pasternak toward the end of his life into a new orbit. He burned up in the atmosphere doing it. This spectacle of a magnificent and proud self-destruction frightened Shostakovich. His immediate and paradoxical comment on Pasternak's death and funeral can be heard in "Descendants" from the song cycle *Satires,* based on the poetry of Sasha Cherny, an early-twentieth-century liberal humorist Shostakovich loved.

"Descendants" mocks the refrain that was heard through the centuries of Russian life: "Things are hard, brother . . . The children / Will live better than us." Suffering patiently for the sake of one's descendants is stupid, the cynical poet exclaims. "I want a little light / for myself, while I'm alive."

In Shostakovich's musical interpretation this message became, as it usually is in his mature works, deeply ambivalent. It seems to mock the official Soviet slogan about the "radiant future" and the sacrifices the achievement of the Communist paradise will entail.* But the music also contains a deeply personal motif, born as a response to Pasternak's untimely death: Really, is the game worth the candle? Will future generations appreciate the sacrifice?

> *I am like an owl on the ruins*
> *Of shattered gods.*
> *Among the unborn descendants*
> *I have no brothers or foes.*

This could have been Pushkin's Pretender from *Boris Godunov* speaking, a desperate, bold, and cynical character. Undoubtedly,

---

*The authorities were so displeased with the allusions of this work that Shostakovich had to add to its title, *Satires,* the evasive subtitle *Pictures of the Past.*

Pushkin recognized some of his traits in himself, which is why the character is written so vividly and succulently. Similar features can be found in Shostakovich's biography as well.

Shostakovich was never a recluse; he constantly wanted to do something besides write music—work for the Composer' Union, help colleagues, get friends and strangers out of trouble. Yet the public activity—travel, representation, appearances—led him to feel like an impostor.

In August 1932, Shostakovich (not yet twenty-six years old) became a member of the board of the newly created Leningrad section of the Composers' Union. From that time, he was always drawn into business and creative problems associated with the organization. The peak of this was his election, sanctioned by Khrushchev, as first secretary of the Composers' Union of the Russian Federation at its founding congress in 1960.

This was a very important step: Shostakovich was responsible for the well-being of over five hundred composers and musicologists. He had always been serious and punctilious, and he plunged into the professional affairs of his colleagues—performance and publication of music, social aid—with total devotion.

It must be added that in 1947, Shostakovich had become the Soviet deputy for Leningrad, first in the Supreme Soviet of the Russian Federation and later in the Supreme Soviet of the USSR. This position was no sinecure, either. He had nothing to do with the elaboration of the country's policies, but there was a lot of work. He had regular office days when he saw constituents who came in a steady stream: People recall that the line stretched from his door out onto the street. This had little relation to music. The constituents who arrived with complaints and requests were hurt and needy. The composer got involved in family conflicts, listened to stories of collapsed ceilings and broken toilets, promised to get medicines, and made inquiries about pensions.

Many times he took action on behalf of the unjustly convicted, writing letters and calling the appropriate agencies; his name opened many doors. A sea of human misery flooded him. How did Shostakovich stand it? How could he, who sometimes resembled nothing more than a bundle of exposed nerves, not lose his mind, common sense, and creative energy?

We know that among Shostakovich's best-loved works by Chekhov were "Ward Six" and "The Black Monk" (he even intended to write an opera based on its themes). Chekhov in these stories described people brought to the edge of madness—they cross that invisible line, leaving the reader certain that the entire world is a madhouse, ward 6.

In "Ward Six" Dr. Ragin thinks about seeing patients just as Deputy Shostakovich must have thought on a difficult day about the endless stream of constituents: "Today you see thirty patients, and tomorrow, you see, there are thirty-five, and the day after, forty, and so on day after day, year after year, and the mortality in the city does not decrease, and the patients do not stop coming. Giving serious help to forty patients between morning and dinner is physically impossible, which means that unwittingly it is sheer deceit."

This of course sounds like an admission of being a pretender—regardless of whether such self-chastisement is justified (Chekhov is ambivalent about it, as usual). But for us, no less important is another theme in "Ward Six," as I think it was important for Shostakovich. Ragin argues with his young idealist friend, who—in the very style mocked by Sasha Cherny—believes that one day, in the future, "the dawn of a new life will rise." To which Ragin responds bitterly, "There will be no prisons or madhouses, and truth, as you chose to put it, will triumph, but the essence of things will not change, the laws of nature will be the same. People will be sick, will age and die just as they do now. Whatever glorious dawn illuminates your life, still in the end you will be hammered into a coffin and tossed into a hole."

When Chekhov wrote this, he was thirty-two. Then, in 1892, the critic Nikolai Mikhailovsky, the idol of the liberal intelligentsia, reviewed "Ward Six" this way: "It all strikes hard on the reader's nerves, but without parsing into definite thoughts and feelings, it does not give artistic satisfaction."[30] The influential critic was disgusted by Chekhov's unorthodox mix of populism and pessimism, making it impossible to reach a single conclusion. Almost seventy years later, fifty-four-year-old Shostakovich found himself in a position similar to Chekhov's. Pessimism and fatalism were taking over a greater part in his life. This was connected, undoubtedly, to his increasingly ill health.

Starting in 1958, Shostakovich was in hospitals more and more. In 1960 he twisted his ankle at the wedding of his son, Maxim, and broke his leg. Ever since then, a mysterious weakness of his arms and legs, never completely diagnosed, made his life miserable.

Everything happened in that *annus horribilis:* illness, a decline in strength and will, the temptations of power. The result was a completely unexpected move that many still consider to be the composer's greatest mistake in public life: In 1960 he joined the Communist Party.

The circumstances of this rather mysterious incident are still not clear. And this is despite the fact that Shostakovich, usually reserved and secretive, tried to dramatize this episode as much as possible.

We know this from his friends Isaak Glikman and Lev Lebedinsky: Shostakovich told them both that he did not want to join the Party at all but was coerced by the authorities. According to his friends, Shostakovich had an extraordinary fit of hysterics: he drank vodka, wept loudly, and created the impression of a character out of Dosto-evsky on the verge of a severe nervous breakdown or suicide.[31]

How it actually happened may never be revealed, even if all the relevant documents from Party archives were to be published: Too much here rests not so much on the corresponding statements—written or at least spoken—but on what went unsaid. (It is like pauses in music: they can be eloquent, but deciphering their meaning is no simple task.)

But we do have an astonishing creative document-commentary: Shostakovich's Eighth Quartet, written down in July 1960, and which many consider one of the composer's greatest opuses (and a pinnacle of the string-quartet genre in general). After the fateful episode of joining the Party, Shostakovich quoted a line from Pushkin in a conversation with a friend: "From the fates there is no defense." These words can serve as an epigraph to the Eighth Quartet, in which we can also hear echoes of Shostakovich's meditation on Pasternak's recent death.

This quartet is the composer's requiem for himself, for which there are precedents in Russian music: Just think of Tchaikovsky's Sixth Symphony. Shostakovich commented on his concept more frankly than Tchaikovsky had, explaining in particular to his daughter, Galina, that he had written a quartet dedicated "to my memory."[32] It is notable that Shostakovich had already written music with a similar idea—in the fateful year of 1948, when he feared arrest and execution. But then he securely hid those requiem pages: they were built into the music for the film *Young Guards,* based on Alexander Fadeyev's popular novel.

The film (and novel) recounted the heroic exploits and tragic end of a group of young underground partisans (who called themselves the Young Guards) in the years of the recent German occupation. The Nazis hunted and shot the Young Guards. That scene in the film gave Shostakovich the opportunity to write a heartrending funeral march called "Death of Heroes."

Young Guards did not please Stalin at first, but after some changes the ruler switched from anger to mercy, giving the film (but not the music) the Stalin Prize First Class. And we can assume that no one would have ever thought to interpret the "Death of Heroes" funeral march as being autobiographical if Shostakovich had not used music from it more than ten years later in his openly autobiographical work, the Eighth Quartet.

This remarkable work consisted almost entirely of self-quotations (and also quotes from Wagner's *Götterdämmerung* and Tchaikovsky's Sixth Symphony). Shostakovich used, too, the popular revolutionary song "Tormented by the Hardships of Prison," the words of which were written in 1876 by poet Grigory Machtet, who then published them in the Russian émigré press in London. An unknown composer set them to music, which became a national funeral march. That march was sung by revolutionary sailors on Kronstadt in 1906, the year Shostakovich was born. The same song, according to legend, was sung by the Young Guards before their execution. In the Eighth Quartet the theme from the autobiographical "Death of Heroes" moves directly into the melody of "Tormented"—the associations, personal and musical, are clear here.

Shostakovich, in a letter listing the self-quotations he used in the Eighth Quartet, mentions themes from the First, Eighth, and Tenth Symphonies, the Piano Trio, the First Cello Concerto, and the opera *Lady Macbeth:* a real autobiography in music. He did not include the key quotation from *Young Guards*—whether consciously or out of forgetfulness, we will never know.

In the poem "Tormented by the Hardship of Prison," dedicated to the memory of student Pavel Chernyshev, who died in a tsarist prison, there are these lines:

> *Like you, we may serve only*
> *As soil for new people,*
> *Only as an awesome prophecy*
> *Of coming new and glorious days.*

This helps us understand the degree to which Shostakovich was in thrall of the idea of self-sacrifice for the sake of the happiness of coming generations. He musically worked this idea from every angle—irony (the song cycle on the words of Sasha Cherny) and tragedy (the Eighth Quartet). Food for thought came from Pasternak's death, Chekhov's "Ward Six," and Pushkin's poetry.

The result is a unique work—simultaneously a musical autobiography and a musical self-obituary, in which the quotations from his own works mark the main milestones of his life. As Shostakovich commented sarcastically, "A fine hodgepodge."

His problem was to keep the heterogeneous material from falling apart. He solved it by introducing as a unifying theme his musical monogram, D-Es-C-H. It plays the function of Virgil, leading the listener through the circles of the composer's hell—through music that is sometimes unbearably gloomy, sometimes supranaturally tranquil and translucent, sometimes nervous, even paranoid.

He wrote the Eighth Quartet in feverish tempo, in just three days, and it resembles a flaming confession in the Russian spirit, Dostoevskian, when the speaker seems to be revealing his bleeding soul to the listener. But the improvisational manner of this work is deceptive; its careful five-part form is sophisticatedly concentrated and symmetrical. Shostakovich, who rarely boasted of his successes as a composer, this time wrote to a friend, still trying to cover his satisfaction in his more usual self-irony: "The pseudo-tragedy of this quartet is such that in composing it, I shed as many tears as urine flows after a half dozen mugs of beer. When I got home, I tried to play it two times or so, and the tears poured again. But now it was not just over its pseudo-tragic nature, but because of my amazement at the marvelous wholeness of its form."[33]

I think that very few people in the Leningrad audience who came on 2 October 1960 for the premiere of the Eighth Quartet understood the mastery of its construction. I also doubt that many got Shostakovich's clues right away: for instance, the juxtaposition in the fourth, penultimate, movement of the song "Tormented by the Hardship of Prison" with the melody from the scene in *Lady Macbeth* that describes the path of convicts to Siberia—a road he had imagined for himself more than once. The audience was simply knocked off its feet by the enormous emotional wave of the music—I was at the premiere and I can attest to that.

I also recall how some professional musicians looked confused: The Eighth Quartet violated their spatial imperative. Many of them guessed at the autobiographical nature of the quartet but did not know how to interpret it. I was a sixteen-year-old schoolboy then, and my review of the premiere of the Eighth Quartet was published in the Leningrad newspaper *Smena*.[34] It was an instant reaction, clumsy but sincere—and I expected serious analysis from my senior colleagues. But they seemed to feel that writing confessional music was somehow . . . indecent.

A book sympathetic to Shostakovich that came out in 1960 made a point of disregarding his monogram theme. "There is no confirmation that this is the composer's intention and not a random coincidence."[35] And even the 1976 monograph by Marina Sabinina, one of the most serious Shostakovich scholars, published after the composer's death, reads, "All authors seem to concur that its 'autobiographical' significance should not be exaggerated."[36] How cautious musicologists can be. (Not only in the Soviet Union, of course.)

The problem of semantic interpretation, intricate and convoluted to begin with, is particularly important for the work of Shostakovich, with its wealth of "latent content." Shostakovich's music, which does not depend exclusively on verbal commentary, nevertheless benefits substantially when it is set in psychological, political, and social context.

Shostakovich knew that very well. He also understood that in the professional musical milieu, with its caste spirit and tendency toward snobbery, his stubborn desire to communicate through his music was met with increasing suspicion. A crisis was brewing in Shostakovich's relationship with his Russian audience.

In part the crisis can be explained by objective causes. Once relatively homogenized, the Soviet audience for serious contemporary music had started fragmenting by the 1960s. A small but influential segment was attracted to the banned, and therefore especially tempting, values of the musical avant-garde establishing itself in the West.

For that part of the audience, it was the height of poor taste to include "Tormented by the Hardship of Prison" in a string quartet. Another part of the audience wanted contemporary art to express opposition to the Soviet regime. These people were affronted by the highly publicized dedication of the Eighth Quartet: "To the memory of the victims of fascism and war."

Shostakovich made a serious tactical error with this dedication. He had thought it would help hide the subtext of his new work from the authorities and that the audience would figure it out for themselves. In essence, it was a continuation of the game of cat-and-mouse with the authorities that Shostakovich had adopted back in the 1930s.

Using Aesopian language had worked successfully before, allowing him to turn public statements about his music into a kind of superfluous side dish: The authorities would eat it and the audiences would overlook it. But a time came when the ploy started backfiring.

The most sensitive part of the audience, the one that used to listen closely, delving into the essence of Shostakovich's music, now demanded that he declare his position with much greater openness. The antifascist theme, which the Soviet regime continued to exploit for propaganda even after the war, no longer seemed relevant to them. The dedication "To the memory of the victims of fascism and war" did the opposite: It did not deceive the authorities; it deceived the audience. For that reason, this most confessional of Shostakovich's works remained misunderstood by many.

For Shostakovich this was a great blow. We must assume that it was at this time that he began thinking of the role of words in his music and of the significance of authorial commentary to it.★

We must also think once again about the social and cultural context. After Stalin's death, huge shifts had taken place in the Soviet Union. Even though the state system remained Stalinist at its deepest core, independent voices could be heard, for the first time in many years, in the public discourse. The central issue remained the attitude toward the Stalin legacy. Whether it was sympathetic or hostile determined a person's political position. Literally every state action, especially in the sphere of ideology and culture, was perceived as a movement either toward the Stalinist line or away from it. This was characteristic of the Khrushchev regime and that of the government that followed in 1964, after a bloodless coup by Leonid Brezhnev, a favorite of the nomenklatura.

★This eventually led to the memoirs that Shostakovich dictated to me in the first half of the 1970s.

Milestones in the dramatic process were the publication of Aleksandr Solzhenitsyn's *A Day in the Life of Ivan Denisovich* (1962), the trials of poet Joseph Brodsky (1964) and writers Andrei Sinyavsky and Yuli Daniel (1966), and the *samizdat* publication of the physicist Andrei Sakharov's *On Progress, Coexistence, and Intellectual Freedom* (1968). Shostakovich's overall participation in this process was significant, albeit contradictory. A description and analysis of his contribution to de-Stalinization and the concurrent zigzags of the composer's complicated creative and civic paths in those years is beyond the scope of this epilogue.

But it is necessary to mention the most important of Shostakovich's musical anti-Stalinist gestures of that era. The primary one is the Thirteenth Symphony ("Babi Yar") for bass soloist, chorus of basses, and orchestra to five poems by the popular young poet Yevgeny Yevtushenko.

The poem "Babi Yar," published by Yevtushenko on 19 September 1961 in the Moscow *Literaturnaya Gazeta,* became an international sensation: No one in the Soviet Union had dared for a long time to speak so openly and publicly about domestic anti-Semitism. Khrushchev attacked the poem. In setting it to music, Shostakovich entered into open confrontation with the authorities, whose anti-Semitic policy went back to Stalin.

A highly charged atmosphere developed around the performance of the Thirteenth. The conductor Yevgeny Mravinsky, up until then Shostakovich's closest interpreter (he had dared to premiere the Fifth Symphony in the dangerous year of 1937 and had supported the composer in numerous dramatic situations afterward), passed on this, which was eloquent evidence of the unstable situation. Kirill Kondrashin, who took on the performance, was subjected to pressure up until the last minute; the authorities tried to prevent the premiere, which was turning (as they had feared) into an impressive demonstration of opposition feelings.[37]

The attention of the Soviet audience and the foreign media was focused on the first movement, Shostakovich's setting of "Babi Yar." That is understandable. But in terms of anti-Stalinist polemic (which is the aspect of Shostakovich's late music that interests us here), it is present throughout the entire symphony, particularly in the fourth movement, "Fears."

Yevtushenko wrote the poetry for "Fears" especially for Shosta-kovich, in fact, with the composer. So it could be said that it expresses Shostakovich's position most accurately. The text deals with the fears that Stalin planted in the hearts of people:

> *I remember them in power and strength*
> *At the court of triumphant lies.*
> *Fears were everywhere, slipping like shadows,*
> *Penetrating every floor.*

Fear in Shostakovich's music turns like the dragon Fafnir in its cave in Wagner's opera *Siegfried*. And using music, reminiscent of the "Stalin" scherzo in the Tenth Symphony, Shostakovich confesses what nightmares pursue him to this day. "Secret fear of someone's denuncia-tion / Secret fear of a knock on the door."

To hear that sung by a bass accompanied by a symphony orchestra from the stage of the Great Hall of the Moscow Conservatory in December 1962 was a shock. The sculptor Ernst Neizvestny said, "It was major! There was a sense of something incredible happening. The interesting part was that when the symphony ended, there was no applause at first, just an unusually long pause—so long that I even thought that it might be some sort of conspiracy. But then the audi-ence burst into wild applause with shouts of 'Bravo!' "[38]

Neizvestny recalled how the Party nomenklatura responded to the seditious concert. "There were a lot of them, those black beetles with their ladies in permanents. I was sitting right behind a group of them. The wives, being more emotional and swayed by success—the whole audience was giving a standing ovation—also rose. And then I saw: Hands flew up—black sleeves, white cuffs—and every official put a hand on his spouse's hip and pushed her back in her seat. They did it as one. It was a Kafkaesque movie!"[39]

That the Russian intelligentsia perceived the symphony through the prism of the polemic with the Stalinist legacy is evident from the letter written in exaltation right after the premiere by the pianist Maria Yu-dina to Shostakovich: "I can say Thank You from the Late Pasternak, Zabolotsky, *innumerable* other friends, from the tortured-to-death Mey-erhold, Mikhoels, Karsavin, Mandelstam, from the nameless hundreds of thousands of 'Ivan Denisoviches,' *they cannot be counted,* the ones

Pasternak called '*tortured alive*'—you know all that, they all live in you, we are all burning in the pages of the Score, you have given it as a gift to us, your contemporaries—for the generations to come."[40]

Shostakovich was always sensitive to the social mood. The success of the Thirteenth Symphony, whose anti-Stalin message came through loud and clear thanks to Yevtushenko's poetry, seemed to confirm his new awareness of the effectiveness and necessity of words as aids in decoding the music. He expressed regret to Yevtushenko that the audiences had not figured on the "latent content" of his Eighth Quartet: Musicologists, he complained, "began interpreting my music, moving the emphasis to Nazi Germany." The Thirteenth Symphony gave Shostakovich, as he told the poet, "the opportunity to express myself not only through music but through your poetry as well. Then no one will be able to ascribe a completely different meaning to my music."[41]

Moving further still in that direction, Shostakovich wrote *The Execution of Stepan Razin* (1964), a vocal-symphonic poem for soloist (a bass again), chorus, and orchestra, again to a poem by Yevtushenko, and the Fourteenth Symphony (1969), for soprano, bass, and chamber orchestra, to the poetry of Federico García Lorca, Guillaume Apollinaire, Rainer Maria Rilke, and Wilhelm Kuchelbecker, a nineteenth-century Russian romantic poet repressed by Nicholas I. But the phenomenal resonance of the Thirteenth Symphony, alas, was not repeated.

The anti-Stalin statements in both new works went unnoticed. The authorities hid their irritation and pretended that nothing special was happening. Burned on the Thirteenth Symphony, they realized that there was no point in giving Shostakovich any more publicity by trying to ban his work. This tactic successfully lowered the liberal intelligentsia's interest in the composer.

Shostakovich was well aware of this. In 1967, with almost Dostoevskian bitterness he wrote to a friend, "I'm disappointed in myself. Rather, I'm convinced that I am a very dull and mediocre composer. Looking back from the heights of my sixty years at 'the road taken,' I can say that twice I had publicity (*Lady Macbeth of Mtsensk* and the Thirteenth Symphony). Publicity that worked very powerfully. However, once everything calms down and takes its rightful place, it is clear that both *Lady Macbeth* and the Thirteenth Symphony are *pffft,* as they say in *The Nose.*"[42]

This self-flagellation (rather frequent in private conversations with the aging composer) could only have increased after the comparatively restrained reception from the right and the left of the Fourteenth Symphony. And yet it was a work of astonishing power, and by Soviet standards, of shocking content: All eleven movements of the symphony are related in one way or another to images of death. (The models here for Shostakovich were Mahler's *Kindertotenlieder* and even more so Mussorgsky's *Songs and Dances of Death,* which Shostakovich orchestrated in 1962.) Shostakovich's opus stands up to comparison with Mussorgsky and Mahler, and to their hopelessness it adds an icy sensation of the ordinariness of meeting violent death that only the late twentieth century could have bestowed.

Here can be found his direct address to Stalin: In the eighth movement ("The Response of the Zaporozhian Cossacks to the Sultan of Constantinople," with its mocking and obscene poem by Apollinaire), Shostakovich continued his dialogue with the dead tyrant, which had become an idée fixe. In music once again reminiscent of the "Stalin" scherzo from the Tenth Symphony, he draws a grotesque portrait of Stalin:

> *Crooked, rotten, and noseless,*
> *You were born when your mother*
> *Had cramps from diarrhea.*

For the officials this was clearly over the line, but for Soviet nonconformists, alas, not enough. Paradoxically, both sides found Shostakovich's obsession with death not to their taste. This rejection was symbolized by two incidents related to the Fourteenth Symphony.

During the dress rehearsal in Moscow, an elderly man staggered out of the hall and died of a heart attack in the foyer. It was Pavel Apostolov, a rather high-placed musical bureaucrat and one of the most vicious persecutors of Shostakovich in the Stalin years. The last movement of the Fourteenth is set to a poem by Rilke, with the line: "Death is omnipotent." In that cultural context, the death of a Stalinist bureaucrat at the dress rehearsal, no matter how accidental, inexorably took on signal significance. It was about that death, and not the music of the Fourteenth Symphony, that all of cultural Moscow was talking.

But that line from Rilke, thundered as the summary of the entire symphony, drew a harsh reaction from Aleksandr Solzhenitsyn, who was present at the performance. The fiercely devout man and radical dissident could not tolerate such a pessimistic conclusion, at odds with the topical problems of struggling against the Soviet regime. "Death is omnipotent." What did that mean? When Solzhenitsyn met Shostakovich, he lambasted him for his atheism and unacceptable social pessimism. This complicated the relations between the writer and the composer, who prized *One Day in the Life of Ivan Denisovich* and was even planning to write an opera based on Solzhenitsyn's story "Matryona's Yard."

Even though Shostakovich and Solzhenitsyn belonged to the same class of the Russian intelligentsia, too much separated them politically and personally. But the most important fact of life that stood between them was that, for all the enormous problems of a dissident struggle in the Soviet state, Solzhenitsyn was in good health—physically at his peak.

Solzhenitsyn described his aggressively messianic sense of self in his autobiographical book *The Oak and the Calf:* "And what cheers me and strengthens me is that it is not I who plans and executes everything, that I am only the sword, well sharpened against the evil spirit, intended to hack it and chase it away. O Lord, grant that I do not break on the blows! That I do not fall from Your hand!"[43]

It is impossible to imagine a greater contrast than Shostakovich's mental and physical state in those years. In 1966, his heart began failing seriously: Doctors diagnosed his first myocardial infarct. His arms and legs moved with greater difficulty, and he spent increasingly longer periods in the hospital. The doctors tried—unsuccessfully—to cure Shostakovich, but managed only to patch up the latest problem. Now every time Shostakovich undertook a new work, he was plagued by the worry that he might not finish it. Would his right hand, his vision (which was also deteriorating rapidly), his heart let him down? The doctors forced him to give up alcohol and smoking, which made him even more nervous and paranoid.

Shostakovich's works written in the last years of his life kept turning into requiems for himself: the elegiac and confessional song cycle to the poems of Alexander Blok and the late quartets—especially the last, the Fifteenth, which is graveside singing, thirty-five minutes of slow, funereal music. In essence, the last, Fifteenth, Symphony and the Viola Sonata, which was not performed until after his death, were in the same vein.

Shostakovich tried not to miss the premieres of his compositions, and audiences observed his physical deterioration with pity and horror. Sometimes it seemed that he was no longer human, but an automaton, with a frozen, crooked mask instead of a face, eyes hidden behind thick glasses, and uncoordinated movements of arms and legs. Profoundly upset by his shocking physical state, he complained to me that he felt he was made of glass and a wrong move could shatter him.

His family and friends could see what efforts he had to expend on the simplest actions (getting up, sitting down, writing a letter, and so on), not to mention executing the creative ideas that continued to excite him. They realized that Shostakovich had marshaled all his spiritual and physical resources to be able to compose. For them, he was first and foremost a great composer; the main goal was for him to write new music. The rest—including Shostakovich's policy of signing all sorts of official public documents, often without even reading them—seemed not important at all. After all, those boring, dull speeches and statements, in a constant stream along a conveyor belt, did no harm to anyone personally.

But not everyone was so forgiving. In dissident circles, where open confrontation with the authorities was becoming the new course, people were irritated with him. In 1973 *Pravda* printed a letter of twelve composers and musicologists against Andrei Sakharov. Shostakovich was among the signers.[44]

There is no doubt that his signature was obtained against his will. There are several versions of this dramatic episode, just as there are about his joining the Party. Some people claim that the officials organizing the anti–Sakharov action printed the musicians' letter without even bothering to get Shostakovich's signature on the document. This practice was prevalent in Soviet times and it was well known. But the fact remains that Shostakovich did not publicly deny his signature under the anti–Sakharov letter.

Shostakovich, who in much more terrible times did not sign a statement condemning the executed Marshal Tukhachevsky as an enemy of the people, now looked cowed and broken in the eyes of the active opponents of the regime. Some especially righteous citizens went even further, publicly shunning him. Lydia Chukovskaya made a statement in *samizdat* that was immediately picked up by the Western media: "Shostakovich's signature under the musicians' letter against Sakharov incontrovertibly demonstrates that Pushkin's question has been answered once and for all: Genius and villainy are compatible."[45] It was put frankly and clearly, but not quite accurately. Pushkin gives the aphorism "genius and villainy are two incompatible things" to Mozart in the play *Mozart and Salieri* as a statement, not a question. Salieri, who violates that postulate (Pushkin has him poisoning Mozart), thereby takes himself out of the circle of geniuses. Pushkin's idea was that once Salieri commits the crime, he reveals himself as a mediocrity, since a true genius is incapable of murder. This aphorism was dear to Shostakovich, who often quoted it. He deeply regretted his signature on the anti-Sakharov letter, but it hardly made him a villain, much less a murderer.

Nevertheless, the outrage of the dissidents was understandable. They did not care that Shostakovich, together with other figures in Soviet culture and science (including, incidentally, Sakharov himself), had signed a letter to Brezhnev against the rebirth of Stalinism.[46] They did not care that he continued to write astonishing, immortal works—not pro-Soviet, not anti-Soviet, but simply "non"-Soviet music that addressed the themes of old age, death, oblivion, return to nature—music of despair and acceptance.

Those in opposition to the Soviet regime did not need music like that. They were concerned with current political problems. Although Shostakovich wasn't proud of his behavior, he wasn't in full agreement with the position of the active political opponents of the regime, either. Hence his statements in his final years that Solzhenitsyn should write instead of getting into a battle with the "Kremlin pack."[47] Hence his hidden hurt and bitterness that sometimes broke through in his attitude toward Solzhenitsyn and Sakharov. And hence his desire to hide, to melt into the flow of dark, funereal, elegiac sounds of his own late works.

Many of the people around him saw this requiem music as escapism. For Shostakovich it was a way into another world. But even in these final opuses, where he seems to be looking down at his own lifeless body, his anger and hatred toward Stalin bursts out. The man, long decomposed, took on almost mystical qualities in Shostakovich's imagination. He became the very symbol of tyranny.

I am speaking of Shostakovich's song cycle to the poetry of Marina Tsvetayeva, composed in 1973. In one day, 6 August, Shostakovich penned two pieces from the cycle—"Poet and Tsar" and "No, the Drum Beat" (he died almost two years to the day later, on 9 August).

The first Tsvetayeva poem deals with Pushkin's conflict with Emperor Nicholas I—a conflict so important for both Shostakovich and Stalin. The second is about Pushkin's funeral:

> *So much honor that there was no room*
> *For his closest friends. At his head, his feet,*
> *On the right and left—standing at attention—*
> *Gendarme chests and mugs.*

Here Shostakovich described the atmosphere of his own funeral with chilling foresight. Unlike Pushkin's, which on Nicholas I's orders was secret and hurried, Shostakovich's service was a very public exercise. Despite the solemnity of the occasion, many of those present were struck by the obscenity of the event. It came from the blatant desire of the authorities to claim the deceased as their own and irrevocably "Sovietize" him.

In the Great Hall of the Moscow Conservatory, Shostakovich's open casket was surrounded by the "honor guard" of the most prominent Party and government officials. I was there, and it was a depressing sight—the same "gendarme chests and mugs," but in monotonous black double-breasted suits.

> *Look then, country, see how, contrary to rumor,*
> *The monarch cares for the poet!*
> *Honor—honor—honor—super-honored*
> *Honor—honor—horror.*

In Shostakovich's Tsvetayeva cycle, the singer shouts out these words, despairingly, challengingly. The day of the funeral, 14 August 1975, the music played in my head like a broken record. This was exactly how Stalin would have buried Shostakovich, if he had outlived him. But Shostakovich had outlived the tyrant by twenty-two years.

It was a feat—in life and in work. It had required all of Shostakovich's abilities: the persistence and zeal of the *yurodivy*, the drive and cunning of the pretender, the genius of the chronicler. These were the role masks that the composer had inherited from the Pushkin-

Mussorgsky *Boris Godunov.* Shostakovich played these parts to the end. Which mask was he wearing when he died?

The first two masks disappeared along with his life, and only historians of culture will ever remember them. The third remained, and it was in that role that he strode into the new millennium with his greatest compositions.

Future generations will learn from Shostakovich's musical chronicles many things: About how entire nations lived precariously in the era of Stalin and, after his death, in the tyrant's shadow, but also about how a single member of the intelligentsia felt as he found himself, yet again, at the crossroads of history. About great fear and great wrath, about love and pity. About the secret of artistic survival in a cruel age. No one had mastered that secret better than Dmitri Shostakovich.

Notes

Preface

1. "Ob opere *Velikaia druzhba* V. Muradeli. Postanovlenie TsK VKP(b) ot 10 fevralia 1948," *Pravda,* 11 February 1948.
2. "Sumbur vmesto muzyki. Ob opere *Ledi Makbet Mtsenskogo uezda,*" *Pravda,* 28 January 1936.
3. *American Record Guide,* September–October 2000, p. 212.
4. Richard Taruskin, *Defining Russia Musically: Historical and Hermeneutical Essays* (Princeton, 1997), p. 508. First voiced by Taruskin in 1987, this equally absurd and offensive definition was repeated by him in print several times, until mounting criticism forced his disingenuous retreat.
5. *Ibid.,* p. 509.
6. *National Post* (Toronto), 15 March 2000.
7. *New York Times,* 2 January 2000.
8. *New York Times,* 9 March 2000.
9. Laurel E. Fay, *Shostakovich: A Life* (Oxford, 2000), p. 269.
10. *Testimony: The Memoirs of Dmitri Shostakovich,* as related to and edited by Solomon Volkov (New York, 1979), pp. xxv–xxvii.
11. *Rossiia/Russia,* 4 (1980), pp. 199–222.

Prologue: Tsars and Poets

1. Quoted in: M.V. Nechkina, *Dekabristy* (Moscow, 1975), p. 134.
2. Quoted in: Georgii Chulkov, *Imperatory: psikhologicheskie portrety* (Moscow, 1995), p. 306.
3. *Pushkin, Pis'ma,* edited and with commentary by B. K. Modzalevsky, vol. 2 (Moscow/Leningrad, 1928), p. 181.

4.   Quoted in: *A. S. Pushkin v vospominaniiakh sovremennikov,* 2 vols., vol. 1 (Moscow, 1974), p. 229.

5.   *Pushkin, Pis'ma,* vol. 2, p. 183.

6.   Dmitrii Volkogonov, *Triumf i tragediia. Politicheskii portret I. V. Stalina,* 2 vols., vol. 2, part 1 (Moscow, 1989), p. 191.

7.   Yuri Lyubimov, in conversation with the author, New York, 1986.

8.   Quoted in: Flora Litvinova, "Vspominaia Shostakovicha," *Znamia,* 1 (1996), p. 171.

9.   Kirill Kondrashin, in conversation with the author, Washington, D. C., 1980.

10.   *Ibid.*

11.   Yevgeny Gromov, *Stalin: vlast' i iskusstvo* (Moscow, 1998), p. 339.

12.   *Ibid.,* p. 342. See also: Volkogonov, *Triumf i tragediia,* vol. 1, part 2, p. 114.

13.   See: Sergei Mikhalkov, *Ot i do . . .* (Moscow, 1998), p. 159; *Muzykal'naia zhizn',* 21–2 (1993), p. 28.

14.   Abel Startsev, letter to the author, 9 July 1997.

15.   Kirill Kondrashin, in conversation with the author, Washington, D. C., 1980.

16.   See: S. M. Khentova, *V mire Shostakovicha* (Moscow, 1996), p. 107.

17.   *Pis'ma k drugu. Dmitrii Shostakovich—Isaaku Glikmanu* (Moscow–St. Petersburg, 1993), p. 62.

18.   Alexander Rodchenko, *Opyty dlia budushchego. Dnevniki. Stat'i. Pis'ma. Zapiski* (Moscow, 1996), p. 363.

19.   G. P. Fedotov, *Sud'ba i grekhi Rossii. Izbrannye stat'i po filosofii russkoi istorii i kul'-tury* vol. 2 (St. Petersburg, 1992), p. 91.

20.   V. A. Sollogub, *Povesti. Vospominaniia* (Moscow, 1988), pp. 495–6.

21.   V. G. Belinsky, *Sobranie sochinenii,* 9 vols., vol. 9 (Moscow, 1982), p. 476.

22.   A. N. Pypin, *Kharakteristiki literaturnykh mnenii ot dvadtsatykh do piatidesiatykh godov* (St. Petersburg, 1890), p. 213.

23.   Quoted in: O. Feldman, *Sud'ba dramaturgii Pushkina* (Moscow, 1975), p. 148.

24.   See: N. K. Shilder, *Imperator Nikolai Pervyi. Ego zhizn' i tsarstvovanie,* vol. 1 (St. Petersburg, 1903), p. 705.

25.   Konstantin Simonov, *Glazami cheloveka moego pokoleniia. Razmyshleniia o I. V. Staline* (Moscow, 1990), p. 111.

26.   *Ibid.*

27.   *Pervyi Vsesoiuznyi s'ezd sovetskikh pisatelei. Stenograficheskii otchet* (Moscow, 1934), p. 716.

28.   Quoted in: M. Lemke, *Nikolaevskie zhandarmy i literatura 1826–1855 godov* (St. Petersburg, 1908), p. 411.

29.   N. Eidelman, *Pushkin. Iz biografii i tvorchestva, 1826–1837* (Moscow, 1989), p. 115.

30.   Eidelman, *Pushkin,* pp. 125–6.

31.   Quoted in: *Novyi mir,* 6 (1994), pp. 198, 202.

32.   Quoted in: Lazar' Fleishman, *Boris Pasternak v dvadtsatye gody* (Munich, 1981), p. 170.

33.   Andrei Platonov, *Masterskaia* (Moscow, 1977), p. 8.

34.   Quoted in: Yevgeny Yevtushenko, *Volchii passport* (Moscow, 1998), p. 522.

35.   A. V. Lunacharsky, *V mire muzyki. Stat'i i rechi* (Moscow, 1958), p. 61.

36.   *Literatura i kul'tura Drevnei Rusi* (Moscow, 1994), p. 79.

37. For this see: K.V. Chistov, *Russkie narodnye sotsial'no-utopicheskie legendy XVII–XIX vv.* (Moscow, 1967).
38. See: Solomon Volkov, "O neizbezhnoi vstreche: Shostakovich i Dostoevskii," *Rossiia/Russia,* 4 (1980), pp. 199–222.
39. Quoted in: A. Orlova, *Trudy i dni M. P. Musorgskogo. Letopis' zhizni i tvorchestva* (Moscow, 1963), p. 591.
40. *Glagol,* 4 (1991), p. 134.
41. *Ibid.,* p. 11.
42. Quoted in: Mikhail Zoshchenko, *Materialy k tvorcheskoi biografii,* vol. 1 (St. Petersburg, 1997), pp. 130–1.
43. For this see: Olga Ivinskaya, *V plenu vremeni. Gody s Borisom Pasternakom* (Paris, 1978), p. 146.

I   Mirages and Temptations

1. Litvinova, pp. 173–4.
2. *Ibid.,* p. 174.
3. Osip Mandelstam, *Sochineniia,* 2 vols., vol. 2 (Moscow, 1990), p. 40.
4. L. Lebedinsky, *Sed'maia i Odinnadtsataia simfonii D. Shostakovicha* (Moscow, 1960), p. 24.
5. L. Lebedinsky, "O nekotorykh muzykal'nykh tsitatakh v proizvedeniiakh D. Shostakovicha," *Novyi mir,* 3 (1990), p. 263.
6. Lev Lebedinsky, "Bessistemnye zapisi" (typewritten copy of manuscript in the archive of Solomon Volkov).
7. *Meierkhol'dovskii sbornik,* issue 1 (Moscow, 1992), p. 24.
8. *Ibid.,* p. 54.
9. *Pis'ma k drugu,* p. 127.
10. Lydia Chukovskaya, *Zapiski ob Anne Akhmatovoi* vol. 2 (Paris, 1980), p. 215.
11. Maria Yudina, *Luchi Bozhestvennoi Liubvi. Literaturnoe nasledie* (Moscow–St. Petersburg, 1999), pp. 470–1.
12. Marietta Shaginian, *O Shostakoviche* (Moscow, 1982), p. 178.
13. I.V. Stalin, *Sochineniia* vol. 6 (Moscow, 1952), pp. 54–5.
14. *N. G. Chernyshevskii v vospominaniiakh sovremennikov* (Moscow, 1982), p. 178.
15. Quoted in: *Pamiatniki mirovoi esteticheskoi mysli* vol. 4, part 1 (Moscow, 1969), p. 294.
16. *N. G. Chernyshevskii v vospominaniiakh sovremennikov,* 2 vols., vol. 1 (Saratov, 1958), pp. 152–3.
17. *V. I. Lenin o literature* (Moscow, 1971), p. 222.
18. *Ibid.,* p. 225.
19. *Literaturnoe Nasledstvo,* vol. 80: *V. I. Lenin i A. V. Lunacharskii. Perepiska, doklady, dokumenty* (Moscow, 1971), p. 313.
20. Valerii Brusov, *Sobranie sochinenii,* 7 vols., vol. 6 (Moscow, 1975), pp. 110–11.
21. *Ibid.,* p. 111.
22. L. Mikheeva, *Zhizn' Dmitriia Shostakovicha* (Moscow, 1997), p. 20.
23. *Tynianovskii sbornik. Tret'i tynianovskie chteniia* (Riga, 1988), p. 299.

24. Alexander Blok, *Sobranie sochinenii,* 8 vols., vol. 6 (Moscow–Leningrad, 1963), pp. 16–17.
25. Quoted from: Dmitri Merezhkovsky, *Bol'naia Rossiia* (Leningrad, 1991), p. 226.
26. *Russkaia mysl',* 14 April 1989.
27. Vladimir Mayakovsky, *Polnoe sobranie sochinenii,* 13 vols., vol. 12 (Moscow, 1959), p. 7.
28. *Literaturnoe Nasledstvo,* vol. 65: *Novoe o Mayakovskom* (Moscow, 1958), p. 573.
29. *Ibid.,* p. 210.
30. Lili Brik, in conversation with the author, Moscow, 1975.
31. Rita Rait-Kovaleva, in conversation with the author, Moscow, 1975.
32. Valentin Katayev, *Almaznyi moi venets* (Moscow, 1980), p. 103.
33. Quoted in: D. Shostakovich, *O vremeni i o sebe* (Moscow, 1980), p. 11.
34. For this, see, for example: A. Bogdanova, *Muzyka i vlast'* (Moscow, 1995).
35. Quoted in: *Vstrechi s proshlym,* issue 5 (Moscow, 1984), pp. 232–60.
36. *Ibid.,* p. 255.
37. Mikhail Zoshchenko, *Uvazhaemye grazhdane* (Moscow, 1991), p. 578.
38. Quoted in: *Dmitri Shostakovich v pis'makh i dokumentakh* (Moscow, 2000), p. 137.
39. *Ibid.,* p. 115.
40. Stalin, *Sochineniia,* vol. 12 (Moscow, 1952), p. 200.
41. *Shostakovich v pis'makh i dokumentakh,* p. 115.
42. *Ibid.*
43. *Vlast' i khudozhestvennaia intelligentsiia. Dokumenty TsK RKP(b), VChK-OGPU-NKVD o kul'turnoi politike. 1917–1953 gg.* Compiled by Andrei Artizov and Oleg Naumov (Moscow, 1999), pp. 6–7.
44. *Ibid.,* p. 6.
45. N. Punin, *Mir svetel liubov'iu. Dnevniki. Pis'ma* (Moscow, 2000), pp. 245–6.
46. *Shostakovich v pis'makh i dokumentakh,* p. 95.
47. *Ibid.,* p. 90.
48. Quoted in: Yevgeny Zamyatin, *Sochineniia* (Moscow, 1988), p. 411.
49. *Ibid.,* p. 562.
50. A. Gvozdev, *Teatral'naia kritika* (Leningrad, 1987), p. 226.
51. *Sovetskaia muzyka,* 6 (1983), p. 91.
52. *Krasnaia gazeta,* 2 September 1929, evening edition.
53. Quoted in: *Sovetskaia muzyka,* 10, (1986), p. 56.
54. Yuri Annenkov, *Dnevnik moikh vstrech. Tsikl tragedii,* vol. 1 (New York, 1966), p. 207.
55. Rodchenko, *Opyty dlia budushchego,* pp. 257–8.
56. Vitaly Shentalinsky, *Raby svobody. V literaturnykh arkhivakh KGB* (Moscow, 1995), p. 54.

II   The Year 1936: Causes and Consequences

1. Quoted in: Vitaly Shentalinsky, *Donos na Sokrata* (Moscow, 2001), p. 280.
2. Mikhail Bulgakov, *Dnevnik. Pis'ma, 1914–1940* (Moscow, 1997), p. 157.
3. *Ibid.,* p. 228.

4. *Ibid.*, p. 230.
5. *Ibid.*, pp. 232–3.
6. *Vlast' i khudozhestvennaia intelligentsiia*, p. 38.
7. *Ibid.*
8. *Ibid.*, p. 87.
9. *Ibid.*, p. 106.
10. *Ibid.*, p. 105.
11. Mikheeva, *Zhizn' Dmitriia Shostakovicha*, pp. 139–40.
12. Bulgakov, *Dnevnik. Pis'ma*, p. 251.
13. *Dnevnik Eleny Bulgakovoi* (Moscow, 1990), p. 167.
14. Quoted in: M. Chudakova, *Zhizneopisanie Mikhaila Bulgakova* (Moscow, 1988), p. 471.
15. *Ibid.*
16. *Teatr*, 12 (1988), p. 111.
17. Maxim Gorky, *Nesvoevremennye mysli. Zametki o revoliutsii i kul'ture* (Moscow, 1990), p. 149.
18. Zamyatin, *Sochineniia*, p. 354.
19. Quoted in: Arkady Vaksberg, *Gibel' Burevestnika. M. Gor'kii: poslednie dvadtsat' let* (Moscow, 1999), p. 253.
20. I. Gronsky, *Iz proshlogo . . .* (Moscow, 1991), p. 152.
21. K. Chukovsky, *Dnevnik. 1901–1929* (Moscow, 1991), p. 148.
22. Zamyatin, *Sochineniia*, p. 355.
23. Quoted in: Lazar' Fleishman, *Boris Pasternak v tridtsatye gody* (Jerusalem, 1984), p. 134.
24. Zamyatin, *Sochineniia*, p. 357.
25. Dmitri Volkogonov, *Sem' vozhdei. Galereiia liderov SSSR*, 2 vols., vol. 1 (Moscow, 1996), p. 265.
26. *Ibid.*, p. 263.
27. *Literaturnaia gazeta*, 17 November 1932.
28. Ivinskaya, *V plenu vremeni*, p. 72.
29. Quoted in: E. Pasternak, *Boris Pasternak. Biografiia* (Moscow, 1997), p. 402.
30. Boris Pasternak, *Perepiska s Ol'goi Freidenberg* (New York, 1981), p. 151.
31. Quoted in: Fleishman, *Pasternak v tridtsatye gody*, p. 221.
32. Viktor Shklovsky, in conversation with the author, Moscow, 1975.
33. Quoted in: Ivinskaya, *V plenu vremeni*, p. 76.
34. Quoted in: Fleishman, *Pasternak v tridtsatye gody*, pp. 144–5.
35. Nadezhda Mandelstam, *Vospominaniia* (New York, 1970), p. 168.
36. *Ibid.*, p. 35.
37. See: Emma Gershtein, *Memuary* (St. Petersburg, 1998), p. 337.
38. Nadezhda Mandelstam, *Vospominaniia*, p. 156.
39. See: N. Vilmont, *O Borise Pasternake. Vospominaniia i mysli* (Moscow, 1989), p. 218.
40. Nadezhda Mandelstam, *Vospominaniia*, p. 156.
41. *Vlast' i khudozhestvennaia intelligentsiia*, p. 275.
42. *Ibid.*, p. 277.
43. *Ibid.*, p. 233.

44. Lili Brik, in conversation with the author, Moscow, 1975.

45. *Pravda,* 5 December 1935.

46. See: Fleishman, *Pasternak v tridtsatye gody,* p. 269.

47. Boris Pasternak, *Vozdushnye puti. Proza raznykh let* (Moscow, 1982), p. 458.

48. *Vlast' i khudozehstvennaia intelligentsiia,* p. 275.

49. Galina Serebryakova, *O drugikh i o sebe* (Moscow, 1971), pp. 309–10.

50. Grigory Maryamov, *Kremlevskii tsenzor: Stalin smotrit kino* (Moscow, 1992), p. 10.

51. *Izvestiia,* 24 September 1933.

52. Sergei Eisenstein, *Izbrannye proizvedeniia,* 6 vols., vol. 4 (Moscow, 1966), p. 564.

53. Berthe Malko, in conversation with the author, New York, 1985.

54. Academician B.V. Asafiev, *Izbrannye trudy,* vol. 5 (Moscow, 1957), p. 118.

55. *New York Sun,* 9 February, 1935.

56. *New York Times,* 6 February, 1935.

57. *Izvestiia,* 24 September 1933.

58. B. Asafiev (Igor Glebov), *Kriticheskie stat'i, ocherki i retsenzii. Iz naslediia kontsa desiatykh-nachala tridtsatykh godov* (Moscow–Leningrad, 1967), p. 242.

59. *Krasnaia gazeta,* 10 February 1934, evening edition.

60. *Ogonek,* 31 (1991), p. 24.

61. Alexander Fadeyev, *Pis'ma 1916–1956* (Moscow, 1973), p. 159.

62. *Komsomol'skaia pravda,* 20 January 1936.

63. Quoted in: V.V. Perkhin, *Russkaia literaturnaia kritika 1930-kh godov. Kritika i obshchestvennoe soznanie epokhi* (St. Petersburg, 1997), p. 141.

64. Bulgakov, *Dnevnik. Pis'ma,* p. 624.

65. *Muzykal'naia akademiia,* 4 (1997), p. 71.

66. Khentova, *V mire Shostakovicha,* p. 121.

67. *Izvestiia,* 3 April 1935.

68. See: Yuri Elagin, *Ukroshchenie iskusstv* (New Jersey, 1988), p. 185.

69. Bulgakov, *Dnevnik. Pis'ma,* p. 625.

70. Mikhail Vaiskopf, *Pisatel' Stalin* (Moscow, 2001), p. 35.

71. Dmitri Shepilov, *Neprimknuvshii* (Moscow, 2001), p. 244.

72. *Novyi zhurnal,* 151 (1983), p. 175.

73. See: *Sto sorok besed s Molotovym. Iz dnevnika F. Chueva* (Moscow, 1991), p. 123.

74. See: A. A. Gromyko, *Pamiatnoe,* vol. 1 (Moscow, 1988), p. 204.

75. About this episode, see: M. Goldshtein, *Zapiski muzykanta* (Frankfurt-am-Main, 1970), p. 28.

76. *Literaturnaia gazeta,* 10 March 1936.

77. This and following responses to "Muddle Instead of Music" are quoted in: *Vlast' i khudozhestvennaia intelligentsiia,* pp. 290–5.

78. *Ibid.,* p. 302.

79. *Ibid.,* p. 304.

80. *Ibid.,* p. 291.

81. Quoted in: Viktor Fradkin, *Delo Kol'tsova* (Moscow, 2002), p. 228.

82. Quoted in: Fleishman, *Pasternak v tridtsatye gody,* p. 349.

83. *Nezavisimaia gazeta,* 27 March 1996.

III   1936: Facing the Sphinx

1. *Pis'ma k drugu,* p. 315.
2. *Ibid.,* p. 316.
3. Vsevolod Ivanov, *Sobranie sochinenii,* 8 vols., vol. 8 (Moscow, 1978), p. 575.
4. See: *Pravda,* 30 March 1936.
5. *Muzykal'naia akademiia,* 4 (1997), p. 73.
6. See: *Sovetskaiia muzyka,* 1 (1989), p. 22.
7. Anna Akhmatova, in conversation with the author, Komarovo, 1965.
8. *Muzykal'naia akademiia,* 4 (1997), p. 72.
9. See: I. Solov'eva, *Nemirovich-Danchenko* (Moscow, 1979), p. 394.
10. K. Chukovsky, *Dnevnik 1930–1969* (Moscow, 1994), p. 141.
11. Mikheeva, *Zhizn' Dmitriia Shostakovicha,* pp. 179–80.
12. Quoted in: Anna Akhmatova, *Requiem* (Moscow, 1989), pp. 108–9.
13. Punin, *Mir svetel liubov'iu,* p. 335.
14. *Vlast' i khudozhestvennaia intelligentsiia,* p. 291.
15. Quoted in: Khentova, *V mire Shostakovicha,* p. 133.
16. Quoted in: Fleishman, *Pasternak v tridtsatye gody,* pp. 388–9.
17. This and following quotes from Yuri Olesha's speech are from: *Ogonek,* 31 (1991), p. 23.
18. See: *Vlast' i khudozhestvennaia intelligentsiia,* p. 289.
19. Quoted in: Mikheeva, *Zhizn' Dmitriia Shostakovicha,* p. 188.
20. P. A. Vyazemsky, *Sochineniia,* 2 vols., vol. 2 (Moscow, 1982), p. 211.
21. *Pis'ma k drugu,* p. 299.
22. *Ibid.,* p. 9
23. Erwin Sinkó, *Roman eines Romans. Moskauer Tagebuch* (Köln, 1969), p. 315.
24. *Ibid.,* p. 326.
25. Grigory Kozintsev, *Sobranie sochinenii,* 5 vols., vol. 4 (Leningrad, 1984), p. 253.
26. Sergei Yutkevich, in conversation with the author, Moscow, 1976.
27. M. Bleiman, *O kino—svidetel'skie pokazaniia* (Moscow, 1973), p. 138.
28. Quoted in: Khrisanf Khersonsky, *Stranitsy iunosti kino. Zapiski kritika* (Moscow, 1965), p. 265.
29. *Vlast' i khudozhestvennaia intelligentsiia,* p. 260.
30. Quoted in: *Rodina,* 2 (2002), p. 96.
31. Lydia Ginzburg, *O starom i novom. Stat'i i ocherki* (Leningrad, 1982), p. 364.
32. *Pis'ma k drugu,* p. 278.
33. Quoted in: Gustav Mahler, *Pis'ma. Vospominaniia* (Moscow, 1964), p. 239.
34. Nikita Zabolotsky, *Zhizn' N. A. Zabolotskogo* (Moscow, 1998), pp. 256–7.
35. *Muzykal'naia akademiia,* 4 (1997), p. 74.
36. Quoted in: Sofia Khentova, *Zhizn' Shostakovicha—v illiustratsiiakh i slove* (Moscow, 1999), p. 62.

37. Related by the writer's son, Vyacheslav Ivanov, in conversation with the author, Los Angeles, 1998.
38. Gromov, *Stalin,* p. 94.

IV   The Tsar's Mercy

1. Quoted in: Fridrikh Ermler, *Dokumenty. Stat'i. Vospominaniia* (Leningrad, 1974), p. 307.
2. Quoted in: *Surovaia drama naroda: uchenye i publitsisty o prirode stalinizma* (Moscow, 1989), p. 494.
3. *Muzykal'naia akademiia,* 4 (1997), pp. 75–6.
4. *Tynianovskii sbornik. Tret'i tynianovskie chteniia,* p. 219.
5. Nikolai Ravich, *Portrety sovremennikov* (Moscow, 1977), p. 153.
6. Grigory Frid, *Dorogoi ranenoi pamiati. Vospominaniia* (Moscow, 1994), p. 175.
7. Ivinskaya, *V plenu vremeni,* p. 146.
8. Fleishman, *Pasternak v tridtsatye gody.* p. 423.
9. Nadezhda Mandelstam, *Vospominaniia,* p. 317.
10. Quoted in: L. V. Nikolaev, *Stat'i i vospominaniia sovremennikov. Pis'ma* (Leningrad, 1979), p. 257.
11. *Sovetskoe iskusstvo,* 4 October 1938.
12. *Sovetskoe iskusstvo,* 2 February 1938.
13. See: *Novyi mir,* 12 (1982), p. 133.
14. Yevgeny Shvarts, *Zhivu bespokoino . . . Iz dnevnikov* (Leningrad, 1990), p. 331.
15. V. N. Toporov, *Akhmatova i Blok (k probleme postroeniia poeticheskogo dialoga: "blokovskii" tekst Akhmatovoi)* (Berlin, 1981), pp. 7–8.
16. A. Glumov, *Nestertye stroki* (Moscow, 1977), p. 317.
17. Quoted in: D. D. Shostakovich, *Sbornik statei k 90-letiiu so dnia rozhdeniia* (St. Petersburg, 1996), p. 127.
18. Khentova, *V mire Shostakovicha,* p. 156.
19. V. V. Shcherbachev, *Stat'i. Materialy. Pis'ma* (Leningrad, 1985), p. 251.
20. A. A. Fadeyev, *Za tridtsat' let* (Moscow, 1957), p. 891.
21. Quoted in: S. Khentova, *Shostakovich. Zhizn' i tvorchestvo,* vol. 1 (Leningrad, 1985), p. 459.
22. *Izvestiia,* 28 December 1937.
23. See: Igor Stravinsky, *Poetics of Music in the Form of Six Lessons* (Cambridge, Mass., 1947), p. 115.
24. Oleg Shishkin, *Bitva za Gimalai. NKVD: magiia i shpionazh* (Moscow, 2000), p. 372.
25. *Zvezda,* 7 (1987), p. 190.
26. *Pod znamenem marksizma,* 6 (1940), p. 54.
27. See: M. M. Bakhtin, *Tetralogiia* (Moscow, 1998), p. 391.
28. Maria Chegodaeva, *Dva lika vremeni* (Moscow, 2001), pp. 268–9.
29. Quoted in: E. Pasternak, *Boris Pasternak,* p. 534.
30. *Vospominaniia o Borise Pasternake* (Moscow, 1993), p. 388.
31. Osip Mandelstam, *Sochineniia,* vol. 2, p. 202.

32. *Ibid.*, p. 406.
33. Boris Kuzin, *Vospominaniia. Proizvedeniia. Perepiska. Nadezhda Mandelstam, 192 pis'ma k B. S. Kuzinu* (St. Petersburg, 1999), p. 532.
34. Solomon Volkov, *Dialogi s Iosifom Brodskim* (Moscow, 1998), p. 33.
35. *Ibid.*, p. 33.
36. Joseph Brodsky, in conversation with the author, New York, 1982.
37. Volkov, *Dialogi s Brodskim*, p. 249.
38. See: L. A. Gordon, E. V. Klopov, *Chto eto bylo?* (Moscow, 1989), p. 179.
39. Ilya Ehrenburg, *Liudi, gody, zhizn'*, vol. 1 (Moscow, 1990), p. 46.
40. *Vlast' i khudozhestvennaia intelligentsiia*, p. 150.
41. A. Matskin, *Po sledam ukhodiazhchego veka* (Moscow, 1996), p. 174.
42. Shentalinsky, *Raby svobody*, p. 41.
43. Quoted in: *Sovetskaia muzyka*, 6 (1990), p. 60.
44. V. E. Meyerhold, *Stat'i. Pis'ma. Rechi. Besedy,* part 2, 1917–1939 (Moscow, 1968), p. 331.
45. V. E. Meyerhold, *Perepiska, 1896–1939* (Moscow, 1976), p. 348.
46. *Shostakovich: mezhdu mgnoveniem i vechnost'iu. Dokumenty, materialy, stat'i* (St. Petersburg, 2000), p. 122.
47. Quoted in: Chegodaeva, *Dva lika vremeni,* p. 305.
48. *Sovetskaia muzyka*, 7 (1982), p. 78.
49. *Sovetskaia muzyka*, 9 (1991), pp. 33–4.
50. Quoted in: E. Pasternak, *Boris Pasternak,* p. 546.
51. *Sovetskaia muzyka*, 9 (1991), pp. 27–8.
52. Shaginian, *O Shostakoviche*, p. 21.
53. *Istochnik,* 5 (1995), pp. 156–8.
54. Anna Akhmatova, in conversation with the author, Komarovo, 1965.
55. Quoted in: D. L. Babichenko, *Pisateli i tsenzory. Sovetskaia literatura 1940-kh godov pod politicheskim kontrolem TsK* (Moscow, 1994), p. 48.
56. B. Pasternak, *Biografiia v pis'makh.* (Moscow, 2000), pp. 266–7.
57. Anna Akhmatova, in conversation with the author, Komarovo, 1965.

V   War: Triumphs and Tribulations

1. Pasternak, *Perepiska s Freidenberg,* p. 197.
2. O. Gladkova, *Galina Ustvol'skaia—muzyka kak navazhdenie* (St. Petersburg, 1999), p. 31.
3. S. Khentova, *Shostakovich. Zhizn' i tvorchestvo,* 2nd ed., expanded, vol. 1 (Moscow, 1996), p. 441.
4. See: *111 simfonii: spravochnik-putevoditel'* (St. Petersburg, 2000), p. 618.
5. Quoted in: *D. Shostakovich o vremeni i o sebe, 1926–1975* (Moscow, 1980), p. 96.
6. *Testimony,* p. 135.
7. *Novyi mir,* 3 (1990), p. 267.
8. *Novyi zhurnal,* 4 (1943), p. 368.
9. *Znamia,* 12 (1996), p. 164.
10. *Novyi zhurnal,* 4 (1943), p. 371.

11.   Yevgeny Mravinsky, in conversation with the author, Leningrad, 1969.

12.   Serebryakova, *O drugikh i o sebe*, p. 311.

13.   *Novyi zhurnal*, 4 (1943), p. 372.

14.   Ehrenburg, *Liudi, gody, zhizn'*, vol. 2, p. 242.

15.   See: E. Pasternak, *Boris Pasternak*, p. 564.

16.   Punin, *Mir svetel liubov'iu*, p. 347.

17.   *Ibid.*, p. 344.

18.   *Pravda*, 13 February 1942.

19.   Alexander Fadeyev, *Materialy i issledovaniia* (Moscow, 1977), pp. 87, 93.

20.   D. A. Tolstoi, *Dlia chego vse eto bylo. Vospominaniia* (St. Petersburg, 1995), p. 164.

21.   Gabriel Glikman, in telephone conversation with the author from Munich, 2002.

22.   D. Ortenberg, *Vremia ne vlastno. Pisateli na fronte* (Moscow, 1975), p. 54.

23.   *Minuvshee*, issue 3 (Paris, 1987), pp. 20–21.

24.   A. Fadeyev, *Leningrad v dni blokady* (Moscow, 1944), p. 40.

25.   *Ibid.*

26.   See: Leonid Girshovich, *Charodei so skripkami* (St. Petersburg, 1997), p. 437.

27.   A. V. Korolkevich, *A muzy ne molchali* (Leningrad, 1965), p. 142.

28.   *New York Herald Tribune*, 18 October 1942.

29.   See: I. R. Shafarevich, *Sochineniia*, 3 vols., vol. 2 (Moscow, 1994), p. 442.

30.   Ehrenburg, *Liudi, gody, zhizn'*, vol. 2, pp. 324–5. In the English translation this comment was erroneously referred to Shostakovich's *Seventh* Symphony.

31.   K. Kh. Adzhemov, *Nezabyvaemoe. Vospominaniia. Ocherki i stat'i* (Moscow, 1972), p. 68.

32.   *Vlast' i khudozhestvennaia intelligentsiia*, p. 289.

33.   Quoted in: L. Mikheeva, *I. I. Sollertinsky. Zhizn' i nasledie* (Leningrad, 1988), p. 110.

34.   Quoted in: Mikheeva, *Zhizn' Dmitriia Shostakovicha*, p. 254.

35.   *Pis'ma k drugu*, p. 291.

36.   The letter is quoted from a typed copy in the archive of Solomon Volkov.

37.   Fadeyev, *Materialy i issledovaniia*, pp. 127–8.

38.   Yuri Lyubimov, in conversation with the author, New York, 1986.

39.   Quoted in: Leonid Maksimenkov, *Sumbur vmesto muzyki. Stalinskaia kul'turnaia revoliutsiia 1936–1938* (Moscow, 1997), p. 296.

40.   *Sovetskaia muzyka*, 1 (1968), p. 21.

41.   *Sovetskaia muzyka*, 4 (1991), p. 108.

42.   Berthe Malko, in conversation with the author, New York, 1985.

43.   D. A. Tolstoi, *Dlia chego vse eto bylo*, p. 103.

44.   *Ibid.*, p. 105.

45.   *Vstrechi s proshlym*, issue 3 (Moscow, 1978), pp. 255–6.

46.   S. S. Prokofiev and N. Ya. Myaskovsky, *Perepiska* (Moscow, 1977), p. 465.

47.   Quoted in: Maryamov, *Kremlevskii tsenzor*, pp. 84–5.

48.   *Vlast' i khudozhestvennaia intelligentsiia*, p. 487.

49.   Sergei Eisenstein, *Memuary*, vol. 1 (Moscow, 1997), pp. 340–1.

50.   *Ibid.*, p. 352.

51.   *Ibid.*, p. 353.

52. Reported by Grigory Alexandrov, in conversation with the author, Moscow, 1975.
53. Maksimenkov, *Sumbur vmesto muzyki*, p. 252.
54. Shentalinsky, *Raby svobody*, p. 58.
55. S. M. Eisenstein, *Izbrannye stat'i* (Moscow, 1956), p. 388.
56. Eisenstein, *Memuary*, vol. 2, p. 399.
57. Maryamov, *Kremlevskii tsenzor*, p. 49.
58. Eisenstein, *Memuary*, vol. 1, p. 15.
59. Quoted in: Viktor Shklovsky, *Eisenstein* (Moscow, 1973), p. 413.
60. *Eisenstein v vospominaniiakh sovremennikov* (Moscow, 1974), p. 413.
61. Mikhail Romm, *Besedy o kino* (Moscow, 1964), pp. 90–1.
62. *Vlast' i khudozhestvennaia intelligentsiia*, p. 582.
63. *Ibid.* See also: Maryamov, *Kremlevskii tsenzor*, p. 74.
64. The first account of this "historic meeting" appeared in: N. K. Cherkasov, *Zapiski sovetskogo aktera* (Moscow, 1953), pp. 379–81. Fuller accounts of the conversation with Stalin are in: Yu. Gerasimov, Zh. Skverchinskaya, *Cherkasov* (Moscow, 1977), pp. 274–8; Maryamov, *Kremlevskii tsenzor*, pp. 84–92; *Vlast' i khudozhestvennaia intelligentsiia*, pp. 612–19.
65. Maryamov, *Kremlevskii tsenzor*, p. 94.
66. *Vlast' i khudozhestvennaia intelligentsiia*, pp. 522–33.
67. *Sovetskaia muzyka*, 4 (1948), p. 15.
68. *Ibid.*, p. 16.
69. M. M. Bakhtin, *Literaturno-kriticheskie stat'i* (Moscow, 1986), pp. 513–14.
70. *Sovetskaia muzyka*, 9 (1976), pp. 17–18.
71. Maryamov, *Kremlevskii tsenzor*, p. 74.

VI   1948: "Look Over Here, Look Over There, the Enemy Is Everywhere!"

1. Chukovskaya, *Zapiski ob Anne Akhmatovoi*, vol. 2, p. 26.
2. *Pravda*, 21 August 1946.
3. Ehrenburg, *Liudi, gody, zhizn'*, vol. 3, p. 34.
4. Chukovskaya, *Zapiski ob Anne Akhmatovoi*, vol. 2, p. iii.
5. *"Literaturnyi front." Istoriia politicheskoi tsenzury 1932–1946 gg. Sbornik dokumentov* (Moscow, 1994), p. 203.
6. *Doklad t. Zhdanova o zhurnalakh "Zvezda" i "Leningrad"* (Moscow, 1946).
7. Babichenko, *Pisateli i tsenzory*, p. 4.
8. G. V. Kostyrchenko, *Tainaia politika Stalina: vlast' i antisemitizm* (Moscow, 2001), pp. 651–2.
9. Solomon Volkov, *Istoriia kul'tury Sankt-Peterburga s osnovaniia do nashikh dnei* (Moscow, 2002), p. 571.
10. *Vestnik Russkogo Khristianskogo Dvizheniia*, 156 (1989), p. 182.
11. Simonov, *Glazami cheloveka moego pokoleniia*, pp. 111–12.
12. *"I primknuvshii k nim Shepilov. Pravda o cheloveke, uchenom, voine, politike"* (Moscow, 1998), p. 137.

13. Quoted in: *Tak eto bylo: Tikhon Khrennikov o vremeni i o sebe*. Dialogues and editing by V. Rubtsova (Moscow, 1994), appendix, p. 3.

14. *Ibid.*, p. 2.

15. *Tynianovskii sbornik. Tret'i tynianovskie chteniia*, p. 218.

16. See: *Tak eto bylo*, pp. 195–201.

17. Kirill Kondrashin, in conversation with the author, Washington, D.C., 1980.

18. See: *Soveshchanie deiatelei sovetskoi muzyki v TsK VKP(b)* (Moscow, 1948); *Muzykal'naia zhizn'*, 13–14, 15–16 (1993).

19. Quoted in: Maksimenkov, *Sumbur vmesto muzyki*, p. 108.

20. *Tak eto bylo*, p. 125.

21. Quoted in: Ehrenburg, *Liudi, gody, zhizn'*, vol. 3, p. 378.

22. *Tak eto bylo*, p. 124.

23. Shepilov, *Neprimknuvshii*, p. 106.

24. *Ibid.*, p. 105.

25. *Pis'ma k drugu*, p. 9.

26. Aram Khachaturian, in conversation with the author, Moscow, 1975.

27. *Muzykal'naia akademiia*, 4 (1997), p. 77.

28. *Rodina*, 2 (2002), p. 95.

29. *Muzykal'naia akademiia*, 4 (1997), p. 77.

30. See: Leonid Girshovich, *Prais* (St. Petersburg, 1998), p. 7.

31. M. Bakhtin, *Problemy poetiki Dostoevskogo* (Moscow, 1972), pp. 268–9.

32. Quoted in: *Vstrechi s proshlym*, issue 5 (Moscow, 1984), p. 249.

33. Andrei Sinyavsky, in conversation with the author, New York, 1996.

34. *Pravda*, 11 February 1948.

35. For this episode, see: Vyacheslav Dombrovsky, "*Ee glaza, vospetye ne raz . . .*" (New Jersey, 2002), pp. 115–16.

36. *Sovetskaia muzyka*, 2 (1948), pp. 35, 45.

37. D. A. Tolstoi, *Dlia chego vse eto bylo*, p. 292.

38. Quoted in: A. Shebalina, *V. Ya. Shebalin. Gody zhizni i tvorchestva* (Moscow, 1990), p. 163.

39. *Sovetskaia muzyka*, 1 (1948), p. 117.

40. Mark Shcheglov, *Studencheskie tetradi* (Moscow, 1973), pp. 58–9.

41. *Ibid.*, p. 59.

42. Shvarts, *Zhivu bespokoino . . .* , p. 331.

43. Khentova, *V mire Shostakovicha*, p. 176.

44. *Sovetskaia muzyka*, 3 (1948), p. 43.

45. Shostakovich, *Sbornik statei k 90-letiiu so dnia rozhdeniia*, p. 369.

46. *Pis'ma k drugu*, p. 77.

VII   Final Convulsions and Death of the Tsar

1. For this episode, see: *Testimony*, pp. 147–8. See also: *Shostakovich v vospominani-akh syn Maksima, docheri Galinu i protoiereia Mikhaila Ardora* (Moscow, 2003), pp. 63–5.

2. See: *Istochnik*, 5 (1995), p. 159.

3. *Sovetskaia muzyka,* 4 (1991), p. 17. See also: A. Shebalina, *V. Ya. Shebalin,* p. 163.
4. Shvarts, *Zhivu bespokoino . . . ,* p. 331.
5. *Novyi mir,* 12 (1982), p. 129.
6. *Testimony,* p. 246.
7. Ehrenburg, *Liudi, gody, zhizn',* vol. 3, p. 115.
8. E. Pasternak, *Boris Pasternak,* p. 502.
9. For this episode, see: Nicolas Nabokov, *Bagazh: Memoirs of a Russian Cosmopolitan* (New York, 1975), pp. 237–8.
10. *Ibid.,* p. 237.
11. *Ibid.,* pp. 235–6.
12. About this idea of Stalin, see: G. M. Adibekov, *Kominform i poslevoennaia Evropa, 1947–1956 gg.* (Moscow, 1994).
13. Ehrenburg, *Liudi, gody, zhizn',* vol. 1, p. 214.
14. *Ibid.,* vol. 3, p. 176.
15. *Znamia,* 12 (1996), pp. 174–5.
16. James Lord, *Picasso and Dora: A Personal Memoir* (New York, 1993), pp. 16, 83, 88.
17. *Muzykal'naia akademiia,* 4 (1997), p. 225.
18. *Sovetskaia muzyka na pod'eme* (Moscow-Leningrad, 1950), p. 8.
19. *Pis'ma k drugu,* pp. 82–3.
20. Shepilov, *Neprimknuvshii,* p. 32.
21. Kirill Kondrashin, in conversation with the author, Washington, D.C., 1980.
22. Lebedinsky, *Bessistemnye zapisi* (typed copy of manuscript in the archive of Solomon Volkov).
23. *Ibid.*
24. See particularly the works of G. Kostyrchenko, based on a wealth of documentary material: *V plenu u krasnogo faraona* (Moscow, 1994) and *Tainaia politika Stalina* (Moscow, 2001).
25. Stalin, *Sochineniia,* vol. 13, p. 28.
26. *Izvestiia TsK KPSS,* 3 (1989), p. 179.
27. Quoted in: Kostyrchenko, *V plenu u krasnogo faraona,* p. 10.
28. *Shostakovich: mezhdu mgnoveniem i vechnost'iu,* p. 35.
29. Lebedinsky, *Bessistemnye zapisi* (typed copy of manuscript in the archive of Solomon Volkov).
30. See: *Shostakovich Reconsidered,* written and edited by Allan B. Ho and Dmitry Feofanov, with an Overture by Vladimir Ashkenazy (London, 1998), pp. 597–640.
31. In particular, about this see: Kostyrchenko, *Tainaia politika Stalina,* pp. 388–95.
32. Eisenstein, *Memuary,* vol. 1, p. 6.
33. Quoted in: Elizabeth Wilson, *Shostakovich: A Life Remembered* (London, 1994), p. 228.
34. *Istochnik,* 3 (1998), p. 120.
35. *Znamia,* 12 (1996), p. 171.
36. *Pravda,* 13 January 1953.
37. *Vlast' i khudozhestvennaia intelligentsiia,* p. 669.
38. Ehrenburg, *Liudi, gody, zhizn',* vol. 3, p. 229.
39. Quoted in: Volkov, *Istoriia kul'tury Sankt-Peterburga,* p. 74.

40. N. Udaltsova, *Zhizn' russkoi kubistki. Dnevniki, stat'i, vospominaniia* (Moscow, 1994), p. 95.
41. Volkov, *Dialogi s Brodskim*, p. 31.
42. See: I. Nestyev, *Zhizn' Sergeiia Prokof'eva* (Moscow, 1973), p. 597; Lebedinsky, *Bessistemnye zapisi* (typed copy of manuscript in the archive of Solomon Volkov).

Epilogue: In the Shadow of Stalin

1. Shepilov, *Neprimknuvshii*, p. 238.
2. Ehrenburg, *Liudi, gody, zhizn'*, vol. 3, p. 230.
3. Anatoli Rybakov, in conversation with the author, New York, 1995.
4. Quoted in: Ivan Zhukov, *Ruka sud'by. Pravda I lozh' o Mikhaile Sholokhove I Aleksandre Fadeeve* (Moscow, 1994), p. 252.
5. Ehrenburg, *Liudi, gody, zhizn'*, vol. 3, p. 130.
6. Zhukov, *Ruka sud'by*, p. 253.
7. *Ibid.*, p. 254.
8. Quoted in: Mikhail Zoshchenko, *Uvazhaemye grazhdane* (Moscow, 1991), pp. 122, 125.
9. *Ibid.*, p. 120.
10. Chukovsky, *Dnevnik 1930–1969*, p. 153.
11. *Pis'ma k drugu*, p. 153.
12. See: Detlef Gojowy, *Dimitri Schostakowitsch* (Reinbek bei Hamburg, 1983), p. 66.
13. See: Shostakovich, *Sbornik statei k 90-letiiu so dnia rozhdeniia*, pp. 228–48.
14. G. Orlov, *Simfonii Shostakovicha* (Leningrad, 1961), p. 271.
15. *Sovetskaia muzyka*, 4 (1954), p. 15.
16. *Sovetskaia muzyka*, 4 (1957), p. 84.
17. N. Vilmont, *O Borise Pasternake. Vospominaniia i mysli* (Moscow, 1989), p. 15.
18. Pasternak, *Biografiia v pis'makh*, p. 311.
19. Quoted in: E. Pasternak, *Boris Pasternak*, p. 605.
20. Pasternak, *Biografiia v pis'makh*, p. 361.
21. Anna Akhmatova, in conversation with the author, Komarovo, 1965.
22. *Pravda*, 26 October 1958.
23. *Literaturnaia gazeta*, 1 November 1958.
24. *Pravda*, 8 June 1958.
25. Nikita Khrushchev, *Vospominaniia. Izbrannye otryvki* (New York, 1979), p. 272.
26. E. Pasternak, *Boris Pasternak*, p. 712.
27. *Ibid.*, p. 710.
28. V. Kaverin, *Epilog. Memuary* (Moscow, 1989), p. 366.
29. E. Pasternak, *Boris Pasternak*, p. 727.
30. Quoted in: A. Turkov, *A. P. Chekhov i ego vremia* (Moscow, 1980), p. 225.
31. For this see: *Pis'ma k drugu*, pp. 160–1; Lebedinsky, *Bessistemnye zapisi* (typed copy of manuscript in the archive of Solomon Volkov).
32. *Shostakovich v vospominaniiakh*, pp. 153–4.

33. *Pis'ma k drugu,* p. 159.
34. *Smena,* 7 October 1960.
35. L. Mazel, *Simfonii D. D. Shostakovicha. Putevoditel'* (Moscow, 1960), p. 122.
36. M. Sabinina, *Shostakovich-simfonist. Dramaturgiia, estetika, stil'* (Moscow, 1976), p. 295.
37. Kirill Kondrashin, in conversation with the author, Washington, D.C., 1980.
38. Ernst Neizvestny, in conversation with the author, New York, 1983.
39. *Ibid.*
40. Yudina, *Luchi Bozhestvennoi Liubvi,* p. 521.
41. Yevtushenko, *Volchii passport,* p. 438.
42. *Pis'ma k drugu,* pp. 225–6.
43. A. Solzhenitsyn, *Bodalsia telenok s dubom. Ocherki literaturnoi zhizni* (Paris, 1975), pp. 407–8.
44. *Pravda,* 3 September 1973.
45. L. Chukovskaya, *Protsess iskliucheniia* (Moscow, 1990), p. 343.
46. For this, see: L. Alexeyeva, *Istoriia inakomysliia v SSSR* (Vilnius/Moscow, 1992), p. 206.
47. Galina Vishnevskaya, *Galina. Istoriia zhizni* (Paris, 1985), p. 435.

Index

A Note About the Author

SOLOMON VOLKOV was born in 1944 in the USSR and was educated at the Leningrad State Conservatory. He came to the United States in 1976 and, in 1979, published *Testimony: The Memoirs of Dmitri Shostakovich,* which was written by him in collaboration with the composer while in the USSR. *Testimony* received the 1980 ASCAP–Deems Taylor Award for excellence in writing about music. Mr. Volkov has also written books on George Balanchine and Joseph Brodsky. He is author, most recently, of *St. Petersburg: A Cultural History.* He lives in New York.

A Note About the Translator

ANTONINA W. BOUIS is the award-winning translator of *Testimony: The Memoirs of Dmitri Shostakovich* and *St. Petersburg: A Cultural History* by Solomon Volkov. Her numerous translations include fiction by Vasily Aksyonov, Sergei Dovlatov, and Yevgeny Yevtushenko and memoirs by Andrei Sakharov, Elena Bonner, and Maya Plisetskaya. She lives in New York.

A Note on the Type

This book was set in a version of the well-known
Monotype face Bembo. This letter was originally cut
for the celebrated Venetian printer Aldus Manutius by
Francesco Griffo, and first used in Pietro Cardinal
Bembo's *De Aetna* of 1495. The companion italic is
an adaptation of the chancery script type designed by
the calligrapher and printer Lodovico degli Arrighi.

Composed by North Market Street Graphics,
Lancaster, Pennsylvania
Printed and bound by Berryville Graphics,
Berryville, Virginia
Designed by Anthea Lingeman